FEMINIST PERSPECTIVES ON CHILD LAW

LIVERPOOL JMU LIBRARY

3 1111 00934 1122

D1549369

Titles in the *Feminist Perspectives in Law* series

FEMINIST PERSPECTIVES ON CHILD LAW

Edited by

Jo Bridgeman, LLB

Lecturer in Law, University of Sussex

and

Daniel Monk, LLB, LLM

Lecturer in Law, Keele University

Cavendish
Publishing
Limited

London • Sydney

First published in Great Britain 2000 by Cavendish Publishing Limited, The Glass House, Wharton Street, London WC1X 9PX, United Kingdom
Telephone: + 44 (0) 171 278 8000   Facsimile: + 44 (0) 171 278 8080
Email: info@cavendishpublishing.com
Website: www.cavendishpublishing.com

© Cavendish Publishing 2000

All rights reserved. No part of this publication may be reproduced, stored in a retrieval system, or transmitted, in any form or by any means, electronic, mechanical, photocopying, recording, scanning or otherwise, except under the terms of the Copyright Designs and Patents Act 1988 or under the terms of a licence issued by the Copyright Licensing Agency, 90 Tottenham Court Road, London W1P 9HE, UK, without the permission in writing of the publisher.

British Library Cataloguing in Publication Data

Feminist perspectives on child law
1 Children – Legal status, laws, etc – England
2 Children – Legal status, laws, etc – Wales
I Title   II Monk, Daniel
344.4'2'0327

ISBN 1 85941 525 3

Printed and bound in Great Britain

SERIES EDITORS' PREFACE

Child law, as the editors of this collection point out, has emerged over the last decade as an area of vibrant study and very much an area in its own right, having struggled out of its origins as a mere child held within the parental concern of family law. Giving the focus to the child, becoming child-centred, has allowed for and required a huge amount of scholarship, uncovering issues and concerns which before had remained hidden or were at best marginalised. But, as child law has come of age, it is now important to keep open issues of how the subject may be constituted and to keep the boundaries of the area in contention. It would be too easy to allow the subject to become 'set' into an agreed agenda, a neat book with neat chapter headings.

Feminist perspectives, along with related critical perspectives, refuse to accept closure of this area of law. Child law remains an area of contention, in which it is recognised that 'the child' appears (and is sometimes there but is made to disappear) in many areas of law and policy which refuse an easy boundary exercise of delineating the subject. This collection does not try to cover all topics which might be brought under the heading of 'child law', but is does introduce some which have not been readily recognised as part of the subject area, as well as bringing to bear tools of analysis to issues which the collection insists are fundamental but which more traditional approaches to the subject might find uncomfortable.

This is an innovative and exciting volume, representing the many strengths of the work which have developed from a critical perspective in this area, as well as new and emerging trends. We are very pleased to have it as part of our series. We have no doubt that it will be a major contribution to the scholarship of child law and a major challenge to those who view the subject as settled and whose main task is now simply to describe the relevant law.

Our thanks to the contributors to the volume, to the editors and to all who have worked on the volume, and the series, at Cavendish. At a conference on women and law, held in June 2000 at Westminster University, Jo Reddy organised a session to discuss the progress of this series. We were pleased to receive very positive feedback from the participants at that conference. So, we take the opportunity here to say that we would both like to thank all those who have read, used and recommended books in the series, as well as to invite potential editors to contact us. In the next year we will be publishing more volumes in the series, but, interestingly, no one to date has put forward a proposal for a family law volume, which is interesting. There must be many factors involved, many contingencies, but we do find it rather intriguing. Meanwhile, we are very pleased to add to the *Feminist Perspectives* series this volume on *Child Law*.

Anne Bottomley and Sally Sheldon

CONTRIBUTORS

Adrienne Barnett works in full time practice as a barrister, specialising in family law. She also teaches at Brunel University, where she is a member of the Centre for the Study of Law, the Child and the Family. Her particular areas of specialist research are child contact and domestic violence.

Jo Bridgeman is Lecturer at the University of Sussex, where she teaches health care law and ethics, law and body politics and tort. Her research interest is feminist perspectives on law, in particular concerning the health of children. Her chapter in this volume is influenced by her research interests and by her children, George and Arthur.

Doris E Buss is Lecturer in Law at Keele University. She has published in the area of feminist international legal theory, women's human rights and war crimes against women. She is currently researching and writing a book (with Didi Herman) on the global politics of the Christian Right.

Richard Collier is Professor of Law at Newcastle University. He has published extensively in the area of law and gender, and is the author of *Masculinity, Law and the Family* (1995) and *Masculinities, Crime and Criminology* (1998).

Alison Diduck researches and teaches law at Brunel University and is a member of the Centre for the Study of Law, the Child and the Family there. She has practised and taught law in Canada and has published articles in both Canadian and British journals. She is co-author (with Felicity Kaganas) of *Family Law, State and Gender* (1999).

Michael Freeman is Professor of English Law at University College London. He is the author of *The Rights and Wrongs of Children* (1983), *The Moral Status of Children* (1997), *Children, their Families and the Law* (1992) and the editor of *Lloyd's Introduction to Jurisprudence*. He is also editor of Current Legal Problems and the International Journal of Children's Rights, and is the General Editor of the *International Library of Medicine, Ethics and Law*.

LIVERPOOL JOHN MOORES UNIVERSITY
LEARNING SERVICES

Hilary Lim teaches child law and equity and trusts at the University of East London. She is co-editor (with Susan Scott-Hunt) of *Feminist Perspectives on Equity and Trusts* (2000, Cavendish Publishing) and her publications include 'Caesareans and cyborgs' (1999).

Daniel Monk is Lecturer in Law at Keele University. He teaches child, education and social work law and is currently writing a book about education, law and childhood. He is co-editor (with Les Moran and Sarah Beresford) of *Legal Queeries* (1998) and co-author (with David Ruebain) of 'Education', in *Atkin's Court Forms Encyclopedia of Civil Proceedings* (forthcoming, 2001).

Katherine O'Donovan comes from Dublin, and teaches law at Queen Mary College in the University of London. Her experiences as a child and as a mother, and of legal research in France, ground her paper in this collection. Other work on children's identity rights is in progress.

Helen Reece is Lecturer in Law at Birkbeck College, University of London. Her research interests include the regulation of the family. Previous publications in this area have focused on children's welfare ('The paramountcy principle: consensus or construct?' (1996)), lesbian and gay parenting ('Subverting the stigmatization argument' (1996)) and divorce ('Divorcing responsibly' (2000)). 'Divorcing responsibly' and her chapter in this collection are part of an ongoing research project into changing notions of personhood within divorce law.

Melanie Roberts is Lecturer in Law at the School for Legal Studies, University of Sussex. Her teaching areas are family law and public law. Her primary research interests are children and family law and the new reproductive technologies.

Jeremy Roche is Lecturer in the School of Health and Social Welfare at the Open University. He writes and researches in the field of children's rights and the law and is co-editor (with Stanley Tucker) of *Youth in Society* (1997) and *Children in Society* (2001) (with Stanley Tucker and P Foley).

Rachel Thomson is Senior Research Fellow in the Social Sciences Research Centre at South Bank University, London. Between 1990–95, she directed the work of the Sex Education Forum and is a member of the feminist research collective responsible for the Women, Risk and AIDS Project and the Men, Risk and AIDS Project. She is currently involved in three major studies on young people (*Youth Values: Identity, Diversity and Social Change*; *Inventing Adulthood – Young People's Strategies For Transition*; and *Consumption, Identity and Values: An Ethnography of Young People in Brazil*).

Anne Worrall is Reader in the Department of Criminology at Keele University and is also Honorary Research Fellow at the University of Western Australia, Perth, where she researched community corrections for six months in 1998. She is author of *Offending Women* (1990); *Have You Got a Minute? The Changing Role of Prison Boards of Visitors* (1994); *Punishment in the Community* (1997); and is co-editor (with Pat Carlen) of *Gender, Crime and Justice* (1987).

ACKNOWLEDGMENTS

We are delighted that this book forms part of Cavendish Publishing's *Feminist Perspectives on Law* series. We wish to thank the series editors, Anne Bottomley* and Sally Sheldon, for recognising the space and need for new feminist engagements with child law and for inviting us to edit this collection. We are also very grateful to Jo Reddy and Ruth Massey at Cavendish for their support, patience and assistance in the production of the collection.

Most of the chapters in this volume were originally presented as papers in June 1999 at a one day workshop at Birkbeck College. We thank Les Moran for his assistance in finding a location for the workshop, and all the people who attended, participated and helped to make it a supportive environment for the exchange of new ideas. Finally, we thank all the contributors to this collection for their enthusiastic engagement with the project and for providing such interesting and challenging ideas.

Jo Bridgeman and Daniel Monk
November 2000

CONTENTS

TABLE OF CASES

TABLE OF STATUTES

TABLE OF ABBREVIATIONS

AC	Appeal Cases
AJIL	American Journal of International Law
All ER	All England Reports
Anglo-Am L Rev	Anglo-American Law Review
BMJ	British Medical Journal
Br J Crim	British Journal of Criminology
Br J Soc	British Journal of Sociology
CEDAW	Convention on the Elimination of All Forms of Discrimination against Women
CFLQ	Child and Family Law Quarterly
CJFL	Canadian Journal of Family Law
CJLS	Canadian Journal of Law and Society
CLJ	Cambridge Law Journal
CLP	Current Legal Problems
CLS	Critical Legal Studies (movement)
CMLR	Common Market Law Reports
CSP	Critical Social Policy
CWA	Concerned Women for America
EHRR	European Human Rights Reports
EJST	European Journal of Social Theory
EL Rev	European Law Review
FCR	Family Court Reporter
FGC	Family group conferencing
FLQ	Family Law Quarterly
FLR	Family Law Reports
FLS	Feminist Legal Studies
FR	Feminist Review
Harv L Rev	Harvard Law Review
HFEA	Human Fertilisation and Embryology Authority

HLR	Housing Law Reports
HRQ	Human Rights Quarterly
ICLQ	International and Comparative Law Quarterly
ICR	Industrial Compensation Reports
IJCR	International Journal of Children's Rights
IJLF	International Journal of Law and the Family
IJLPF	International Journal of Law, Policy and the Family
IJSL	International Journal of the Sociology of Law
JCL	Journal of Child Law
JLE	Journal of Legal Education
JLS	Journal of Law and Society
JSWFL	Journal of Social Welfare and Family Law
LGR	Local Government Reports
LRB	London Review of Books
LS	Legal Studies
LQR	Law Quarterly Review
MLR	Modern Law Review
NGO	Non-governmental organisation
NLJ	New Law Journal
NSPCC	National Society for the Prevention of Cruelty to Children
OJLS	Oxford Journal of Legal Studies
PL	Public Law
QB	Queen's Bench
QCA	Qualifications and Curriculum Authority
RP	Radical Philosophy

Table of Abbreviations

SLS	Social and Legal Studies
Stan L Rev	Stanford Law Review
UNCRC	United Nations Convention on the Rights of the Child
Web JCLI	Web Journal of Current Legal Issues
WLR	Weekly Law Reports
YBEL	Yearbook of European Law

CHAPTER 1

INTRODUCTION: REFLECTIONS ON THE RELATIONSHIP BETWEEN FEMINISM AND CHILD LAW

Jo Bridgeman and Daniel Monk

WHAT IS CHILD LAW?

Over the past decade, child law has become a discrete category of legal practice and academic study, notably distinct from family law. This development can be understood as a simple process of consolidation of issues relating to children across a number of more established legal categories and, in addition, as a reflection of increased specialisation and juridification. More broadly, and perhaps optimistically, this development can also be understood as a reflection of the influence of children's rights and feminist engagements with law which, albeit in different ways, have to a limited extent encouraged a 'child-centred' focus wherein children are seen as individuals and not simply as family members or passive 'objects of concern'. Yet, more critically, the development of child law can be understood as a reflection not simply of heightened social and political concern for *children,* but, less tangibly and more problematically, as a reflection of an increase in the importance of *childhood* as a category of cultural and governmental significance for society as a whole. These various explanations indicate that child law is more than a 'common sense' category. Significantly, it is far more than simply the law relating to children, which is to say that 'law' is not merely functional and descriptive and that the 'child' is not always easily identifiable; rather, it is a complex and frequently contested and continually shifting discursive construction.

We wish to make clear from the outset that this collection of essays does not claim to represent a comprehensive coverage of the many topics and issues which are currently understood to be part of child law.[1] However, by

---

1   The enormous breadth of these issues can be seen from a survey of the contents lists of textbooks devoted to the subject (eg, Bainham, A, *Children: The Modern Law*, 1998, Bristol: Jordan; Fortin, J, *Children's Rights and the Developing Law*, 1998, London: Butterworths; Hayes, M and Williams, C, *Family Law: Principles, Policy and Practice*, 1999, London: Buterworths; Freeman, M, *Child Welfare and the Law*, 1998, London: Sweet & Maxwell), the articles published in journals which include child law within their remit (eg, CFLQ; JSWFL; Family Law; IJLPF; IJCR) and by the research projects undertaken by centres for the study of the law relating to the child (eg, Centre for the Study of Law, the Child and the Family, Brunel University; Centre for the Study of the Child, the Family and the Law, University of Liverpool; Children's Legal Centre, Essex University).

giving prominence to questions about the coherency and genealogy of child law, and by recognising the contingency and complexity of terms such as 'children' and 'childhood', this collection of essays seeks to enable familiar issues to be examined and analysed in new ways and for overlooked or silenced voices and perspectives to be explored.

As mentioned above, child law is no longer perceived as being merely one aspect of family law, but traverses the boundaries of established academic categories. This is reflected within this collection, which contains chapters relating to human rights,[2] health care law,[3] education law,[4] criminal justice[5] and tort.[6] Furthermore, those chapters that do explore issues contained within the traditional boundaries of family law do so from original perspectives, for example, by questioning the meanings and uses of 'fatherhood'[7] and 'motherhood',[8] and by exploring how law is produced not only in its traditional texts,[9] but also in legal practice.[10] In order to explore these issues, a broad range of methodologies are utilised. Consequently, alongside a variety of feminist and critical theoretical perspectives such as discourse analysis, autopoiesis and poststructural and comparative approaches are chapters which draw on empirical research. And, while many of the chapters take traditional legal sources such as cases and statutes as their starting point, others draw on legal practice, literature and popular media. Notwithstanding this breadth, all of the chapters, albeit in distinct ways, are informed by feminism and raise a number of questions about the relationship between feminism and childhood, some of which we highlight and explore in this introduction.

WHAT IS A CHILD?

'Expensive nuisance, slave and super-pet'?[11]

The question 'what is a child?' is an extremely important one, but one that is rarely asked. Our experiences, as children or as adults surrounded by or

---

2   See Lim and Roche, Chapter 12 and Buss, Chapter 14, in this volume.
3   See Roberts, Chapter 3, in this volume.
4   See Monk, Chapter 10, in this volume.
5   See O'Donovan, Chapter 4, Worrall, Chapter 8 and Thomson, Chapter 9, in this volume.
6   See Bridgeman, Chapter 11, in this volume.
7   See Collier, Chapter 6, in this volume.
8   See O'Donovan, Chapter 4, in this volume.
9   See Reece, Chapter 5, in this volume.
10 See Diduck, Chapter 13 and Barnett, Chapter 7, in this volume.
11 Holt, J, *Escape from Childhood*, 1975, Harmondsworth: Penguin, p 15, quoted in James, A, Jenks, C and Prout, A, *Theorizing Childhood*, 1998, Cambridge: Polity, p 210.

coming into contact with children, appear to render the question unnecessary.[12] As Chris Jenks, one of the leading 'new' sociologists of childhood, explains, the category of child has been, and continues to be, seen as natural. From this perspective, childhood is viewed as a perfectly ordinary, and expected, period through which we all go prior to becoming adults.[13] Consequently, the sociology of the child has long been dominated by theories of development and socialisation from a state of biological and psychological immaturity to adult maturity.[14] And childhood has accordingly, and without question, been perceived simply as a period of acquiring the skills, characteristics and behaviour of adulthood.

But attitudes towards children, expectations of them and understandings of their capacities are not unitary, fixed or static. Rather, they are contingent, negotiable and contested and the understandings of and meanings given to childhood are culturally and historically specific; which is to say that childhood is socially constructed.[15] What is understood by childhood – the activities of its members, the spaces they are permitted to occupy, the characteristics they are believed to possess – differ, depending upon the point in time and the culture of the childhood being considered;[16] and, furthermore, at any point in time, a number of discourses may present understandings of childhood which may be conflicting or contradictory.[17] While one of the competing discourses will often come to be the dominant understanding,[18] legal, spatial and temporal boundaries enable alternative and conflicting constructions to coexist.[19] The way in which discourses construct childhood has an impact upon the lives of children as they and adults change their behaviour in response. This does not mean that there is a universal experience for children. Children actively shape their own lives and have different experiences which may depend upon, for example, their sex, race, ethnicity, religion or class. A social constructionist analysis of childhood should not lose sight of the reality of children's embodied lives, identities and subjectivities.

---

12 Jenks, C, *Childhood*, 1996, London: Routledge and Kegan Paul, p 6.

13 *Ibid*.

14 The most influential exponent of this approach is Piaget; see, eg, Piaget, J, *The Language and Thought of the Child*, 1924, London: Routledge; Piaget, J, *The Moral Judgment of the Child*, 1932 (4th reprint 1965), London: Routledge.

15 *Ibid*, Jenks; James, A and Prout, A (eds), *Constructing and Reconstructing Childhood: Contemporary Issues in the Sociological Study of Childhood*, 1997, London: Falmer; *op cit*, James *et al*, fn 11; Buss, Chapter 14, in this volume.

16 For a critical perspective, see *op cit*, James *et al*, fn 11.

17 Trinder, L, 'Competing constructions of childhood: children's rights and children's wishes in divorce' (1997) 19 JSWFL 219.

18 *Ibid*, Jenks, p 69.

19 See O'Donovan, K, 'The child as legal object', in *Family Law Matters*, 1993, London: Pluto. Compare, eg, the girl child as constructed by education law, in criminal justice and in laws concerning the heterosexual age of consent in Monk, Chapter 10, Worrall, Chapter 8 and Thomson, Chapter 9, respectively, in this volume.

Additionally, Chris Jenks argues that a social constructionist analysis of childhood provides further insights, in that the position afforded to children within society is revealing of the nature of the society in which the child is situated:

> [T]heories of the child are ... pointers towards the social construction of reality. Just as I have argued that the child is neither simply 'natural' nor merely 'normal', we may claim to have established, in addition, that the child is not neutral but rather always moral and political. Thus the way that we treat our children is indicative of the state of our social structure, a measure of the achievement of our civilisation or even an index of the degree to which humanism has outstripped the economic motive in everyday life. Similarly, the way that we control our children reflects, perhaps as a continuous microcosm, the strategies through which we exercise power and constraint in the wider society.[20]

Chris Jenks argues that the child has been repositioned to a central place in meeting the needs of adults. He terms this 'nostalgia', in that the child appears to offer all that adults want but which adults lack: dependency, love, care, stability and security. And the particular concern for childhood evident in our society demonstrates, he suggests, adult concern for stability and security, embodied by the child, in an otherwise disrupted world:

> As we need children we watch them and we develop institutions and programmes to watch them and oversee the maintenance of that which they, and they only, now protect. We have always watched children, once as guardians of their/our future and now because they have become the guardians.[21]

The law is one of the institutions which performs this task.

Law and childhood

The law does not intervene simply by regulating a pre-existing child but, rather, legal discourse is heavily implicated in the production of the category childhood. At a very basic level, the law sets the boundaries of childhood by defining the legal age of majority, an age which differs across time and across cultures.[22] Yet the age of majority, currently 18 in the UK, is one of many temporal boundaries found in law. The separate age limits relating to, for example, smoking, drinking alcohol, driving, compulsory schooling, employment, consent to medical treatment and criminal justice sentencing challenge the notion that there is an absolute, temporal, binary distinction

---

20 *Op cit*, Jenks, fn 12, p 69.
21 *Op cit*, Jenks, fn 12, p 108.
22 The Family Law Reform Act 1969, s 1, reduced the age of majority from 21 to 18.

between adulthood and childhood.[23] To this extent, law admits to and enables a degree of fluidity in the construction of childhood. More significantly, however, these incremental temporal and legal boundaries reflect and uphold an understanding of childhood as a series of developmental stages on the road to becoming an adult. That this characterisation of childhood is generally perceived as 'common sense' attests to the overriding influence of the scientific discipline of developmental psychology in contemporary understandings of childhood. Within this discipline, child development is conceptualised as a natural process in which children acquire cognitive competencies according to universal and stratified sequences based largely on age. Critical analyses have highlighted how this 'ideology of development'[24] or 'developmentalism'[25] imposes rigid boundaries between adulthood and childhood and between children of different ages.[26] As Chris Jenks comments, 'real children are subjected to the violence of a contemporary mode of scientific rationality which reproduces itself at the expense of their difference'.[27] While these critiques have provided, and continue to provide, insights into contemporary understandings, they have had notably little impact on professional and political discourse and practises. The law, as a legitimising discourse, arguably contributes to the silencing of alternative perspectives.

One of the implications of the dominance of the discourse of developmental psychology and its construction of childhood as a process which ends when a child becomes an adult is that children are perceived in terms of lack and, consequently, as vulnerable and in need of protection. Once again, law and legal discourse reflects and upholds this image. This is particularly the case in the context of those aspects of child law contained within the Children Act 1989. The Children Act, which consolidated much of the law relating to children and was consequently perceived and heralded as representing a 'child focused' approach in its structure and application, makes a clear distinction between private law and public law. The former deals with changes in familial structure through divorce and separation and issues of parental responsibility such as change of name, and the latter with circumstances where State intervention is justified or required. In both locations, the image of the child as vulnerable and in need of protection prevails. Alison Diduck demonstrates how, in the context of divorce

---

23 For a clear summary of these provisions and others, see Children's Legal Centre, 'At what age can I ...?' (1999) Information Sheet, University of Essex.

24 *Op cit*, Jenks, fn 12, p 25.

25 Stainton Rogers, W and Stainton Rogers, R, 'Word children', in Lesnik-Oberstein, K (ed), *Children in Culture: Approaches to Childhood*, 1998, London: Macmillan.

26 *Op cit*, Jenks, fn 12; *ibid*, Stainton Rogers and Stainton Rogers; Burman, E, *Deconstructing Developmental Psychology*, 1994, London: Routledge.

27 *Op cit*, Jenks, fn 12, p 25.

proceedings, the child is objectified as a 'passive potential trauma victim'.[28] More explicitly, in public law proceedings, the threshold for intervention is determined by assessments of 'need'[29] and 'harm'.[30]

We are not in any way suggesting that children do not suffer harm or are not in need of protection; rather, we seek to highlight the significance of the dominance of the image of the child as vulnerable and passive, which serves to restrict and silence children's involvement and obscures the extent to which assessments of children's harm uphold normative constructions, not only for children,[31] but for fathers and, in particular, mothers.[32]

What these insights into the construction of the child as passive, vulnerable and needy demonstrates is the extent to which child law is dominated by adult perceptions of the child, as a non-adult or future adult. The protection afforded to the child is consequently motivated not simply by the present reality of children's lives, but in more complex ways, by a desire to safeguard the personal and political potential which the child embodies.[33]

This critical approach towards childhood and the work of the 'new' sociologists of childhood is explicitly referred to by many of the contributors to this volume. However, while the child as 'victim' can be identified in chapters dealing with domestic violence,[34] the broad focus of the collection as a whole moves away from a child protection perspective. Once again, it is important to stress that this does not represent a lack of concern for the real harms that are inflicted on real children. The perspectives adopted by these essays represent recognition of a need in legal scholarship relating to children for alternative approaches which reveal the disciplinary role of law implicit in the construction of the child, as opposed to an emphasis upon the saving role of law. For example, Doris Buss explores how the discourse of children's rights is perceived as dangerous by Christian rights organisations; Rachel Thomson explores how children themselves perceive law's protectionism in the context of sexual activity; Melanie Roberts implicitly questions who is protected by laws relating to new reproductive technologies; and Helen Reece demonstrates how it is not just children but adults who are increasingly objectified and infantilised by law's 'protective' role.

---

28 See Diduck, Chapter 13, in this volume.

29 Children Act 1989, s 17.

30 *Ibid*, s 31.

31 See Freeman, Chapter 2, Worrall, Chapter 8, Thomson, Chapter 9 and Bridgeman, Chapter 11, in this volume.

32 See Freeman, Chapter 2, Collier, Chapter 6, O'Donovan, Chapter 4, Barnett, Chapter 7, Diduck, Chapter 13 and Buss, Chapter 14, in this volume.

33 Oakley, A, 'Woman and children first and last: parallels and differences between children's and women's studies', in Mayall, B (ed), *Children's Childhoods: Observed and Experienced*, 1994, London: Falmer, p 23.

34 See Diduck, Chapter 13 and Barnett, Chapter 7, in this volume.

FEMINIST PERSPECTIVES

Feminist thought encompasses a rich and wide ranging variety of perspectives, characterised by a concern with the social, political and legal position of women. In all forms, feminism adopts a critical stance upon the subject of its gaze, seeking to reveal and develop an understanding of the conditions of women's lives and, by undertaking this critique or, more specifically, in advocating reform, suggest how it might be otherwise. A central theme of this collection is to question the stability of the child as the subject or object of child law.[35] In our view, feminist perspectives and the chapters in this volume provide insights into this issue in two distinct ways.[36]

First, the tools of feminist analysis can be employed to question the centrality of the child, that is, whether the law is more effective in protecting the interests of others, principally the adults who care for the child, than in safeguarding the child.[37] Secondly, feminist perspectives challenge the gender neutrality of law. Liberal feminism accepted the existence of natural or essential differences between the sexes but sought equal treatment of the sexes within the law. Radical feminism located the explanation for the oppression of women within the differences between the sexes. A constructivist approach sees differences as socially constructed and seeks, by exposing the way in which discourses construct subjects differently, to create the space for alternative understandings to emerge. Consequently, feminist perspectives may expose treatment of the child within the law as pre-gender or gender neutral, masking the extent to which the identity and experiences of the male and female child are distinct.

The law as a cause of harm?

The requirement imposed by legislation to consider, and in the determination of cases to give effect to, the welfare or best interests of the child reflects a desire on the part of adults to protect children. Yet, as the perspectives and experiences of children remain excluded, it might be that the law is ineffective in protecting children from harm as felt, understood, experienced and defined by children as distinct from adults.

---

35 *Op cit*, O'Donovan, fn 19.

36 Freeman, Chapter 2, in this volume, specifically addresses the lack of a feminist analysis of child law and suggests ways in which feminism could provide useful insights.

37 *Op cit*, O'Donovan, fn 19, p 90; Herring, J, 'The welfare principle and the rights of parents', in Bainham, A, Day-Sclater, S and Richards, M (eds), *What is a Parent? A Socio-Legal Analysis*, 1999, Oxford: Hart; Freeman, Chapter 2, Roberts, Chapter 3 and O'Donovan, Chapter 4, in this volume.

What is harmful is not 'a transcendental notion which is automatically knowable and recognisable at any moment in history by any member of a culture';[38] rather, conceptions of harm change over time and between cultures. Carol Smart,[39] for example, discusses the lack of response within law to the sexual abuse of children in the early part of the 20th century. She argues that the failure to recognise the abuse of children as harmful at that time (and not until the 1970s) arose from a belief that children were not affected by events which occurred to them as children: children, by their nature, could not be harmed. Furthermore, the subsequent behaviour of children who had been exposed to sexual conduct, rather than being seen as caused by the abuse they had experienced, was attributed to their evil nature, which permitted the responsibility for the abuse to be placed upon the child. Whilst her analysis supports an understanding of harm as contingent and contestable, what is further notable is the resistance which Carol Smart identifies amongst the participants within the criminal justice system at that time to challenges to the exclusion of abuse of children from conceptions of harm. Harm may, therefore, be experienced differently by members within society but is legally recognised as such, depending upon the scope given to the concept of harm by those possessing the power to give harm definition.

In her work, Robin West has explored the failure of the law to recognise the gender specific harms suffered by women.[40] She argues that the law recognises and provides protection where women suffer the same harms as are suffered by men, that is, the invasion of the boundaries of the separate self, but fails to extend protection to harms specifically experienced by women. These harms, she argues, are different in cause, consequence and effect from those harms which are suffered by men and in respect of which the law does provide redress.[41] West argues that the consequences of the failure of the law to recognise the specific harms experienced by women are twofold. First, the silence of the law is legitimating. That is, the failure of the law to acknowledge the harm signals that no harm has been done, thereby legitimising the conduct. Secondly, women are thus doubly harmed: once by the harm itself, then by the failure of the law to respond. She concludes: '... we need to articulate what harms us, and how, and by how much, and what the law could do to minimise those harms.'[42] This feminist analysis raises pertinent and important questions about the harms suffered by children.

---

38 Smart, C, 'A history of ambivalence and conflict in the discursive construction of the "child victim" of sexual abuse' (1999) 8 SLS 392; see, also, Freeman, Chapter 2, in this volume.

39 · *Ibid*, Smart.

40 West, R, 'Jurisprudence and gender' (1988) 55 Chicago UL Rev 1; West, R, *Caring for Justice*, 1997, New York: New York UP, particularly 'The concept of harm'.

41 *Ibid*, West, 1997, p 98, identifying 'harms of invasion' (sexual assault and unwanted pregnancy), 'private altruistic harm' (including dependency leading to a fear of abandonment), 'harms of separation' (arising from the connections with others).

42 *Ibid*, West, 1997, p 176.

First, laws which are aimed at the protection of children or their interests may not only fail to achieve this aim, but may be positively damaging to children. One obvious example is provided by the Cleveland Inquiry, which identified that children were additionally harmed by examinations undertaken to detect abuse and, thereby, by systems aimed at protecting them. Caroline Sawyer emphasises the importance of being aware of this possibility and the need to change the 'protective' processes of the law:

> [T]he legal process should not, in the course of collecting evidence as to what had happened in the past, do further damage to the child. Ignoring the child might mean the court reaching the 'wrong' decision through lack of information, but, separately, it might mean that the child's experience of the process was a damaging one, confirming to the child a sense of powerlessness and unimportance.[43]

A further example is provided by Adrienne Barnett's analysis of contact orders where there has been domestic violence.[44] Her argument is that the law takes from scientific discourses ideas about the welfare of the child and employs them in an effort to reproduce the nuclear family. Consequently, fathers are permitted contact with their children even where they have in the past been violent. In doing so, the law adopts one perspective from contested, contradictory and confusing scientific evidence, silencing the accounts of others, in particular the accounts of women and children about abusive men.

Secondly, children may be harmed in ways that are not so manifestly obvious as the harm caused by physical, emotional or sexual abuse. Richard Collier, for example, discusses the concerns that the efforts undertaken by parents who are 'anxious' to protect their children may in themselves cause harm.[45]

A better understanding of the nature of the harm arising from the specificities of children's lives can only be achieved if we listen to children.[46] Participatory models are premised upon hearing the voices of children, involving them by empowering them and supporting them in the extent to which they wish to become involved in issues affecting them. Participatory models present a challenge to the perception that adults know what is best for children and provide the means to best accommodate the interests and wishes of children in issues affecting their lives.

---

43 Sawyer, C, 'Conflicting rights for children: implementing welfare, autonomy and justice within family proceedings' (1999) 21 JSWFL 99, p 103. Christina Lyon comments on *South Glamorgan CC v W and B* [1993] 1 FLR 574 that we are confronted with the 'spectre of further potential abuse perpetrated this time by the very system which is supposed to protect children': Lyon, C, 'What's happened to the child's "right" to refuse? *South Glamorgan County Council v W and B*' (1994) 6 JCL 84, p 87.

44 See Barnett, Chapter 7, in this volume.

45 See Collier, Chapter 6, in this volume.

46 See Freeman, Chapter 2, Lim and Roche, Chapter 12, Diduck, Chapter 13 and Bridgeman, Chapter 11, in this volume.

Dependent/interdependent?

The perspective of the child as immature, dependent and in need of protection distinguishes the child as 'other' to the adult. This dichotomy ignores the extent to which adults are likewise dependent upon others, including their children, practically, emotionally and when, for example, sick or old. It further hides the capacities and agency of children.[47] Children are treated as if they are not thinking, active, determining beings, but non-subjects awaiting adulthood.[48] However, we only need to look to the children who themselves care for dependent adults or siblings, or to children whose earnings are an essential contribution to the family income, or to consider the extent to which children themselves play a formative role in what is culturally valued, to begin to understand children differently.[49]

Judith Ennew's discussion of the structured activities of children leads her to the conclusion that children do not spend endless hours in 'idle play'; they work in school, doing jobs around the home and participating in organised activities:

> The artificial split between children and adults is based on a mystification, or fetishisation, of 'play' as the core of childhood, being opposed to work as the 'hub of the adult world'. By trivialising childhood activities, marginalising and economically devalorising children, adults in industrial societies reproduce the power relations that enable them to take hold of children's time, organise it, curricularise it and simultaneously control the next generation on behalf of an economic system that depends for its very existence on the subdivision of human energy into units of labour time.[50]

Here, there is a clear parallel, exposed by feminists, with the failure to recognise or reward the work which women do in the home; cooking, cleaning, washing and emotionally supporting men and children. Work which is essential for the functioning of the economy and nurturing of the future workforce. Contrary to the view of the dependent and, hence, 'unproductive' child, James, Jenks and Prout identify three major facets of the employment of children in industrialised societies:[51] first, that children contribute to the economy when they are able to care for themselves, as opposed to relying

---

47 See Diduck, Chapter 13, in this volume, for a discussion of the ways in which children of divorce are denied agency.

48 Qvortrup, J, 'Childhood matters: an introduction', in Qvortrup, J, Bardy, M, Sgritta, G and Wintersberger, H (eds), *Childhood Matters: Social Theory, Practice and Politics*, 1994, Aldershot: Averbury, p 4.

49 A point made by Lim and Roche, Chapter 12, in this volume.

50 Ennew, J, 'Time for children or time for adults', in *ibid*, Qvortrup *et al*, p 143.

51 *Op cit*, James *et al*, fn 11, pp 112–14. They also discuss the place of work in the lives of children in developing countries.

upon an adult to provide that care; secondly, that children do undertake the care of sick or disabled adults;[52] thirdly, that legislation which seeks to limit the participation of children in renumerated employment is widely flouted.[53] Recognition of the productivity and contribution made by children disrupts the perception of children as only and always dependent, and provides the possibility of reconceptualising the relationship between adults and children as one of interdependency.[54]

Talking with children

Questioning the reality of the perception of children as mere dependents should not lead to the conclusion that children should be treated in law as if they were adults by extending to them equal rights with adults.[55] A claim to equal treatment begs the question of 'equal to what?' and feminists have exposed the legal norm as one which is framed by male characteristics, behaviours and values. The societal disadvantages faced by women are not overcome by treating women as if they were men. Likewise, the appropriate response to the social conditions of children is not to treat them as if they are adults. Children should not have to fit into adult categories when their values, priorities, interests and desires may be different. However, concern about the interests of children does not ensure that the terms in which those interests are considered are any different. Ann Oakley suggests that the focus upon children in the children's rights movement, and, similarly, in child law, often adopts the same perspective of the child as endangered, dependent and vulnerable:

> Women's studies grew directly out of the political movement for women's liberation; it emerged out of the politics of experience. But children's studies are not rooted in the same way in the movement of children to claim their own liberation. Although there are some instances of children acting politically to secure their rights, the children's rights movement is not a political movement initiated primarily by children themselves. By and large, it is adults who are making representations on behalf of children – in their 'best interests' to re-use the traditional phrase. Children are coming to the fore in adult's minds, but the danger is that adults may continue to be the protectors of children, the

---

52 See, also, Dearden, C and Becker, S, 'The needs and experiences of young carers in the UK' (1998) 148 Childright 15; Dearden, C and Becker, S, 'Protecting young carers: legislative tensions and opportunities in Britain' (1997) 19 JSWFL 123.

53 Children and Young Persons Act 1933, s 18, as amended by the Children (Protection at Work) Regulations 1998 (SI 1998/276).

54 See Lim and Roche, Chapter 12, in this volume.

55 Or treating children as if they were adults, eg, in criminal justice policy. See Fionda, J, 'R v Secretary of State for the Home Department ex p Venables and Thompson: the age of innocence? The concept of childhood in the punishment of young offenders' (1998) 10 CFLQ 77.

representers of their interests, rather than facilitators or active seekers out of children's own perspectives and voices.[56]

A view that adults know where the best interests of the child lie and can best represent the interests of children by speaking for them coexists with a sense that, because we have all been children, as adults we have experiences which give us a privileged position from which to speak. However, as adults, our understanding of childhood derives from memories which have been reinterpreted in the light of adult experience and influenced by contemporary ideas about childhood.[57] To challenge the adult view and allow different understandings to emerge, it is necessary, first, to enable children to express their views and detail their experiences of, for example, the law; and, secondly, to ensure that analysis of what they have to say is not framed by understandings and expectations of children held by adults.[58]

Ann Oakley argues that it is necessary to effect a shift from children as the objects of study to children as subjects of study: to 'study the world from the standpoints of children both as knowers and as actors'.[59] This requires imagination on the part of researchers to formulate research projects which permit children to express (and not necessarily orally) their understandings and experiences.[60] It demands sensitivity on the part of researchers to their own perspectives of childhood to ensure that their findings are not reinterpreted through adult understandings of children's lack of capacity.[61] Further, Ann Oakley suggests that it is necessary to undertake not only those studies which dip into particular points in the lives of children taking a snapshot of an age, but also longitudinal studies which map the changing views and experiences of children over time.[62] Rachel Thomson's research study, in which children spoke about the age of consent to heterosexual intercourse, identifies tensions within what the children had to say in relation to the gendered differences upon which the law is premised, that is, of male agency (out of control) and female passivity (in need of protection), with the ways in which they thought about themselves and their sexual identities.[63]

---

56 *Op cit*, Oakley, fn 33, p 20.

57 *Op cit*, Oakley, fn 33, p 28.

58 *Op cit*, Qvortrup, fn 48, p 2.

59 *Op cit*, Oakley, fn 33, pp 24–25; see, also, Alanen, L, 'Gender and generation: feminism and the "child question"', in *op cit*, Qvortrup *et al*, fn 48, pp 35–36. See, eg, Smart, C, Wade, A and Neale, B, 'Objects of concern? – children and divorce' (1999) 11 CFLQ 365; James, AL and Richards, MPM, 'Sociological perspectives, family policy, family law and children: adult thinking and sociological tinkering' (1999) 21 JSWFL 23.

60 See the examples given by Oakley in *op cit*, fn 33, pp 25–26.

61 Alderson, P, 'Researching children's rights to integrity', in *op cit*, Mayall, fn 33.

62 *Op cit*, Oakley, fn 33, p 27.

63 See Thomson, Chapter 9, in this volume.

Whilst expressing doubts about the ability of the law to accommodate the individuality encapsulated by the way in which the children whom she spoke with talked about sex, she argues that this understanding is important for discussion about sexual conduct and sexual health policy and practice.[64]

Women and children – a relationship of conflict or care?

The focus of feminism has been upon the experiences of women. Where feminism has considered children, it is often in relation to the implications for women of their 'mothering' role of begetting, bearing, birthing, caring and nurturing children. This has resulted in perceptible tensions between, on the one hand, the importance and value to women of their caring relationships with children and, on the other, feelings of constraint through confinement to the domestic sphere whilst desiring alternative roles. In its liberal form, feminism sought equality for women through, for example, legal rights, reproductive autonomy and self-determination. Challenging the perception that women's natural role was in the domestic sphere, liberal feminism claimed access for women to the public sphere. Rather than be confined to the roles of wife, mother and carer, equal access was sought to participation in the public realm of education, the professions, industry and politics. To be freed from the shackles of the domestic realm and have the choice to pursue other activities required the provision of contraception, access to abortion and alternative childcare. In its radical form, feminists, such as Shulamith Firestone in *The Dialectic of Sex*,[65] argued that the oppression of women was located in their reproductive role. Others argued that it is not the reproductive abilities of women as such which result in oppression, but male control over female reproductive abilities.[66]

Both liberal and radical feminism thus appear to be premised upon a perception of the child as an obstacle to the social positioning of women.[67] This approach can similarly be seen in feminist legal scholarship, which, for example, identified the disciplinary and restrictive implications for women of interpretations of the child's best interests in custody/residence disputes. From such perspectives, children remained an object of feminist thought, whilst action was directed at improving the position of the female subject. Yet,

---

64   The importance of children's perspectives in developing responsive legal approaches is also acknowledged by Lim and Roche, Chapter 12 and Bridgeman, Chapter 11, in this volume.

65   Firestone, S, *The Dialectic of Sex*, 1970, New York: Bantam.

66   Rich, A, *Of Woman Born: Motherhood as Experience and Institution*, 1976, New York: WW Norton. As the title of her book suggests, Rich makes a distinction between the institution of motherhood, which, in her view, is oppressive, and the experience, which need not be; O'Brien, M, *The Politics of Reproduction*, 1981, Boston: Routledge and Kegan Paul.

67   *Op cit*, Oakley, fn 33, p 22; *op cit*, Alanen, fn 59, pp 32–34.

despite the tensions within feminism about the relationships between women and children, there are similarities between the social conditions of women and children which mean that feminism can provide insights into the position of children in society, including in law. These include being denied equal rights, being constructed as lacking capacity, having decisions made on their behalf in their best interests and being treated as a social problem.[68]

What seems to us to be particularly instructive is the ways in which feminist thought, rather than being limited to attempts to reconcile the perceived conflict between women and children in the favour of one or the other, has insisted upon the need to challenge the terms of the debate. One method is the constructionist turn within feminism which explores the way in which the subject is constituted by discourses as, for example, the 'good' mother[69] or the 'self-sacrificing' mother.[70] This has been discussed above, but it is worth repeating here to emphasise that one of the insights provided by discourse analysis of the law is an acknowledgment that the law does not benefit one subject all of the time but produces different subjects against which the individual is judged.

Secondly, the perception of relationships between women and children as characterised by conflict may not be consistent with the experience of the relationships which many women have with children. Despite the resolution in law of issues concerned with children in terms of their welfare, the domination of adversarial approaches to legal problems means that the law is instrumental in creating and sustaining a conflictual relationship. An alternative which permits reconceptualisation of problems, decision making processes and solutions is provided by the ethic of care theorised by Carol Gilligan.[71] A developmental psychologist, Carol Gilligan was concerned that women achieved lower levels of moral development, as measured on the scale determined by Harvard's Lawrence Kohlberg. Moral maturity, in his understanding, was represented by determinations in terms of universal conceptions of justice, whereas women tended to focus upon positive relationships with others, which he positioned halfway up his six point scale.[72] A further observation that the scale of moral maturity was derived from studies exclusively upon men[73] led to her own studies of moral decision

---

68 *Op cit*, Oakley, fn 33, pp 14–18; see, also, *op cit*, Alanen, fn 59, p 35.

69 Smart, C, 'The woman of legal discourse' (1992) 1 SLS 29.

70 Diduck, A, 'Legislating ideologies of motherhood' (1993) 2 SLS 462; for consideration of the relevance of this for the study of children, see *op cit*, Alanen, fn 59, p 35.

71 Gilligan, C, *In a Different Voice: Psychological Theory and Women's Development*, 2nd edn, 1993, Cambridge, Mass: Harvard UP.

72 *Ibid*, p 18.

73 *Ibid*. See Kohlberg, who studied 84 males over a period of 20 years (Kohlberg, L, *The Philosophy of Moral Development*, 1981, San Francisco: Harper and Row); and, similarly, Piaget before him (*op cit*, Piaget, 1932, fn 14).

making, which sought to redress this by listening to the approaches of women, as well as men, to moral problems.[74] From what she heard, she identified an alternative trajectory or, as she called it, a 'different voice'. In contrast with abstract individualistic rationalisations, the different voice spoke in terms of an ethic of care. This ethic:

> [F]ocuses on the dynamics of relationships and dissipates the tension between selfishness and responsibility through a new understanding of the interconnection between other and self. Care becomes the self-chosen principle of a judgment that remains psychological in its concern with relationships and response but becomes universal in its condemnation of exploitation and hurt. ... This ethic [the ethic of care], which reflects a cumulative knowledge of human relationships, evolves around a central insight, that self and other are interdependent.[75]

A concern with relationships necessitates appreciation of attachment, connection and interdependence. From the perspective of the ethic of care, resolution of moral problems is dependent upon contextualisation in terms of the responsibility of caring – both for others and for the self. Broadly stated, the ethic of care approach, identified by Carol Gilligan, involves addressing the consequences for all involved, seeking a resolution which avoids hurting and taking responsibility for the decision.

Appreciating the centrality of conceptions of justice, premised upon equality and rights in Western liberal democracies, Gilligan suggests incorporation, not replacement – that the law should accommodate both justice and care. What is of particular interest is the potential application of the ethic of care in resolving issues concerning children: suggesting frameworks for resolution of legal problems which are not centred around adversarial battles between competing rights.[76] Furthermore, it is important to recognise that caring is both an emotional state and a physical activity. As Carol Smart *et al* observe, this is particularly important where children are concerned, as they can be actively caring whilst, because it is not expected of them, not in the act of providing care.[77] Recognition of the contribution made by children caring

---

74 A study of 25 college students, both male and female, which sought to explore the relationship between ideas and attitudes to moral problems and the experience of making decisions; the abortion decision study of women considering the termination of a pregnancy; the rights and responsibility study of both sexes, across the ages, exploring hypothetical and real moral problems. For a summary of the studies, see *op cit*, Gilligan, fn 71, pp 2–3 .

75 *Op cit*, Gilligan, fn 71, p 74.

76 A great deal of feminist work has taken up this idea, particularly within feminist legal theory. Eg, the implications for substantive law are explored by Martin, R, 'A feminist view of the reasonable man: an alternative approach to liability in negligence for personal injury' (1994) 23 Anglo-Am L Rev 334; the implications for lawyering are considered by Menkel-Meadow, C, 'Portia in a different voice: speculating on women's lawyering process' (1987) 1 Berkeley Women's LJ 39. See, also, Lim and Roche, Chapter 12, Diduck, Chapter 13 and Bridgeman, Chapter 11, in this volume.

77 See, eg, *op cit*, Smart *et al*, fn 59, p 369.

permits acknowledgement of children as active, determining subjects as opposed to simply the 'objects of concern'. And it brings into focus the interdependency between adults – considering the needs of their children and provide care – and children, thinking about the needs of their parents even if they are not actively caring for them.[78]

Good girls and bad boys

Feminists have provided a critique of the understanding of law as a neutral universally applicable set of rules. The constructionist approach reveals that, in relation to different legal issues, different legal subjects are constructed, against which the individual is measured. In the first place, the Woman of Legal Discourse is produced, who stands in opposition to the male norm. Secondly, the law constitutes different types of women, depending upon the issue and who are measured against the Ideal Woman.[79] The ideal woman and the types of women that are constructed by legal discourse, however, bear little relation to the lives of women.

Whilst the production by discourses, including law, of differently gendered and sexed subjects has been at the centre of much feminist analysis of the law, the gender or sex of the child subject has not received the same scrutiny. Indeed, even in child and family law textbooks which adopt a broad socio-legal approach, rarely, if at all, is there any mention of 'boys' or 'girls'; rather, the gender neutral construction of the child remains unchallenged. In relation to many issues, the sex and gender of the child would appear to be irrelevant in the understanding of the law. This arises from a primary positioning of the child in contradistinction to the adult. In other words, what characterises all children, both girls and boys, appearing before the law is a perception of the child as immature, dependent and in need of protection. The myth of the gender neutral child makes the law blind to the specific identities of the individual boy or girl child. Feminist perspectives on child law raise the same question as has been asked in relation to the impact of law upon women: despite the appearance of neutrality in the application of universally applicable rules, what impact does the sex/gender of the child have upon the understanding of their welfare?

Analysis reveals that, in relation to some issues, differential treatment is meted out not only because of a failure to address the specificities of childhood identities, but because of an understanding of differences existing between the boys and girls. The perception of boys as out of control and in need of a firm hand appears to be the understanding of legislators and to be reflected in practice, for example, in school exclusions. This perception,

---

78 James, A, 'Parents: a children's perspective', in *op cit*, Bainham *et al*, fn 37.
79 *Op cit*, Smart, fn 69.

embodied by a few individuals such as 'rat boy',[80] justifies more punitive measures and obligations imposed upon parents.[81] One of the media's favourite shockers, concern with teenage pregnancy, seems to hold similar influence in the treatment of the girl child in law.[82] The girl child is subjected to regulation, for example in criminal and education law,[83] motivated by a desire to prevent teenage pregnancy. Sex, rather than crime, violence or disruptive behaviour is seen as the problem for girls. This does not, however, mean that the girl is considered to be an agent, actively choosing to engage in sexual activity or to enter into motherhood; rather, legal intervention is necessary to protect girls from the sexuality of the male. As Rachel Thomson discusses in this volume, the protective reach of the law is incompatible with the sexual identity of girls, the ways in which girls experience and perceive themselves.[84] Recognising the different identities of boy and girl children may present an effective challenge to the belief of the law as neutral and universally applicable. Yet, even when the law does recognise sex differences, there is no guarantee that they will bear any relation to the particularities of girl and boy children.

A number of the chapters in this collection explore this issue. Anne Worrall analyses changing constructions of female juvenile delinquency; Daniel Monk looks at law's role in the context of the moral panic regarding boys 'failure' in education; Rachel Thomson explores the distinctions between boys' and girls' perceptions of the legal provisions relating to the heterosexual age of consent; and Doris Buss comments on the significances of the girl child in the context of international human rights law.

FEMINIST PERSPECTIVES ON CHILD LAW

The contributors to this volume have adopted a range of feminist perspectives, showing the diversity and range of feminist thought. What they share is a critical approach to substantive law and legal practice, presenting a challenge to traditional approaches to child law.[85]

---

80 See Collier, Chapter 6 and Worrall, Chapter 8, in this volume.

81 Such as parenting orders: Crime and Disorder Act 1998, s 8.

82 Who automatically falls foul of the ideal mother of legal discourse, who is married, financially and emotionally supported by her husband.

83 See Worrall, Chapter 8 and Monk, Chapter 10, in this volume.

84 See Thomson, Chapter 9, in this volume. See, also, Worrall, Chapter 8 and Buss, Chapter 14, in this volume.

85 The relationship between feminist thought and the sociology of childhood is considered by Oakley, *op cit*, fn 33, and by Alanen, *op cit*, fn 59. Freeman, Chapter 2, in this volume, specifically addresses the relationship between feminism and child law.

Through the different issues which are addressed in the chapters, a number of themes can be identified, including: the entrenchment by the law of the nuclear family;[86] the perception of the child as fundamentally different from the adult;[87] children's identities;[88] dependency;[89] the constitution of the legal subject;[90] and the adult/legal desire to protect.[91] A number of influences are apparent: the 'new sociology of childhood';[92] the 'ethic of care';[93] and the participation of children in decisions affecting them.[94]

This collection is not, and could not be, comprehensive in its coverage of issues of the law relating to children. What is clear from law – in both its legislative and judicial forms, government policy, academic writing and the media is that there is currently, within different sectors of society, much concern about children. What we hope this volume does achieve is to demonstrate the value of feminist perspectives in providing insights into the nature of those concerns and suggesting alternative means of addressing them.

---

86 See Roberts, Chapter 3, Diduck, Chapter 13, Barnett, Chapter 7, Buss, Chapter 14 and Monk, Chapter 10, in this volume.

87 See Lim and Roche, Chapter 12, Thomson, Chapter 9, Buss, Chapter 14 and Bridgeman, Chapter 11, in this volume.

88 See Roberts, Chapter 3, O'Donovan, Chapter 4 and Thomson, Chapter 9, in this volume.

89 See Lim and Roche, Chapter 12, and Collier, Chapter 6, in this volume.

90 See Diduck, Chapter 13, Thomson, Chapter 9, Bridgeman, Chapter 11 and Monk, Chapter 10, in this volume.

91 See Freeman, Chapter 2, Lim and Roche, Chapter 12, Collier, Chapter 6, Thomson, Chapter 9, Diduck, Chapter 13, Buss, Chapter 14 and Bridgeman, Chapter 11, in this volume.

92 See Collier, Chapter 6, Buss, Chapter 14, Bridgeman, Chapter 11 and Monk, Chapter 10, in this volume.

93 See Lim and Roche, Chapter 12, Diduck, Chapter 13 and Barnett, Chapter 7, in this volume.

94 See Lim and Roche, Chapter 12, Diduck, Chapter 13, Thomson, Chapter 9 and Bridgeman, Chapter 11, in this volume.

CHAPTER 2

FEMINISM AND CHILD LAW

Michael Freeman

INTRODUCTION

There are feminist accounts of most legal territories now, but, strikingly, though perhaps not surprisingly, there is no feminist analysis as such of child law. Feminists have looked at child abuse,[1] at children's rights[2] and at institutions like adoption,[3] and some principles of child law have been scrutinised – Helen Reece's critical examination of the paramountcy principle is an outstanding example.[4] But none of this is surprising, for there are obvious takes on 'abuse' and on 'rights', and the ways in which paramountcy may have undermined the interests of parents, perhaps to the particular detriment of mothers (or at least some mothers),[5] is worthy of deconstruction. This, then, is unsurprising. But we lack a feminist account of child law, in the way that we now have an account (or accounts) of contract law,[6] labour law,[7]

---

1   See Ashe, M and Cahn, NR, 'Child abuse: a problem for feminist theory' (1993) 2 Texas J Women and the Law 75.

2   See Minow, M, 'Rights for the next generation: a feminist approach to children's rights' (1986) 9 Harvard Women's LJ 1; Olsen, F, 'Children's rights: some feminist approaches with special reference to the Convention on the Rights of the Child', in Alston, P, Parker, S and Seymour, J (eds), *Children, Rights and the Law*, 1991, Oxford: OUP. See, also, Lim and Roche, Chapter 12, in this volume.

3   Luker, K, *Abortion and the Politics of Motherhood*, 1984, Berkeley: California UP is the classic source.

4   Reece, H, 'The paramountcy principle – consensus or construct?' (1996) 49 CLP 267.

5   In particular, lesbians.

6   See Frug, M, 'Rescuing impossibility doctrine: a postmodern feminist analysis of contract law' (1992) 140 Pennsylvania UL Rev 1029; Brown, B, 'Contracting out/contracting in: some feminist considerations', in Bottomley, A, *Feminist Perspectives on the Foundational Subjects of Law*, 1996, London: Cavendish Publishing. On obligations more generally, see (2000) 8 FLS 1, pp 1–131 (Special Issue).

7   See Morris, A and O'Donnell, T (eds), *Feminist Perspectives on Employment Law*, 1999, London: Cavendish Publishing; Conaghan, J, 'The invisibility of women in labour law: gender-neutrality in model-building' (1986) 14 IJSL 377.

the law of property,[8] tort law,[9] international law,[10] etc.[11] Why has the discipline of child law escaped feminist scrutiny? The subject is, of course, relatively new – indeed, of about the same vintage as feminist legal literature – but this cannot explain why it has been overlooked. Have feminists avoided exploring the area because the issues are too obvious? Or because, already marginalised, they wished to avoid an obvious legal ghetto? Or because they can translate the issues into broader concerns (patriarchy, mothering, marriage and family law generally) or narrower ones (child abuse and children's rights)? Whatever the explanation, it cannot be because the subject is not intrinsically interesting, for it has both a rhetoric and a silence with enormous potential for feminist mining (and, need it be said, undermining).

SOME FEMINIST CONCERNS

Insofar as one cannot ignore the social constructions of 'male' and 'female', any essay looking at the law relating to children and feminism would review the feminist project. Although not my remit, some introductory comments must be offered.

We are reminded by Pateman that the public/private dichotomy is what feminism is all about.[12] The dualism is, of course, problematic, even illusory.[13] That the parent-child relationship has been regarded as quintessentially private is beyond dispute.[14] What, however, has been often overlooked is that it is the State which determines what is private; as Deborah Rhode puts it, what forms of intimacy deserve protection.[15] So, for example, only those forms of child abuse which the State wished to proscribe are categorised as

---

8   See Green, K, 'Being here: what a woman can say about land law', in *op cit*, Bottomley, fn 6.

9   See Bender, L, 'A lawyer's primer on feminist theory and tort' (1988) 38 JLE 3; Finley, L, 'A break in the silence: including women's issues in torts course' (1989) 1 Yale J Law and Feminism 41.

10 See Charlesworth, H, Chinkin, C and Wright, S, 'Feminist approaches to international law' (1991) 85 AJIL 613; Engle, K, 'Female subjects of public international law: human rights and the exotic other female' (1992) 26 New England L Rev 1509.

11 Eg, bankruptcy law (see Gross, K, 'The debtor as modern day peon: a problem of unconstitutional conditions' (1990) 88 Michigan L Rev 1506); tax law (see Beck, RCE, 'The innocent spouse problem' (1990) 43 Vanderbilt L Rev 317); public law (see Millns, S and Whitty, N, *Feminist Perspectives on Public Law*, 1999, London: Cavendish Publishing); and, of course, of family law (a recent excellent example of which is Bartlett, KT, 'Feminism and family law' (1999) 33 FLQ 475).

12 Pateman, C, *The Disorder of Women*, 1989, Cambridge: Polity, p 118.

13 Boyd, SB (ed), *Challenging The Public/Private Divide: Feminism, Law and Public Policy*, 1997, Toronto: Toronto UP.

14 Fineman, MA, *The Neutered Mother, the Sexual Family and Other Twentieth Century Tragedies*, 1995, New York: Routledge.

15 Rhode, D, 'Feminist critical theories' (1990) 42 Stan L Rev 617.

within the public arena: children are protected against physical abuse, but not against so called reasonable corporal chastisement,[16] though the line may be difficult – even impossible – to draw, and often the label (or social construction) is imposed retrospectively. Defining what amounts to sexual abuse[17] or emotional abuse[18] is equally problematic. Nor, and this is often forgotten, is categorising something as 'public' necessarily a guarantee that the State will interfere and protect: labelling a nude photograph of a child as 'art' will protect as public freedom of expression an artefact that others will deem child pornography and, thus, abuse.

Feminism is about inequalities. But inequality, which, as we will see, is imbricated within child law (and not always to the disadvantage of women or girl children), is not just a legal mistake. It is no more irrational than, for example, violence against women is irrational. As Ann Scales observed, 'the injustice of sexism is not irrationality', but 'domination'.[19] It is her view, which I endorse, that law must embrace a version of equality that focuses on the real issues – domination, disadvantage and disempowerment – instead of differences between the sexes.

Heather Wishik suggests a number of questions posed by feminist jurisprudence. For the purposes of this chapter, I would wish to emphasise her second question: 'What assumptions, descriptions, assertions and/or definitions of experience – male, female or ostensibly gender neutral – does the law make in this area?'[20] It is clear that laws, norms and judgments often reinforce patriarchal assumptions and sexual double standards. This is less so now than in the past, even the recent past, but examples remain. The claim that the law is patriarchal does not mean that women or their interests (and it is difficult to avoid the essentialist trap)[21] have been ignored by the law, but rather that the law's cognition of women is refracted through the male eye (male legislators, male judges, male bureaucrats, or women who think as men), rather than through women's experiences and definitions.

The answer does not lie, I believe, in creating a new (legal) language, as argued for by some French feminists.[22] Rather, it requires, in the words of

---

16   *R v Hopley* (1860) 2 F & F 202.

17   The most commonly quoted definition is by Schechter and Roberge: '... the involvement of dependent, developmentally immature children and adolescents in sexual activities that they do not fully comprehend and to which they are unable to give informed consent or that violate the social taboos of family roles.' (In Helfer, R and Kempe, CH, *Child Abuse and Neglect*, 1976, Cambridge, Mass: Ballinger, p 60.)

18   And all sexual abuse is also severe emotional abuse: Glaser, D and Frosh, S, *Child Sexual Abuse*, 1988, Basingstoke: Macmillan.

19   Scales, A, 'The emergence of feminist jurisprudence: an essay' (1986) 95 Yale LJ 1373.

20   Wishik, H, 'To question everything: the inquiries of feminist jurisprudence' (1986) 1 Berkeley Women's LJ 64.

21   See, eg, particularly in relation to Gilligan, Harris, A, 'Race and essentialism in feminist legal theory' (1990) 42 Stan L Rev 581.

22   Eg, Luce Irigaray (see *The Sex Which Is Not One*, 1985, Ithaca: Cornell UP).

Lucinda Finley, 'critical engagements with the nature of legal language'.[23] As she puts it, with cogency:

> ... The more we can find openings to argue from the perspective of those often overlooked by legal language, such as the people upon whom the legal power is being exercised, or those disempowered or silenced or indeed rendered invisible by the traditional discourse, the more the opportunities to use the engine of fairness and equity to expand the comprehension of legal language.[24]

THE PAST – AND SOME OF ITS HANGOVERS

Child law has no beginning; no obvious single source. There is no one text, statute, code, case or institutional source (as Hale's *Pleas of the Crown* could be pointed to by those examining the marital rape immunity).[25] For some of our concepts and practices we can detect biblical origins. Thus, both Hebrew scriptures in the Old Testament and passages from the New Testament have sustained for centuries the defence of physical punishment.[26] And what is one to make of one of the most famous stories in the Bible (or anywhere): the attempted sacrifice of Isaac by his father, Abraham? Alice Miller's response repays consideration: 'Our awareness of the child's victimisation is so deeply rooted in us that we scarcely seem to have reacted at all to the monstrousness of the story ...'[27] Sons' obedience to fathers is a recurrent biblical theme.[28] As Philip Greven points out, God's punishments provided 'the paradigm for parental discipline of children, a model that became most explicit in the proverbs attributed to Solomon, the king of Israel'.[29] Ironically, the proverbial 'Spare the rod and spoil the child' is 17th century English[30] and not biblical at all, but there are plenty of substitutes in the Bible.[31] Jesus felt a deep love and compassionate concern for children,[32] and nowhere in the New Testament does he approve of the infliction of pain upon children in order to correct

---

23 Finley, L, 'Breaking women's silence in law: the dilemma of the gendered nature of legal reasoning' (1989) 64 Notre Dame L Rev 886.

24 *Ibid*, p 898.

25 See Freeman, MDA, 'Doing his best to sustain the sanctity of marriage', in Johnson, N (ed), *Marital Violence*, 1985, London: Routledge, p 124.

26 Greven, P, *Spare The Child*, 1991, New York: Alfred A Knopf.

27 *The Untouched Key: Tracing Childhood Trauma in Creativity and Destructiveness*, 1990, New York: Doubleday, p 141.

28 Eg, Deuteronomy 8:5–6 or II Samuel 7:14–15.

29 *Ibid*, Greven, p 47.

30 It comes from Samuel Butler's poem 'Hudibras', published in 1664 (see Gibson, I, *The English Vice: Beating, Sex and Shame in Victorian England and After*, 1978, London: Duckworth, p 49).

31 Eg, in Proverbs 29:17; 3:11–12; 10:13; 19:18.

32 See Matthew 18:10–11, 14.

them, but arguments for corporal punishment as the Christian method of discipline can be found in New Testament texts other than the Gospels. There are few,[33] but, with Greven, we must wonder 'if it is likely that the chastisement and scourging of Jesus before his Crucifixion would become the model for Christian parents to follow with their children in the centuries to come'.[34] The relationship between God and man is clearly reflected in that between parent and child: obedience and submission are expected and are to be enforced by the rigours of punishment. God's punishments for disobedience, graphically described in the Old Testament,[35] are matched by those which fathers and mothers can inflict upon disobedient sons:

> If a man have a stubborn and rebellious son, which will not obey the voice of the father, or the voice of the mother, and that, when they have chastened him, will not hearken unto them: Then shall his father and mother lay hold on him, and bring him out unto the elders of the city, and unto the gate of his place; And they shall say unto the elders of the city, This our son is stubborn and rebellious, he will not obey our voice; he is a glutton, and a drunkard. And all the men of his city shall stone him with stones, that he shall die: so shalt thou put evil from among you; and all Israel shall hear, and fear.[36]

Despite references to mothers[37] and the seeming limitation to 'sons', what is constructed here is a metaphor for patriarchy, with the relationship between parent and child having many of the characteristics with which we associate the social constructions of male and female: domination, disadvantage, disempowerment. The child has no voice. He is expected to submit, to conform, to obey. We are told that this law was never once carried out,[38] but in terms of constructing a relationship that is unimportant. Children belong to their parents.[39] And this, we find from other texts, is the more so with female children. So, for example, in Deuteronomy we read:

> If a man find a damsel that is a virgin, which is not betrothed, and lay hold on her, and lie with her and they be found; then the man that lay with her shall give unto the damsel's father fifty shekels of silver, and she shall be his wife.[40]

This law is presented as an advancement, a humane step beyond the culture of heathen society. The text prohibits the man divorcing a wife he so marries. And yet, it is clear that it was designed to protect a man's property rights in his daughters. Are not the origins of all rape laws thus?

---

33   Hoyles, JA, *Punishment in the Bible*, 1986, London: Epworth.
34   *Op cit*, Greven, fn 26, p 50.
35   Eg, Deuteronomy 8:5–6; or 8:20.
36   Deuteronomy 21:18–21.
37   Following the Fifth Commandment.
38   This is certainly traditional Jewish teaching.
39   As in the disgraceful episode described in Judges 19.
40   Deuteronomy 22:28–29.

Earlier in the same chapter is a yet more graphic (and certainly more brutal) demonstration of the status of daughters.[41] Where a man 'hateth' his bride because he alleges she is not a virgin, the following distinction is set down. If the wife's parents can produce 'tokens' of her virginity – some commentators insist that this is not to be taken literally but is a metaphorical expression for clearly establishing the falsity of the charge by witnesses and expert evidence[42] – he is corporally punished and has to pay the father 100 silver shekels. But, if her virginity is not satisfactorily established, she is to be stoned to death (we are not told the fate, if any, of the man who took her virginity, perhaps by rape). We are, though, given an explanation of why so severe a penalty is to be inflicted upon the woman: she has 'wrought a wanton deed in Israel, to play the harlot in her father's house'.[43] She is, in other words, a threat to the 'entire social and economic fabric of a rigidly male-dominated society'.[44] As Eisler explains:

> ... these laws regulating women's virginity were designed to protect what were essentially economic transactions between men. By requiring compensation to the father if the accusation against the woman was proven false, the law provided a punishment for falsely slandering the man's reputation as an honest merchant. It also offered the father a further protection. If the accusation was untrue, the merchandise in question (his daughter) could now never be returned. On the other hand, by having the men of the city stone his daughter to death if the accusation *was* true, the law also protected the father. Since the dishonoured bride could not be resold, provision was made for the destruction of this now economically worthless asset.[45]

Of course, those who made these rules did not talk in this economic language but said that they were the word of God. It was the word of God, too, that told the Children of Israel, having triumphed over Midian, to 'kill every male among the little ones and kill every woman that hath known man by lying with him', but to 'keep alive for [them]selves' all female children who were virgins.[46] A standard commentary explains that this was in order to employ them as domestic servants,[47] but does not explain why only virgins could, in Reg Graycar's memorable phrase, take up hoovering (or its equivalent) as a hobby.[48] Virgins were clearly valuable booty, marketable as concubines, slaves, and even wives.

---

41 Deuteronomy 22:13–21.

42 Hertz, JH, *The Pentateuch*, 1956, London: Soncino, p 844.

43 Deuteronomy 22:21. Hertz quotes Sifri thus: 'She did not merely degrade herself, but every virgin in Israel.'

44 Eisler, R, *The Chalice and The Blade*, San Francisco: Harper, p 97.

45 *Ibid*.

46 Numbers 31:17–18.

47 *Ibid*, Hertz, p 705.

48 Graycar, R, 'Hoovering as a hobby and other stories – gendered assessments of personal injury damages' (1997) 31 British Columbia UL Rev 17.

The birth of a female child is also treated differently in the Old Testament. Leviticus tells us that a woman who has given birth to a child is unclean and must be ritually purified, lest her impurity contaminate others.[49] (In parenthesis, it may be noted that the quintessentially female act is unclean: there is no such suggestion in the case of men who kill, rape or pillage.) Her 'uncleanness' lasts twice as long where she gives birth to a female child.[50] The standard commentary can offer no satisfactory explanation for the difference.[51] There are many more examples which could be drawn upon; lack of space prevents their excavation.

It is important to return to these sources. They may not be read overmuch nowadays but they remain as cultural underpinnings in ways that other classical sources do not. But any discussion of the law relating to children cannot overlook the fact that classical civilisations treated women throughout their lives as children. Thus, Harrison, writing of the law of Athens, observes:[52]

> There can be no doubt that a woman remained under some sort of tutelage during the whole of her life. She could not enter into any but the most trifling contract, she could not engage her own hand in marriage, and she could not plead her own case in court. In all these relations, action was taken on her behalf by her *kyrios*,[53] and this was so during her whole life.

It was little different in Roman law and culture.[54] Children born of *iustae nuptiae* were subject to the *patria potestas* of their father. *Patria potestas* was lifelong: those subject to it had their lives almost 'wholly controlled by their paterfamilias'.[55] His *potestas* included the power of life and death; Crook indicates that this was a reality in Republican times. He explains:

> His household jurisdiction, with a family council, dealt with offences of its members (such as sexual offences) that threatened the reputation of the family, and he could inflict chastisements and even death ... It was the right of the *paterfamilias* to decide whether new-born children should be reared or exposed ...[56]

---

49 Leviticus 12:2–6.

50 Eighty days in the case of a female child; 40 days in the case of a male child.

51 See *op cit*, Hertz, fn 42, p 460. But, he says, it is not because a female was regarded as more defiling than a male.

52 Harrison, ARW, *The Law of Athens Volume I: The Family and Property*, 1968, Oxford: Clarendon, p 108. See, also, Just, R, *Women in Athenian Law and Life*, 1989, London: Routledge.

53 Ie, when it is used adjectivally, literally, 'having power or authority over'; when used as a substantive, it means 'master', 'controller', 'possessor'.

54 Gardner, JF, *Women in Roman Law and Society*, 1986, London: Croom Helm.

55 See Crook, JA, *Law and Life of Rome*, 1967, London: Thames and Hudson, p 107. See, also, Lacey, WK, '*Patria potestas*', in Rawson, B, *The Family in Ancient Rome*, 1986, London: Croom Helm.

56 *Ibid*, Crook, pp 107–08.

These powers were exercised over both male and female children: there is no evidence that they were exercised differentially, that there was gendericide, for example, but this cannot be ruled out. Certainly, in the case of marriage, there was discrimination against female children. Sons could not be forced to marry particular persons. This is formally clear from the *Digest*[57] and is also implied by Gellius,[58] when he discusses the moral duty of a son. But, Crook observes, 'fathers could be jolly angry and make things difficult', and, he adds, 'all the more might they make things difficult for daughters'.[59] Roman law was less clear on this. The *Digest* says that a daughter's consent is necessary for betrothal, but indicates that anything short of positive resistance is taken as consent, and consent can only be refused if the proposed bridegroom is morally unfit.[60] Crook adds, 'Little girls of 12 can have had small practical chance to refuse; but it must be remembered that your children *in potestate* might not be little girls or boys'.[61]

Emancipation was also possible, though it was not the norm – in the Republican age, it was usually a penalty for misbehaviour – but emancipation did not extend to daughters, only to sons.[62]

THE COMMON LAW

At common law, parental rights in respect of a legitimate child were vested in the father and were almost absolute. Of course, we are not talking (as previously) of rights over life and death, but, in an old graphic case of 1804, it was held that a father could claim from the mother custody of a child at the breast.[63] It was only in exceptional cases that his right could be forfeited.[64] A further exception at common law was in the so called 'age of discretion' cases in *habeas corpus* proceedings, where it came to be accepted[65] that a court would not order a child who had reached that age to return to the father if he or she did not wish to do so. That age was fixed differentially, at 14 for boys and 16 for girls. It would be difficult to justify any distinction, but, given what we know of the cognitive and social developments of the genders, we might

---

57 *Digest* 23.2.21.

58 *Noctes Atticae II*, pp 7, 20.

59 *Op cit*, Crook, fn 55, p 108.

60 *Op cit*, Crook, fn 55, quoting *Digest* 23.1.11–12.

61 *Op cit*, Crook, fn 55, p 108.

62 But Hallett, JP, *Fathers and Daughters in Roman Society*, 1984, Princeton, New Jersey: Princeton UP shows that elite Roman daughters were highly valued as daughters of their fathers.

63 *R v De Manneville* (1804) 5 East 221.

64 *R v Greenhill* (1836) 4 Ad & El 624, p 640.

65 *R v Howes ex p Barford* (1860) 3 E & E 332.

have expected any difference to have been the other way round. It is not why 14 was a boy's age of discretion – at different stages of English history, 10 and 12 may have been the ages of majority and, in medieval times, a distinction was drawn between sons of knights and sons of inferior classes, the former of whom came of age at 21,[66] the latter of whom were regarded as late as the 12th century as of full age at 14 or 15. But with girls, 16 was in line with the offence, property based of course, of abduction of girls, which an Act of 1557[67] fixed at 16. It would be unwise to develop discussion of the age of discretion concept any further, but the question which nags is, why could 19th century judges look no further than an Elizabethan statute? This may have upheld the value of conceptual coherence, but did it not fly in the face of their experiences?

The high water mark of common law bias in favour of fathers is *Re Agar-Ellis*.[68] Here, the Court of Appeal was not prepared to interfere with a father who unreasonably refused to allow free access and correspondence between his 17 year old daughter and her mother because he was afraid that the mother would alienate the daughter's affections from him. But there had already been limited statutory incursions. Legislation in 1839[69] empowered the Court of Chancery to give the mother custody until the child reached the age of seven, provided that she had not committed adultery. There was, of course, no judicial divorce in England at this time; when it was introduced 18 years later, it continued this policy of treating male and female infidelity differently.[70] In 1873, the age was extended to 16 and the proviso relating to adultery was not re-enacted.[71] Meanwhile, the first divorce legislation gave the Divorce Court the power to make custody orders up to the age of 21 on such terms as seemed to it just, thus enabling it to give either parent custody. What would have seemed just to Victorian judges will not necessarily cohere with ours and we have no empirical evidence. But it is not likely, I think, that mothers were automatically preferred – a common allegation later. More significant still was the Guardianship of Infants Act 1886: it gave the mother rights concerning guardianship and it directed that, in hearing her claim, the court was to have regard to, *inter alia*, the welfare of the child.[72]

The cumulative effect of these pieces of legislation was, as is apparent in *R v Gyngall*,[73] to weaken the father's rights and to strengthen those of the

---

66 See Pollock, F and Maitland, FW, *The History of English Law*, 1968, Cambridge: CUP, Vol II, pp 438–39.

67 Abduction Act 1557.

68 (1883) 24 Ch D 317.

69 Talfourd's Act (the Custody of Infants Act 1839).

70 Matrimonial Causes Act 1857.

71 Custody of Infants Act 1873.

72 See Guardianship of Infants Act 1886, s 5. The first statutory reference to the child's welfare was in the Custody of Infants Act 1873.

73 [1893] 2 QB 232.

mother, but even more so to promote the welfare of the child. It was this policy, according to Lord Upjohn in *J v C*,[74] which prevailed 'behind the closed doors of the Chancery Division'. The welfare principle has often been criticised for being indeterminate and vague. It was supposedly upheld in *Re Thain*[75] (decided immediately after the 1925 legislation[76] and affirming the paramountcy of the child's welfare). But *Re Thain* decided that the parental right of an unimpeachable parent should take priority over considerations that we would certainly attribute to a child's welfare. The father in this case, unable to cope after the death of the mother, had handed his eight month old daughter to his brother-in-law and the latter's wife and, six years later, had sought her return. Eve J, ordering the delivery up of the child, remarked:

> It is said that the little girl will be greatly distressed and upset at parting from Mr and Mrs J. I can quite understand it may be so, but, at her tender age, one knows from experience how mercifully transient are the effects of partings and other sorrows, and how soon the novelty of fresh surroundings and new associations effaces the recollection of former days and kind friends, and I cannot attach weight to this aspect of the case.

On what experience was the learned Chancery judge relying? His own, perhaps, on being transported to 'prep' school?

It is interesting to speculate whether *Re Thain* would have been decided the same way if a mother had handed her child to relatives in similar circumstances. I doubt it. She would have been expected to put caring for her child before her career. Nevertheless, mothers who surrendered their children for adoption and then changed their minds were held, until the 1970s, not to be acting unreasonably unless they could be said to be callous or culpable in some way.[77] This may have been a reflection of attitudes towards adoption as a second class institution, as much as an emphasis on the pseudo-science of the blood-tie[78] (though the latter is not finally dead, as the so called 'Zulu boy' case in the mid-1990s showed all too apparently).[79]

Courts continued to discriminate against mothers throughout the 20th century. 'Unimpeachable' parents – a totem in many contested custody cases – were always fathers (though, to be fair, this may have been required symbolism to wrest a child from a mother, particularly in days when

---

74 [1970] AC 668, p 723.

75 [1926] Ch 676.

76 Guardianship of Infants Act 1925. This was passed in order to inject some equality into the rights of parents; see Brophy, J, 'Parental rights and children's welfare: some problems of feminists' strategy in the 1920s' (1982) 10 IJSL 149.

77 Until *Re W* [1971] AC 682 and *O'Connor v A and B* [1971] 2 All ER 1230.

78 Reflected in the notorious case of *Re C (MA)* [1966] 1 All ER 838.

79 *Re M* [1996] 2 FLR 441.

Bowlbyism reigned).[80] So, in 1962, Lord Denning, in an outburst of moral fundamentalism, could reason thus:

> It would be an exceedingly bad example if it were thought that a mother could go off with another man and then claim as of right to say: 'Oh well, they are my two little girls and I am entitled to take them with me. I can not only leave my home and break it up and leave their father, but I can take the children with me and the law will not say to me "nay".' It seems to me that a mother must realise that, if she leaves and breaks up her home in this way, she cannot as of right demand to take the children from the father.[81]

The language is colourful, but doubtless mothers who committed adultery were being denied custody of their children by other judges, perhaps in less florid (and, therefore, less reportable) language. Few, it seems, noted how very close this was to the legislation of 1839, though now, of course, it was justified – if not by Lord Denning, whose sentiment gelled with early Victorianism – in terms of the child's welfare. There is no reference in Lord Denning's 'sermon' to the children's best interests: significantly, twice in his judgment he used the expression 'as of right', and he went on to refer to the case as 'a matter of simple justice' between mother and father. But it was also clear at this time that fathers could be wronged much more easily than mothers.

To cope with the indeterminacy of the 'best interests' test, the common law evolved a number of presumptions. Young children should be placed in the custody of their mothers.[82] Older children, especially boys, should be brought up by their fathers.[83] Whether, in general, the law favoured mothers, as is often claimed, or whether decisions to give custody to the mother reflected an understandable desire to protect the status quo, it was (and still is) mothers who usually got/continued to care for children after divorce. For women, divorce perpetuates the inequalities inherent in marriage:[84] it is much easier for men to rebuild their lives. That women's caring and nurturing role continued is what, said the judges, nature had 'ordained'.[85] It is an unproblematic given, an unquestionable (and a long unquestioned) truth. Stamp LJ explained why in 1978: '... however good a man may be, he cannot perform the functions which a mother performs by nature in relation to her own little girl.'[86]

---

80   Bowlby, J, *Child Care and the Growth of Love*, 1953, Harmondsworth: Penguin.

81   *Re L* [1962] 3 All ER 1, pp 3–4.

82   *Re B* [1962] 1 All ER 872; *Re S* [1958] 1 All ER 783; *Re O* [1971] Ch 748 (the more so when she was not gainfully employed: see p 752).

83   *Re C (A)* [1970] 1 All ER 309.

84   Delphy, C, 'Continuities and discontinuities in marriage and divorce', in Barker, DL and Allen, S (eds), *Sexual Divisions and Society: Process and Change*, 1976, London: Tavistock, p 90.

85   *M v M* [1978] 1 FLR 77.

86   *Ibid.*

The presumptions have gone. They have been replaced by 'considerations'. Thus, Butler-Sloss LJ in *Re S* could still talk, in 1991, of its being 'natural' for young children to be with their mothers, but, she added, 'where it is in dispute, it is a consideration ... not a presumption'.[87] She explained this further in *Re A*:

> In cases where the child has remained throughout with the mother and is young, particularly when a baby or a toddler, the unbroken relationship of the mother and child is one which it would be very difficult to displace, unless the mother was unsuitable to care for the child. But, where the mother and child have been separated, and the mother seeks the return of the child, other considerations apply, and there is no starting point that the mother should be preferred to the father ...[88]

And she stressed again that there is no presumption which requires the mother, 'as mother', to be considered as the primary caretaker in preference to the father. Even so, it is rare for the father to be preferred to the mother where the child is young. When this happened in 1998 in *Re K*,[89] the decision attracted considerable media attention. The child had been with his mother for a considerable period of his life, though not the whole of it, but he had never been in the exclusive care of his father. *The Times* commented, 'Mother's Day has gone, says custody judge',[90] and it noted that twice as many men were looking after their children compared with five years earlier. Actual numbers were not disclosed but they remain small. In the US, the tender years presumption may have been displaced because of feminist demands that men and women be treated equally.[91] There is no evidence that the attenuation of the doctrine in England – for that is what the replacement of presumptions by considerations amounts to – can be similarly explained.

THE CHILDREN ACT 1989

Most disputes about children are decided in terms of their best interests. Section 1 of the Children Act 1989 provides that, when a court determines questions of a child's upbringing, the child's welfare shall be the paramount consideration. This guiding principle – the culmination of a century in which focus on a child's best interests had intensified, and rightly so – has been variously criticised by feminists and others. Critics have emphasised its indeterminacy, its vagueness, its values and its absence of normative

---

87   *Re S* [1991] 2 FLR 388.
88   [1991] 2 FLR 388, p 390.
89   [1999] 1 FLR 583.
90   (1998) *The Times*, 27 November.
91   This is the view of Mason, M-A; see *The Custody Wars*, 1999, New York: Basic, Chapter 1.

content.[92] In an important article, Helen Reece[93] attacked it for allowing other policies and principles, for example negative attitudes towards lesbianism, to 'smuggle themselves'[94] into children's cases. She and others have wondered why the interests of children should be prioritised over the interests of adults. There are difficult cases, of course; one will be referred to shortly. But, in general, I do not have any difficulty with placing children's interests on a pedestal. Nor do I see why feminists should object to the paramountcy principle as such, though I agree that there may be problems with its interpretation.

A problem does occur where a case concerns more than one child and the interests of the two are not congruent. *Birmingham CC v H* was one such case.[95] The mother was herself a child (she was 15). It was in her interests that she should retain contact with her baby boy because she might harm herself otherwise, but not, so it was thought, in his. The law said that the welfare of both was paramount. The House of Lords held that it was necessary to identify the child who was the subject of the application (in this case, the baby) and promote his welfare. This is hardly good reasoning, for everything turns on the nature of the application. But it enabled the court to put the baby's welfare above that of his mother, and that is, I maintain, right. Nor is it as difficult to justify the paramountcy principle as its critics maintain. It has, for a start, enormous symbolic importance: take away the paramountcy principle and we would slide back towards seeing children as property. Take away the paramountcy principle and we would soon reach the stage where disputes about children would be argued in terms of rights ('he is mine') or justice ('she is responsible for the breakdown of the marriage' or 'I am an unimpeachable parent'). Children do not ask to be litigated over and can demand, justifiably, that such disputes should be governed only by what is best for them. Even if, in general, children do not have a special right to have their welfare prioritised[96] (I think that they do, but it is not necessary to my argument here), in the context of litigation about them it is not difficult to construct a right that their welfare should assume overriding importance.

This is not to say that the paramountcy principle is not sometimes misused. Not so long ago, a judge made a residence order in favour of a father because he disapproved of the mother's and her new partner's attitude to nudity and communal bathing. The Court of Appeal, not surprisingly, allowed the appeal.[97] Where did the judge get his values from? At least in one of the

---

92 Most famously, Mnookin, R, 'Child-custody adjudication: judicial functions in the face of indeterminacy' (1975) 39 Law and Contemporary Problems 226.

93 *Op cit*, Reece, fn 4.

94 *Op cit*, Reece, fn 4, p 268.

95 [1994] 1 FLR 224.

96 This is Reece's argument; see *op cit*, fn 4.

97 *Re W* [1999] 2 FLR 869.

cases where sexual orientation was at issue,[98] Balcombe LJ addressed this. After advising that it was necessary to apply the moral standards of the community (though he did not say why or how he discovered these), he continued:

> It is still the norm that children are brought up in a home with a father, mother and siblings (if any) and, other things being equal, such an upbringing is most likely to be conducive to their welfare. If, because the parents are divorced, such an upbringing is no longer possible, then a very material factor in considering where the child's welfare lies is which of the competing parents can offer the nearest approach to the norm.[99]

It was, he said, 'clearly the father', since the mother was living in a lesbian relationship. The father would offer 'a normal home by the standards of our society'. This is dangerous reasoning, and not just to lesbians. What of the white mother who left the white father to live with a black partner? Bringing up a child as a vegetarian or a Jew or in a household without a television are all outside 'the norm'. It is clear that no woman in a lesbian relationship could ever be awarded a residence order if Balcombe LJ's standard was upheld. They clearly are – that there are no recent cases suggests change without challenge, the reasons for which would be worth investigating.[100]

The 1989 Act injected normative content into the paramountcy principle in the form of a checklist.[101] The issue is thus not left at large, but the discretion of the courts is structured by a checklist of factors to be considered before making a decision about a child. This requires a court to have regard in particular to such matters as a child's wishes and feelings; her needs; the likely effect of any change of circumstances; her age, sex and background; any harm suffered or risk of harm; and the capability of her parents and any other relevant person of meeting her needs, as well as the range of powers open to the court. The list reflects a broad based consensus of both professional and popular opinion. It is child-centred and there is no reference to parental conduct (or rights or justice between the parties), to sexual orientation or to new relationships.

The paramountcy principle is self-limiting: it only applies to questions relating to a child's upbringing. This has been construed narrowly. Thus, where the issue is a child's paternity, this, it has been held,[102] only indirectly concerns a child's upbringing, and so falls outside the paramountcy test. But if knowledge of one's identity is to be relegated in this way, what are the

---

98 *C v C* [1991] 1 FLR 223.

99 *Ibid*, p 231.

100 Curiously, the courts take a much more liberal attitude to homosexuality in the context of adoption: see *Re W* [1997] 2 FLR 406.

101 Children Act 1989, s 1(3).

102 *S v Mc* [1972] AC 24.

implications? Since maternity is rarely in doubt (at least in a system like that in operation in England),[103] in effect the law is assisting men who wish to deny their fatherhood. It is also discriminating against women. Unlike Katherine O'Donovan,[104] I do not think that the answer lies in giving women anonymity rights; it would be far better for women and for children, not to mention the State (the Child Support Agency, most notably), if the paternity of all children was determined at birth.[105]

Another interpretation which served to protect the interest of parents (in this case a well known father) rather than promote the interests of children is the case of *Re Z*[106] (the length that the courts go to to protect well known men exemplified by calling the case 'Z'!). At issue in *Re Z* was whether a court could stop a mother publicising the activities of the Peto Institute in Budapest by allowing her daughter, who had cerebral palsy, to participate in a television programme about the remarkable work of the Institute. Because of who the father was, it was obvious that the programme would attract a lot of interest and, it was thought, redound to the benefit of children with cerebral palsy, including the child in this case. Not surprisingly, the father (whose political career had been adversely affected by earlier stories about his relationship with the mother and his responses to his child) had sought an injunction restraining the media from publishing information which would expose the child's identity. At issue was whether this injunction could now be lifted. The Court of Appeal refused to do so. Ward LJ noted that the law had 'so developed that there is this category where freedom of publication always prevails over the welfare of the child. The child may be harmed by the realisation that he is related to the object of the publicity ... but ... that has to be accepted as part of the slings and arrows of misfortune of life'.[107] But this case did not fall into that category.

The court did not, of course, indicate why, if freedom of the press was so fundamental, it could triumph over a child's welfare but not, it seems, over the interests of a well known politician. But 'Z' did not come into this category. Since the case related to the child's upbringing ('the central issue [was] one which relates to how the child is being reared'),[108] the Children Act 1989 applied and welfare was the paramount consideration. And then, in a wonderful twist, the court concluded that the welfare of the child would be

---

103 Compare the French system, where women can give birth as 'X'.

104 See O'Donovan, Chapter 4, in this volume.

105 And see Okin, SM, *Justice, Gender and the Family*, 1989, New York: Basic, p 178, following Ellwood, D, *Poor Support: Poverty in the American Family*, 1988, New York: Basic, pp 163–74.

106 [1996] 1 FLR 191.

107 *Ibid*, p 212.

108 *Ibid*, p 213.

LIVERPOOL JOHN MOORES UNIVERSITY
LEARNING SERVICES

'harmed and not advanced'[109] by her involvement in the film. How convenient! Imagine the criticisms if the court had said that the interests of the father were more important than those of his (disabled) child. Even with paramountcy, conclusions can be reached which run counter to informed professional opinion (and lay intuition). Take paramountcy away and I fear a trend away from upholding the interests of children.

Some of the most hotly contested disputes about children concern contact. Nearly all of these will centre on a father's contact. In 1962, the Court of Appeal was clear that access (as it was then called) was a non-custodial parent's right,[110] but, by 1973, it was being viewed as the right of the child,[111] so that no court was to deprive a child of access to a parent unless wholly satisfied that it was in the child's interest that there should be none. It has meant, for example, that courts have imposed obligations on mothers to send photographs, school reports and the like, and to read fathers' letters to the child.[112] Disputes over contact have intensified. Many men now think differently about their role as fathers and their relationship with their children which they wish to survive the breakdown of their relationship with their partner. Perhaps, as a result, more men are demanding contact. But we have also become much more aware of domestic violence; perhaps this features in a quarter of the marriages which end in divorce and may increase after proceedings commence.[113] Yet, only recently has domestic violence been raised in (reported) contact cases.[114] It is clear that contact may be used to perpetuate the violence of a marriage or relationship. Contact orders have enabled violent men to pursue battered partners to refuges. Not surprisingly, what has been dubbed the 'implacably hostile' mother has emerged, prepared to resist contact at all costs.[115] The case of *Morgan v Foretich*[116] in the US became a *cause célèbre*: the allegation in this case was of sexual abuse of the child rather than violence against the mother, and this is increasingly raised in England, too.

The courts do not react favourably to implacable hostility. Thus, in *Re O*,[117] the Master of the Rolls said: 'Neither parent should be encouraged or

---

109 *Ibid*, p 215.

110 *S v S and P* [1962] 2 All ER 1, p 3.

111 *M v M* [1973] 2 All ER 81, p 85. For critical discussion, see Barnett, Chapter 9 and Diduck, Chapter 13, in this volume.

112 *Re O* [1995] 2 FLR 124.

113 The Law Commission said in 1998 that 22% end in divorce (see *Facing The Future*, Law Com No 170, 1998, Appendix C).

114 See Kaye, M, 'Domestic violence, residence and contact' (1996) 8(4) CFLQ 285. See Barnett, Chapter 7, in this volume for discussion of the views of barristers of such cases.

115 See Wallbank, J, 'Castigating mothers: the judicial response to "willful" women in disputes over paternal contact in English law' (1998) 20 JSWFL 357.

116 On which see Groner, J, *Hilary's Trial*, 1991, New York: Basic.

117 [1995] 2 FLR 124.

permitted to think that the more unco-operative they are, the more likely they are to get their own way.' In *Re P*,[118] this reluctance to allow implacable hostility to prevail led the Court of Appeal to order supervised contact to a father with a history of psychiatric illness, alcohol and drug abuse and who, to boot, had pronounced Nazi sympathies (on contact visits he dressed his sons, aged five and eight, in Nazi regalia). The court conceded that contact would cause the mother stress and anxiety, which would communicate itself to the children, whose welfare would suffer detriment as a result.

Because of the many allegations of implacable hostility, there is a danger that opposition to contact by a mother will attract this label even where she has genuine and rationally held fears for her child or for herself. Thus, the courts have been reluctant to refuse contact because of domestic violence. But this may be about to change. In *Re M*,[119] in 1999, Wall J expressed this opinion:

> Often in these cases where domestic violence has been found, too little weight ... is given to the need for the father to change. It is often said that, notwithstanding the violence, the mother must nonetheless bring up the children with full knowledge and a positive image of their natural father and arrange for the children to be available for contact. Too often ... the courts neglect the other side of the equation, which is that a father ... must demonstrate that he is a fit person to exercise contact; that he is not going to destabilise the family; that he is not going to upset the children and harm them emotionally.

This is an important *per curiam* statement. But it will be noted that not included in the changes is any reference to behaviour towards the mother. Domestic violence in the context of contact poses a dilemma for feminists: on the one hand, seeing the dangers of the liberties of men being upheld at the expense of woman; on the other, recognising the importance of relationships and the values of nurturing, and the needs of children. It is not a dilemma which lends itself to an easy solution.

TREATING CHILDREN AS WOMEN

One of the rallying cries of feminist jurisprudence is to question the difference that difference makes.[120] We all know that children, or at least small children, are different to adults. But what should hinge on this difference? In the mid-1980s, the House of Lords decided the *Gillick* case.[121] The decision should have been applauded by feminists, but it was virtually ignored. Was this

---

118 [1996] 2 FLR 314.

119 [1999] 2 FLR 321.

120 On which see Rhode, D, *Justice and Gender*, 1989, Cambridge, Mass: Harvard UP, pp 111, 319.

121 [1986] AC 112.

because the granting of rights to adolescents was seen as diversionary; or because legal equality (if that is what it was) was no substitute for substantive equality; or because rights are individualist or reliance on them is ineffective? It cannot have been that the decision was protecting the 'wrong' right (for, if it focused on a right at all, it was on the right of adolescents, and clearly this meant girls, to seek contraceptive advice and treatment when competent to do so).[122]

The leading judgment in *Gillick*[123] tied *Gillick* competence, as it has come to be known, both to understanding and intelligence and – and one would have thought that feminists would have seized on this – to experiential wisdom.[124] *Gillick* was a watershed decision: it recognised the personality of children; it undercut their dependence; it defined their decision making abilities. It was a liberating judgment. Children now had, John Eekelaar claimed, 'that most dangerous but precious of rights: the right to make their own mistakes'.[125] Four years later, the Children Act 1989 in part endorsed this philosophy. It recognised, as part of the normative structure of paramountcy, the importance of a child's wishes and feelings, modelling this on *Gillick* and thus linking it to age and understanding.[126] It gave *Gillick* competent children the right to refuse to consent to medical examinations and assessments.[127] Although not seen as such, these can be interpreted as feminist victories. When the history of the battle to uphold bodily integrity and autonomy is written, *Gillick* and the Children Act 1989 will rank aside *St George's*[128] as high points.

But there are troughs as well. These victories have been forgotten in a retreat from *Gillick* that we should perhaps have been able to predict – the decision did, after all, fly in the face of the opinion of the day[129] – though no one did. So, when the opportunity presented itself for the courts to test the implications of *Gillick*, they froze. In *Re R*[130] and *Re W*,[131] and subsequently in

---

122 The case was brought by Gillick to challenge a governmental circular which permitted doctors to give contraceptive advice and treatment to underage girls without informing their parents.

123 *Gillick v West Norfolk and Wisbech AHA* [1986] AC 112.

124 *Ibid*, p 186.

125 Eekelaar, J, 'The emergence of children's rights' (1986) 6 OJLS 161.

126 See Alderson, P and Goodwin, M, 'Contradictions within concepts of children's competence' (1993) 1 IJCR 303.

127 Children Act 1989, ss 38(6), 43(8), 44(7); Sched 3, paras 4(4)(a), 5(5)(a). See, also, Brasse, G, 'Examination of the child' (1993) 23 Fam Law 12.

128 *St George's Healthcare NHS Trust v S* [1999] Fam 26.

129 At the time, a national campaign to 'protect the family from interference from officialdom' was established (see (1985) *The Times*, 28 May). Pre-*Gillick*, concerns were expressed by Mount, F, in *The Subversive Family*, 1982, London: Jonathan Cape.

130 [1992] Fam 11.

131 [1993] Fam 64.

other cases,[132] most recently the heart transplant case of *Re M*,[133] they held that, although a *Gillick* competent child could consent to medical treatment on her own behalf, she could not refuse to consent to treatment. As a result, as Brazier and Bridge observe, 'the right to be wrong applies only where minors say yes to treatment'.[134]

But, both here and elsewhere, the courts raised the level of *Gillick* competence beyond that which is required to consent to treatment. Indeed, the more far reaching the effects of refusal, the higher the level of competence is raised. In *Re R*, where the evidence was that, without the treatment, the girl (who was 15) would lapse into a dangerously psychotic state, Lord Donaldson MR said that what was required was not merely an ability to understand the nature of the proposed treatment, 'but a full understanding and appreciation of the consequences both of the treatment in terms of intended and possible side effects and, equally important, the anticipated consequences of a failure to treat'.[135] This went way beyond what was envisaged in *Gillick*, and is also more stringent than the test laid down for mentally disordered adults.[136] That test, first articulated by Thorpe J in *Re C* (1994), has been used by courts to test the competence of 16–18 year olds, but not to supplant that laid down in *Re R* (1992) for adolescents under 16.[137]

The test formulated by Lord Donaldson in *Re R* demands more of adolescents than is required of adults in another respect, too. He himself accepts that an adult's capacity to decide about treatment has to be assessed at the time that the decision is made.[138] But, in *Re R*, he held that what was required was a permanent state of competence: where this fluctuates, as it did in *Re R*, the adolescent cannot be judged by her capacity on her 'good days'.[139]

Despite *Gillick*, and in the face of legislation,[140] the courts evince a reluctance to give rein to a child's autonomy. Where the child is under 16, they do this by concluding that the child is not *Gillick* competent. This is well illustrated by two Jehovah's Witnesses blood transfusion cases. In the first, *Re E*,[141] a boy of 15, though of sufficient intelligence to be able to take decisions about his own well being, was not, it was held, *Gillick* competent, because

---

132 *Re E* [1993] 1 FLR 386; *Re S* [1994] 2 FLR 1065. Discussed further by Bridgeman, Chapter 11, in this volume.

133 [1999] 2 FLR 1097.

134 Brazier, M and Bridge, C, 'Coercion or caring: analysing adolescent autonomy' (1996) 16 LS 84, p 88.

135 *Re R* [1992] Fam 11, p 18.

136 *Re C* [1994] 1 FLR 31.

137 *A Metropolitan Borough Council v DB* [1997] 1 FLR 767, p 773, *per* Cazalet J; *Re C* [1997] 2 FLR 180, p 195, *per* Wall J.

138 *Re T* [1992] 2 FLR 458, p 470.

139 *Re R* [1992] Fam 11, p 26.

140 Children Act 1989 and the Family Law Reform Act 1969, s 8.

141 *Re E* [1993] 1 FLR 386.

there was a range of decisions confronting him which lay outside his full comprehension. Said Ward J: 'He may have some concept of the fact that he will die, but as to the manner of his death and the extent of his and his family's suffering I find he has not the ability to turn his mind to it nor the will to do so.'[142] In *Re S*,[143] a girl of 15, who had suffered from thalassaemia virtually since birth, became a Jehovah's Witness and decided to cease having blood transfusions. She said that forcing them on her was 'like rape'.[144] But Johnson J saw S as 'a child' with the 'integrity and commitment of a child and not of somebody who was competent to make the decision that she tells me she has made. She still hopes for a miracle. My conclusion is, therefore, that she is not "*Gillick* competent"'.[145] Her capacity, he concluded, was not 'commensurate with the gravity of the decision which she has made'.[146] In effect, as she perceived it, she could be judicially raped.

In *Re E* (1993), the boy died shortly after his 18th birthday, when treatment could no longer be imposed upon him.[147] It is possible that the same fate befell S. Both cases were decided upon what the courts deemed to be in the child's best interests, but whether either of the adolescents involved would have seen it that way or, had they lived, would have come as adults to see it in that way, may be doubted.

Perhaps the most troubling example of this trend is the case of *Re W*.[148] W was an 16 year old anorexic. *Gillick* competence was not in issue, and it was thought that legislation[149] had made the law clear: at 16, an adolescent could take her own decisions in relation to medical care. But, in *Re W*, the Court of Appeal decided that we laboured under a misapprehension and, even though the girl was 16, the local authority was granted leave to make an application for the exercise by the court of the High Court's inherent jurisdiction. An anorexic, with sufficient understanding to make an informed choice, could be force fed. The decision shows scant understanding of *anorexia nervosa*. The anorexic is typically lacking in self-confidence. She may suffer 'the basic delusion of not having an identity', of not even 'owning' her body and its sensations. What unites those who suffer the disease (though its causes differ) is 'the urgent need to be in control of their own lives and have a sense of identity'.[150] We know that W wanted control over her own life. She wanted to stay in the adolescent psychiatric unit and decide when she would eat. The

---

142 *Re E* [1993] 1 FLR 386, p 391.

143 *Re S* [1994] 2 FLR 1065.

144 *Ibid*, p 1072.

145 *Ibid*, p 1076.

146 *Ibid*, p 1076.

147 This fact was revealed in *Re S, ibid*, p 1075.

148 *Re W* [1993] Fam 64.

149 Family Law Reform Act 1969, s 8(1).

150 See Bruch, H, *Eating Disorders*, 1974, London: Routledge and Kegan Paul.

ability to take these decisions were taken from her. Her life may have been saved, but at the price of further undermining her identity and integrity. Indirectly, decisions like those in *Re W* will create more anorexics, more disturbed adolescents.

Why, then, are decisions like those in *Re W* made? One clue is found in the judgments in *Re R* and *Re W*, particularly in those of Lord Donaldson MR. Doctors need protection against litigation (in *Re W*, he uses the metaphor of a legal 'flak jacket').[151] This 'protects the doctor from claims by the litigious, whether he acquires it from his patient, who may be a minor over the age of 16, or a '*Gillick* competent' child under that age, or from another person having parental responsibilities, which include a right to consent to treatment of a minor'.[152] The interests of the medical profession (still, of course, predominantly male) are prioritised over the interests of adolescent patients (who are, in most of the difficult cases, girls). A *Gillick* competent girl of 15 cannot object to a male doctor touching her if one of her parents gives consent. A 17 year old could be forced to undergo an abortion against her will. This is a hair-raising scenario and Lord Donaldson MR, aware of it, himself dons a flak jacket, this time that of medical ethics: doctors would not let this happen 'unless the abortion was truly in the best interests of the child'.[153] But to fall back on medical ethics to protect when we know that many girls have been needlessly sterilised is unconvincing; it was, it will be remembered, only chance intervention by an educational psychologist, financed by the National Council of Civil Liberties, that brought this practice to the attention of the courts.[154]

The protection of the medical profession is only part of the putative answer. The test relies on there being a valid distinction between consent and refusal. But the distinction drawn is simplistic and illogical. Adults have an absolute right 'to choose whether to consent to medical treatment, to refuse it or to choose one rather than another of the treatments being offered'.[155] Broadmoor patients suffering from chronic paranoid schizophrenia,[156] prisoners[157] and pregnant women who are potentially endangering their unborn children[158] may refuse recommended treatment; not so competent children, even those of 16, whom legislation empowered in 1969.[159] The argument that refusing treatment can harm whilst agreeing to treatment

---

151 *Re W* [1993] Fam 64, p 78.
152 *Ibid*.
153 *Ibid*, p 79.
154 *Re D* [1976] Fam 185.
155 *Re T* [1992] 2 FLR 458, p 460, *per* Lord Donaldson MR.
156 *Re C* [1994] 1 FLR 31.
157 *Home Office v Robb* [1995] 1 FLR 412.
158 *St George's Healthcare NHS Trust v S* [1999] Fam 26.
159 See the Family Law Reform Act 1969, s 8(1).

cannot is unconvincing:[160] as the law stands; it allows a *Gillick* competent adolescent to consent to treatment which may well harm her. Jane Fortin gives the example of a child suffering from leukaemia who finds a consultant prepared to carry out an unproven form of treatment with a small chance of success, which is also likely to cause considerable further suffering and not prolong life. Her parents could not veto her, and a court could only do so if it found her incompetent or by reinterpreting *Gillick*.[161] The former solution would be disingenuous; the latter unprincipled.

I suspect that a court might well adopt the first of these solutions: it would not have great difficulty in negating rationality where it thought the decision making process flawed. Gillian Douglas[162] is surely right to reject the consent/refusal distinction. She gives three reasons for doing so. First, there are often differing medical opinions on the benefits of any proposed treatment. Secondly, even when medical opinions are in agreement, others may not be. Thirdly, the rejection of refusal inevitably involves a gross infringement of bodily integrity and self-determination. And this point is accepted by the courts. Thus, in *Re W*, it was said that the courts would normally assume that it was in the best interests of a *Gillick* competent child 'to make an informed decision that the court should respect its integrity as a human being and not highly override its decision on such a personal matter as medical treatment, all the more so if that treatment is invasive'.[163]

CHILD ABUSE

No account of feminism and child law can conclude without a consideration of perhaps the most contentious problem area – that of child abuse.[164] Child abuse is a social construction; whether something comes within its perimeters depends on the actions of political actors. All sorts of explanations and rationalisations were posited to deny the significance of sexual abuse,[165] which was not properly recognised as a form of abuse until the Cleveland affair in the mid-1980s.[166] Whether a particular child has been abused

160 As argued by Lowe, N and Juss, S, 'Medical treatment – pragmatism and the search for principle' (1993) 56 MLR 865, pp 871–72.

161 Fortin, J, *Children's Rights and the Developing Law*, 1998, London: Butterworths, pp 104–05.

162 Douglas, G, 'The retreat from *Gillick*' (1992) 55 MLR 569.

163 *Re W* [1993] Fam 64, p 88, *per* Balcombe LJ.

164 Despite the title of their article, Ashe and Cahn (*op cit*, fn 1) do not really address the issues.

165 Smart, C, 'A history of ambivalence and conflict in the discursive construction of the "child victim" of sexual abuse' (1999) 8 SLS 391.

166 Freeman, M, *The Moral Status of Children*, 1997, The Hague: Kluwer, Chapter 13.

depends upon how official agencies (doctors, hospital personnel, the police, social workers and coroners) classify the term 'abuse'. The agent's moral beliefs and stereotypic definitions influence his or her definitions of, and reactions to, people's behaviour, and certain individuals are more likely to be defined as abusers than others. Whether a particular behavioural act is an accident or an abusive incident is, thus, far from value-free. The poor are more likely to reveal abuse, whether or not they are more likely to commit it.[167] Of course, if the poor are more likely to reveal abuse and have their abuse officially perceived, then characteristics become identified with the so called abuse 'syndrome' that are overrepresented in the poor population. Abusers are found to be socially isolated or mother-headed families or unemployed (often a combination of all three). This has a spiralling effect, for families with these characteristics are necessarily perceived to be 'at risk'. A family with these characteristics is more likely to find that an injured child is perceived as having been deliberately traumatised than classified as 'accidentally' hurt.

Women are often blamed for child abuse, whether as perpetrators or as bystanders, implicated in their partner's abusive behaviour. This is but an extension of the thinking which blames battered women (she provoked him, deserved it or didn't leave). As far as the physical abuse and neglect of children is concerned, women may well be overrepresented as abusers because of 'beliefs about their roles, responsibilities and natures'.[168] In fact, children in two parent families are more likely to be physically abused by fathers (or step-fathers) than mothers.[169] Few victims of sexual abuse are abused by women. Research into cases of female sexual abuse of children concluded that women who did abuse did so for similar reasons to men: these included security and power, in addition to needs for intimacy.[170]

Official reporting figures suggest that girls are more subject to abuse than boys.[171] More boys may be physically abused than girls – a legacy of corporal punishment practices – but girls are overwhelmingly the victims of sexual abuse. There is no satisfactory explanation of why this should be: outside the West, it has been suggested that it is girls' lesser economic utility that accounts for their abuse.[172] This cannot explain it in Britain. The answer may lie in discovering why abuse is perpetrated at all.

---

167 Freeman, M, 'Child welfare: law and control', in Partington, M and Jowell, J (eds), *Welfare Law and Policy*, 1979, London: Frances Pinter, p 223.

168 Corby, B, *Child Abuse: Towards a Knowledge Base*, 1993, Buckingham: OU Press, p 65.

169 Creighton, S and Noyes, P, *Child Abuse Trends in England and Wales 1983–1987*, 1989, London: NSPCC, p 21.

170 Krug, R, 'Adult male report of childhood sexual abuse by mothers: case descriptions, motivations and long-term consequences' (1989) 13 Child Abuse and Neglect 111; see, also, Banning, A, 'Mother-son incest: confronting a prejudice' (1989) 13 Child Abuse and Neglect 563.

171 See *ibid*, Corby, p 81.

172 Finkelhor, D and Korbin, J, 'Child abuse as an international issue' (1988) 12 Child Abuse and Neglect 3.

There are three models of abuse:[173] the psycho-pathological one, which finds something 'wrong' with the abuser; the socio-environmental stress model, which links abuse to the stress caused by poverty and its correlates; and the cultural model. In the context of sexual abuse, this offers particular insights. Most perpetrators are men, and most victims are female. It would not, therefore, be surprising if the general source of the abuse were located in masculine sexuality. And yet it is surprising – though feminists would say it is not – that the gender of the perpetrator is so rarely made explicit. For example, discussion relating to Cleveland was invariably about 'parents'.[174] In part, this is because women are blamed, even though they do not abuse: they 'allow' it to occur. It is common to find mother-blaming in the orthodox literature on child sexual abuse. Nelson notes that 'professionals cling to the collusive wife theory like drowning men grasping at flotsam'. Could it be, she asks, because 'it is such a powerful defence against admitting the male abuse of power? And because, without it, family therapists might be like emperors without clothes?'.[175]

Feminism not only offers a different interpretation of child sexual abuse, but also challenges the responses of orthodoxy, in particular those of 'family systems' theory and family therapy. For feminists, child sexual abuse is an example of the inequality between the sexes produced by a patriarchal social system.[176] Thus, Wattenberg writes: 'The father rapes, abuses, brutalises and assaults the children and the mother, but somehow it is the mother's or child's fault.'[177] Men have been taught that they have the right to have their sexual needs satisfied. Belief that there was open access to wives led to the marital rape immunity surviving until 1991;[178] the extension to that other chattel, the daughter, seems quite rational, particularly if the wife is unavailable.[179] And the structure of the family is such that both wife and children are trapped within dependency. An understanding of abuse requires an understanding of power.

Feminism has been less interested in other forms of abuse. In part, this may be because they have not been seen as starkly in gender terms, but also

---

173 Freeman, MDA, *Violence in the Home: A Socio-Legal Study*, 1979, Farnborough: Saxon House, pp 21–32.

174 A good example, just before Cleveland erupted, is Baker, A and Duncan, S, 'Child sexual abuse: a study of its prevalence in Great Britain' (1985) 9 Child Abuse and Neglect 457.

175 Nelson, S, *Incest: Fact and Myth*, 1987, Edinburgh: Stramullion, p 108.

176 Campbell, B, *Unofficial Secrets: Child Sexual Abuse – the Cleveland Case*, 1988, London: Virago; see, also, the special (1988) 28 FR.

177 Wattenberg, E, 'In a different light: a feminist perspective on the role of mothers in father-daughter incest' (1985) 64 Child Welfare 203, p 206.

178 *R v R* [1991] 4 All ER 481.

179 See the case in (1988) *The Times*, 29 November, and others discussed in *op cit*, Freeman, fn 166, p 296.

because of the existence of policies (noticeable particularly in the US) to extend the categories of abuse to target the behaviour of women when pregnant.[180] There is no doubt that the use of drugs by a pregnant woman or smoking during pregnancy is abusive. But then neither is there any doubt that the consumption of drugs by men can affect the children whom they father or that a man who smokes in the presence of a pregnant woman or a child may harm the foetus or child.[181] It is, however, women's behaviour which is targeted, sometimes even criminalised. It is right to draw attention to differential policies – Cynthia Daniels and Janet Golden point to ways in which responses to men are couched in terms of pity[182] – but equally wrong, I believe, to exonerate women. They may have the right to smoke during pregnancy; they also have the responsibility not to exercise that right.

English law does not define child abuse. Nor does it set out parental responsibilities or rule out any practice associated with child rearing, except female circumcision.[183] A girl, even one who is *Gillick* competent, cannot consent to any form of genital mutilation. This restriction on autonomy, whatever its cultural repercussions, ought to be applauded, though the legislation is increasingly criticised.[184] There is no restriction on male circumcision. It would be wrong to equate the two, for here, surely, is a difference which can be justified. English law also imposes a limit on corporal punishment, which must be 'reasonable';[185] with such a vague standard, it would be difficult to detect any gender differentiation, though, in the days when corporal punishment was allowed in schools, many schools did use different chastisement practices.

State intervention into parent-child relations is pitched high. The trigger for intervention is significant harm.[186] This rules out minor shortcomings and focuses on that which has, or is likely to have, serious and lasting effects upon the child. Harm may be significant in a number of ways: in amount, in effect and in importance. There has not been much debate about the meaning of

180 Johnsen, D, 'The creation of fetal rights: conflicts with women's constitutional rights to liberty, privacy, and equal protection' (1986) 95 Yale LJ 599.

181 Ezra, DB, 'Sticks and stones can break my bones but cigarette smoke can kill me: can we protect children from parents that smoke?' (1993) 13 St Louis U Public L Rev 547.

182 Daniels, C and Golden, J, 'The politics of paternity: foetal risks and reproductive harm', in Freeman, M and Lewis, A, *Law and Medicine*, 2000, Oxford: OUP, p 363.

183 Prohibition of Female Circumcision Act 1985.

184 Eg, Sheldon, S and Wilkinson, S, 'Female genital mutilation and cosmetic surgery: regulating non-therapeutic body modification' (1998) 12 Bioethics 263; Green, K and Lim, H, 'What is this thing about female circumcision?' (1998) 7 SLS 365.

185 But this standard is now said to be insufficient to protect children: see *A v UK* [1998] 1 FLR 2; and Freeman, M, 'Children are unbeatable' (1999) 13 Children and Society 130.

186 Children Act 1989, s 31(2).

'significant'. Feminism could make a valuable contribution here, but has not done so. Little, if anything, has as yet been said about the impact of abuse on relationships and the role that this can play in determining whether harm is significant. Feminism may also be able to offer some insight into the effect of abuse on identities.

The feminist interpretation of 'abuse' may lead to different activities being construed as abuse from those so classified within orthodox thinking. This should have led to feminists joining the corporal punishment debate and calling for English law to be brought into line with the Swedish model, where hitting children is unlawful.[187] That it has not done so is sad; is it also explicable in terms of a fear that the stick would be turned on mothers? Feminist views on what constitutes sexual abuse will also be different. What a judge labelled 'vulgar and inappropriate horseplay'[188] – to distinguish it from sexual abuse – would be seen for what it is, a misuse of power, silly perhaps, but abuse nevertheless.

Feminists could usefully contribute, too, to the debate about standard of proof. The House of Lords' ruling in *Re H*[189] that, when assessing probabilities, a court should have in mind that 'the more serious the allegation, the less likely it is that the event occurred and, hence, the stronger should be the evidence before the court concludes that the allegation is established on the balance of probability'[190] is bizarre, even perverse, for the worse the danger the child is in, the less likely the courts are to remove her from it. Where the House of Lords went wrong was in believing that sexual abuse of step-daughters was a rare event. On this they were wrong. But they also identified the question wrongly: this related not to the probability of *any* step-daughter being sexually abused, but the step-daughters in the case. A better comparator population than step-daughters as a whole would have been step-daughters in cases where other girls within the family have complained.

CONCLUSION

A full account of feminism and child law remains to be written. What this chapter has demonstrated is that the subject is rich in history and the legacies of history and that an examination of child law in England today repays

---

187 A precedent followed by legislatures in Norway, Finland, Austria, Cyprus, Denmark, Croatia, Latvia, and also by Supreme Courts in Italy and in Israel.

188 [1988] 1 FLR 462.

189 [1996] AC 563.

190 *Ibid*, p 586. See Hayes, M, 'Reconciling protection for children with justice for parents' (1997) 17 LS 1.

critical scrutiny. The answers are not obvious or always forthcoming, but the insights are many. I have cast light on a neglected conjunction but much more can and, I hope, will, be said.

CHAPTER 3

CHILDREN BY DONATION: DO THEY HAVE A CLAIM TO THEIR GENETIC PARENTAGE?

Melanie Roberts

INTRODUCTION

Increasing numbers of children are being born as a result of techniques involving medically assisted reproduction.[1] Where a couple's own sperm and ova are used to achieve pregnancy, there is no separation of genetic and social parentage. In these cases, medical assistance is merely a tool used to achieve pregnancy and the involvement of medical technocrats[2] is simply an incident in the parents' life.[3] Where donated gametes are used, the link between genetic and social parentage is partially broken; with embryo donation, there is no link between genetic and social parentage. Medical assistance involving donation is not simply an incident in the parents' life but has long term implications for them and for any resulting children. Medically assisted reproduction changes human relations and what has traditionally been the family – children with one mother and father, with adoption providing an accepted anomaly.[4] The techniques available mean that a child could have up to six different 'parents': a genetic mother or mothers (cells from two women can create one egg);[5] a gestating mother; a social mother; a genetic father; and a social father. Recognition and respect needs to be given to the roles which different people may perform in a child's life.

---

1 Approximately 2,500 children are born each year in the UK as a result of licensed treatments using donated gametes or embryos: HFEA, *Annual Report*, 1997.

2 A term used to describe doctors, scientists and researchers involved in assisted reproduction by Spallone, P, *Beyond Conception: The New Politics of Reproduction*, 1989, London: Macmillan.

3 Medically assisted reproduction raises further issues which are beyond the scope of this chapter, such as medical power, allocation of resources, access to treatment, and which are of relevance whether their own, or donated, gametes are used.

4 For a brief discussion of the history of families, see Dickens, BM, 'Reproductive technology and the "new" family', in Sutherland, E and McCall Smith, A (eds), *Family Rights*, 1990, Edinburgh: Edinburgh UP. See O'Donovan, Chapter 5, in this volume, who compares French law – which distinguishes between maternity (giving birth) and motherhood (being a mother) – with English law – which conflates the two, both at common law and in legislation concerning adoption and medically assisted reproduction.

5 'Baby created from two mothers raises hopes for childless' (1998) *The Sunday Times*, 14 June; 'Fertility doctors create babies with two mothers' (1999) *The Sunday Times*, 16 May.

The law has succeeded in defining the legal parentage of children born as a result of donation.[6] Children know who their legal parents are, but what about their genetic origins? Do children by donation have a claim to their genetic parentage? The regulation of medically assisted reproduction has been mainly concerned with protecting the patients (those seeking treatment for infertility) and the donors who make treatment possible. However, gamete and embryo donations are not like organ, tissue or blood donation; genetic links are established. The use of donated gametes and embryos raises issues about the interests and needs of children by donation to be told about their genetic background, the interests of parents in withholding that information and the interests of donors in having anonymity.

Reproduction is essentially a private matter contained within the domestic sphere; and so it is, traditionally, beyond the scope of legal regulation, although a private issue may become a matter of public concern and hence the object of legal regulation.[7] The use of medical technology in reproduction has led to an element of control and regulation of reproductive freedom. An examination of the legal framework which regulates medically assisted reproduction is necessary to assist in an understanding of the way in which the three parties – prospective parents, donor and child – are perceived. The concepts of secrecy, anonymity and identity will be employed in order to explore the different positions of those involved. The concept of secrecy reflects the interests of the prospective parent, the concept of anonymity reflects the interests of the donor, whilst questions of identity arise in relation to the child.

THE LEGAL FRAMEWORK

The Human Fertilisation and Embryology Act 1990 (the Act) regulates medically assisted reproduction using donor gametes and embryos. In general, medical practice is rarely regulated by statute in England and this Act

---

6   Human Fertilisation and Embryology Act 1990, ss 27 and 28. The gestational mother is the legal mother, whether or not she is also the genetic mother and whether or not she intends to be the social mother (s 27). Identifying the legal father is more complicated. Section 28(6)(a) ensures that the donor of sperm used in accordance with the provisions of the Act is not the legal father. If the woman being treated is married, her husband is presumed to be the father (s 28(5)(a)). This presumption can be rebutted, but, if the husband consented to the treatment, he is the legal father (s 28(2)). If a woman is not married but receives treatment services provided for her and a man together, using donor sperm or embryo, her partner is deemed to be the father (s 28(3)). Legitimacy of the child conceived by donation is solved by the Act, although succession to hereditary titles and honours are excluded (s 29(4)).

7   See O'Donovan, K, *Sexual Divisions in Law*, 1985, London: Weidenfeld & Nicolson, cited in Bridgeman, J and Millns, S, *Feminist Perspectives on Law*, 1998, London: Sweet & Maxwell, p 24.

provides a significant exception. The infertile parents are seen as the subject of the legislation, with the focus being on their needs;[8] a child is seen as successful treatment.[9] As donor gametes are able to 'cure' many instances of infertility, there is a need to encourage donation, and it is thought that, in order to do so, it is necessary to protect donor anonymity. Confidentiality in the relationship between doctor and patient is interpreted as being owed to the future parents and to the donor.[10] Concern lies with the prospective parents and the donors, whilst concern with the child's welfare is somewhat ambiguous.

There was no reference to the child's welfare in the Human Fertilisation and Embryology Bill. Pressure from the 'moral right' to restrict the access of single or lesbian women to infertility treatment resulted in an amendment to take *'account* of the welfare of any child who may be born as a result of the treatment (including the need of that child for a father)'.[11] The primary concern of legislators was with access to services, rather than with the welfare of the child. One of the reasons for regulating reproductive technologies, and donor insemination in particular, has been concern about the creation of families that differ from the traditional heterosexual family.[12] Fears of autonomous motherhood are apparent in the Warnock Report, which wanted to ensure that medically assisted reproduction would only be available to women together with a partner.[13] The 'welfare of the child' is a rhetorical consideration, dependent upon the subjective view of the decision maker and reflecting personal moralities and ideologies. The concept of the welfare of the child is, arguably, a shield behind which social judgments are made as to maternal fitness and concerns about paternity.[14] The Act allows doctors and counsellors to make value laden judgments as to who they will allow to become a parent. However questions of 'welfare' are not just about how the child's parents may relate to her, or what type of environment the child may live in (and, in fact, should not concentrate on this aspect of 'welfare'), but

---

8   Spallone, *op cit,* fn 2, argues that the subject of the Act is not children or women, but eggs and sperm.

9   For a discussion of the use of the language of disease and cure in respect of infertility, see Overall, C, *Ethics and Human Reproduction: A Feminist Analysis,* 1987, Boston: Allen & Unwin, pp 140–42.

10 HFEA, *Code of Practice,* 4th edn, July 1998, London: HFEA.

11 Human Fertilisation and Embryology Act 1990, s 13(5) (emphasis added). Only an 'account' is to be taken of the child's welfare. The child's welfare is not paramount, as it is under the Children Act 1989 (s 1), or even the first consideration, as in adoption (Adoption Act 1976, s 6).

12 Snowden, R and Mitchell, GD, *The Artificial Family,* 1981, London: Allen & Unwin, p 119.

13 *Report of the Committee of Inquiry into Human Fertilisation and Embryology,* Cmnd 9314, 1984, paras 2.9–2.11.

14 See *op cit,* Bridgeman and Millns, fn 7, pp 131–45, for discussion of access to treatment.

should extend to consideration of a right for the child to know the circumstances of her conception and a claim to her genetic parentage.

Guidance on the welfare of the child is given by the Human Fertilisation and Embryology Authority (HFEA) in its *Code of Practice*,[15] which includes a list of factors that clinics should consider when assessing the welfare of the child.[16] The code sets out additional factors where donated gametes are to be used, including 'a child's potential need to know about their origins and whether or not the prospective parents are prepared for the questions which may arise while the child is growing up'.[17] However, there is no requirement that the prospective parents tell the child of the means of her conception. Also, there is no requirement for the child's birth certificate to indicate that donor gametes were used: the intending parents are registered as the legal parents.[18] The Warnock Committee recommended that parents might insert the words 'by donation' on the birth register; however, Parliament did not endorse this suggestion. Whilst counsellors may espouse openness,[19] there are pressures on parents against this, not least from some medical professionals. Medically assisted reproduction and the legal framework in which it operates is concerned with protecting the anonymity of the donor, in order to ensure a supply of gametes so that treatment can take place. The focus is not upon the child who may be created and, thus, is not upon issues for the child such as identity and a child's potential need to know about her origins. If parents have not told anyone of the way in which the child is conceived, then they are unlikely to tell the child. Even where parents have told members of their families and/or friends, they may still not tell the child.

What information about donors is presently available to children by donation?

The Act does not apply where conception as a result of donor insemination takes place on a do it yourself basis, with a woman using the sperm of a friend or acquaintance without the need for medical assistance.[20] Where there is self-insemination, the parents of the child will usually know the identity of the donor, so it will be up to the child's parents to decide the information which they will provide to the child about the donation and the donor. It is a

---

15 The *Code of Practice* is not legally binding, although it has been argued that failure to comply with the Code would constitute a breach of duty (Kennedy, I and Grubb, A, *Medical Law: Text with Materials*, 1994, London: Butterworths, p 793).

16 *Op cit*, HFEA, fn 10, paras 3.12–3.17.

17 *Op cit*, HFEA, fn 10, para 3.18.

18 See above, fn 6.

19 Blyth, E, *Infertility and Assisted Conception: Practice Issues for Counsellors*, 1995, Birmingham: British Association of Social Workers, p 67.

20 Where insemination does not take place in a licensed centre, the donor is the legal father.

different matter where donor gametes are used in accordance with the Act, with donors being nearly always anonymous. A statutory obligation is placed upon the HFEA to keep a register of information relating to the users of their services; this includes identifying information about its patients, the donors and any resulting children.[21] However, access to this information is strictly limited to members and employees of the HFEA and staff at clinics licensed by the HFEA.[22] This means that there is absolute anonymity; neither the donor, the recipients, nor any child born as a result of the donation can be identified. However, s 31(4) of the Act provides that, on reaching 18 years of age, children can discover whether they were born as a result of treatment using donated sperm, ova or embryos. Children aged 16 or over can be told whether they could be genetically related to someone whom they intend to marry.[23]

The register was established on 1 August 1991 and contains information concerning children conceived using donated gametes as of that date; therefore, the earliest the register can be accessed is 2007. The Act provides that the HFEA may give any information, which would include identifying information, as is required by regulations.[24] Regulations can be made retrospectively to provide non-identifying information,[25] but identifying information cannot be retrospectively disclosed.[26] Therefore, a donor of gametes will know at the time of donation whether or not their identity may subsequently be divulged to any child. To date, no regulations have been made. This means that, at present in the UK, a child (when 18 (or 16 if marrying)) will only have access to information revealing that she was conceived by donation. No information about a child's genetic background or information linking an individual child with an individual donor is obtainable. It is expected that secondary legislation permitting disclosure of extra information, although not identifying information, will have been passed by 2007.[27] However, a child who has not been told that she was conceived by donation will not know that there is relevant information about genetic parentage to be had.

The Warnock Committee was unable to decide what information ought to be given to children about their genetic background and, thus, it took an uneasy middle ground. The Committee concluded that no identifying

---

21 Human Fertilisation and Embryology Act 1990, s 31(1) and (2).

22 *Ibid*, s 33.

23 *Ibid*, s 31(6) and (7). Counselling is to be offered to people seeking this information: s 31(3) and (6).

24 *Ibid*, s 31(4)(a).

25 Non-identifying information includes medical details, physical characteristics, occupation and interests.

26 Human Fertilisation and Embryology Act 1990, s 31(5).

27 The Department of Health and the HFEA are jointly considering what information should be disclosed to children by donation and are preparing a paper that may be used as the basis of a consultative exercise should there be public consultation (telephone communication with Mike Evans, Department of Health, September 2000).

information about the donor should be available to a child by donation[28] but recommended that, on reaching the age of 18, the child should have access to certain 'basic information' about the donor's ethnic origin and genetic health.[29] Children by donation would be given information about the health and ethnic origin of the donor, but nothing about their genealogical background, such as the donor's personality, appearance, interests and family life history.

The information that the Warnock Committee recommended be available opens up too many questions. Some recipients of donor sperm have expressed concern that, unless the child could be given full information, including the donor's identity, there would be no point in telling the child anything about her conception, as this would leave too many unanswered questions.[30]

The information presently obtained from donors by the HFEA is fairly sparse.[31] All donors are required to fill out a form that contains identifying information required by the HFEA.[32] There is a section where donors may write something about themselves, a description of their lives and interests, which could later be passed on to any child born as a result of the donation.[33] As retrospective regulations could be made to disclose non-identifying information, it is likely that this optional description of the donors would be part of what is disclosed.[34] As the form makes clear, the self-description by the donor is optional, and studies show that only a small number of donors are completing this part of the form, with the consequence that some children would receive a description of their genetic parents whilst others would not.[35] These studies have important implications for parents who want to tell their

---

28   Op cit, Report of the Committee of Inquiry into Human Fertilisation and Embryology, fn 13, para 4.26.

29   Op cit, Report of the Committee of Inquiry into Human Fertilisation and Embryology, fn 13, para 4.21.

30   Op cit, Blyth, fn 19, Chapter 5.

31   Some centres collect more information; see op cit, Blyth, fn 19, p 99 and Maclean, S and Maclean, M, 'Keeping secrets in assisted reproduction – the tension between donor anonymity and the need of the child for information' [1996] CFLQ 243, p 245.

32   This includes ethnic group, eye colour, hair colour, skin colour, height, weight, occupation and interests (one line is provided for listing interests).

33   The Code of Practice (op cit, fn 10, para 3.43) states that donors should be encouraged to provide non-identifying biographical information about themselves.

34   Ibid, Maclean and Maclean, pp 245–46.

35   Maclean and Maclean, ibid, found that less than 20% of donors are completing the descriptive section of the form but that the larger centres offering treatment with donated gametes have a higher completion rate. This suggests that the culture at these larger centres may be more encouraging of providing this information. A study conducted at the Lister In-Vitro Fertilisation Unit, London, found that 94% of egg donors did not respond to the last question, which asked for a brief description of themselves, leaving only profession and interests as information to be given in the future. See Abdalla, H, Shenfield, F and Latarche, E, 'Statutory information for the children born of oocyte donation in the UK: what will they be told in 2008?' (1998) 13 Human Reproduction 1106.

child of her origins. Unless there is a legal obligation to provide this descriptive information, there will be a lack of consistency in the information which children by donation receive about their genitor.

The only time a child may come to know a donor's identity is where the court requires the HFEA to disclose the identity of a donor to enable a child to bring an action against the donor for his or her negligence under the Congenital Disabilities (Civil Liability) Act 1976.[36] This may arise where the screening of donated sperm failed to detect a genetic defect, which the donor had failed to disclose, and the child inherited the disease.[37] A child who is the subject of a 'parental order' under s 30 of that Act will be allowed a copy of their original birth certificate on reaching the age of 18.[38] They therefore have the same rights as adopted children under s 51 of the Adoption Act 1976, but they are the only children born as a result of medically assisted conception who have been granted this right. Some children could, therefore, obtain the identity of their genetic parents, but this raises questions of equity for all donor children. As information relating to donors' identities exists, it would be possible for Parliament to repeal the Act and enact primary legislation permitting disclosure of the identity of donors, and to apply this retrospectively, as occurred in relation to adoption.[39]

SECRECY – THE PARENTS

Donation is surrounded with secrecy. When artificial insemination by donor was first introduced, it was assumed that secrecy was the best stance to take and was taken for granted. Secrecy stems from fear: fear that the child will reject the social parent in favour of the genitor; fear that the genitor will interfere; and fear of societal disapproval. As use of donor sperm far outweighs the use of donor ova, it is the infertile man in particular who is protected by a policy of secrecy. There is some evidence that there may be particular problems in relation to openness and male infertility. Western culture attaches much significance to the association between fertility and

---

36 Human Fertilisation Embryology Act 1990, s 35. Perhaps this exception to donor anonymity exists because, if there was no one to pursue for negligence, the State would have to support the disabled child.

37 The donor's identity is protected more stringently than that of the patient parent or any child born. For further discussion on this point, see *op cit*, Kennedy and Grubb, fn 15, pp 811–15.

38 Parental Orders (Human Fertilisation and Embryology) Regulations 1994 (SI 1994/2767), amending the Adoption Act 1976, s 50. These children will have been born by surrogacy and may be the genetic child of both their social parents or of only their father. However, where gamete donation was used, the genetic parents will not be shown on the birth certificate.

39 Children Act 1975.

power.[40] Male infertility is thus seen as a source of shame and weakness, with feelings of masculinity being damaged by the discovery of infertility.[41] The myth that fertility and virility are related and the attitudes of others means that couples often wish to keep the problem of infertility and the means of conception secret.[42] A quest for 'normality' can result in secrecy and dishonesty. For men, parenthood means genetic parenthood. Secrecy stems from patriarchal concern to protect male pride in hiding male infertility and what is considered a failure: the inability to pass on one's genetic heritage.[43] Where donor sperm is used, men place more importance on having a donor with a similar genetic background than women do when using donor ova.[44] Mason argues that in a patrilineal society there is far less concern as to the origin of female genes than is attached to the male genetic line, as 'not even the esoteric problems of the inheritance of titles of honour would be disturbed by ovum donation in the UK'.[45] This emphasis on genetics in Western culture means that sperm donation is seen as breaking a taboo, which needs to be covered up by secrecy.[46]

Not only are medical professionals involved in the maintenance of secrecy; so, too, is the State. Where children are born by donation, birth certificates are issued in the name of the legal parents, thus deliberately falsifying the birth register, as the genetic parents (where they differ from the legal parents) are not recorded. Where children are adopted, new birth certificates are issued (although the original is always maintained), yet the birth records of children by donation are genetically inaccurate from the start. Freeman argues that a birth register is not, in any event, a source of genetically accurate information,[47] since there are entries which fail to disclose the father's name and no checks are made as to whether the information given is genetically correct. However, the collusion of the State in the falsification of birth records is a practice far more questionable than failure on the part of the State to investigate the accuracy of the information provided. Glazebrook advocates that, instead of leaving children to discover by chance, or to suspect, that they

40 Dewar, J, 'Fathers in law? The case of AID', in Lee, R and Morgan, D (eds), *Birthrights: Law and Ethics at the Beginnings of Life*, 1989, London: Routledge, p 116.

41 Snowden, R and Snowden, E, *The Gift of a Child*, 1984, London: Allen & Unwin. The Warnock Committee felt that a change in attitude to male infertility was required (*op cit*, fn 13, para 4.28).

42 *See op cit*, Blyth, fn 19, pp 66–67, for a discussion of how infertility affects men.

43 Thevoz, J, 'The rights of children to information', in Evans, D (ed), *Creating the Child*, 1996, The Hague: Kluwer, p 198.

44 Adair, VA and Purdie, A, 'Donor insemination programmes with personal donor: issues of secrecy' (1996) 11 Human Reproduction 2558.

45 Mason, JK, *Medico-Legal Aspects of Reproduction and Parenthood*, 1998, Aldershot: Dartmouth, p 241.

46 *Ibid*, Thevoz, p 198.

47 Freeman, M, 'The unscrambling of egg donation', in McLean, S (ed), *Law Reform and Human Reproduction*, 1992, Aldershot: Dartmouth, p 280.

are not the genetic offspring of both their legal parents, it ought to be a requirement that resulting births of donation be registered as such.[48]

Denial and secrecy can involve deception, which can cause tension, stress and problems within the family. Secrecy carries the danger that a child by donation will discover her status and, as a consequence, never trust her parents again.[49] Secrecy can destroy the trust on which all good family relationships are built and a child by donation is likely to feel cheated if deceived about her origins. Some parents feel that ensuring that the donor remains unknown helps to diminish his or her importance.[50] The donor may remain a constant shadowy figure, of uncertain significance, in their lives. The psychological cost to parents of maintaining secrets is also high.[51] A policy of secrecy arises from the stigmatisation of infertility in the way that illegitimacy was stigmatised in the past.[52] Secrecy implies that there is something shameful about infertility and donation, yet keeping donation a secret further fuels society's ignorance and the stigmatisation of the infertile.

How do women view donation and the genetic link? A Dutch study found that men and women in donor insemination families held different opinions about secrecy and donor anonymity: men, more often than women, were secretive about the use of a donor, and men, more often than women, were in favour of donor anonymity.[53] An American study of women who had had donor insemination found that there were significant differences in attitudes towards disclosure, with more single than married women reporting that they would tell the child about using donor sperm to conceive.[54] The married women may have been protecting their husbands, sensing that they would feel threatened if the circumstances of conception were revealed to the child – the husbands would perhaps feel that the children were not theirs if the children knew that the husband was not the genetic father. Women who seek to use reproductive technology may do so, not so much because they want children who are theirs, but because they desire the experiences of pregnancy,

---

48 Glazebrook, PR, 'Human beginnings' [1984] CLJ 209, p 211.

49 Haimes, E, 'Secrecy' (1988) 2 IJLPF 46.

50 *Op cit*, Snowden and Snowden, fn 41. Interviews with couples where sperm donation had been used revealed that fathers often refer to the donor as being the 'real father', whilst at the same time expressing the view that the child was 'their' child, indicating that fathers feel somewhat confused about the paternity of the child.

51 For a discussion of the need for openness by a mother of sperm donor children, see Mays, A, 'Secrecy is not an option: trust in the truth', in Blyth, E, Crawshaw, M and Speirs, J (eds), *Truth and the Child 10 Years On: Information Exchange in Donor Assisted Conception*, 1998, Birmingham: British Association of Social Workers.

52 O'Donovan, K, 'A right to know one's parentage?' (1998) 2 IJLPF 27.

53 Brewaeys, A, Golombok, S, Naaktgeboren, N, de Bruyn, JK and van Hall, EV, 'Donor insemination: Dutch parents' opinions about confidentiality and donor anonymity and the emotional adjustment of their children' (1997) 12 Human Reproduction 1591.

54 Klock, SC, Jacob, MC and Maier, D, 'A comparison of single and married recipients of donor insemination' (1996) 11 Human Reproduction 2554.

childbirth and caring for a newborn. From their point of view, the problem of adoption, especially of an older child, is not that the child is not genetically related, but rather that these experiences must be forgone.[55] However, when women are faced with fertility problems, they are more inclined than men to consider adoption, which suggests that genetic links are less important to women than they are to men.[56] Traditionally, in most households, women have been the primary carers of children and nurturing and caring for the child on a daily basis forges a bond between mother and child. Where the father has less nurturing contact with the child, he may be more anxious to rely upon genetic links to create a relationship with the child. Perhaps with fathers becoming more involved in the nurture and care of their children, men will become less anxious about genetic links.

Are recipients of eggs or embryos able to be more open regarding a child's genetic parentage? A woman who is implanted with an embryo (from a donor's egg and her partner's sperm) or a donated embryo is in a different position from the male recipient of donor sperm. The woman in this position contributes to the creation of the child during pregnancy and gives birth to the child; the social, non-genetic father contributes nothing to the creation of the child.[57] In such a situation, the bond between mother and child, established during pregnancy, can prevail over the lack of a genetic link. This bond may give the non-genetic mother the confidence to be more open about the donation and the child's genetic heritage. Further, the relationship between the egg donor and the recipient differs from that between sperm donor and the social father. Egg donation is comparatively rare and, when it occurs, it does so frequently between related women, where the issue of anonymity does not arise. Often,women want to know who they are getting the egg from or who they are giving their egg to.[58] Secrecy is unlikely to be an issue where donor eggs are used.

ANONYMITY – THE DONOR

The Human Fertilisation and Embryology Act 1990 was drafted with the interests of the infertile parents foremost in mind; it is concerned with medical treatment and not child care. The policy of anonymity of gamete donors is

55 *Op cit*, Overall, fn 9, p 152.

56 Stanworth, M, 'The deconstruction of motherhood', in *Reproductive Technologies: Gender, Motherhood and Medicine*, 1987, Cambridge: Polity, p 22; and Crowe, C, 'Women want it: in vitro fertilisation and women's motivations for participation', in Spallone, P and Stenberg, DL (eds), *Made to Order*, 1987, Oxford: Pergamon, p 87.

57 The Warnock Committee was of the view that egg donation had an advantage over sperm donation, in that both partners contribute to the birth of the child (*op cit*, fn 13, para 6.5).

58 *Op cit*, Thevoz, fn 43, p 198.

justified on the basis of confidentiality of medical treatment and has been regarded by medical personnel as necessary in order to recruit donors. Policies of anonymity reflect societal concern with the genetically related family as the 'norm'. Anonymity ensures that the child cannot trace the donor, thus, no one need know of the involvement of the donor and the family is able to appear to be a 'natural', genetically related family. Anonymity encourages a belief that donation is a furtive way of forming a family. This means that families often do not tell the child the method of her conception for fear of exposing the child and themselves to stigmatisation. Donation is not always anonymous, since the Act does allow the use of donor sperm or egg where the donor is known to the recipients. However, when deciding whether or not to use a known donor, the clinics are directed towards 'the implications for the welfare of the child if the donor is personally known within the child's family and social circle'.[59] This additional element of scrutiny indicates that it is thought that anonymous donation is more desirable.[60]

IS THERE A NEED FOR DONOR ANONYMITY?

Is there any reason to suspect that donors would not participate in donation if they were not given anonymity? The Swedish Law on Insemination 1985 has given children by donation the right to know the identity of the sperm donor, when mature enough (no age is specified). It is considered that the right of the child overrides other interests such as the donor's right to secrecy.[61] The central interest is that of the child born as a result of the donation; it is considered that a child's interests require disclosure of parentage. However, whilst encouraged to disclose details of conception to the child, parents are not required to do so. The concern that the number of donors would fall with the removal of anonymity was temporarily realised, although numbers have since gradually increased[62] and the character of donors has changed from largely young students to maturer men, who are more altruistically motivated.[63] Recent studies elsewhere have found that, if anonymity were removed, a number of donors would no longer donate, but the majority would still do so.[64]

---

59 *Op cit*, HFEA, fn 10, para 3.18(c).

60 Indeed, the Warnock Committee recommended that donors be anonymous, although they made an exception to the principle of donor anonymity where the egg was donated by a sister or a friend (*op cit*, fn 13, para 6.7).

61 Bradley, D, *Family Law and Political Culture*, 1996, London: Sweet & Maxwell, p 112.

62 McWhinnie, A, '"Who am I?" Genealogical disadvantage for children from donated gametes', in *op cit*, Blyth *et al*, fn 51.

63 *Op cit*, Maclean and Maclean, fn 31, p 248.

64 Kirkland, A *et al*, 'Comparison of attitudes of donors and recipients to occyte donation' (1992) 7 Human Reproduction 355; Robinson, JN *et al*, 'Attitudes of donors and recipients to gamete donation' (1991) 6 Human Reproduction 307; for a summary of a number of studies, see *op cit*, Blyth, fn 19, p 82.

There are marked differences in the number of, and motivation of, sperm donors and egg donors. Women have one egg a month, whilst men release millions of sperm per ejaculation. This, in itself, may mean that men and women regard their gametes in different ways. The difference in method of donation is vast. Egg donors must undergo drug treatments to stimulate their ovaries in order to produce a number of eggs, followed by an invasive procedure, often under general anaesthesia, to collect the eggs. Egg donors face medical risks to which sperm donors are not exposed.[65] Sperm donation involves the simple and pleasurable act of masturbation.

Research indicates that financial incentives are important for sperm donors,[66] despite the small amount of payment currently permitted.[67] As the procedure for donating eggs carries medical risks, there is a shortage of donated eggs. This has led to women being offered inducements such as free IVF treatment, or treatment at a reduced cost, shorter waiting lists for treatment, or treatment in a private hospital if they donate some of their eggs.[68] These practices clearly go beyond the definition of 'donor', as women in this situation are only donating in order to receive treatment themselves. Egg sharing could cause tremendous distress for the donor if the recipient conceived and the donor was unsuccessful in her attempts at a pregnancy.

There are gender differences in motivation to donate, with men donating anonymously, whilst women often donate for family and friends.[69] There are no provisions in the Act for informing donors as to the outcome of the donation. Yet, Price and Cook found that almost two-thirds of the women in their study who had donated anonymously wanted to know something about the outcome of the donation.[70] These women donors were actively envisaging a future child born of their donation and had expectations and concerns about the child and the women who gave birth to it.[71]

---

65 Balen, AH, 'Ovarian hyperstimulation syndrome' (1999) 14 Human Reproduction 1138.

66 Lui, SC and Weaver, SM, 'Attitudes and motives of semen donors and non-donors' (1996) 11 Human Reproduction 2061.

67 Human Fertilisation and Embryology Act 1996, s 12(e). After a consultation exercise, the HFEA decided to retain the limit of £15, plus reasonable expenses: HFEA, *Annual Report*, 1999.

68 The HFEA confirmed, in December 1998, that women can receive cut price or free fertility treatment in exchange for donating some of their eggs: see 'IVF authority allows women to share eggs' (1998) *The Times*, 10 December; Ahuja, KK, Mostyn, BJ and Simons, EG, 'Egg sharing and egg donation: attitudes of British egg donors and recipients' (1997) 12 Human Reproduction 2845.

69 For personal accounts of women who have donated eggs ensuring that their identity is known to the resulting child, see Nelson, L, 'Truth and the surrogate child'; Ledger, D, '... when somebody is there in front of you in black and white ... there is no mystery', both in *op cit*, Blyth *et al*, fn 51.

70 Price, F and Cook, R, 'The donor, the recipient and the child – human egg donation in UK licensed centres' [1995] CFLQ 145.

71 *Ibid*, p 149.

Price and Cook found that one-fifth of anonymous egg donors expressed a personal preference that the child be told that she was born of a donation, whereas almost all of the known donors preferred that the child was not told the circumstances of her conception.[72] The difficulty which personal donors have with the child being informed of their role in her creation may centre upon uncertainty about the relationship they may then be expected to have with the child. Being identified as the child's genetic parent does not mean that a social relationship must follow, as the existence of a genetic tie does not, in itself, merit the creation of a social relationship. A policy of anonymity, which implies that there is something almost underhand about donation, perpetuates uncertainty about the nature of this relationship. Society's attitude towards infertility and donation makes it difficult for recipients and donors to forge the novel relationships that medical technology has given rise to. A study in New Zealand found that 78% of known sperm donors agreed to being identified to the child, although this was qualified with regard to the age of the child. Reasons for identification were given as avoidance of family secrets and the rights of the child to have information concerning their conception. For both recipients and donors, the advantages of having a personal donor related to openness within the relationship. For the recipients, this focused on knowledge of the donor's background and, for related couples, having a common genetic relationship. For donors, the advantages given were knowing the child's environment, having access to the child and the ability to choose recipients. A disadvantage for donors and recipients was the possibility of a change in the relationship.[73] It is questionable whether the difference in response to identification between the two studies is gender related. The reasons for the difference are more likely to be due to a general emphasis in New Zealand on rights to information held by the State and the fact that, in New Zealand, the use of potentially identifiable donors is the norm.[74] This would explain why donors and recipients are able to feel more comfortable with openness and identification of the donor than in the UK, where anonymity is the norm.

The use of the word 'parent' in describing the role of the donor is inappropriate. The donor has no intention to parent at all.[75] A different terminology is needed to describe 'genetic parents' and 'social parents' which

---

72 The study consisted of 75 women: 57 had donated anonymously; 15 had donated to specific women; and three had yet to donate.

73 *Op cit,* Adair and Purdie, fn 44.

74 Blyth, E, 'Access to genetic origins information in donor assisted conception – international perspectives', in *op cit,* Blyth *et al,* fn 51, p 72.

75 The role of the donor cannot be compared to that of the birth mother, who relinquishes her parenthood when a child is adopted, but is a parent until then. The donor is never a parent.

recognises and respects the role that each has to play. A more appropriate term for the donor is 'genitor'. To employ this term would help to make it clear that the child's parent is the social parent, emphasising the importance of the commitment involved in bringing up a child over the genetic link. The fact that women often donate to known recipients may help to change attitudes towards donation. Recipients of donor eggs are less concerned with secrecy than male recipients and egg donors clearly want some information about the child. Thus, attitudes of openness on the part of female recipients and the ability for egg donors to see their donation in terms of a child should help to change society's view of the need for secrecy and anonymity and to accept children by donation as simply one way of forming a family.

IDENTITY – THE CHILD BY DONATION

What information do children want? Does the child by donation simply want to know about the method of her conception or does she want to know about her genetic parentage? How important is knowledge of blood ties for the development of identity?

The Warnock Committee recommended that parents be open about the means of conception[76] and, as discussed above, openness is needed to ensure an honest and healthy relationship between parents and child. It is also vital that children be told that they were conceived with donor gametes for purposes of medical history, which could otherwise be life threatening.[77] However, it is necessary to distinguish between openness in respect of the child's conception (secrecy) and medical history, on the one hand, and access to identity of the donor (anonymity), on the other.

Analogy with adoption

Policies of anonymity were a part of the institution of adoption until 1975.[78] Adoption legislation now provides the right of access to the adoptee's original birth certificate,[79] thereby recognising that adoptees have a claim to their genetic parentage. In contrast, the register maintained by the HFEA includes the identity of the donors, yet this is withheld, denying children by donation a claim to their genetic parentage. Can the rights of access to adoption records be applied, by analogy, to children by donation? Is it possible to argue that

---

76 *Op cit*, fn 13, paras 4.25 and 6.8.
77 The need for knowledge of medical history was emphasised by the Warnock Committee: *op cit*, fn 13, para 4.21.
78 Children Act 1975, s 26.
79 Adoption Act 1976, s 51. Access is provided to the adopted person when they are 18.

children by adoption should have the right to learn the identity of their genetic parents but that children by donation should not have the same right?

There are differences between adoption and medically assisted reproduction. Adoption involves finding parents for children who already exist; assisted reproduction involves creating children for prospective parents. With embryo donation, as with adoption (excluding step-parent adoption) but unlike sperm or egg donation, neither parent is genetically related to the child. This type of donation can be viewed as pre-natal adoption, but embryo donation is different to adoption, as the legal and social mother will have carried the child during the term of pregnancy and will have given birth to the child, creating a gestational bond which does not exist between adoptive parents and adopted children. With adoption there may have been some early bonding with the genetic parents; there is no such bonding between the child by donation and the donor. Adoption and donation also differ because, with donation, the social mother is also the woman who carries the pregnancy to term (except, of course, where full surrogacy is used). An important difference between donation and adoption is that adopted children have to come to terms with the fact that they were relinquished by their biological mother. Adopted children often ask, 'why was I given up?'. It is frequently the search for the answer to this question which drives them to find their birth mother. Children by donation do not have to cope with the knowledge of having been rejected: a child by donation is wanted and created. Are these differences sufficiently profound to justify a difference in treatment of children by donation and children by adoption in respect of a claim to their genetic parentage?

Adoption was traditionally a secretive process, similar to that of donation today. Secrecy ensured that childless couples would avoid the shame of infertility, unmarried mothers would avoid social stigma and the child would avoid the stigma of illegitimacy. The baby would be 'matched' with adopters in, for example, physical appearance, temperament and intelligence in an attempt to emulate a 'natural' family, so that the adopted status would not be readily ascertainable.[80] There was concern to protect the façade of the genetically related family, foreshadowing the approach to donation today. In recent years, there has been a decline in the number of babies available for adoption, due to abortion and the erosion of the stigma of single parenthood. The majority of adoptions now involve older children who remember their birth families and, therefore, know their origins. There is no pretence that these children are the genetically related children of their adoptive parents. Adoptions of babies tend to be from overseas and, again, usually due to the different ethnic origins of the adoptive parents and the child, there is no

---

80 O'Donovan, K, 'What shall we tell the children? Reflections on children's perspectives and the reproduction revolution', in *op cit*, Lee and Morgan, fn 40.

pretence that the child is the genetic child of the adoptive parents. It is current adoption practice to recommend that children be told of their adoptive status as early as possible. This is to avoid damaging the child and relationships within the family should the child discover the truth later on. It is national policy for all adoption agencies to obtain from prospective adoptive parents a commitment to tell adopted children that they are adopted and the circumstances of their adoption. Adoptive parents are given fairly detailed information about the child's background for them to pass on to the child. Openness and removal of policies of anonymity demonstrate that, within the adoption context, there is no longer a perceived need to try to emulate the genetic family. There is a now a recognition that adoptive families are just another way of creating a family. This has important repercussions for families created by donation.

Today, adoption legislation, practice and policy[81] is based on the belief, emphasised by Triseliotis,[82] that there is a psychological need to know genetic origins in order to develop identity. This psychological need is tied to the importance placed in Western culture on the blood tie and is, as Katherine O'Donovan argues, socially constructed.[83] There are no official figures showing how many adopted children make enquires about their birth relatives or make contact with them.[84] It has been estimated that 40–50% of adopted people have sought background information or contact with a birth relative.[85] There are few studies of numbers and characteristics of people who search for information relating to their genetic background. Triseliotis found that the need for access to records or meetings with genetic parents was frequently a characteristic of those who were not given reasonable explanations and information about their origins, or those who had gone through some major crisis in their lives.[86]

There is general agreement that more women than men search for information about their genetic background – it has been suggested that this is at a ratio of at least 2:1.[87] However, Feast and Howe report that their small study of English adoptees found a much higher percentage of adopted men seeking information and contact with a birth relative than previous studies, most of which were North American.[88] Interestingly, Harper's study of

---

81 Adoption Act 1976.

82 Triseliotis, J, *In Search of Origins*, 1973, London: Routledge.

83 *Op cit*, O'Donovan, fn 80.

84 If an adopted person knows their original name and the agency which placed them, they can bypass the official route for access to a record of their birth certificate.

85 Feast, J and Howe, D, 'Adopted adults who search for background information and contact with birth relatives' (1997) 12 Adoption and Fostering 8.

86 *Ibid*, Triseliotis.

87 *Ibid*, Feast and Howe.

88 54.6% of women and 45.4% of men.

adopted and non-adopted children aged between 6–15 found that girls tended to want more information and greater detail about their genetic parents than did boys.[89] As it is usually a significant event that triggers the search for genetic origins, such as marriage, death of an adoptive parent or birth of a child, it may be that women are more affected by these events. Particularly when adopted women have children themselves, issues are raised in relation to their own adoption. Furthermore, perhaps more women than men go in search of their origins, as women's particular closeness to family medical history raises issues of medical and genetic history.[90]

Disclosure of information to adoptees has been justified on the basis of a notion of identity which emphasises genetic ties. As the importance which society places on the genetic tie is socially constructed, it could be argued that information about the donor's identity should not be provided, as this reinforces the importance of the genetic link. However, denying children information about genitors is not the way in which to diminish the importance placed on the genetic tie and to raise the importance of the social family. Concepts of anonymity and secrecy reinforce the importance of the blood tie. These concepts fuel the notion that the genetic family is the 'norm' and any other family formation is 'unnatural' and must be hidden. Recognition of, and respect for, the different ways in which families can be formed is needed, and the way to achieve this is to be honest and open about the formation and structure of families.

Genealogical background does form a part of who a child is and recognition of this does not displace the importance of the social family. Little is known about the development of children by donation, but, nonetheless, children by donation will have one or more genetic parents who are not their social parent(s) and it is likely that children by donation will want information about their origins,[91] in the same way that children by adoption do, as part of the narrative of who they are.[92] Parents of donor children should be given information about the donor, in the same way as adoptive parents are given information about the genetic parents of the child. This enables parents to give this information to the child, as and when appropriate.

---

89 Harper, J, 'What does she look like? What children want to know about their birth parents' (1993) 7 Adoption and Fostering 27.

90 *Op cit*, O'Donovan, fn 80, p 108.

91 For personal accounts of sperm donor children, see Whipp, C, 'Offspring's perspective on secrecy in assisted conception'; Lauren, 'Issues for donor inseminated offspring', both in *op cit*, Blyth *et al*, fn 51.

92 For a discussion of the concepts of fixed and narrative identities, see Wilson, S, 'Identity, genealogy and the social family' (1997) 11 IJLPF 270.

Many children may not seek the identity of their genitors but may be satisfied to know something of their genetic origins and to have some information about their conception and the donor, in the same way that many adopted children are satisfied with knowing of their conception and some broad detail but are not curious to know the identity of their biological parents. But, for those that do want information, including the identity of their genitor, it is difficult to comprehend why children by adoption should have access to this information whilst children by donation are presently denied any information about their genetic origins.

Due to the incidence of step-families, fostering and adoption, many children are being raised in families without one or both genetic parents. However, most of these children will know something of their genetic parentage. Case law concerning genetic identity during childhood is in favour of the child being told of her genetic origins. The courts' view is that knowledge of the truth regarding genetic parentage is beneficial to the child's welfare.[93] Children born as a result of conception using donor gametes are the only people who are denied information about their genetic origins by law.

A RECONCILIATION OF INTERESTS?

Whilst reproductive technologies are capable of making women's roles in reproduction 'discontinuous', they also have the potential to confound existing assumptions about parenting.[94] Novel relationships are generated by the use of donor gametes, yet there is little recognition of this. The legal framework places donation securely within the medical context and does little to acknowledge the social context of donation. The regulatory framework is based on the separation of donor and recipient; donation is a 'cure' for infertility, with little regard being had for the child that is created following the donation.

Reproductive technology affects family formation, yet legislation and the practice of medically assisted reproduction does not acknowledge the unique relationship that exists between the three parties – donor, recipient(s) and child. The policies of secrecy and anonymity are related to conventional ideas concerning family structure. There is a clear paradox in the way in which the legislature views genetics. The statutorily protected anonymity of donors reflects society's emphasis on the blood tie and the importance of genetics. Yet there is an acceptance that the social role, rather than the genetic role, of parenting is prominent; there is a recognition that intention to parent can

---

93 See *Re H (Paternity: Blood Test)* [1996] 2 FLR 65 and *Re G (Parentage: Blood Sample)* [1997] 1 FLR 360. Discussed in Fortin, J, *Children's Rights and the Developing Law*, 1998, London: Butterworths, pp 323–26.

94 *Op cit*, Bridgeman and Millns, fn 7, p 122.

displace the blood tie as the test of parentage.[95] Rather than trying to emulate a 'natural' family, by disguising the means of conception and the involvement of donor gametes, reproductive technologies offer alternatives to family relationships that go beyond the traditional heterosexual marital union. As Stanworth acknowledges, reproductive technologies carry the threat (or the promise) of delegitimating genetic parenthood.[96] A number of different people may contribute to the creation and upbringing of a child and all should be viewed as playing an important part in the child's life. It appears that women recipients of donor gametes are able to be more open about the use of donor gametes than men are and that genetic origins are less significant to women. Genetic origins are only a part of 'who' the child is and will become, but information about her conception, heritage and identity of genetic parentage is needed as part of the child's story of herself. This appears to be particularly important for the girl child.

Legislators tend to impose one position about donor anonymity on all participants: either all donors are anonymous or all donors are identified. An alternative policy which has been suggested is to let the parties decide for themselves. Donors may choose between anonymity or identification and recipients can opt for an anonymous or identifiable donor.[97] Pennings suggests that this 'double track' policy for anonymity represents the best attempt to balance the rights of donors, recipients and the child.[98] However, the rights of the child are not being preserved; the child is not able to make the decision as to whether or not she wishes to know the identity of the donor, as the decision is made prior to her conception. There is no recognition of the potential importance to the child of knowing the identity of the donor. The egg donor, whilst envisaging a child from her donation, appears uncertain about losing her anonymity. This undoubtedly arises from a concern with the way in which donors are perceived by society and from an uncertainty with what role, if any, she should have in the child's life.

The whole donor process should be more open. Openness would give value and dignity to donors. Rather than medical personnel deciding whether or not a child should be conceived using donor gametes, the donor and the recipient can share in making the decision, so that each receives information about the other and can decide whether or not they want the treatment to go ahead. In the same way that a mother is consulted when placing a child for adoption, the donor can be consulted over whether a woman or a couple should receive their gametes.[99] Openness regarding a child's conception and

---

95 Human Fertilisation and Embryology Act 1990, ss 27–29. See *op cit*, Overall, fn 9, p 206.
96 Stanworth, M, *Reproductive Technologies: Gender, Motherhood and Medicine*, 1987, Cambridge: Polity, p 21.
97 Pennings, G, 'The "double track" policy for donor anonymity' (1997) 12 Human Reproduction 2839.
98 *Ibid.*

birth is vital for a child's well being and psychological health. Whether or not to tell a child that she was conceived by the use of donated gamete(s) is not a decision for parents to make; children are not commodities owned by their parents.[100] Children must be respected for themselves, and this means that they must be told about their conception, including information about their genetic parentage. Legislation which focuses on the child is needed to encourage new ways of approaching families and the formation of families.

---

99 See *op cit*, Blyth, fn 19, pp 81–82, where he discusses the various models for deciding who should have access to treatment services.

100 *Op cit*, Blyth, fn 19.

CHAPTER 4

CONSTRUCTIONS OF MATERNITY AND MOTHERHOOD IN STORIES OF LOST CHILDREN

Katherine O'Donovan[1]

INTRODUCTION

> A newspaper delivery boy found a newborn girl abandoned in bushes. Police began an immediate search for the baby's mother.[2]

How often have these, or similar words, appeared in news reports and been accepted without question? 'Common sense' suggests that mother and child should be together. Interview responses from police and social workers contain reassuring words about the mother: 'She may be in need of medical attention' and we would ask her to come forward as soon as possible.'[3] 'Our prime concern is her care and welfare. She may need medical attention, and she will be dealt with with the utmost consideration ... Our aim is to reunite her with her child.'[4] The words of official reaction and newspaper accounts conjure up a picture of a young person, delivering her child alone, and taking desperate measures of abandonment. There are assumptions that mother and child are one, as they have been during pregnancy, and that adverse circumstances, but not choice, have parted them. The friendly police words of encouragement to the woman to come forward demonstrate these assumptions about maternity and motherhood which are shared by a large majority of the population of Britain.

How different are the attitudes and words where a mother abandons an older child. Where a child was left in a wood for 30 hours, the mother was sentenced to five years' imprisonment for cruelty.[5] There can be no doubt that the child in question, aged three, suffered fear, cold, scratches and bruises. The

---

1   I would like to thank Richard Collier for reading an earlier draft of this chapter and for many suggestions which, I hope, have improved it. Much of my interest in this topic has been stimulated by visits to the centre for family law at the University of Lyon. Particular thanks are due to Professor Jacqueline Rubellin-Devichi, the director, who has helped me in innumerable ways. I would also like to acknowledge the help of Alber Wei, who is concerned with these issues in US law, and who has provided information about the changing legal situation there.

2   (1996) *The Guardian*, 27 December, p 6.

3   *Ibid.*

4   Detective Inspector Phil Jones of Leyton CID, quoted in (1998) *The Guardian*, 2 January, p 5, after a baby had been found in East London.

5   Under the Children and Young Persons Act 1933.

Crown Court judge told the mother: 'You went against the basis of all maternal emotion and abandoned your child to its fate.'[6] The language of 'abandoned to fate' harks back to interpretation of the first statute to make this a specific crime, where abandonment was defined as 'leaving the child to its fate'.[7] The construction of 'maternal emotion' conjures up images of the normal mode of 'being a mum' in British society. Both elements will be investigated further below.

In 1997, 65 infants were abandoned by women who had given birth, of whom 52 were traced by the police.[8] Few prosecutions result from the desertion of a newborn. A clinical psychologist commented that the mother would need professional help to assess why she had behaved in this manner: 'There needs to be an assessment to unearth what led her to do this, because she won't be feeling very good about herself.'[9] Most judgments about mothers who abandon newborns centre on their physical and mental states, against a backdrop of what are considered to be adequate State-provided support systems for mothers. An idyllic view of maternal love coexists with cosy assumptions about the Welfare State as 'mumsy' to all mothers.

Amongst the assumptions about a woman who abandons a newborn is that she needs help. She is depicted as a victim herself, who can be helped to come to terms with motherhood. On the one hand, she must learn to mother her child. On the other, she is already a mother by virtue of giving birth. A mother who abandons an older child does not receive the same sympathy, for she is assumed to have already learned motherhood. Her action is a denial of society's beliefs about mother love and is condemned outright.

This chapter examines the attitudes to child abandonment in English and in French law. Despite the adherence to the United Nations Convention on the Rights of the Child (UNCRC) by both States, there are very different provisions and institutions dealing with the identity rights of children born to women who do not wish to raise them. French law permits the mother to remain anonymous and protects her right to do so. English law has no such provisions. In investigating these differences, it is not intended to advocate one system or the other. Rather, the object is to highlight cultural differences expressed as a step in legal reasoning existing in France, but not in England. Differences in constructions of the concepts of family and motherhood emerge from this study.

---

6   (1999) *The Guardian*, 22 May, p 5.
7   *Mitchell v Wright* (1905) 7 F 568.
8   Hall, S, *The Guardian* (1998) 2 January, p 5.
9   Clinical psychologist, Kathleen Cox, cited *ibid*.

SOME REFLECTIONS ON THE HISTORY OF
ENFANTS TROUVES IN EUROPE[10]

Child abandonment has not received much attention from legal scholars. The absences of children from history have been commented on by many historians. As Laslett reflects, 'these crowds and crowds of little children are strangely absent from the written record'.[11] Although there have been valiant attempts to rescue children from silence and absence, like other unknown peoples of history, they are hard to recover.[12] Their absences can be attributed to the power of those who were recorded and the attitudes of those who made the records. This is not an accident of history, but a reflection of perceived unimportance.

There is evidence that child abandonment played a significant part in early modern culture and society. Studies of foundling hospitals provide some information, as do the recordings in writing of myths, oral traditions and fairy tales. *Enfants trouves* by the roadside, or in the forest, must be distinguished from children left in foundling hospitals. We know little of lives outside institutions, and reasons for abandonment have to be surmised. Even today, empirical research is lacking. Respect for privacy, sympathy with tragedy and lack of legal records hamper investigation.[13] The majority of cases of abandonment are not followed by legal proceedings, either because the woman is not found, or because she is perceived to need support not punishment.

That there has long been a human understanding about lost children is evident from folklore and stories. Moses, Oedipus, Romulus and Remus, Gretel and Hansel, as names, evoke a history still appreciated today. That Moses, Romulus and Remus went on to be leaders, and that their stories are told without stigmatising their origins, tells something about past and present attitudes. Oedipus reflects the incest taboo and marriage requirements of exogamy. Gretel and Hansel stand for the stories of many children abandoned because of famine, but also for the demonisation of deserting mothers. All can be said to form part of the symbolic codes that permeate culture and its stories.

---

10 The expression *'enfants trouves'* is used in French to signify children abandoned by their parents or families and then found. It is interesting to note that, in English, we do not have an equivalent expression. When I have wanted to focus on the child, I have used the expression 'lost children'. In general, the language of abandonment is used when focusing on adult actions, regarded as blameworthy, if not criminal.

11 Laslett, P, *The World We Have Lost*, 1971, London: Methuen, p 140.

12 Cunningham, H, *Childhood and Children in Western Society*, 1995, London: Longman; Hendrick, H, *Children, Childhood and English Society, 1880–1990*, 1997, Cambridge: CUP.

13 This is my experience, also, in earlier research on infanticide. See O'Donovan, K, 'The medicalisation of infanticide' [1984] Crim LR 259.

Where lost children are concerned, fairy tales can be a source of information and understanding. Yet the use of fairy tales in this way is contested. To Carolyn Heilbrun, stories regularly repeated in our culture fashion our identities:

> Let us agree on this: that we live our lives through texts. These may be read, or chanted, or experienced electronically, or come to us, like the murmurings of our mothers, telling us what conventions demand. Whatever their form or medium, these stories are what have formed us all, they are what we must use to make our new fictions.[14]

This is a view shared by many chroniclers of the origins and histories of fairy tales. Through these texts, heard and read as children, we are taught to read and attempt to realise our own lives.[15] These stories circulate in multiple versions and are retold with different purposes and different effects.[16] Versions of a tale may be found in China, Europe, the Middle East and Asia,[17] but, to Andrea Dworkin, our formation by the ancient world of fairy tales prepares women for passivity and acceptance of stereotypical roles:

> ... We ingested it as children, whole, had its values and consciousness imprinted on our minds as cultural absolutes long before we were in fact men and women. We have taken the fairy tales of childhood with us into maturity, chewed but still lying in the stomach, as real identity. Between Snow White and her heroic prince, our two great fictions, we never did have much of a chance. At some point the great Divide took place: they (the boys) dreamed of mounting the Great Steed and buying Snow White from the dwarfs; we (the girls) aspired to become that object of every necrophiliac's lust – the innocent, *victimised* Sleeping Beauty, beauteous lump of ultimate, sleeping good.

Ontological possibilities for women may have been stereotyped by the literary fairy tale initially recorded and published by men.[18] The older tales, however, were part of an oral tradition maintained as a 'domestic art' by women. As Marina Warner has noted, Plato in *Gorgias* referred to 'old wives' tales' told by nurses to amuse and frighten children.[19] 'Lady storytellers' were the sources for the men who compiled fairy tales.[20] There is evidence that the tales were adapted to carry instructional and moral messages, which inevitably involved the construction and opposition of 'good' and 'evil'. Although the colonisation of old wives tales by male literary writers may have served the interests of

14 Heilbrun, C, 'What was Penelope unweaving?', in *Hamlet's Mother and Other Women*, 1990, New York: Columbia UP, p 109.

15 Zipes, J, *Fairy Tale as Myth, Myth as Fairy Tale*, 1994, Lexington: University of Kentucky, p 4: 'Consciously and unconsciously we weave the narratives of myth and folktale into our daily existence.'

16 Carter, A, *The Vintage Book of Fairy Tales*, 1990, London: Virago, p x.

17 Tatar, M, *The Classic Fairy Tales*, 1999, New York: Norton, pp ix–xii.

18 Zipes, J, *Happily Ever After*, 1997, New York: Routledge.

19 Warner, M, *From the Beast to the Blonde*, 1994, New York: Farrar, Strauss & Giroux, p 19.

20 *Ibid*, Zipes.

patriarchy, according to the analysis of Jack Zipes,[21] the tales seem to have escaped the bounds set for them. To Alison Lurie, the tales reflect gender equality with older women seen as powerful: 'Gretel, not Hansel, defeats the Witch; and for every clever youngest son there is a youngest daughter equally resourceful.'

Tradition and folk tales are a source of information about the history of abandonment, which will never be fully written. The demographic data is impossible to reconstruct. We shall never know how many children lost their parents through desertion, nor what the outcomes for them were. John Boswell, who has attempted to synthesise what is known, reflects that the printed stories provide 'extremely valuable clues about many details of abandonment', and 'correspond closely to the facts recoverable from more traditional historical sources'.[22]

Gretel and Hansel is one of many stories about parents, unable to feed children, then deciding to desert them. In this genre can be found Tom Thumb, Molly Whuppie, Sleeping Beauty in the Wood, The Juniper Tree, The Rose Tree and Pippety Pew. Various versions exist, but the 'classic' tale, as amended frequently by the Brothers Grimm, is said by Jack Zipes to demonise women, extol patriarchy and reconcile children to hierarchy.[23] This view is based on the conclusion to the tale in which the children are reunited with their father, the mother/stepmother having conveniently died. Yet it is Gretel who has the quick wits to push the witch into the oven and who persuades the little duck to take them home across the river, thus saving Hansel and herself. The demonisation point can be read variously. In the original oral version of the tale, it was the children's mother who proposed that they be left in the wood. Because of their concern with morality and instruction, the Grimms removed the mother and introduced a stepmother.[24] As ever, interpretation remains with the reader. Nevertheless, it seems that the idea of a mother who abandons her child became hard to bear by the late 19th century. The evidence from history and fairy tales is that, in late antiquity and the early modern period, this action was understood in ways that cannot be borne today. This goes to constructions of childhood and motherhood.

---

21 *Op cit*, Zipes, fn 18.

22 Boswell, J, *The Kindness of Strangers: The Abandonment of Children in Western Europe from Late Antiquity to the Renaissance*, 1988, London: Pantheon, p 429.

23 *Op cit*, Zipes, fn 18, Chapter 2.

24 *Op cit*, Zipes, fn 18, Chapter 2.

ABANDONMENT IN ENGLISH LAW

Abandoning or exposing an infant under two is a specific criminal offence under s 27 of the Offences Against the Person Act 1861. At common law, if an abandoned child survived exposure, conviction of the parent did not necessarily follow. In *R v Renshaw*,[25] a mother left her child of 10 days at the bottom of a ditch, alongside which ran a path. Parke J said that:

> ... there were no marks of violence on the child, and it does not appear in the result that the child actually experienced any inconvenience, as it was providentially found soon after it was exposed and, therefore, although it is said in some of the books that an exposure to the inclemency of the weather may amount to an assault, yet, if that be so at all, it can only be when the person suffers a hurt or injury of some kind or other from the exposure.

Other reported cases from the mid-19th century emphasise endangerment to life or health as a necessary element of proof.[26] The act of abandonment did not, in itself, constitute an offence. Even after the enactment of a specific criminal offence of abandonment, evidence of injury was read into the statute.[27] The reluctance of the courts to convict where no injury to the child was evident suggests an attitude to parent-child relations different from that which prevails today.

Burdening the Poor Law seems to have been the hidden assumption behind the enactment of a specific offence of abandonment. In *R v Hogan*,[28] prior to the 1861 Act, the indictment alleged:

> ... that the prisoner, intending to injure the inhabitants of the parish of B and to burthen them with the maintenance of a bastard child of the prisoner, four days old, ... did abandon and desert the same child without having any means for its support.[29]

Injury to the ratepayers seems to have been of greater concern than the needs of the child. This highlights how children are constructed in theories today and how laws may reflect this. Motherhood is constructed in relation to theories about childhood, whereas maternity retains elements of ideas about hormones, infanticide, distress and a need for counselling.[30]

---

25 (1847) 2 Cox CC 285.
26 *R v March* (1844) 1 Car & Kir 496; *R v Cooper* (1849) 1 Den 459; *R v Hogan* (1851) 2 Den 277, (1851) 169 ER 504.
27 *R v Falkingham* [1870] LR 1 CCR 222.
28 (1851) 169 ER 504.
29 Similar indictments are to be found in the reports of *R v Philpot* (1853) 169 ER 504 and in *R v Gray* (1857) 169 ER 1017.
30 (1998) *The Guardian*, 2 January, p 5, reports: '... women who have abandoned their children are given counselling before the infants are returned to them and "for as long as is deemed necessary", according to the Department of Health.' There is something slightly ominous in these words.

The distinction between maternity and motherhood made in this essay is the distinction between giving birth and being a mother. In common parlance in Britain, this distinction is not made, nor even seen. Nor is it made in law. However, in France, this distinction has meaning in everyday life, and in law.

THE CONFLATION OF MATERNITY AND MOTHERHOOD IN ENGLISH LAW

Giving birth makes a woman a mother in English law. Even if the child is to be placed for adoption, or is born to a woman acting as a surrogate for another, or is not genetically related to the birth giver, parturition makes motherhood under common law. There is a legal obligation, sanctioned by criminal law, on the mother and on those who assist her in giving birth, to enter her name on the birth certificate. It is not sufficient to record that an infant has been born on a particular date in a particular place. Where the woman who gives birth is not genetically related to the child because of egg donation, statute prescribes the same rule as common law.[31] The mother's identity and details will be recorded on the birth certificate, notwithstanding that she is not the genetic parent. Although a new birth certificate may be issued on adoption or 'parental order' transferring legal parentage, the original certificate remains as an historic document. To give up her child officially, the mother must consent and observe legal forms.

A woman who does not wish to be a mother, even if only for six weeks – which is the legal delay before consent can be given to adoption or parental order – may choose abortion. What she cannot do is to give birth and refuse legal motherhood. Nor can she refuse to be named on the birth certificate. In common parlance, she is 'the real mother'. The rights of the child to know the identity of its 'real mother' are tied in to discussions of adoption and abandonment. The constructions of identities and of relationships involved in this language of 'real' accounts in part for the conflation of maternity and motherhood.

---

31 Under common law, the rule is *mater semper certa est* – the mother is always certain by virtue of giving birth. Statute provides that, in cases of medically assisted reproduction in a licensed clinic or hospital, the woman who gives birth is the mother: Human Fertilisation and Embryology Act 1990, s 27. See Roberts, Chapter 3, in this volume.

THE SEPARATION OF MATERNITY AND
MOTHERHOOD IN FRENCH LAW

French law (like the law of Italy, Luxembourg and Spain) offers a choice to women who give birth not to become legal mothers.[32] It is possible to enter a hospital in France without revealing one's identity where delivery is imminent. This possibility is perceived as a woman's right and exists also in Italian law. The right is protected under the French Civil Code by Art 341-1, whereby 'at the time of her delivery a mother may demand that the secret of her admission and of her identity be preserved'.[33] The right is referred to as *'accouchement sous X'*, because the mother will be recorded on the birth certificate as X, an anonymous woman. Article 341 precludes a child born anonymously (*ne sous X*) from establishing any legal tie to the mother, even if her identity should be discovered. This is important, because legal ties in French law give rise to automatic rights of succession. The action to establish a legal bond with a mother (*action en recherche de maternité*) cannot be instituted by a child born to X and, if it should be, a court is legally required to refuse it. It is legally barred. There is a comparable *'action en recherche de paternité'* which remains open.[34]

The reasons for this exceptional denial to X children of this action to establish their legal mothers lie in French history and in legal conceptions of parent-child relations. French legal reasoning contains a step between birthing and mothering. The notion of a family traditionally involves a decision by parents on admittance. Acceptance into a family contains legal and emotional resonances. Men not married to women who give birth to their genetic child have traditionally been able to refuse to recognise the child, even where they are obliged to provide financial support.[35] Although this has changed with the increased emphasis on the child's rights, there remain cases where the child's

---

32 In the case of Spain, it is only the unmarried woman who has the right to ask for the secrecy of maternity.

33 Articles 341 and 341-1 were first introduced into the Civil Code in 1993, codifying a traditional right of silence when giving birth.

34 The Civil Code, Art 340, provides that paternity outside marriage may be judicially declared, but proof can only be brought where there are serious presumptions or indications, such as evidence of sexual relations at the time of conception. Article 340 has opened up possibilities of paternal filiation as a result of the Law of 8 January 1993, in response to the Child Convention. Previously, the cases of judicial declaration of paternity were limited to abduction, rape, seduction (accompanied by an abuse of authority or breach of promise), written proof of paternity, stable co-habitation and evidence of conduct of a father towards the child. There are time bars to the *'action en recherche de paternité'*. See Rubellin-Devichi, J, *Droit de la Famille*, 1999, Paris: Dalloz, paras 1491, 1522, 1528.

35 *Reconnaissance* is separate from genetic fatherhood. Under current law, the 'natural' child and the child born of an adulterous relationship (*l'enfant adulterin*) are in regimes of their own, each separate from the legitimate child.

father is known but no affiliation takes place because of legal difficulties.[36] Thus, the establishment of legal parentage is subject to a series of prior legal concepts and parental choices. Interviews with young French women show that they perceive anonymity as a choice open to all women who give birth in France, whereas interviews in England show that no such step in reasoning exists.[37] Both legal jurisdictions are subject to the UNCRC, which contains provisions on children's identity rights.

THE UNCRC AND CHILDREN'S IDENTITY RIGHTS

Articles 7 and 8 of the UNCRC – the Child Convention – are denoted the provisions on identity rights. Article 7 provides for registration after birth, and rights to name, nationality and 'as far as possible, the right to know and be cared for by his parents'.[38] Art 8 denotes 'the right of the child to preserve his or her identity, ... including family relations ...'.[39]

To many commentators, Art 7 gives rights to know the identities of genetic parents.[40] English law takes an ambivalent attitude to this issue. No open public debate has taken place in Parliament or elsewhere. On the one hand, adopted children have rights of access to their original birth certificates and an

---

36   See *op cit*, fnn 34 and 35. See the discussion in Report of the Working Group on Family Law, *Renover le Droit de la Famille*, chaired by Francoise Dekeuwer-Defossez, to the Minister of Justice, September 1999, pp 43–44.

37   Interviews in Lyon, November 1999. Discussions with students in London 1998–99.

38   The full text of Art 7 is as follows:

    The child shall be registered immediately after birth and shall have the right from birth to a name, the right to acquire a nationality and, as far as possible, the right to know and be cared for by his parents.

    States Parties shall ensure the implementation of these rights in accordance with their national law and their obligations under the relevant international instruments in this field, in particular where the child would otherwise be Stateless.

39   The full text of Art 8 is:

    (1) States Parties undertake to respect the right of the child to preserve his or her identity, including nationality, name and family relations as recognised by law without unlawful interference.

    (2) Where the child is illegally deprived of some or all of the elements of his or her identity, States Parties shall provide appropriate assistance and protection, with a view to speedily re-establishing his or her identity.

40   Fortin, J, *Children's Rights: The Developing Law*, 1998, London: Butterworths; Freeman, M, 'The new birth right?' (1996) IJCR 1; Masson, J and Harrison, C, 'Identity: mapping the frontiers', in Lowe, N and Douglas, G (eds), *Families Across Frontiers*, 1996, The Hague: Martinus Nijhoff.

adoption contact register has been established by law.[41] Official help is available to adopted children in attempting to establish the identities of their birth parents and to get in touch with them. On the other hand, children conceived through donated gametes do not have rights to know the identities of their genetic parents, because it is believed that donors need protection.[42] In addition, there will always be a small group of children, abandoned at birth, who will be unable to know their parents, and a further group whose fathers are unknown to them, if not to their mothers.[43] Nevertheless, the official position today in English law, upheld by judicial rhetoric, is that children have a right to know the identities of their birth parents.[44]

The debate in France in 1993 about the implementation of the UNCRC was based on a principled desire to re-write family law in the light of the rights of the child.[45] There has been a large measure of success in so doing and further reforms are envisaged in an attempt to place all children on an equal footing so far as possible. One difficulty is the highly developed and elaborate filiation law which gives rise to membership rights, such as name and succession, within the family. Other family members are considered to be affected by the acceptance of a non-marital child. Although, as indicated above, the law on paternal filiation has been modified in the child's interests, anonymous birthing has raised issues of the rights and plight of the woman who gives birth, but does not wish to be a legal mother.

In the course of the debate on Art 7 of the UNCRC in the Assemblée Nationale, members were divided into two opposing groups. There were those who wished to implement Art 7 fully, by repealing the right to give birth anonymously which was contained in the Family Code, but not the Civil Code. Opposed were those who pointed to the words 'as far as possible' in Art 7, qualifying the child's right to know her parents. The outcome was the strengthening of the right to give birth anonymously. Article 341 was modified, and Art 341-1 entered the Civil Code, ensuring not only that the

---

41 Adoption Act 1976, s 51. The adoption contact register was established by an amendment to the Adoption Act 1976 (s 51A) inserted by the Children Act 1989, Sched 10, para 21.

42 The HFEA announced that a consultation paper on this issue will soon be published. See Roberts, Chapter 4, in this volume, who argues that the focus of the Human Fertilisation and Embryology Act 1990 is the medical needs of the prospective parents and, hence, the need to secure a supply of donated material. The legislation is characterised by secrecy and anonymity, at the expense of any concern for the identity needs of the child by donation.

43 About one-quarter of children born outside marriage do not have the father's name on the birth certificate, that is, less than 10% of all births. It does not necessarily follow that they do not know who their fathers are. Estimates of the numbers of children with the wrong father's name on the birth certificate vary from 10% upwards.

44 *Re F (A Minor) (Blood Tests: Parental Rights)* [1993] Fam 314; *Re H (A Minor) (Blood Tests: Parental Rights)* [1996] 2 FLR 65; *Re R (Blood Test: Constraint)* [1998] 1 FLR 745.

45 Rubellin-Devichi, J, 'Le principe de l'interet de l'enfant dans la loi et la jurisprudence françaises' (1999) I *La Semaine Juridique* 3739.

mother may demand anonymity and confidentiality, but, also that should her identity become known to the child, no filiation links can be legally established.[46]

Accounting for changes in a legal system with which one is only partially familiar must be tentative. Intervening as an interpreter of another legal culture requires sensitivity to structures of meaning, to ways of doing and being, and to the means used subsequently in reporting on one's understandings.[47] My exposé of *accouchement sous X* starts with puzzlement that a debate on children's identity rights led to reinforcement of a woman's right to choose anonymity. Further reading has created the realisation that history and tradition play a part in the interpretation of, and location of, the UNCRC within a legal culture. To acquire some understanding of why English and French law differ in their approaches to anonymity, records of birth and identity in the construction of motherhood, we must look to the past. First, let us note the particular history of abandonment in France. Then, broader reflections on sources of history will be made, with proposals as to how this affects the constructions of the mother-child dyad.

THE TRADITIONAL PROTECTION OF ANONYMOUS MOTHERS IN FRANCE

Under the National Convention of the French Revolution, a law was passed in June 1793 to open refuges in every district 'where the pregnant girl might go in secret to give birth, [where] she could enter at any time of her pregnancy, according to her wishes'.[48] The rule of secret pregnancy and birth was precise. The law stated that 'it will be provided by the nation for the need of the mother during her stay, which may last until she is perfectly recovered from giving birth; the most inviolable secret will be preserved on all that concerns her'.[49] This law was passed at the behest of the women who participated in the first national UNCRC, for its subsequent history shows that, after

---

46 For an account, see *op cit*, Rubellin-Devichi, fn 45.

47 Legrand, P, in 'Comparative legal studies and commitment to theory' (1995) 58 MLR 262, observes: 'Scholars who engage in comparative work about law face an exigent challenge. First, having been prepared for another legal culture, they need to amplify their appreciation for different structures of meaning, to the point where they will ultimately be in a position to report on discrepant cognitive processes in an apperceptive mode. Secondly, comparatists, acting as cultural intermediaries, must determine how to convey their acquired understanding of another legal culture within the inconsonant parameters of their own.'

48 See Neirinck, C, 'L'accouchement sous X: le fait et le droit' (1993) 392 *La Semaine Juridique* 143; Rubellin-Devichi, J, 'Droits de la mère et droits de l'enfant: reflexions sur les formes de l'abandon' (1991) Revue Trimestrielle de Droit Civil 90.

49 Bonnet, E, 'La loi de l'accouchement secret' (1995) Les Dossiers de l'Obstetrique, Mai, p 20.

Robespierre excluded women from public life, the law was no longer observed.

A charitable practice of permitting women to give up their infants anonymously prevailed in France and Italy throughout the Middle Ages. The *tour* consisted of a hole in a wall with a wheel and a door. From the outside of the wall, which usually surrounded a convent, the door could be opened and the infant placed on the wheel, which was then turned inwards. From the interior, the child could be collected whilst preserving the anonymous identity of the mother. A bell could be rung to alert those inside the wall of the infant's arrival. Examples of the *tour*, and of the notes sometimes attached to the babies, can be seen at the Museum of Public Assistance in Paris. There is evidence that some mothers hoped for reunion with the children in the future for, sometimes, half a note or token was left, to be matched later with the half retained. The *tour* was finally abolished in France in 1904.[50]

The tradition of anonymous birthing was revived in France during the 1870s, after the Franco-German war. Popular sentiment favoured protection of young mothers and their children, particularly where the latter's fate was likely to be infanticide or exposure. Once again the development of sanctuaries for anonymous birthing was placed on the political agenda. A hospital circular issued in December 1899 reminded women about to give birth that they could choose to place their identity documents in a sealed envelope, to be returned on leaving hospital. Subsequently, refuges for secret delivery were established. These were legalised between 1914 and 1924.[51]

The Vichy Government of occupied France in the 1940s followed a pro-natalist policy. A Law of 2 September 1941 was adopted on the protection of birth. This permitted anonymous birthing in public hospitals without cost to the woman involved, for two months' duration, if necessary. This law was repealed in 1953, but the protection of secret maternity continued. Sympathy for maternity in distress, allied to the idea of choice in becoming a mother, has a long history in France.

Similar provisions to those enacted by the Vichy Government were passed in 1953, as part of the Family Code. Article 47 of the Social Services Code, passed on 6 January 1986, provides that the expenses of accommodation and delivery of women who have asked for anonymity shall be borne by the social services of the local *departement*.[52] This presupposes the possibility of anonymity without stating it directly as a right. The general principle of medical confidentiality is interpreted in France as applying to maternity patients who ask for their identity to be kept secret. That a choice of

---

50 Dreifuss-Netter, F, 'L'accouchement sous X': *Liber amicorum à la memoire de Daniele Huet-Weiler*, 1994, Paris: PUS/LGDJ, p 100. In Italy, the wheel was known as the *ruota*.

51 *Op cit*, Bonnet, fn 49, p 20.

52 Code de Famille, Art 47, is still in force today.

anonymity in giving birth is respected in French law is evident from the Family Code. The entry of a right into the Civil Code through Art 341-1, whereby 'the secret of her admission and her identity' can be demanded on delivery by a woman, is confirmation of what was previously understood but not formulated as a right.

The denial to the X child of the *action en recherche de maternité* is an extension of the woman's right. Article 341 was amended during the debates in the National Assembly. Previously, it provided for the filiation of the 'natural child' with the mother based either on proof of a *de facto* relationship or by witnesses. In the latter case, serious indications or written evidence were required before the action could be initiated. The Article has been amended to make proof of maternal filiation easier, but with the contradictory addition of the absolute block to the action where the child was born to X.

A debate has ensued among French feminists, amongst others, who are divided on this issue. A major empirical study, which involved interviews with some of the women who have given birth anonymously, was undertaken between 1986 and 1989. Although official figures estimate the number of children born to an anonymous woman as a minimum of 600,[53] scholars of family law put the figure nearer 1,000.[54] The study was published as a book entitled *Gesture of Love* and the author, Catherine Bonnet, concluded that *accouchement sous X* as a choice for women protects children from exposure, infanticide and abuse.[55] Her view is also that patriarchal attitudes in some communities put the life of a woman who has a child outside marriage in danger.

Bonnet argues that the right to give birth anonymously is a fundamental freedom. She sees this as linked to privacy, to a right to renounce forever the motherhood of a particular child, an autonomous choice. Given that legal parentage is treated as a juridical concept in France, with elements of choice for both men and women, such an argument is possible. Indeed, some feminists see this as part of the equality of the sexes, because there has traditionally been an element of choice in accepting the child for men who are not married to the woman who gives birth.[56] However, the asymmetry of the sexes affects not only matters of procreation, but also the way in which French law distinguishes paternity from maternity.

---

53 *Op cit,* Dekeuwer-Defossey, fn 36.

54 Information received from Professor Rubellin-Devichi, November 1999.

55 Bonnet, C, *Geste d'Amour,* 1991, Paris: Editions Odile Jacob.

56 This choice has effect on the entry on the birth certificate, the recognition of the child and the family name of the child. It is only since 1993 that 'natural children' have been able to bring an action to establish filiation links with the father under the Civil Code, Art 340.

The rights of *accouchement sous X* have been put back in question by two recent reports. Irene Thery, a feminist sociologist, is the author of a report for the Ministry of Justice and the Ministry of Employment jointly. Entitled *Couple, Filiation and Parenthood Today*, the report examines how the family both changes and remains.[57] Thery sees the introduction of the right to give birth anonymously into the Civil Code in 1993 as symbolically reinforcing the absolute character of the right of a woman to hide her maternity. Her view is that the right negates the objective fact of birth giving, and clashes with the right of children to know their origins. Part of the argument turns on the reforms of 1993, which enlarged the possibilities of a declaration of paternal filiation outside marriage. In Thery's view, anonymous maternity prevents the child from establishing filiation links with the father, and thus undoes the effects of the new Art 340, which was undoubtedly an advance for children's rights.[58] Thery is also concerned about the child born to a married woman, on which the texts are silent.[59]

The strongest language used by Thery concerns the child born to X. To her, empty filiation, and the secret organised by the law, are a source of acute suffering for children born thus:

> Perhaps it is worse to know that the effacement of one's origins was organised by society, than to be faced with the silence of the unknown, as with lost children.[60]

Admitting that the debate on *accouchement sous X* is controversial and passionate, Thery proposes that Art 341-1 be repealed. The effect of this would be to abolish women's right to anonymous birthing.

Thery's report has contributed to, rather than resolved, the controversy over *accouchement sous X*. The majority of family lawyers who have written on this subject, mostly women, favour the continuation of the right.[61] A recent report by Françoise Dekeuwer-Defossey proposes a compromise. As chair of a committee of lawyers and a psychoanalyst, she recently reported to the Ministry of Justice on the renewal of family law.[62] The report proposes that existing distinctions in the child's filiation rights, according to the sex of the parent, be eliminated where possible.[63] However, it is proposed that the right of *accouchement sous X* be retained and distinguished from filiation. In other

---

57 Thery, I, *Couple, Filiation et Parente Aujourd'hui*, 1998, Paris: Editions Odile Jacob, p 9.

58 Cour d'Appel, Riom, 16 December 1997. A recent case has shown that the woman can, by anonymous birthing, prevent the establishment of paternity, even where the father would have undertaken an ante-natal recognition.

59 *Ibid*, Thery, p 179.

60 *Ibid*, Thery, p 179. Translation by this writer.

61 *Op cit*, Rubellin-Devichi, fn 48; see, also, the articles cited *op cit*, fnn 48–50.

62 *Op cit*, Dekeuwer-Defossez, fn 36.

63 *Ibid*, p 36.

words, should the child somehow come to know the identity of the birthgiver, she or he would not be faced with the absolute legal bar to bringing the *action en recherche de maternité*. That part of Art 341 which prevents the establishment of a link of filiation with X would be repealed.

A second aspect of choice in French law is the entry on the birth certificate. At present, whether or not paternity or maternity should be recorded is a choice for the father not married to the women who gives birth, and for her.[64] In theory, this absence of parental name on the birth certificate only applies to the 'natural child'. No change to this aspect is proposed, but, where the mother does accept the child through birth registration, it is proposed that this should be a sufficient sign of admission to her family.[65]

The tradition of family law in France has been of collective family rights, particularly in succession, with admittance to the family, for the most part, dependent on the will of the patriarch. As the Dekeuwer-Defossez report notes, French law on filiation is based on voluntary parental acceptance, and has hesitated in allowing free access to the establishment of forced filiation. Court actions for the establishment of parentage 'have been surrounded by a luxury of precautions and restrictions which have given way little by little'.[66] A patriarchal conception of the family is beginning to give way, despite family suspicions of intrusions over its threshold. Nevertheless, the reforms of 1993, in response to the UNCRC, retained traces of the reticences of the past. The new conception of the child's rights attempts a compromise between the choice of genitors whether or not to accept the child and the child's right to belong to the family of birth. Individual history and fundamental elements of identity for the child receive greater respect today and this will be augmented if the latest proposed reforms are introduced.[67]

CONSTRUCTIONS OF CHILDHOOD

Scholars of childhood are today agreed on its constructed nature throughout its history. Being a child does not have, and has not had, the same meaning according to time and space.[68] In other words, history and place affect how childhood is presented and seen. The evidence is that the same is true of parent-child relations. An argument along the lines of 'did the parents of the

---

64 Civil Code, Art 57.

65 *Op cit*, Dekeuwer-Defossez, fn 36, pp 58–59, 67. At present, the name on the birth certificate is not enough to prove maternal filiation. It must be accompanied by additional proof.

66 *Op cit*, Dekeuwer-Defossez, fn 36, p 36. Translation by this writer.

67 *Op cit*, Dekeuwer-Defossez, fn 36. This paragraph is a summary by this writer.

68 Jenks, C, *Childhood*, 1996, London: Routledge and Kegan Paul; James, A and Prout, A (eds), *Constructng and Reconstructing Childhood*, 1997, London: Falmer.

past love their children?' used to take place among social historians. Many suggest that the infant under two was not loved as an older child might be, because infant mortality led parents to guard against the emotional pain of loss.[69] It is not necessary to enter into these debates here. Constructions are the point. Just as the story of Gretel and Hansel has had many versions, and as each version has had many interpretations, so too are there multiple constructions of mother love.

Where two jurisdictions are subject to the same international convention, history and culture will lead to different interpretations. The ways in which the family and parent-child relations are understood in England and France are not the same. This may lead to different consequences for mothers and children. As Claude Neirinck says: '... to take the measure of *accouchement sous* X today it is not enough to describe it. One must analyse the significance for the woman and for the child to whom she gave birth.'[70]

Catherine Bonnet's study of X women shows that many are young, at school, or university, not yet in employment and financially dependent on their families.[71] The majority discover themselves to be pregnant late in the second or third trimester of pregnancy and, therefore, outside the period during which French law permits elective abortion.[72] A psychosocial explanation is offered by Bonnet for the failure of her X respondents to notice the changes in their bodies when they were pregnant. She refers to this as 'denial'. Her explanation goes back to the childhoods of the women involved. Very often, experiences of physical, sexual or emotional abuse, or of parental neglect, blocked the capacity to anticipate the future as a sexual being or a mother. These misfortunes made awareness of pregnancy a late discovery and created a possibility of infanticide. To Bonnet, *accouchement sous* X protects both child and woman, particularly where the latter comes from a community which cannot accept her sexuality outside marriage.

The majority of the X women do not wish to reveal their identity and do not see themselves as mothers. They believe that adoption is the best solution for the child and do not wish to have meetings later in life. It is true that adoption lies behind some of the official discussions of the X facility. Adoption pressure groups wish to retain the possibility of anonymous birth, because the issue of consent of the mother does not arise.[73]

---

69 Hunt, D, *Parents and Children in History: The Psychology of Family Life in Early Modern France*, 1970, New York: Harper; *op cit*, Hendrick, fn 12, p 21: '... until well into this century, "newborns" were not usually viewed as persons and, therefore, were not always loved as "children"'. Aries, P, *The History of Childhood*, 1973, London: Jonathan Cape, takes the view that children had to pass their second birthday to be seen as persons and family members.

70 *Op cit*, Neirinck, fn 48.

71 *Op cit*, Bonnet, fn 55.

72 Elective abortion is available on request during the first 12 weeks of pregnancy. Thereafter, medical reasons must be found: Law of 17 January 1975.

73 *Op cit*, Dekeuwer-Defossez, fn 36, p 61.

From Bonnet's work, which is the only systematic study of the X women, we see a particular construction emerge. These women are victims, but also agents. They take advantage of the possibilities offered by the law. The current discourse in France emphasises these aspects, although there are signs of the entry of the discourse of mother regret favoured in Britain. In this discourse, the emphasis is on the long term: the subsequent regret of X that she gave up her child and the suggestion that the action was a short term impulse from which the woman will later suffer. This discourse is based on the presumption of mother love, a presumption which perhaps human individuals must make for their own psychological health.

Attention is paid also to Art 7 of the UNCRC and the child's rights of knowledge. Pressure groups of X children exist and are growing in strength, with regular meetings.[74] The Dekeuwer-Defossez report confronts this seeming clash of rights with the proposal that an acceptable balance of rights be found.[75]

CONCLUSION

The imperative of English law is for women who give birth to be mothers. Being a mother means accepting the child out of 'natural' love. No route of non-acceptance is open, other than giving up the child for adoption. In such cases, the birth mother is construed as the 'real mother'. The regulatory impact of legal provisions on birth registration contains a particular meaning. Mothers and children are monitored and surveyed; their individual biographies are fused with broader social goals. If the pregnant woman is perceived as an agent, this agency refers to the abortion decision rather than to giving birth.[76] Determination of 'normality' in English discourses of the social pre-supposes the natural; the love of a woman for the infant to whom she gives birth.

French discourse does not assume mother love as a natural given in all cases. The law contains a different conception of 'family'. This appears as an institution to which one is admitted by birth plus the will of other members, rather than by birth alone. It might be argued that two conceptions of the family are being compared in this chapter and that the French conception retains the element of admission to the extended family. Sustenance of this argument must confront the agency of individual women who decide alone whether or not to become mothers.

---

74 Interview with Nadine Lefourcheur, Paris, November 1998.

75 See the discussion in *op cit*, fnn 62–67.

76 Even the abortion decision is not constructed as one for the woman as agent. Under the Abortion Act 1967, it is legally constructed as a medical decision.

Political debates about abortion rights, schoolgirl mothers and irresponsibility might have been introduced into the discourse of this chapter. I have tried to avoid these aspects, whilst being conscious that all academic research can be hijacked into policy making. I am not advocating the introduction of the X possibility into English law, nor automatic birth registration of mothers into French law. Rather, my object is to attempt an understanding of the cultural assumptions made in the society in which I am living.

CHAPTER 5

DIVORCING THE CHILDREN

Helen Reece

INTRODUCTION

On 17 June 1999, the Lord Chancellor announced in a response to a question from Lord Wedderburn that the divorce reforms contained in Pt II of the Family Law Act 1996 would not be implemented in 2000. This was because the preliminary research results of the pilot projects, designed to test the operation of the information meetings, were 'disappointing'.[1] How has it happened that a reform the kernel of which has been in the public domain since 1988[2] seems to have fallen at the last hurdle? It is not as if the reform was enacted without debate: the fate of the Family Law Bill hung in the balance on several occasions during its passage through Parliament. Introduced in the dying days of Conservative rule, the Bill was only saved by the support of the Labour Opposition, given in return for various amendments.[3]

When we examine what has been in dispute during the last 11 years of discussion over divorce, the puzzle deepens: there has been uniform agreement on at least one of the principal aims of a civilised divorce law, that the law should give greater weight to the interests of children.[4] The Family Law Act 1996 accordingly embodies a far more child-centred divorce law than

---

1   *Hansard* 17 June 1999 Col WA 39, HL.

2   Law Commission, *Facing the Future: A Discussion Paper on the Ground for Divorce*, No 170, 1988, London: HMSO.

3   Primarily a provision to create powers to split pensions, a requirement for a cooling off period between the information meeting and the making of the statement, an exhortation to couples to consider reconciliation and exceptions for victims of domestic violence from aspects of the Bill: see Copley, J, 'Ministers forced to climb down on divorce' (1996) *The Daily Telegraph*, 1 May; Jones, G, 'Mackay bows to divorce defeat' (1996) *The Daily Telegraph*, 26 April; White, M, 'Rebel lords hit divorce bill' (1996) *The Guardian*, 1 March; Smithers, R, 'Divorce: a law nobody wants' (1996) *The Guardian*, 18 June; Smithers, R, 'Divorce bill in fresh crisis' (1996) *The Guardian*, 17 May; Smithers, R, 'Tory divorce bill rebels rally allies' (1996) *The Guardian*, 20 April; Smithers, R, 'Ministers agree counselling change to Family Law Bill' (1996) *The Guardian*, 1 May; Leader, 'Labour joins the right: divorced from reality' (1996) *The Independent*, 29 May; 'Four cabinet ministers vote for divorce defeat' (1996) *The Guardian*, 25 April; 'Four cabinet ministers join divorce revolt' (1996) *The Times*, 25 April; 'Ministers defy Tory pressure to ditch Divorce Bill' (1996) *The Independent*, 26 April; 'MPs threaten to mangle Divorce Bill' (1996) *The Independent*, 26 April.

4   See Reece, H, 'Divorcing responsibly' (2000) 8(65) FLS 1 for discussion of another of the agreed aims of a civilised divorce law, that couples should divorce responsibly.

any previous UK statute. This is apparent from a great many of its provisions.[5] Most strikingly, s 11(3) heralds the first introduction of the 'paramountcy principle' into the law of divorce. Section 11(2) gives the court the power to postpone divorce indefinitely if the circumstances are likely to require the court to exercise any of its powers under the Children Act 1989, the court is not in a position to do so without further consideration, and the circumstances are exceptional. In deciding whether the circumstances are likely to require the court to exercise its powers, the court is instructed by s 11(3) to treat the child's welfare as paramount.

This is an important development because many people who are supportive of the paramountcy principle in general would accept that divorce is an area where adults' interests should predominate. Alexander McCall-Smith distinguishes child-centred from adult-centred parents' rights. He argues that the former find their justification in the furtherance of children's welfare, while, in the case of the latter, the parent is accorded a wide range of discretion to pursue goals that society might find undesirable, but will nevertheless tolerate.[6] Andrew Bainham develops this distinction. He agrees with McCall-Smith that there are spheres of parental control that have more to do with the way in which adults want to live their lives than with promoting children's welfare. He describes these as areas in which the parents' interests are primary, and suggests that we should not try to answer questions of conflict between children's welfare and parents' rights in the abstract but, rather, identify the appropriate category for a particular right by identifying

---

5   Family Law Act 1996, s 1, which sets out the general principles to which the court or any person exercising functions under Pts II or III of the Act shall have regard, is inclusive of children. In particular, s 1(c) provides that a marriage should be brought to an end with minimum distress to the children affected and in a manner designed to promote as good a continuing relationship as possible between the parties and any children affected, while s 1(d) instructs that any risk to any children of violence from one of the divorcing spouses should be removed or diminished so far as is reasonably practicable. Orders preventing divorce under s 10 have likewise been amended to include children. In general, the length of time that the couple has to wait before the divorce depends on the interests of their children: s 7(11)–(13) extends the period of reflection and consideration by six months where there is a child of the family under 16. One of the grounds on which this extension can be waived is that the court is satisfied that delaying the divorce would be significantly detrimental to the welfare of any child of the family and another is that an occupation order or non-molestation order is in force in favour of a child of the family and against one of the spouses. Under s 7(14), any extension comes to an end when the youngest child of the family reaches the age of 16. In determining whether to adjourn any proceedings connected to the divorce, s 14(2) directs the attention of the court in particular to the need to protect the interests of any child of the family. Schedule 1, paras 2 and 4 focus on children's interests in determining whether the requirement to settle financial arrangements before the divorce order can be waived. Schedule 1 makes it clear that under no circumstances can the divorce order be granted until arrangements for the children have been settled pursuant to s 11.

6   McCall-Smith, A, 'Is anything left of parental rights?', in Sutherland, E and McCall-Smith, A (eds), *Family Rights: Family Law and Medical Advance*, 1990, Edinburgh: Edinburgh UP.

the beneficiary of that right.[7] If this is the correct approach,[8] then the question of whether or not a parent is able to divorce represents the paradigm of the parent's primary interest. Indeed, Bainham gives this question as an example.[9]

Despite the importance of the introduction of the paramountcy principle into the law of divorce, I will concentrate in this chapter on a less overt respect in which recent divorce reform has been child-centred. In what follows, I begin by arguing that the debates about divorce reform constructed the divorcing couple as children and that this construction facilitated the enactment of a divorce process more suited to punishing children than re-ordering the lives of adults. I then turn to an examination of the roots of this construction and argue that they are to be found in the post-liberal fusion of duty and interest and corresponding separation of autonomy from adulthood. Clearly, the construction is in conflict with reality: divorcees are not naughty children! The Lord Chancellor's announcement may indicate that, by attempting to treat them as such, Pt II of the Family Law Act 1996 has fallen on its own sword. One of the consequences of constructing divorcees as children has been to call into question the implementation of Pt II of the Family Law Act 1996.

DIVORCE DEBATES: CHILD BRIDES AND YOUTHFUL DIVORCEES

The image that the legislature has of the divorcing couple could not be clearer. Throughout the parliamentary debates that preceded the Family Law Act 1996, divorcees were continually and consistently described as 'young people',[10] 'the young',[11] 'youth',[12] 'young couples',[13] 'young married

---

7   Bainham, A, 'Non-intervention and judicial paternalism', in Birks, P (ed), *Frontiers of Liability*, 1994, Oxford: OUP. See, also, Bainham, A, '"Honour thy father and mother": children's rights and children's duties', in Douglas, G and Sebba, L (eds), *Children's Rights and Traditional Values*, 1998, Aldershot: Dartmouth.

8   For criticism, see Herring, J, 'The Human Rights Act and the welfare principle in family law – conflicting or complementary?' (1999) 11 CFLQ 223.

9   *Ibid*, Bainham,1998, p 174.

10 Eg, Duke of Norfolk, *Hansard* 30 November 1995 Vol 567, HL, p 751; Lord Gisborough, *Hansard* 30 November 1995 Vol 567, HL, p 755; Lord Ashbourne, *Hansard* 30 November 1995 Vol 567, HL, p 772; Baroness Young, *Hansard* 29 February 1996 Vol 569, HL, p 1638; 23 January 1996 Vol 568, p 950; Edward Leigh, *Hansard* 24 April 1996 Vol 276, HC, p 455; Angela Rumbold, *Hansard* 24 April 1996 Vol 276, HC, p 466.

11 Eg, Baroness Young, *Hansard* 29 February 1996 Vol 569, HL, p 1638; Baroness Young, quoted in White, M, 'Rebel Lords hit Divorce Bill' (1996) *The Guardian*, 1 March, p 1.

12 Eg, Lord Simon, *Hansard* 22 February 1996 Vol 569, HL, p 1196.

13 Eg, Lord Northbourne, *Hansard* 2 July 1996 Col 1426, HL.

couples'[14] and 'children'.[15] The following picture from the Duke of Norfolk gives a good illustration of the prototype:

> ... the likelihood of divorce needs to be lessened by ... helping young people to acquire the necessary social skills of communication to deal sensibly and maturely with conflicts and to develop an understanding of what commitment means in terms of changing and adapting within the marital relationship as the couple grow up.[16]

If the divorcing couple were viewed as youthful, then the bride and groom could be little more than children, hence Lord Elton's reference to 'the need for some form of preparation during education for the responsibilities of marriage now that it comes so early in life'. 'Indeed,' he continued, 'parenthood often comes before the end of a school career.'[17] These youthful couples were presumed to have contracted their marriages in the heat of the moment. So Lord Simon hoped that if the skills of communication could be acquired then 'the flame of passion of the early years of marriage may subside to form a warm glow of companionship'.[18] Angela Rumbold provided a memorable thumbnail sketch of the flighty bride and groom: 'Young people are already saying, "Let us have a happy marriage. Let us float down the aisle in white dresses. If it all gets too difficult and we do not enjoy ourselves later on, that does not matter: we can always get out of it".'[19] Therefore, it was inevitable that the bride and groom had to be helped. The Duke of Norfolk wanted 'marriage counselling to start with advice being given by the social welfare people and, of course, by the churches, to try to assist the very young before they become engaged'.[20]

It is worth comparing this image of divorcing and marrying couples with the reality. The average age of divorcees has been steadily increasing, so that, by 1997, it had reached 40 for men and 37 for women. Only 0.1% of divorcing couples were under the age of 20 and only 6.5% were under the age of 25.[21] The average age of marriage has also been rising consistently, so that, by 1996, the average groom of 34 married an average bride of 31. Of course, a large proportion of marriages are second marriages, but even for first marriages the

---

14 Eg, Lord Elton, *Hansard* 23 January 1996 Vol 568, HL, p 991.

15 Eg, Lord Gisborough, *Hansard* 30 November 1995 Vol 567, HL, p 755; Lord Stallard, *Hansard* 25 January 1996 Vol 568, HL, p 1192; Duke of Norfolk, *Hansard* 29 February 1996 Vol 569, HL, p 1705.

16 *Hansard* 30 November 1995 Vol 567, HL, p 751.

17 *Hansard* 4 March 1996 Vol 570, HL, p 56.

18 *Hansard* 29 February 1996 Vol 569, HL, p 1660. See, also, 22 February 1996, p 1196.

19 *Hansard* 24 April 1996 Vol 276, HC, p 466. See, also, Lord Ashbourne, *Hansard* 30 November 1995 Vol 567, HL, p 772; Mackay (Lord), 'Family law reform' (1996) 128(3) Law and Justice 10.

20 *Hansard* 22 January 1996 Vol 568, HL, pp 833–34. See, also, Lord Northbourne, *Hansard* 2 July 1996 Col 1426, HL.

21 Office of Population, Censuses and Surveys, *Population Trends*, Spring 1999.

average male age was 30 and the average female was 28. Both of these averages for first marriages had increased by two years since 1993. In only 4.1% of marriages was even one of the parties under the age of 20.[22]

But, given that weddings and GCSEs were treated as contemporaneous, preparing children for marriage in the classroom was seen as the only solution. Edward Leigh welcomed the suggestion that children should be educated about their future responsibilities[23] and Lord Jakobovits felt that 'some teaching in the responsibilities of marriage should also be included as an essential subject in school instructions'.[24] In 1998, *Supporting Families* proclaimed that 'education about parental and personal responsibility can help prepare children for entering adult relationships'[25] and promised 'greater emphasis in the curriculum ... at the first opportunity'.[26] The recent Learning and Skills Act 2000 provided an opportunity, s 148 of which mandates guidance designed to secure that, when sex education is provided, children 'learn the nature of marriage and its importance for family life and the bringing up of children'. While controversy raged up until the last minute over whether the Act would explicitly rank marriage above other stable relationships, there was almost no opposition to the central plank of s 148, that children should be educated about marriage at school.[27]

Given the emphasis on, first, the youthfulness of the married couple and, secondly, on educating children for marriage, the line between future and present married couples eventually became blurred and the distinction between adult and child fuzzy, as the following extract from Lord Elton illustrates:

> The first thing that we have to do is to teach people what marriage is about. Even that has an element of the classroom in it because marriage is about human relationships ... we discussed the fact that children were entering reception and nursery classes insufficiently educated within the family to be able to have conversations or to play with their contemporaries. That is a disaster and it must be tackled. Those children will eventually become young married couples, so the problem has to be tackled in the school.[28]

---

22 Central Statistical Office, *Social Trends*, 1996.

23 *Hansard* 19 December 1997 Col 579, HC.

24 *Hansard* 30 November 1995 Vol 567, HL, p 722. See, also, Lord Stallard, *Hansard* 11 January 1996 Vol 568, HL, p 280; 22 January 1996, p 820; 30 November 1995 Vol 567, p 744; Lord Jakobovits, *Hansard* 6 July 1999 Col 788, HL.

25 Home Office, *Supporting Families: A Consultation Document*, 1998, London: HMSO, p 17, para 1.55.

26 *Ibid*, p 17, para 1.56.

27 See Kallenbach, M and Sparrow, A, 'Peers back guidelines on sex education in schools' (2000) *The Daily Telegraph*, 19 July.

28 Lord Elton, *Hansard* 23 January 1996 Vol 568, HL, p 991. Lord Jakobovits, *Hansard* 23 January 1996 Vol 568, HL, p 988; 6 July 1999 Col 788; Viscount Brentford, *Hansard* 6 July 1999 Col 788, HL.

The line between adult and child became still fuzzier when the divorcing couple were allotted a place in the family structure. Either they were constructed as parents, in which case the emphasis was placed exclusively on the needs of their children, or they themselves were allotted the role of children within the family. Lord Stallard had accordingly 'discovered that first marriages often break up because children did not listen to their parents' advice and the second marriage was a success because they realised that they should have listened to parents in the first place'.[29]

Richard Collier has argued that, on embarking on the divorce process, the individual is entering a point of regulation, a central aim of which is to foster certain modes of self-identification, and that one key self-identification is that of the good citizen.[30] But who is the good citizen? Lauren Berlant recognises that 'something strange has happened to citizenship ... a nation made for adult citizens has been replaced by one imagined for foetuses and children'.[31] Intimate issues such as marriage and family values have become vital to defining how citizens should act; citizenship has become downsized and privatised. Berlant suggests that, because 'this national icon is still innocent of knowledge, agency and accountability and thus has ethical claims on the adult political agents who write laws, ... the foetal/infantile person is a *stand in* for a complicated and contradictory set of anxieties and desires about national identity'.[32] Therefore, the 'most hopeful national pictures of "life" circulating in the public sphere are not of adults in everyday life, in public or in politics, but, rather, of the most vulnerable minor or virtual citizens ... persons that, paradoxically, cannot yet act as citizens'.[33] She concludes that the infantile citizen's naïve citizenship surfaces constantly as the ideal type of patriotic personhood.[34] It could be argued, then, that the Family Law Act 1996 constructs the divorcee as a child because the child is today's ideal citizen, and so the next best citizen to the actual child is the virtual child.

So, divorcees were constructed as virtual children. Once this construction had been accomplished, whenever the figurative family was unable to exert influence over the virtual children, no further justification was necessary for the legislature to step into *loco parentis*. According to Lord Gisborough:

> ... the Government could offer a range of services to help prepare young people
> for the responsibilities of marriage ... children are often loath to take advice

---

29 *Hansard* 25 January 1996 Vol 568, HL, p 1192. See, also, Duke of Norfolk, *Hansard* 29 February 1996 Vol 569, HL, p 1705.

30 Collier, R, 'The dashing of a "liberal dream"? The information meeting, the "new family" and the limits of law' (1999) 11(3) CFLQ 257, p 261, fn 20.

31 Berlant, L, *The Queen of America Goes to Washington City: Essays on Sex and Citizenship*, 1997, North Carolina: Duke UP, p 1.

32 *Ibid*, p 6.

33 *Ibid*, p 5.

34 *Ibid*, p 21.

from their parents who, since the days of Adam, have been thought old and out of touch, but a third party is sometimes better heeded.[35]

THE DIVORCE PROCESS: PUNISHING NAUGHTY CHILDREN

The period of reflection or time out

Douglas Riley, in *The Defiant Child: A Parent's Guide to Oppositional Defiant Disorder*,[36] recommends 'time out' as the main form of punishment:

> Time out is best conceptualised as a period a child must spend thinking about how his thoughts and behaviors have gotten him into trouble and how to replace those thoughts and behaviors with others that will not cause trouble ... It should be used by your child to sit and think about how to make better decisions and about how to use the replacement behaviors and replacement thoughts you have previously urged him to use.[37]

Of course, it is preferable to encourage children to take time out before they have transgressed. For these purposes, Douglas Riley suggests 'the time machine game':

> I ask the child to imagine that he is getting ready to do something negative ... Then I ask him to imagine that, just before he does it, he jumps into the time machine and goes forward 10 minutes to see what might happen if he does. Children are almost always able to outline the negative outcome their behaviour will precipitate.[38]

Older children progress from the time machine game to 'forward thinking':

> The idea of forward thinking is the same, but without the game like trappings used to engage younger children. I tell older children and teenagers that we all have negative or anti-social impulses we are tempted to act upon, and the difference between the person who stays in trouble and the one who stays out of trouble is that they learn to think forward in a way that lets them anticipate what the outcome will be.[39]

---

35 *Hansard* 30 November 1995 Vol 567, HL, p 755. See, also, Baroness Young, *Hansard* 29 February 1996 Vol 569, HL, p 1638; 23 January 1996 Vol 568, p 950; Angela Rumbold, *Hansard* 24 April 1996 Vol 276, HC, p 469.

36 Riley, D, *The Defiant Child: A Parent's Guide to Oppositional Defiant Disorder*, 1997, Dallas, Texas: Taylor. I am grateful to Geraldine Crabbe for assistance with this section of the article.

37 *Ibid*, p 91. See, also, Fontana, D, *Your Growing Child: From Birth to Adolescence*, 1990, London: Fontana, p 434; Hartley-Brewer, E, *Positive Parenting: Raising Children with Self-Esteem*, 1995, London: Cedar, p 164.

38 *Ibid*, pp 116–17.

39 *Ibid*, p 117. See *ibid*, Hartley-Brewer, p 165 regarding the related concept of 'stickability' or 'task commitment'.

This is known otherwise as the period of reflection and consideration, which is 'a period for the parties ... to reflect on whether the marriage can be saved and to have an opportunity to effect a reconciliation'.[40] According to the Government White Paper, *Looking to the Future: Mediation and the Ground for Divorce*, the key aspects of the Government's proposals are that they will 'require couples to think through and face the consequences of divorce before it happens'.[41] Since brides and grooms have been constructed as lacking maturity, it is unsurprising that *Supporting Families* ushers the bride and groom into a mini version of time out, with its proposal that couples should have to give a minimum of 15 days' notice of their intention to marry: 'This would allow couples more time to reflect on the nature of the commitment they are entering into and to take up marriage preparation, if they wished to do so.'[42]

The meetings

According to Douglas Riley, 'time out should always begin with a brief, clear description of the behaviors that have gotten the child in trouble along with an explanation of how long the time out will be'[43] because 'they need to have the consequences of their behaviour made clear to them, and to take responsibility for what they decide to do'.[44] For divorcees, this converts into the information meeting that precedes the period of reflection, which gives the prospective divorcee the opportunity and encouragement to have a meeting with a marriage counsellor, and information on, among other things, marriage counselling and other marriage support services; the importance to be attached to the welfare, wishes and feelings of children; how the divorcee may acquire a better understanding of the ways in which children can be helped to cope with the breakdown of the marriage; protection, support and assistance available with respect to violence; and mediation.[45] The divorcing couple have to wait at least three months after the information meeting before

---

40 Family Law Act 1996, s 7(1)(a). See 'Marriage of true mindlessness' (1996) *The Guardian*, 20 June, p 6, for recognition that a cooling off period is more appropriate for children.

41 Lord Chancellor's Department, *Looking to the Future: Mediation and the Ground for Divorce*, Cm 2799, 1995, London: HMSO, p v. See, also, p 17, para 3.1.

42 *Op cit*, Home Office, fn 25, pp 34-35, para 4.27.

43 *Op cit*, Riley, fn 36, p 91.

44 *Op cit*, Hartley-Brewer, fn 37, p 165.

45 Family Law Act 1996, s 8(9). See Cretney, S, 'Divorce on demand' (1993) *The Times*, 14 December; and Barton, C, 'Until mediation us do part' (1993) *The Times*, 8 March, for recognition of the paternalistic nature of the requirement to attend an information meeting.

beginning the period of reflection[46] because 'children will need time to assimilate the information – to fully understand and make it their own'.[47]

Supporting Families proposes that prospective spouses would also have to attend an information meeting in order to enable the registrar to provide information on available guidance and to refer both partners to pre-marriage support at the earliest possible stage[48] because:

> ... marriage is a serious business, and it is important that people who plan to marry have a clear idea of the rights and responsibilities they are taking on. This could be done through a simple and clear guide to the implications of getting married ... made available through register offices, churches and other places of worship, and other bodies providing advice to married people[49] ... The purpose of marriage preparation is to ensure that couples planning to marry have considered, and reached an understanding on, the major issues that affect married life. Couples may consider how their finances should be organised; where they will live; whether they will have children; and what arrangements they might make, for example, for one or other parent to reduce or stop work when the children are born.[50] This would allow time for thought and discussion by the couple before the ceremony itself.[51]

But one meeting may be insufficient for prospective divorcees, so *Supporting Families* suggests two.[52] The first meeting would concentrate on information to help the couple decide whether their marriage is over,[53] while the second meeting would be a group presentation at which the couple would be given detailed information about issues concerning their children, finances, property and mediation at a time when they were ready for this information. This would be, at the very least, after they had already embarked on divorce.[54]

Moreover, for both the naughty child and the recalcitrant divorcee, it may be necessary to hold supplementary meetings in the middle if the message has not been absorbed. For the child:

> When the basic time out fails to help your child change his behavior, it is time to reconsider whether the intensity of the time out is sufficient ... ask yourself how your child is spending the time out period. Is he actually thinking of new ways to act and think, or is he drawing, reading books or taking a nap? ... Far too often, a parent simply sends a child to his room, waits 20 minutes, and then

---

46 Family Law Act 1996, s 8(2).
47 Miller, J, *Never Too Young: How Young Children Can Take Responsibility and Make Decisions: A Handbook for Early Years Workers*, 1996, London: Save the Children, p 18.
48 *Op cit*, Home Office, fn 25, p 34, para 4.27.
49 *Op cit*, Home Office, fn 25, p 32, para 4.13.
50 *Op cit*, Home Office, fn 25, p 32, para 4.17.
51 *Op cit*, Home Office, fn 25, p 34, para 4.26.
52 *Op cit*, Home Office, fn 25, pp 35–36, paras 4.29–4.33.
53 *Op cit*, Home Office, fn 25, p 35, para 4.31.
54 *Op cit*, Home Office, fn 25, p 35, para 4.33.

shouts up to him that he can come out. Maybe he was using the time productively. But, if his behaviour remains oppositional, chances are he used the time out period to check out his baseball card collection, or listen to the latest CD on his headphones ... If your child is not using time out in a productive way, give him explicit instructions on how to use it. Again, tell him that he is to think about how his behavior and thinking got him into trouble and about how he might replace the faulty behaviors and thoughts.[55]

For the divorcee:

... after the court has received a statement, it may give a direction requiring each party to attend a meeting arranged in accordance with the direction for the purpose ... of enabling an explanation to be given of the facilities available to the parties for mediation in relation to disputes between them; and ... of providing an opportunity for each party to agree to take advantage of those facilities.[56]

Imparting information is not sufficient: the way in which information is imparted is crucial. Penelope Leach emphasises that a great deal of children's naughtiness is caused by lack of comprehension.[57] According to another child rearing manual:

If children are to make informed decisions, adults need to consider carefully what information they will need and how this can be presented in ways that are engaging and meaningful.

We cannot rely just on telling children things. They need:

- to see things demonstrated;

- to handle information in as concrete a form as possible; and

- to experience things at first hand.[58]

Lord Mackay made it clear that, for divorcees as well, it was not enough to rely on telling them things:

I wish ... to try to ensure that people do not just obtain the information but that they obtain it in such a way that they understand it ... It is important ... that they have taken that information on board. There is a limit to what anyone can do about that matter, but that is why I have suggested an information session. The first point is to try to obtain some method by which people do not merely have pieces of paper presented to them, but that some effort is made on behalf of the State to ensure that they have assimilated the information as it affects them.[59] If the information has been given effectively, I would hope that the

---

55   *Op cit*, Riley, fn 36, p 92.

56   Family Law Act 1996, s 13(1).

57   Leach, P, *Getting Positive About Discipline: A Guide for Today's Parents*, 1997, Ilford: Barnardo's.

58   *Op cit*, Miller, fn 47, p 18.

59   *Hansard* 22 January 1996 Vol 568, HL, p 836; see, also, p 837; Baroness David, *Hansard* 22 January 1996 Vol 568, HL, p 832.

parties would not forget it[60] ... I believe it is extremely important that these matters should be effectively communicated and that people are not left with an ineffectual communication of information. We are all familiar with the situation of receiving pieces of paper, sometimes in fairly large quantities, where perhaps we do not always study them as fully as the importance of the information they contain would require.[61]

Indeed, Lord Stallard went so far as to propose that one of the objectives contained in s 1 of the Family Law Act 1996 should be to ensure that the parties understood what mediation could do for them.[62] Although this proposal was rejected, the sentiment behind the proposal found expression in the requirement that some divorcees should attend a supplementary meeting:

> The court may realise, once the matter comes before it, that the parties have not really understood what mediation can do for them in the particular circumstances ... if the court feels that the parties, notwithstanding our efforts to inform them, do not really appreciate or have understood the efforts that have been made ... the court should invite them to attend a meeting at which that would be clearly explained to them[63] ... I think it is extremely important that, in this area, any refusal is an informed refusal. I do not want people just to say, 'I do not like the sound of mediation'. We want them to understand precisely what is involved ... It is important that parties are put in a position of fully understanding mediation.[64]

Divorcees, just like children, needed to experience things at first hand. Lord Stoddart was concerned at one point in the debate on information meetings that, 'as the amendment stands, a person ... could rely upon hearsay information. He or she might receive it over the telephone, or someone else might telephone and pass on the information second hand. Under these circumstances, unless the person were to attend the session face to face, he might receive quite the wrong information through third parties'.[65]

The entire divorce process was, in fact, designed to enable the couple to experience things first hand, to see things demonstrated and to handle information in as concrete a form as possible. John Dewar explains that the explicit purpose of the requirement that all relevant information be lodged with the original statement was 'to force the parties to face the harsh realities of their position sooner rather than later'.[66] This explanation is supported by

60 *Hansard* 22 January 1996 Vol 568, HL, p 837.
61 *Hansard* 22 February 1996 Vol 569, HL, p 1184.
62 *Hansard* 11 January 1996 Vol 568, HL, p 280. See, also, *op cit*, Lord Chancellor's Department, fn 41, p 56, para 7.1 and p 66, para 7.33.
63 Lord Mackay, *Hansard* 23 January 1996 Vol 568, HL, p 1023.
64 Lord Mackay, *Hansard* 4 March 1996 Vol 570, HL, pp 95–96.
65 *Hansard* 22 January 1996 Vol 568, HL, p 836. See, also, *op cit*, Lord Chancellor's Department, fn 41, p 56, para 7.4.
66 Dewar, J, *Law and the Family*, 2nd edn, 1992, London: Butterworths, p 263.

Lord Coleraine's hope that the proposals in general would 'give couples the chance to experience, before the divorce takes place, the sadness and sense of failure which so many decent divorced couples have been shown to feel after it is all over'.[67]

Arrangements for the future

Normally, time out, or the period of reflection, will end when the time limit is up. But:

> There is one serious exception to these time limits. If you tell your child that she has to go into her room for a 20 minute time out and she spends the 20 minutes slamming doors, throwing things, yelling at you to let her out, or crying hysterically enough to alarm the neighbors, from my perspective, she has not completed time out[68] ... It should end with a brief discussion of the decisions your child has come to about new behaviors, new thoughts, and how to stay out of trouble.[69]

Other child rearing manuals have further emphasised the 'vital importance of discussion' as a form of discipline.[70] *Looking to the Future: Mediation and the Ground for Divorce* recommends, similarly, that 'the divorce process ... should enable couples to consider their future in an environment that allows them to address together what went wrong with the marriage',[71] and suggests that, under the proposals, couples 'are encouraged to talk about the issues in their own way, using language which is familiar, thus enabling them both to say what they want to each other'.[72] As we have seen, to encourage dialogue further, at the end of the period of reflection, the court can refuse to grant the divorce because it might need to make orders about the children under the Children Act 1989. Moreover, the court will not make a divorce order unless the couple have agreed on arrangements for the future concerning their finances and their children.[73]

---

67 *Hansard* 30 November 1995 Vol 567, HL, p 723. See, also, *op cit*, Lord Chancellor's Department, fn 41, p 18, paras 3.5–3.6.

68 *Op cit*, Riley, fn 36, p 92.

69 *Op cit*, Riley, fn 36, p 91.

70 Lansdown, R and Walker, M, *Your Child's Development from Birth to Adolescence*, 1996, London: Frances Lincoln, p 447.

71 *Op cit*, Lord Chancellor's Department, fn 41, pp 9–10, para 2.17.

72 *Op cit*, Lord Chancellor's Department, fn 41, p 38, para 5.6.

73 Family Law Act 1996, s 9. For exceptions to the requirement to agree financial arrangements, see Family Law Act 1996, s 9(7) and Sched 1.

POST-LIBERAL THEORY: WE'RE ALL CHILDREN NOW

Despite the apparent diversity of different forms of post-liberal theory, principal forms share an emphasis on the particular, the local and the social nature of both the self and reality, in opposition to the dominant themes within traditional versions of liberalism of abstraction, universalism and individualism.[74] In essence, post-liberal theorists discover and value *connectedness* where liberals found and safeguarded separateness. To varying degrees, within different versions of communitarianism and post-liberal feminism, the self is regarded as constituted by his or her society. Therefore, people are fundamentally connected, both to others and to the community which they inhabit.[75]

If we are constituted by our community, then it is impossible to separate our own interests from the interests of the community. This leads communitarians to downgrade the liberal distinction between rights and good, interest and duty. This tendency is particularly pronounced within the civic republican strand of communitarianism, which emphasises commitment to a substantive conception of the common good.[76] Adrian Oldfield, who exemplifies this strand of communitarian thinking, explains that individuals are free only when their duty and interest coincide.[77] However, this coincidence is not the automatic accompaniment of physical maturity.[78] And this leads Oldfield to reject another of 'the central tenets of the liberal individualist tradition of political thinking ... that, once children reach and pass the threshold of adulthood, the courtesy is paid of regarding them as fully responsible moral agents'. He explains that, within the broad frame of liberal individualist thinking, the young are encouraged to become aware of themselves as moral agents, able and willing to take on the responsibilities of the adult world, but that it is 'this ability, but above all this willingness, that civic republicanism challenges'.[79]

---

74 See Hutchinson, A and Green, L, 'Introduction', in Hutchinson, A and Green, L (eds), *Law and the Community: The End of Individualism?*, 1989, Cambridge, Mass: Harvard UP, p 2; Frazer, E and Lacey, N, *The Politics of Community: A Feminist Critique of the Liberal-Communitarian Debate*, 1994, Buffalo, New York: Toronto UP, p 2.

75 *Ibid*, Frazer and Lacey.

76 *Ibid*, Frazer and Lacey.

77 Oldfield, A, *Citizenship and Community: Civic Republicanism and the Modern World*, 1990, London: Routledge, p 153.

78 *Ibid*.

79 *Ibid*, p 152.

LIVERPOOL JOHN MOORES UNIVERSITY

Education and participation

Fuzziness between adult and child is further compounded by, first, the extension of education into adulthood and, secondly, the substitution of participation for education in childhood. For Oldfield, since freedom exists only at the intersection of duty and interest, and since this co-existence is not the automatic accompaniment of adulthood, an understanding and acceptance of one's duty is a pre-condition to becoming a citizen:[80] '... individuals *become* citizens by taking their civic duties seriously.'[81] He recognises that civic republicanism might seem inappropriate to the modern world, given the demise of religious belief, which used to generate an understanding and acceptance of duty.[82] But he responds that this merely 'suggests that one must build on whatever religion is available, and that a different social institution must be brought into focus: education[83] ... Even if religion is not necessary to provide the motivation, some form of moral or civic education is'.[84] Because of this, he continues, education for freedom has to continue into, and indeed throughout, adult life:

> Freedom, in this sense, ... involves apprenticeship and ... periodic retraining ... Human beings not only have to be taught what moral autonomy means as a practice, but, being weak and shortsighted, they also have to be reminded of what it is that they have been taught ... The practice of citizenship, which is what moral autonomy means within civic republicanism, is an unnatural practice for human beings and Rousseau was correct to say that their 'natural' character has to be 'mutilated' before they will engage in it. This is the cost of the practice of citizenship. It is not surprising that liberal individualists will not pay it: it is an unwelcome entrance fee to social living. Liberal individualists object to having their characters systematically mutilated (as if this did not already take place); civic republicans know that it is worth paying the price[85] ... The moral character which is appropriate for genuine citizenship does not generate itself; it has to be authoritatively inculcated. This means that minds have to be manipulated. People, starting with children, have to be taught what citizenship means for them.[86]

Thus, childhood is no longer the exclusive province of education: adults must continue their education. However, even with respect to children's education,

---

80 *Op cit*, Oldfield, fn 77, p 145.

81 *Op cit*, Oldfield, fn 77, p 159 (emphasis added).

82 *Op cit*, Oldfield, fn 77, p 153.

83 *Op cit*, Oldfield, fn 77, p 154.

84 *Op cit*, Oldfield, fn 77, p 164.

85 *Op cit*, Oldfield, fn 77, pp 153–54.

86 *Ibid*, p 164. See, also, Etzioni, A, *The New Golden Rule: Community and Morality in a Democratic Society*, 1998, New York: Basic, pp 52 and 74, for the argument that education should take precedence over coercion within a communitarian society in order to preserve the communitarian conception of freedom.

Michael Sandel makes it clear that this serves a different purpose for the communitarian than for the liberal:

> On some issues, the two theories may produce different arguments for similar policies. For example, ... where liberals might support public education in hopes of equipping students to become autonomous individuals, capable of choosing their own ends and pursuing them effectively, communitarians might support public education in the hope of equipping students to become good citizens, capable of contributing meaningfully to public deliberations and pursuits.[87]

In the light of this aim for education, it should no longer surprise us that increasing emphasis is being placed on educating children about marriage and relationships.

We can now also make sense of the slippage in the divorce debates between educating children and educating adults for marriage. But, adult education is not enough. According to Oldfield, theory has to be coupled with practice; education in one's duty has to be accompanied by active participation in citizenship. Participation, as well as an acceptance of duty, is a precondition of citizenship: to be a citizen *is* to participate; citizenship is something that follows from participation, so that citizenship is not a condition of participation but one of participation's richest fruits.[88] Oldfield argues that, if individuals are empowered through education for citizenship, then a virtuous circle of participation breeding participation will result. Participation feeds back into education: the process of participating is educative in itself – 'the more one participates, the more one develops the attitudes appropriate to a citizen'.[89] Participation *per se* is insufficient; citizenship is participation in a specific mode, that is, participation with public responsibility, with attention to the common good.[90] Neither education nor participation is adequate individually to generate commitment to the practice of citizenship, however: '... what is required is a much broader educative effort to inculcate both knowledge of the duties of citizenship and willingness to perform them.'[91]

The educative nature of participation operates in both directions. According to Geoff Mulgan, 'if you want children to come out of [schools] understanding good and bad, you don't teach them morals as if they were chemical equations: you encourage them to learn through working with

---

87 Sandel, M, 'Morality and the liberal ideal' (1984) *New Republic*, 7 May, p 15.

88 *Op cit*, Oldfield, fn 77, p 160.

89 *Op cit*, Oldfield, fn 77, p 155. See, also, Berry, C, *The Idea of a Democratic Community*, 1989, Hemel Hempstead: Harvester.

90 *Op cit*, Oldfield, fn 77, p 160.

91 *Op cit*, Oldfield, fn 77, p 156.

others'.[92] Modern child rearing manuals are unanimous in proclaiming the virtues for children of participation:

Benefits for children

- Participation offers children the opportunity to express and understand their own feelings and needs. Only when they are able to do this can they consider the feelings and needs of others.

- Participation helps children to develop the skills of communication, debate, negotiation and compromise and so to achieve a balance between their own needs and those of others.

- Through participation, children gain information that helps them to understand both possibilities, and constraints ...

- By choosing among various options, children develop the skill of decision making, both individually and as part of a group.

- When children's ideas, feelings and capabilities are treated with respect, their confidence and self-esteem grow.[93]

Importance was placed on children's classroom participation in education for marriage specifically:

So many noble Lords have referred to education for marriage. I should like to end by saying something really positive, so here is a suggestion. It arises out of the question: how can young people learn of the benefits of marriage when a growing number of them have never seen marriage at work? With this problem in mind, an initiative has been taken to introduce married couples to volunteering sixth formers who wished to have the opportunity to discuss the institution of marriage ... there is a hunger to learn about marriage.[94]

Illusory autonomy

Within post-liberal theory, since identities are interconnected, the liberal conception of the independent autonomous individual is incoherent.[95] Yet, post-liberal theory still needs some conception of self-determination. Nedelsky explains that this is of particular importance within feminist theory:

---

92 'Our built in moral sense is the basic we should go back to' (1994) *The Guardian*, 4 August, p 22.

93 *Op cit*, Miller, fn 47, p 16.

94 Lord Craigmyle, *Hansard* 24 March 1999 Col 1322, HL.

95 See, eg, Benhabib, S and Cornell, D, 'Beyond the politics of gender', in Benhabib, S and Cornell, D (eds), *Feminism as Critique*, 1987, Cambridge: Polity, p 12; Hewitt, J, *Dilemmas of the American Self*, 1989, Philadelphia: Temple UP, p 29; Kitwood, T, 'Psychotherapy, post-modernism and morality' (1990) 3 J Moral Education 3; *op cit*, Oldfield, fn 77, p 153.

Indeed, feminists are centrally concerned with freeing women to shape our own lives, to define who we (each) are, rather than accepting the definition given to us by others (men and male-dominated society, in particular). Feminists, therefore, need a language of freedom with which to express the value underlying this concern.[96]

The problem, then, for feminism is the tension between the value accorded to self-direction and the precept that relationships are central in constituting the self.[97] Nedelsky attempts to resolve the tension by embracing it, her argument being that the collective is in fact an important source of autonomy:

> If we ask ourselves what actually enables people to be autonomous, the answer is not isolation, but relationships ... that provide the support and guidance necessary for the developments and experience of autonomy ... We see that dependence is not, as our tradition teaches, the antithesis of autonomy, but a literal precondition of autonomy, and interdependence a constant component of autonomy.[98]

'The task, then, is to think of autonomy in terms of the forms of human interactions in which it will develop and flourish.'[99] For communitarians and civic republicans, as well as many feminist theorists, it is the family that is most conducive to post-liberal autonomy because it is within the family that we experience the closest connection and greatest commitment to others.[100] Elshtain illustrates this point well with her assertion that the family involves 'links between particular persons that cannot be reduced to instrumental terms [and] stands as one barrier between human beings and the flattening out of their social world under the demands of untrammeled self-interest'.[101] Clearly, feminist writers are quick to emphasise that they are not advocating

---

96 Nedelsky, J, 'Reconceiving autonomy: sources, thoughts and possibilities', in *op cit*, Hutchinson and Green, fn 74, p 221.

97 *Ibid*, p 222. See, also, *op cit*, Benhabib and Cornell, fn 95, p 12.

98 *Ibid*, p 225.

99 *Ibid*, pp 225–26.

100 Eg, Etzioni, A, *The Spirit of Community: Rights, Responsibilities and the Communitarian Agenda*, 1993, New York: Random House; *op cit*, Etzioni, fn 86, pp 52 and 74; Fowler, RB, *The Dance with Community: The Contemporary Debate in American Political Thought*, 1991, Kansas: Kansas UP; Elshtain, J, 'Feminism, family, and community' (1982) 29 Dissent 442; Elshtain, J and Buell, J, 'Families in trouble' (1991) 38 Dissent 262; Minow, M and Lyndon Shanley, M, 'Relational rights and responsibilities: revisioning the family in liberal political theory and law' (1996) 11 Hypatia 4; Albert, M, 'In the interest of the public good? New questions for feminism', in Reynolds, C and Norman, R (eds), *Community in America: The Challenge of Habits of the Heart*, 1988, Berkeley, Cal: California UP. See Friedmann, M, 'Feminism and modern friendship: dislocating the community' (1989) 99 Ethics 275; Struering, K, 'Feminist challenges to the new familialism: lifestyle experimentation and the freedom of intimate association' (1996) 11 Hypatia 135; Greschner, D, 'Feminist concerns with the new communitarians: we don't need another hero', in *op cit*, Hutchinson and Green, fn 74, for criticism of the emphasis on family as community. See Gutmann, A, 'Communitarian critics of liberalism' (1985) 14 Philosophy and Public Affairs 308, p 309, for a critique of the discussion.

101 *Ibid*, Elshtain, p 447.

the traditional patriarchal family premised on the subordination of women but are, rather, supporting a critical view of the family.[102] They express differing views over what aspect of the family best encapsulates the ideal community. Albert argues that we should consider marriage as the model for civic commitment because it is 'our most personal experience of committing to another person ... an obligation we must assume; to be married, we can no longer be absolutely "freely choosing"'.[103] In contrast, Nedelsky suggests that the most promising symbol for autonomy is child rearing, because it encapsulates the emergence of autonomy through relationship with others.[104]

John Dewar argues that Pt II of the Family Law Act 1996 seeks to pursue two objectives simultaneously: first, behaviour modification, the use of divorce law and procedure to ensure that divorcing couples are made to honour their responsibilities to each other; and, secondly, the delegalisation of divorce. He concludes:

> ... in short, the 1996 Act seeks both to give the parties greater autonomy, while at the same time seeking to influence how they use it ... The principle ... represents a significant departure from the previous model in that it seeks explicitly to use the divorce process itself as a means of affecting divorcing behaviour. Gone is the idea that the role of law is to facilitate and implement private decisions: it now seeks to influence the decisions themselves.[105]

Similarly, John Eekelaar documents a growing belief that the court system has a role to play in influencing outcomes for the divorcing couple. He suggests that this can be viewed either as regulation, in that obstacles are placed along the way, or retreat, in that the couple's own solutions are accepted.[106] Dewar sees rich possibilities of potentially unworkable contradictions in pursuing the twin objectives of behaviour modification and party control 'because behaviour modification implies precisely a loss of party control or autonomy'. He sees it as, therefore, paradoxical that an emphasis on party control has been associated with a more interventionist divorce procedure.[107]

The paradox that Dewar identifies is explicable once we realise that the Family Law Act 1996 offers post-liberal autonomy, for which child rearing is the symbol and dependence the precondition. On close examination, we find

---

102 *Op cit*, Albert, fn 100; *op cit*, Elshtain, fn 100, p 446; *op cit*, Fowler, fn 100, p 98; *op cit*, Greschner, fn 100, p 133.

103 *Op cit*, Albert, fn 100, p 94.

104 *Op cit*, Nedelsky, fn 96, p 225. See, also, *op cit*, Fowler, fn 100, p 98; *op cit*, Greschner, fn 100, p 132.

105 Dewar, J, 'The normal chaos of family law' (1998) 61 MLR 467, pp 476–77.

106 Eekelaar, J, *Regulating Divorce*, 1991, Oxford: Clarendon, p 154. See Cretney, S, 'Divorce reform in England: humbug and hypocrisy or a smooth transition', in Freeman, M (ed), *Divorce: Where Next?*, 1996, Aldershot: Dartmouth, for the view that, in reality, the Family Law Act 1996 introduces party control hidden behind a façade of behaviour modification.

107 *Ibid*, Eekelaar, pp 477–78.

that post-liberal autonomy indeed resembles the autonomy that child rearing specialists recommend for children:

> This [eight to 11] is the time for self-management, rather than external control, when standards of behaviour are developed by the child[108] ... 'Knowing', in the sense of being told, the difference between right and wrong, is not enough either: 'knowing' does not mean we will *choose* to do right, and true self-discipline means that we should be able to evaluate such things for ourselves.[109]

Therefore, children should be given a high degree of control and decision making power:

> Most parents reckon it's impossible to know 'who started it', so school yourself to let them sort things out for themselves[110] ... If you give an allowance or pay for chores, let children spend the money as they wish ... so that they can learn money management by trial and error and let your children help to choose their own clothes ... even if you think their taste often leaves a lot to be desired[111] ... There is no reason for children to make what parents would consider to be sensible choices about how they spend their money. Your children probably think you make some pretty weird choices in how you spend your money ... it is fair, in principle, that children should spend their own money however they choose ... if the chocolate bar they buy is revolting, then they have to live with their choice. If they wish they had not blown all their pocket money on yet another plastic figure, then that, unfortunately, is life[112] ... Children are more likely to learn the value of money and of a considered decision if you let them make some mistakes.[113]

But, clearly, this autonomy is illusory. Even at its highest, it exists only within strict boundaries:

> ... school yourself to let them sort things out for themselves, *unless you really think one child might injure the other.*[114]

> ... let your children help to choose their own clothes, *within sensible limits* ... let children spend the money as they wish (*except for junk food or anything else potentially harmful*)[115] ...

> ... [but] whilst children are your responsibility, you may wish to place limits on the principle of 'spend your own money how you like'. You may well say an absolute 'No' to an air rifle or to a pet snake. You may put a limit on the

108 Bullivant, A and Bullivant, B, *Helping Children at Home*, 1996, Northampton: Home and School Council, p 22.
109 *Op cit*, Hartley-Brewer, fn 37, p 164.
110 *Op cit*, Leach, fn 57, p 41.
111 Spock, B, *Parenting*, 1990, London: Penguin, p 138.
112 Lindon, J and Lindon, L, *Your Child from Five to Eleven*, 1993, London: Headway, p 73.
113 *Ibid*, p 74.
114 *Op cit*, Leach, fn 57, p 41 (emphasis added).
115 *Ibid*, Spock, p 138 (emphasis added).

number of sweets, especially if you have firm rules about when these can be eaten.[116]

More often than not, it exists only so long as the favoured decision is reached:

I have found the most satisfying way of dealing with my children's mistakes or unacceptable behaviour is to allow them to sort it out. When something is spilled, I hand them the cloth. If, rarely, one of them should hurt another child, I invite them to decide what they want to do about it. Invariably, they want to hug, and kiss and say sorry.[117]

And, in its most Machiavellian form, the autonomy actually exists in order to ensure that children reach the favoured decision:

By this time [eight to 11], a child should have some idea of money management, which can only be acquired successfully if he actually has some money to manage. Helping to draw up a shopping list, and checking the goods against a till receipt, will make money real. Parents can help him to plan the spending of his own money, reminding him of the things he has to cover: bus fares, dinners, comics, etc, depending on what it has been agreed that the money is to cover. The amount given to a child as 'spending money', should always be open to negotiation from time to time, though, once agreed as reasonable, the amount ought to be adhered to for a period. Weekly pressures should be resisted. One lesson children have to learn is that they cannot be given everything they want at the moment they want it and that they may need to 'save up' for some special purchase.[118]

... In one research project directed solely at the issue of tidying up, it was found that very few children co-operated at a parent's first request. Although some jumped to it when faced with 'negative parental action', the best strategy was one of 'non-coercive, positive action', such as getting down on one's hands and knees and tidying up oneself.[119]

It is hard not to hear echoes from the child rearing literature in the following quotation from Lord Mackay:

The best that I can do is to ensure that people get all the information available about the services on offer. You cannot compel them to take any particular service – that must be a matter for them – just as you cannot compel them to do other things that you might think was in their interest. They have to see to that themselves ... The emphasis should be that we provide them with all the information that they need, as effectively as we can, and then leave them to use it[120] ... it seems from experience that, in practice, it is not uncommon for parties to say no to mediation if asked in very general terms ... However, once parties have met with a mediator and had the opportunity to discuss what is

---

116 *Op cit*, Lindon and Lindon, fn 112, p 73.
117 Jackson, D, *Do Not Disturb: Benefits of Relaxed Parenting for You and Your Child*, 1993, London: Bloomsbury, pp 185–86.
118 *Op cit*, Bullivant and Bullivant, fn 108, p 22.
119 *Ibid*, Jackson, p 146.
120 *Hansard* 23 January 1996 Vol 568, HL, p 997.

involved and its benefits, they often change their minds and become willing at least to try one or two sessions.[121]

CONCLUSION

I have argued that the divorce reforms in Pt II of the Family Law Act 1996 are based on an illusory notion of autonomy, of the type that we associate with bringing up children. We are now in a position to return to the starting point and ask why the implementation of the reforms has been called into question. The Lord Chancellor announced that the preliminary research results of the pilot projects were 'disappointing'. What was it that was so 'disappointing'? It was that 39% of the 7,000 volunteers whose attendance at information meetings the pilot projects had surveyed said that they were more likely to see a solicitor than before, while only 7% went on to mediation and 13% to marriage counsellors.[122] But, as Richard Collier points out, this presentation was based on a highly selective reading of the results of the pilot projects: 'Other findings might equally have been highlighted to reveal a rather more mixed picture. For example, over 90% of attendees stated that they found the meetings useful.'[123] When dealing with children, however, the aim of providing information is to manipulate, rather than to inform, their decisions. We can now appreciate why Baroness Hollis, who was asked to explain the Government's decision to postpone implementation, put great store on the consideration that 'that was not the original intention of the meetings'.[124]

The similarity between the proposed divorce procedure and child rearing practice is no coincidence. Remarkably, the law has suggested a mechanism that compels competent adults to delay and think things over before making a decision.[125] Although we might expect our friends to counsel caution and deliberation, as competent adults, we expect the law to allow us to act and bear the consequences. Most child rearing manuals make use of logical punishments, where the parent deliberately sets up events so that children

---

121 *Hansard* 4 March 1996 Vol 570, HL, p 96. See Raitt, F, 'Domestic violence and divorce mediation' (1996) 18 JSWFL 11; Raitt, F, 'Informal justice and the ethics of mediating in abusive relationships' [1997] Juridical Rev 76 for discussion of the dangers that post-liberal autonomy holds for women in particular.

122 *Hansard* 17 June 1999 Col WA 39, HL; Lord Chancellor's Department, *Information Meetings and Associated Provisions within the Family Law Act 1996: Summary of Research in Progress*, 1999, London: HMSO, p vii.

123 *Op cit*, Collier, fn 30, p 266.

124 *Hansard* 6 July 1999 Col 781, HL.

125 See Richards, M, 'Private worlds and public intentions – the role of the State at divorce', in Bainham, A, Pearl, D and Pickford, R (eds), *Frontiers of Family Law*, 1995, Chichester: Wiley, p 15, for recognition that there is no reason to think that people generally do not think hard and struggle with alternatives before divorcing.

experience the consequences of their naughtiness. For example, the parent warns the child that, if he dawdles on the way home from the shops, he will miss his favourite television programme, and then the parent allows this to happen. For adults, the law had previously, and properly, allowed life to be its own logical punishment.

CHAPTER 6

ANXIOUS PARENTHOOD, THE VULNERABLE CHILD AND THE 'GOOD FATHER': REFLECTIONS ON THE LEGAL REGULATION OF THE RELATIONSHIP BETWEEN MEN AND CHILDREN

Richard Collier[1]

INTRODUCTION

This chapter presents an investigation of the way in which certain ideas about what is deemed to constitute a desirable relationship between men and children have become bound up within what I suggest has been a mutual reconfiguration of understandings of childhood and parenthood within the social conditions of late modernity.[2] What follows is an exploration of those forces which have produced a particular constellation of ideas about 'good fatherhood'. I shall argue that these are ideas which have been central to the broader debate presently taking place around the legal regulation of the relationship between men and children. The argument draws on a literature recently termed 'the new sociology of childhood' and family practices, although it does not seek to serve as a discussion of the general scope of this work *per se*. Nor does what follows present an overview of the multifarious ways in which law regulates the relationship between adults and children on a daily basis. It seeks, rather, to map out the way in which a circulation of discourses of childhood and parenthood are presently serving – within the field of the popular knowledge, the media and at the level of official government discourse – to constitute the relationship between men and children in some problematic and contradictory ways.

The argument is structured in three sections. The first seeks to locate contemporary debates about the relationship between men and children within the broader context of what I term the experience of 'anxious parenthood'. It seeks, in particular, to unpack the mutual interdiscursive reconceptualisation of childhood and parenthood central to this process. The second section shifts the focus to the social and legal *re*-construction of the idea of the 'good father' which has taken place over the past 15 years (at least). This is something which has had a number of effects on how perceptions of

---

1   I would like to thank Jo Bridgeman and Daniel Monk for their helpful comments on an earlier version of this chapter. Note: this article was written before the public protests which took place during the summer of 2000 following the decision of the British newspaper, *The News of the World*, to 'name and shame' known sex offenders in the aftermath of the murder of eight year old Sarah Payne.

2   See, further, Giddens, A, *Modernity and Self-Identity*, 1991, Cambridge: Polity.

risk and dangerousness in relation to family practices are understood to be gendered. The concluding remarks in the third section address the ways in which the shifting experiences of childhood and parenthood have themselves become bound up within a broader questioning of understandings of the relationship between men, children and the social. It is the aim of this chapter to surface something of the *contested* nature of the shifting interface between an (always, already) contingent nexus of ideas of (masculine) dangerousness, childhood (innocence) and understandings of social (dis)order.

THE ANXIOUS PARENT AND THE INNOCENT CHILD

Do you live in fear for your children? Send us your stories. We will be publishing a dossier later this week ... There cannot be a parent, faced with lengthy news reports about paedophilia, who does not ask themselves if they want to know that much detail or whether it is their duty to read on and face the terrible reality *for their children's sake.*[3]

Throughout the 1990s, a particular mythologising of locale informed constructions of Britain's 'dangerous places'[4] as communities and spaces associated with high profile crimes both by and against children. In so doing, some familiar conflations of ideas about family life and socio-economic privilege have pervaded understandings of respectability, security and public safety in accounting for the relationship between children and social order[5] (with the murder, in 1993, of two year old James Bulger by the 10 year old boys Robert Thompson and Jon Venables continuing to have an especial significance in this regard).[6] I have argued elsewhere[7] that, within this context, the ontological importance given to the idea of the heterosexual family as an institutional source for the preservation and reproduction of moral order has been central to the discursive construction of 'the social'. Yet, surrounding these broader debates about the relationship between children, crime and sociality has also been something else; a construction of the experience of parenthood as involving a perpetual – and, it would seem, an increasingly heightened – state of anxiety and vigilance.

To clarify the meaning of 'anxious parenthood'; within both press and governmental discourses throughout the 1990s, and across a number of contexts, parenthood has increasingly appeared as an ontologically insecure

---

3   (1998) *The Express*, 15 April.

4   Campbell, B, *Goliath: Britain's Dangerous Places*, 1993, London: Virago.

5   Scraton, P (ed), *'Childhood' in 'Crisis'?*, 1998, London: UCL; Collier, R, *Masculinities, Crime and Criminology*, 1998, London: Sage, Chapter 3.

6   See King, M, 'The James Bulger murder trial: moral dilemmas, and social solutions' (1995) 3 IJCR 167; Young, A, *Imagining Crime*, 1996, London: Sage; Morrison, B, *As If*, 1997, London: Granta.

7   *Ibid*, Collier.

state when seen in comparison with previous historical periods. A number of elements have underscored the construction of what are some specific parental anxieties. Taken together, these are now widely understood to be important – indeed, to be *inescapable* – elements of contemporary 'family life'.[8] Uniting each of these fears and anxieties is one central idea or theme; that of the 'loss of childhood' seen as resulting from a series of specific and general threats to the child. That is, pervading these constructions of (anxious) parenthood has been a notion of the child, and in particular of the *body* of the child,[9] as an essentially vulnerable and innocent entity. Implicitly, the *idea* of child*hood* itself appears as a pre-discursive ontological state in this depiction. It is something which once existed but is now said to have been 'stolen':[10]

> Childhood, as we once understood it, no longer exists: instead, there is only the vague unease of an extended adolescence that seems to start at five and finish not at all.[11]

Such a phantasm of childhood lost is by no means a new phenomenon. Yet, in some particular ways, it has come to encircle a range of recent concerns about parental anxiety. Parental anxiety is enmeshed with the notion of the loss of childhood most clearly perhaps by threats which are perceived as originating from outside the heterosexual family. Here, the domain of 'safe' parenting, the heterosexual familial sphere, is seen as that which is most threatened. In this context, the figure of the paedophile assumed an iconic significance during the 1990s in Britain, and elsewhere, as embodying a threat and risk which has, as is all too evident in the debates which have surrounded the release of known sex offenders from prison,[12] impacted both on concerns about the well being of specific children within particular localities, as well as on 'what is happening to' childhood, and 'responsible' parenthood more generally:

> Can there be a parent in the land who does not fear for their children? Fear to let them walk on the streets, play their games in the parks or stand too long at the school gate lest they get molested, mugged or abused.[13]

---

8   By 'inescapable' I mean the way in which such anxiety around the care and protection of the child is now widely seen to be an inevitable part of the experience of parenthood within contemporary social conditions.

9   See Bridgeman, Chapter 11, in this volume.

10   See, eg, 'Whatever happened to childhood?' (1999) *The Independent on Sunday*, 18 July.

11   (1998) *The Express*, 15 April.

12   Collier, R, 'The release of convicted sex offenders from prison: towards an ontology of the paedophile', in Alldrige, P and Brants, C (eds), *Personal Autonomy, the Private Sphere and the Criminal Law: A Comparative Study*, forthcoming, Oxford: Hart.

13   'Editorial' (1998) *The Express*, 15 April.

In August 1999, the 'Full Stop' media campaign conducted by the British charity the National Society for the Prevention of Cruelty to Children (NSPCC) met with considerable criticism precisely because it was seen as heightening deep rooted but, it was argued, unjustified parental anxieties about the dangers represented by the presence of the paedophile and paedophilia in society. If, as its detractors claimed, the NSPCC campaign encouraged over-protective behaviour on the part of the anxious parent,[14] it also fed into a perception that certain threats to the idea of childhood originate not so much from outside the family, but from within the familial domain itself; that is, more specifically, as a direct result of the very behaviour of the 'anxious parent'.

From this latter perspective, it is parental activity (or inactivity) which is called into question. Illustrations of the pervasiveness of concerns about such problematic parenting were not hard to find during the late 1990s. In October 1999, for example, it was announced that the very technology presently being used by the police to regulate the movements of known sex offenders following their release from prison, an electronic tagging system, would itself be used on a trial basis by a major supermarket chain in Britain. The aim, it was said, was to protect children and to reassure the fears of parents who enter its stores. The rather cruel irony of such a development was not lost on those who had for some time expressed concerns about the ways in which it is now increasingly parents themselves who are becoming the 'unwitting jailers' of their children. Parents are simultaneously seen as responsible for the policing and surveillance of their children (in the form, for example, of video links with schools or nurseries, where they can see what they are up to) and as being constituted as potentially irresponsible and, importantly, legally liable[15] when such surveillance is seen to fail: 'Britain is becoming a generation of battery children ... Parents frightened of crime are keeping youngsters cooped up like hens for their own safety.'[16] At the same time, such *over*-protection on the part of parents – 'making their kids too soft to survive' – has been seen as resulting not just in a diminution in children's interactive skills with adults, but also in a marked reduction in the temporal and spatial parameters of children's play. This question of children's play or, more accurately, the regulation and policing of the body of the child in ostensibly public space, has assumed an increasing significance within these debates about childhood.[17] Organisations such as the Children's Society, the Children's Play Council and

---

14 (1999) *The Observer*, 8 August.

15 See, further, Gelsthorpe, L, 'Youth crime and parental responsibility', in Bainham, A, Day-Sclater, S, Bainham, A and Richards, M (eds), *What is a Parent? A Socio-Legal Analysis*, 1999, Oxford: Hart, p 217.

16 (1998) *The Express*, 15 April.

17 See Monk, Chapter 10, in this volume.

the Early Years Network have each produced initiatives in recent years explicitly designed to promote play and to highlight the extent and potentially damaging psychological effects of parental fears and anxieties focused on the problem of 'stranger danger' (the danger epitomised by the figure of the paedophile).[18] Yet, far from protecting children, as a report by the Mental Health Foundation concluded, the result of such excessive parental restrictions on unsupervised play has been rising levels of stress and other serious psychological problems in the very children whom the measures were designed to protect.[19] Each of these issues about the surveillance, control and spatial regulation of the body of the child have combined with broader concerns about the question of 'what is happening' to childhood to some powerful, and at times contradictory, political effects. A recurring theme has been a belief that, relative to earlier historical periods,[20] children are now increasingly 'cut off' from the communities in which they live. As a result of this, it has been argued, they now experience greater pressures to become involved in crime, to face poverty by living in a lone parent household, to eat unhealthy food[21] or, indeed, to then have to educationally succeed[22] in order to obtain the very credentials which might reduce such risks in the first place!

It is possible, at this stage, to make a number of points. First, the 'anxious parent' being constructed in these debates is arguably very much a middle class (and, indeed, white) parent. Many of the concerns about childhood and child development being presented within the anxious parent discourse are mediated by questions of socio-economic and ethnic positioning. Questions of child health, food intake, the spatial parameters of play, cultural identification, educational attainment, access to leisure, and so forth, do not necessarily play out the same way for all sections of the population. Indeed, the very debate is premised on certain assumptions of (relative) affluence and of a particular relationship to paid employment existing within the household (the unemployed parent is curiously invisible in these debates). In a number of respects, these concerns can also be seen to be linked to parental age changes, with older parents being assumed to experience anxiety and responsibility in a particularly acute way.

Secondly, and related to the above, the underlying good parent(al) ideal – the parent who will, or should, act in certain ways in certain circumstances – is implicitly contrasted with a notion of the 'bad' parent. For example, and notwithstanding the existence of a now well established and persuasive

---

18 'NSPCC accused of fuelling parents fears' (1999) *The Guardian*, 9 August; 'Lack of risk in play damaging children' (1999) *The Guardian*, 24 June.

19 Mental Health Foundation, *Too Safe For Their Own Good*, 1999, London.

20 'Children experience the pros and cons of modern life' (1999) *The Guardian*, 14 January.

21 'Feeding parental fears' (1999) *The Guardian*, 29 July.

22 'Play is out, early learning is in' (1999) *The Guardian*, 23 June.

academic critique, the legacy of the concept of the underclass would appear ideologically alive and well in the New Labour Government's representation of 'bad' parents as requiring disciplining, sanction and (re)education (as embodied particularly clearly in the provisions of the Crime and Disorder Act 1998).[23] Of course, such a disciplining of social life via the normative regulation of family practices has historically taken different forms across different populations, mediated notably by the contingencies of youth, class, race and ethnicity. Not all families have been deemed 'suitable' or 'respectable' in the same way, with a disproportionate number of working class, black and lone parent families historically attracting State intervention, scorn and blame.

Yet, thirdly, and to bring together these points, of direct relevance to my concern in this chapter is the fact that the phenomenon of anxious parenthood has itself been *gendered* in some particular ways across diverse areas and contexts. In relation to crime, for example, ideas of motherhood and fatherhood continue to be gendered in ways dependent on ontological presuppositions of sexual difference and familial function. The good father and good mother continue to be seen as having different, albeit overlapping, roles in inculcating discipline and order in their children, with the still culturally resonant anxious/over-attentive mother being ascribed blame and responsibility for youthful criminality.[24] At the same time, the figure of the 'feckless' irresponsible father, the 'deadbeat' dad, has become increasingly visible within law and order debates, albeit in a way that has sidestepped fundamental questions about what it means to speak of paternal 'presence' in the first place.[25] In terms of the broader cultural constructions and experience of parental anxieties, an ongoing, high profile debate about the impact of working parents on the psychological and educational well being of children has clearly been predicated on the differential positioning of women and men as mothers and fathers. This dominant research paradigm has constituted 'working mothers' and 'working fathers' as socially problematic in some very different ways.

My argument at this stage, in short, is that a number of concerns have coalesced around the idea that it is *parenthood* itself, as well as childhood, which is now understood to be an increasingly problematic and fraught social experience. The experience of 'being a parent' has become, for both women and men (although, as we shall see, in different ways), emblematic of those forces of fragmentation, disaffection and individualisation widely seen to have marked the social conditions of late modern advanced capitalist societies. It is,

23 *Op cit*, Gelsthorpe, fn 15.

24 On representations of motherhood in the context of the murder of James Bulger see, further, *op cit*, Young, fn 6.

25 See, further, Morgan, D, 'The "family man": a contradiction in terms?', Fifth Jacqueline Burgoyne Memorial Lecture, February 1994, Sheffield: Sheffield Hallam University.

I recognise, important on one level not to overestimate how new this development is in the way in which it concerns anxieties relating to crime. Addressing the fear of crime has, of course, historically long involved the State in a balancing of individual rights with questions of public protection. However, the power of any particular discursive construction (say, that of the anxious or good parent) is such that, if it has not (and cannot) been owned by a political executive, then it can most certainly be shaped by different political rationalities as an object amenable to programmatic intervention. With this in mind, it is possible to see the political *effects* to which a particular representation of anxious parenthood and familial responsibility is presently being put as having involved not only the development of a distinct moral agenda around notions of (privatised) family life, but also no less than the promotion – indeed, an explicit attempt to *produce* – a particular subject; that of the good parent as a 'responsible citizen'.

Nowhere is this normative reconstruction of parental subjectivity clearer than in relation to contemporary criminal justice and family policy. Indeed, the notion of the good parent as a responsible citizen has been bound up, more generally, within what has been termed 'third way' political thought, notably in relation to the idea of the new democratic family.[26] This theme has traversed such diverse legislative provisions as the parenting orders and youth crime provisions contained within the Crime and Disorder Act 1998[27] and the notion of the good (divorcing) parent implicit in the Family Law Act 1996.[28] With regard to the latter, the legal promotion of the harmonious (as possible) divorce, a particular idea of parental responsibility can be seen as being constituted in the context of the promotion of a social subject who will, in certain instances, be deemed to be in need of training by a range of 'experts' who will themselves, in various ways, counsel, encourage and assist in the promotion of good parenting practice. The State is directly involved in the administrative regulation of this good parent(hood), with local authorities, State agencies and voluntary groups working together to make parents 'meet their responsibilities', whether it is – to take recent examples – in encouraging them to balance the competing demands of work and family life;[29] in preventing crime; in divorcing in an (economically) responsible manner; or, more generally, in the provision of guidance as to what constitutes 'good'

26 Giddens, A, *The Third Way*, Cambridge: Polity.

27 *Op cit*, Gelsthorpe, fn 15.

28 See Collier, R, 'The dashing of a "liberal dream"? The information meeting, the "new family" and the limits of law' (1999) 11(3) CFLQ 257; Reece, Chapter 5 and Barnett, Chapter 7, in this volume.

29 Collier, R, 'Feminising the workplace? (Re)constructing the "good parent" in employment law and family policy', in Morris, A and O'Donnell, T (eds), *Feminist Perspectives on Employment Law*, 1999, London: Cavendish Publishing, pp 161–81.

parenting practice.[30] Importantly, underscoring this normative reconstruction of parenthood is a social subject conceptualised as an individual, not so much one in whom needs are to be met and nurtured, but an individual as a consumer, an individual(ised) subject in whom personal choices must be cultivated, a personal self fulfilled and a quality of life maximised. Parenthood can be seen as just one, albeit significant, part of such a project of the self. In this normative reconstruction it is not simply a matter of the experience of parenthood having become fraught with certain tensions and contradictions. The very experience of anxious parenthood itself appears as a prerequisite for a governmental strategy based on a normative reconstruction of what is deemed to be desirable familial practice. In such a context, it is no wonder that parenthood can be seen as having become a particularly problematic and ontologically significant part of late modern projects of the self. It is important not to underestimate the psychosocial resonances of the experience of becoming, the desire to become, or, indeed, to not become, a parent in terms of the social responsibilities it is seen as demanding, the rewards it is seen as entailing and the anxieties which it is seen as (inevitably) attending. Yet a number of questions remain about this question of the *gendering* of anxious parenthood. More specifically, how does it relate to perceptions of the changing relationship between men and children?

To explore these issues, I first examine what has been termed the 'new sociology of childhood'. This recent work, which is centrally concerned with the changing concept of childhood within the social conditions of late modernity, has shed some interesting light on understandings of how social change impacts on family practices, and how family practices themselves impact on social change.[31] Secondly, in the subsequent section, I consider those writings on governmentality, risk and subjectivity which have sought to explore the construction of social subjects at particular moments in history.

Childhood(s) lost

From their post-Enlightenment positioning as unequivocal sources of love, the new sociological accounts of childhood have presented the child within late modern cultural configurations as signifying both a 'nostalgia' for innocence lost,[32] as discussed above, and also, notably in the form of the criminality of

---

30 Note, eg, the formation of the National Family and Planning Institute and plans to enhance the role of health visitors in the provision of family support.

31 James, A, Jenks, C and Prout, A, *Theorising Childhood*, 1998, Cambridge: Polity; James, A and Prout, A (eds), *Constructing and Reconstructing Childhood*, 1997, London: Falmer; Jenks, C, *Childhood*, 1996, London: Routledge; Qvortrup, J, 'Childhood and modern society: a paradoxical relationship?', in Brannen, J and O'Brien, M (eds), *Childhood and Parenthood*, 1995, London: Institute of Education.

32 Jenks, C, 'The post-modern child', in Brannen, J and O'Brien, M (eds), *Children in Families: Research and Policy*, 1996, London: Falmer.

(largely male)[33] youth, a heightened sense of social breakdown and moral dislocation.[34] Chris Jenks has suggested that the figure of the child has come to assume a particular significance across discourses concerned with the maintenance and security of the social bond.[35] Indeed, it is this concept of the child which has been identified as the site for the relocation of a number of discourses concerned with questions of stability, integration and the maintenance of sociality. What is taking place at present, it has been argued, is no less than a fracturing and reforming of the socially constructed childhood of modernity. Whereas children used to cling to us for guidance into their/our futures, now we, the adults, in Jenks' words:

> ... cling to them for 'nostalgic' groundings because such change is both intolerable and disorienting for us. They are lover, spouse, friend, workmate and, at a different level, *symbolic representations for society itself* ... We need children as the sustainable, reliable, trustworthy, now outmoded treasury of social sentiments that they have come to represent. Our 'nostalgia' for their essence is part of a complex, late modern rearguard attempt at the resolution of the contradictory demands of the constant re-evaluation of value with the pronouncement of social identity.[36]

In contrast to the highly visible threats to the innocence of childhood discussed above, many of which continue to be routinely depicted as embodying a pre-modern sense of 'evil' (this is particularly clear in relation to the categories of the paedophile and the child killer, for example), the post-modern child appears fixed as permanent and dependable, the incarnation of a nostalgic vision of childhood which, Jenks argues, has now come to preserve no less than the meta-narrative of society itself.[37] Of course, if it is the case that the innocence of the child should be seen as having grounded a sense of sociality at a time of otherwise intolerable and disorientating change, it is no wonder that the abuse and destruction of such innocence should be seen to strike so powerfully at the remaining vestiges of the social bond; nor that what should then result should be more general expressions of collective pain at the loss of social identity per se.[38] This is something which has pervaded recent understandings of phenomena such as the sexual abuse of children and, with a particularly heightened symbolic power and, it would seem, frequency across societies, the sudden and very public deaths of children (the murders of children at Dunblane Primary School in Scotland and Columbine High School

---

33   Although see Worrall, Chapter 10, in this volume, for an analysis of young women and crime.

34   *Op cit*, Collier, fn 5, especially Chapter 3.

35   *Op cit*, Jenks, fn 31.

36   *Op cit*, Jenks, fn 31, pp 20–21 (emphasis added).

37   *Op cit*, Jenks, fn 31, p 20.

38   *Op cit*, Jenks, fn 31.

in the US, as well as elsewhere, serving as cases in point).[39] In short, it is no wonder that what should surface in the aftermath of such events should be a concern with the loss of childhood itself.

It is interesting how, within this process charted by new sociologies of childhood, it has largely been in terms of the issue of anxious parenthood that a dominant, overarching explanatory framework has been constructed. Importantly and revealingly, however, any question of the *gendering* either of anxious parenthood itself or of these crimes – or, indeed, of the fact that it is predominantly, though not exclusively, the actions of *men* which constitutes the source of the majority of those threats to children within the anxious parent discourse – is a matter which tends to be routinely effaced. That is, any consideration of the crimes of men *as men* continues to be rare,[40] notwithstanding the recent emergence of academic criminology's 'masculinity turn'. Before discussing this question, it is necessary to explore further how a particular kind of parental subjectivity has been conceptualised within this process and, in particular, what this means for the shifting regulation of the relationship between men and children, whether in relation to the 'private' (familial) or the 'public' domain.

RETHINKING THE MEN-CHILD RELATIONSHIP: FATHERHOOD, RISK AND THE FEAR OF CRIME

The increasing discursive visibility of anxious parenthood is revealing not just of changes around the concept of childhood, as discussed above, but also of some broader developments in and around understandings of family, the fear of crime and social change. Encircling questions of parental fear and childhood innocence, as outlined above, has been an entwining of some specific and general threats to the child with a heightened parental concern in the context of more general anxieties now associated with the fear of crime in contemporary society. Hollway and Jefferson argue that these are fears which connect not just to the realities of becoming the victim of any specific crime or threat.[41] Rather, they relate to broader historical, socio-political formations in which questions of social order and control – and the very meaning and lived experience of crime and the fear of crime – have each been socially and politically constructed within an overall context of risk management.[42] Much

---

39 See, further, Collier, R, 'After Dunblane: crime, corporeality and the (hetero)sexing of the bodies of men' (1997) 24(2) JLS 177.

40 See, further, Newburn, T and Stanko, EA (eds), *Just Boys Doing Business? Men, Masculinities and Crime*, 1994, London: Routledge; *op cit*, Collier, fn 5.

41 Hollway, W and Jefferson, T, 'The risk society in an age of anxiety: situating fear of crime' (1997) 48(2) Br J Soc 255, p 256.

42 *Ibid*, p 257.

criminological literature on the fear of crime has tended to be pitched largely at a descriptive, empirical level.[43] Yet the idea that risk may be managed or, more specifically, regulated (by appropriate use of legal sanction) is itself, I would suggest, of some use in seeking to make sense of the kinds of concerns which are presently being expressed within the ostensibly gender neutral discourse of anxious parenthood.

Fear is here conceptualised as 'not simply a quantity, of which one possesses larger or smaller amounts: rather it is *a mode of perception*, even perhaps a constitutive feature of personal identity'.[44] Following Beck's influential depiction of risk as a central analytic tool in understanding ways of dealing with the hazards and insecurities introduced by modernity and late modernity,[45] and in seeing risk itself as being fundamentally 'written into' the social forms of contemporary capitalist societies, it is from within this perspective of risk management that the transformations 'of the routines of everyday life and the pleasures that they have brought' can be seen to have created new uncertainties and fears.[46] These are uncertainties, importantly, in which some particular and, I shall argue, *gendered* ideas of dangerousness have been injected into the social fabric of society in ways which have 'continued to produce a series of infections of varying degrees of intensity'.[47] The iconic figure of the paedophile and the threat which *he* is seen as representing to the child can be seen as illustrative of this point.

The paedophile and the 'dangerous masculine'

The risks focused on in the fear of crime discourse have tended 'to have had individual identifiable victims and individual identifiable offenders which makes them knowable'.[48] Yet many of the threats to childhood presently being articulated within the discourse of anxious parenthood constitute risks which are, at once, both 'knowable' and 'unknowable'. With regard to the 'unknowable', a figure such as the paedophile appears as a particularly powerful (and, in terms of criminal justice policy, undeniably influential) phenomenon in the threat that it (he) is seen as posing to the body of the child and to the idea of childhood. The paed*ophilia* this man is seen as embodying

---

43 Sparks, R, 'Reason and unrealism in "left realism": some problems in the constitution of fear of crime', in Matthews, R and Young, J (eds), *Issues in Realist Criminology*, 1992, London: Sage; *op cit*, Hollway and Jefferson, fn 41.

44 *Ibid,* Sparks, p 14 (emphasis added).

45 Beck, U, *The Risk Society*, 1992, London: Sage.

46 Pratt, J, *Governing the Dangerous*, 1997, Sydney: Federation, p 150.

47 *Ibid,* p 3.

48 *Op cit*, Hollway and Jefferson, fn 41, p 260 (emphasis in original).

appears ubiquitous, potentially penetrating all spheres of life,[49] via the internet,[50] into the home, the children's bedroom, the school,[51] the charity and the voluntary organisation[52] and other spaces (constituted as 'safe'). In relation to the legal regulation of cyberspace and the laws of international relations concerning sex tourism,[53] this is a public space which itself has encouraged the 'promenade' of bodies which has created such a 'suburban criminal [who] blends in with the environment': 'We have convinced ourselves that "they" are everywhere, in scout troops, schools, any institution involving children.'[54] The 'criminal life support system' of a figure such as the paedophile may be less visible than for other offenders, but it is, arguably, one which would appear to threaten most acutely the basic trust which residents feel for others who live in their (our?) community. As such, the paedophile embodies a 'downside' of urban life in a world in which strangers are encountered on public streets and in places which, increasingly, pose profound and unsettling questions about the possible dangers and personal harms that they might represent.[55] Importantly, the paedophile embodies a threat which transcends the traditional boundaries of family, community and State in some particularly disturbing ways: where, ultimately, is there left that might be called 'safe'? Whilst attempts may be made to expunge the body of the paedophile from society, in the form of expulsion, for example, from the local community into which he is to be introduced on his release from prison,[56] the danger and risk represented by paedophilia (the threat he is seen as embodying) appears, in short, much more evasive, powerful and threatening, a hazard which cannot be confined to any particular time, space or locale in the danger it poses for the well being of children and the vigilance it calls for on the part of adults.

---

49 A point encapsulated in headlines such as 'Nightmare on *Any* Street' (1997) *The Guardian*, 10 June (emphasis added).

50 An issue which received considerable attention following a series of arrests in September 1998 in Britain, the US, Germany, Portugal, Italy, Australia, Austria, Belgium, Finland, France, Norway and Sweden, resulting from the (chance) police discovery of the 'Wonderland Club'. The technological sophistication of this child pornography group was described as shocking and led to calls for greater regulation of internet usage and provision.

51 In relation to which it has been claimed by both teachers and child protection experts that, during the 1990s, there was an increase in the numbers of children sexually abusing their classmates, a problem being 'swept under the carpet' by schools: 'Schools ignoring classroom sex abuse' (1999) *The Independent*, 26 June.

52 In July 1999, the National Criminal Intelligence Service reported evidence that paedophiles were joining aid agencies in order to facilitate access to children overseas, stating that the problem has the potential to become as serious as that of 'sex tourism': 'Paedophiles infiltrate aid charities' (1999) *The Guardian*, 22 July.

53 'Child sex tourists escape UK law' (1998) *The Independent*, 13 July.

54 Marr, A, 'The paedophile who has our imagination' (1998) *The Independent*, 9 April.

55 See Karp, D, Stone, G and Yoeb, W, *Being Urban: A Sociology of City Life*, 1991, New York: Praeger.

56 *Op cit*, Collier, fn 12.

The case of the paedophile is taken here as illustrative of the ways in which the spatiality of the threat to the idea of childhood has been bound up within the broader socio-political reconstruction of parenthood presently taking place in the social conditions of late modernity. It also has a direct bearing, importantly, on the way in which this has, throughout, been a gendered phenomenon which has, as I have suggested, positioned men and women in some very different ways. At the present moment complex social relations are transforming the ways in which parenthood is conceptualised, ways which cannot be confined to such familiar and symbolic foci of public concern and anxiety such as the category of 'youth'. Rather, and turning to focus on the question of the relationship between *men* and children, what is of particular significance at the present moment is how understandings of what are seen to constitute desirable healthy relationships between men and children are themselves being transformed. And this is taking place within a context in which there exists, simultaneously, a continuing depiction of parenthood as a distinctly *gendered* experience – in the form, for example, of the historically established and familiar ontologies of motherhood and fatherhood – and, also, in marked contrast, the increasing representation of parenthood in terms of gender neutrality, as a *gender neutral* phenomenon.

Making the 'father figure': fatherhood and gender neutrality

Nowhere is this tension between gendered and gender neutral conceptualisations of parenthood clearer, perhaps, than in the debates which presently encircle legislative interventions and judicial decisions in the field of child and family law. However, it is a tension which is all too evident in – for, indeed, it has become central to – the contestations which are presently taking place around the meaning of fatherhood across a range of debates about government policies in Britain concerned with the relationship between men, parenthood and children.[57] The New Labour Government has embraced some specific and targeted initiatives aimed explicitly at the promotion of 'active parenting' on the part of men. This has involved a series of measures based on an explicit recognition of the need to change the behaviour of men as fathers in ways which are seen to be more in keeping with the social, cultural, ethical, political and economic imperatives of the 21st century. Implicitly, there has been a conceptualisation – however ill thought out and vague it may be at times – of there being a 'men problem' in the first place. It is an issue which pervades such diverse concerns as the search for a 'balance' between 'work and family life' and the promotion of equal opportunity and equality in the

---

57 See, eg, Lord Chancellor's Department, *Court Procedures for the Determination of Paternity: The Law on Parental Responsibility for Unmarried Fathers – Consultation Paper, 1998*, London: HMSO; Burgess, A and Ruxton, S, *Men and Their Children: Proposals for Public Policy*, 1996, London: Institute for Public Policy Research.

workplace and the family. It is also an issue which has coalesced around, and become of crucial importance in, consideration of how the concept of fatherhood is presently being transformed by complex social shifts resulting from changing practices of economic and social (re)production.

To clarify: over the past 20 years, though arguably, with a heightened resonance during the 1990s, a range of economic, cultural and technological changes (not least around new reproductive practices)[58] have been widely interpreted as bringing about new adaptations, new forms of attachment and new ways in which subjective commitments are mobilised towards modes of belonging and integration such as legal marriage and the heterosexual family. In this process there has occurred a widespread reconsideration of the place of men within the family in which the status, position and very meaning of the father and fatherhood has assumed a central role. Of course, any discussion of the relationship between men and children cannot be confined to a question of fatherhood. Nonetheless, an increasingly *politicised* debate about the legal status, rights and responsibilities of fathers has been central to, and bound up within, the broader shifts around understandings of parenthood and childhood discussed above. In a context in which ideas about social life traditionally central to notions of normative gender roles are increasingly being contested and disengaged from hitherto 'categories of givens', ideas about what constitutes the gender neutral 'good parent' have become issues about much more than historically familiar questions of the disciplining, regulation and surveillance of the 'good enough' mother.[59] They have also involved the problematising of the meaning of the 'good father' with the result that, and without overstating the case, the consideration of the cultural and legal meanings, responsibilities and experience of fatherhood has emerged as a major political conversation. The positioning of the concepts of both fatherhood and parenthood within these cultural and legal discourses is, however, far from straightforward and has notably involved some frequently contradictory narratives.

On the one hand, the father figure continues to be situated within dominant discourses as a major guarantor of both social and familial order. The practices associated with fathering remain, in particular, firmly within the context of conventional (heterosexual) masculine behaviour. The father continues to be located as, *a priori*, being 'within' rather than 'outside' society in the way in which men's parenting practices continue to be constituted via the making of powerful and still resonant assumptions about paternal

---

58 See Roberts, Chapter 4, in this volume.

59 Fineman, M, *The Neutered Mother, the Sexual Family and Other Twentieth Century Tragedies*, 1995, New York: Routledge; Diduck, A, 'In search of the feminist good mother' (1998) 7(1) SLS 129; Wallbank, J, 'The campaign for change of the Child Support Act 1991: reconstituting the "absent" father' (1997) 6(2) SLS 191.

presence/absence, heterosexual marriage, economic status, the meaning of emotionality and the nature of sexual difference. It is taken as axiomatic, for example, that a 'family man's' primary commitment and identification will be, and should be, with paid employment rather than full time child care and that being a father will involve a temporal and spatial trade off between the domains of work and family. In terms of the *legal* subject, ideas of the 'good father' have been constituted historically through reference to some socially and economically specific ideas of the respectable masculine and sexual propriety, ideas which have their roots in ostensibly archaic notions of paternal authority (not least, of course, in the perception of the father and fatherhood as a principal guarantor of social cohesion).[60] The discursive production of such a normative masculine familial subject has, in turn, historically served to actively participate in the construction of heterosexual men as a category more generally, involving a way of seeing sexual difference, sexuality and gender which has been constructed hegemonically through the mobilisation and consolidation of various practices and, of course, the exclusion of others. In terms of the *lived experience* of parenting as a sexed (as different) phenomenon, family practices would appear, as numerous empirical studies have suggested, to frequently involve some distinct and differential experiences, routines and obligations for women and men.[61] Thus, whether it is in relation to the economic demands of work, the cultural pull of the homosocial or the well documented psychological distancing which has traditionally been associated with ideas of heterosexual masculinity within Western cultures, what appears from this perspective is a father figure marked by a sense of paternal *absence* rather than presence in the family. In short, a range of economic, cultural and legal discourses undoubtedly continue to position men as social agents who, if not effectively free, are at least being 'dissociated' in a number of important respects from the emotional and material encumbrances in relation to children which mark out understandings of heterosexual family life.

However, it is important to recognise not just those demographic changes which are taking place in and around men's and women's parenting practices, but also how ideas of what constitutes good fatherhood are themselves being transformed and challenged by changes taking place within ideas of parenthood, childhood and the broader redefinitions of the parameters of the family. It is possible to make a number of points in this regard.

First, the gender neutral model of parenting underscoring contemporary family and criminal justice policy has 'cut off' a number of the traditionally gender specific attributes of parenting from the sexed specificity of an individual man or woman's presence in constituting understandings of family

---

60 Collier, R, *Masculinity, Law and the Family*, 1995, London: Routledge; *op cit*, Wallbank, fn 59.

61 See, eg, Smart, C and Neale, B, *Family Fragments*, 1999, Cambridge: Polity.

practices. At the risk of simplifying, it is now assumed that men can and do 'parent' just as well as women. Accordingly, and as we have seen, it is a 'good thing' to promote active fathering by bringing men into the family. This gender neutral parenting ideal may well stand in a problematic relationship to what research suggests is actually *happening* in family practices 'on the ground', as it were. It has nonetheless served to reposition the father in some far reaching ways.

Secondly, the notion of active and gender neutral parenting on the part of men has served, in the context of a large scale family restructuring away from legal marriage, to displace the combination of an ontology of sexual difference, hierarchy and normative heterosexuality – the trinity historically central to the discursive constitution of father-presence as socially desirable in the first place.[62] In so doing, the door has been opened to readings of 'transformations of intimacy' which *cannot* now be confined to changing contours of heterosexuality and which, importantly, embrace forms of 'confluent love' which do not have to be heterosexual.[63] The 'space' of the heterosexual family is thus itself being fractured and reformed in a process in which a different kind of space, open to new possibilities and new familial subjects, is being constituted.[64]

The question remains however, without this epistemologically foundational father figure, without the 'family man' whose presence has historically, both legally and culturally, constituted the heterosexual family as socially normative entity (and we need think only of continuing stigmatising representations of lone motherhood to see how culturally and legally resonant this has been), what happens to understandings of the heterosexual family as a discursively 'safe space'? What happens, in particular, when the good father of modernity, as it were, is recast as a very different kind of being? Not *simply* as one who is failing to spend enough time with his children, one who is failing to 'pull his weight' domestically, someone whose social behaviour, whether in the family or in work, is widely seen to be out of step with the economic and ethical imperatives of the day (and each of the above areas, it is to be remembered, have been the subject of recent legislative intervention); but, also, as a man who is himself increasingly seen as a potentially *dangerous* familial figure in the first place; a man who, far from signifying safety and protection, would appear from empirical research and from the testimonies of women and children to so often be the source of dangers to and anxieties concerning 'familial' well being.

---

62 *Op cit*, Collier, fn 60.
63 Giddens, A, *The Transformations of Intimacy*, 1992, Cambridge: Polity.
64 Note, eg, *Fitzpatrick v Sterling Housing Association Ltd* (1999) *The Times*, 2 November.

None of this is to overstate the empirical reality of men's violence. It is to ask what a reconsideration of men's and women's 'everyday' gendered lives, particularly in terms of the material and emotional dependencies which surround child care (and, increasingly, elder care), means for developing an understanding of the ways in which perceived threats to the child and the idea of childhood should be interpreted not as issues of the changing relationship between men and children, but in terms of a dominant (degendered) discourse of anxious parenthood. And why, moreover, it should be around men's and women's differential relationships to/with *children* that these sexed *as different* experiences of heterosexual relationships should presently surface in such powerful, contested and politicised ways.

Reconfiguring the spatiality of 'masculine risk'

Drawing on the impact of feminisms, it is via this discourse of the 'dangerous father' that traditional ideas of good fatherhood have come under increasing critical scrutiny in recent years. Although of an arguably ambiguous status in a number of respects,[65] the idea that the father figure might himself be a dangerous presence in the lives of children, and constitute a particular kind of (gendered) threat (notably in the form of domestic violence and sexual abuse), has secured a strong cultural resonance in the light of feminism. This 'dangerous father' now figures prominently across a range of cultural artefacts (for example, in talk shows, newspaper and magazine articles, television dramas, popular novels and films). Furthermore, it is around this idea of dangerous fatherhood that the broader issue of 'how men are' with children has, more generally, fed into debates about the care and protection of children. In this process, issues have been raised about what is deemed to constitute the normative masculine which transcend the parameters of the public and private domains. They involve, importantly, questions about the relationship between men and children which directly address the experience of anxious parenthood. For example, how are understandings of the dangers that men can and do constitute to children to be perceived and guarded against? What is now considered to be a safe/dangerous male presence in the lives of children? How is 'masculine risk' to be assessed? What are the acceptable and unacceptable boundaries of physical intimacy between men and children, whether in the family or in public institutions/settings?[66] In what circumstances is such contact permissible or to be encouraged?[67]

---

65 By this I mean that dominant constructions of fatherhood continue, in a number of ways, to make certain assumptions about what are presumed to be, in all instances, the 'natural' qualities of father love. This has been particularly evident in cases where men have killed members of their families and then themselves, where media depictions are commonplace of men 'who loved too much'.

66 See, eg, 'British men fear to touch children' (1999) *The Observer*, 25 July.

67 See *op cit*, Morrison, fn 6, pp 180–86.

Each of the above, although frequently not spoken of, are questions central to conversations about the legal regulation of child welfare across diverse domains. Perhaps most visibly, such concerns have figured prominently in relation to debates about men in institutional contexts such as the playgroup, the nursery and the primary school. These are locations where the very presence of men has been discursively positioned as potentially, if not inherently, problematic in particular contexts.[68] Hitherto subjugated knowledges are presently articulating the point that 'strangers' have historically been a significant problem in the lives of many young men and women in terms of sexual abuse in locations such as the youth club, the school, the church, children's homes and so forth.[69] Yet it is nonetheless *within* the family and the familial domain that the rupture between men and children is being most rigorously and pervasively experienced and where such issues have had their greatest resonance in questioning notions of the normative masculine. And it is here that they can be seen as most profoundly disturbing and challenging understandings and assumptions about the social good of a dominant conceptualisation of gender neutral parenting.

At the very moment when formal gender neutrality is now in the ascendant, and when men are increasingly being brought into the heterosexual family as both 'good fathers' and 'good workers',[70] the relationship between adults and children itself has become a contested terrain. And what appear to be contestations around childhood are routinely reformed as questions about the (re)constitution of social *per se*, as a mutually constituted reconfiguration of the meanings of both childhood and parenthood, has rendered problematic precisely that which had hitherto been unspoken, natural, inviolable and unquestioned within familial ideology: the relationship between men and children within the heterosexual(ised) family. One consequence of disturbing the normative gendering process of men and women as familial social subjects in the way attempted in this chapter (what does it mean to be a good mother or a good father?) has been a rethinking and politicisation of a gendered ideology of 'care' which has itself historically played out differently for men and women. Furthermore, these issues about the relationship between men and children cannot be confined to a discourse of the father*less* family, although father absence continues to be associated

---

68 Skelton, C, 'Sex, male teachers and young children' (1994) 6(1) Gender and Education 87.

69 In Britain, growing evidence of abuse in State run children's homes, going back at least 20 years, prompted the inquiry by Sir William Utting. The subsequent Report, published in 1997, chronicles accounts of widespread abuse: (1997) *The Independent*, 20 November; 'Care system fails children' (1997) *The Guardian*, 20 November; Davies, N, 'Public figures named in paedophile ring' (1997) *The Guardian*, 15 October. Note, also, 'Priest jailed for sexual abuse of boys' (1998) *The Guardian*, 1 May; 'Nuns abused hundreds of children' (1998) *The Independent on Sunday*, 16 August.

70 *Op cit*, Collier, fn 29.

with social breakdown and atrophy far more than it is seen to signify any positive opportunity on the part of the lone mother. Ultimately, given the centrality of the figure of the child to the familial(ised) experience of material and emotional dependencies which surround heterosexual relating more generally, it is unsurprising that it should be in and around the dangers associated with men's physical presence/proximity to the body of the child that the relationship between men and children should have become such a problematic issue. For in a context in which 'the enhanced interest in men's relationship to children and of men in children' grows,[71] and where the construction of (hetero)masculinities are being subjected to increasing critical scrutiny within both the academic and popular discourse, the iconic status of the child has become the disputed territory around which a more general assessment of the contribution of men to the social is taking place. In other words, it is in the light of these *adult* investments, not least the emotional dependence of parents upon children, that the various 'betrayals' of the child encapsulated in the experience of anxious parenthood would now appear to be so deeply felt.

CONCLUSION

Is a father allowed to miss his children *physically*? Should I feel guilty that I do?[72]

By way of conclusion, I will make three broad comments. First, the gendered concepts of motherhood and fatherhood are not (and have never been) uncontested categories in law. Their 'explanation' does not reside in pre-determined categories of identity and experience. Rather, such categories can themselves be seen as sites of negotiation, contestation and reconstruction. Each has the potential to be mobilised in such a way as to create, as Segal has argued in relation to heterosexuality,[73] a space for a politics of pleasure and desire as much as, or as well as, a politics of oppression. The contested and ideological nature of the idea of fathers 'being there' with children, for example, is by no means straightforward and has meant different things in different contexts.[74] And, importantly, men's and women's differential positioning to children and child care within the discourses of modernity, their (our) experiences of familial 'inevitable dependencies'[75] have been constituted in terms of sexed embodiment and differentially gendered lives. Historically, the encoded as familial male subject has been, in many respects, constituted as

---

71 *Op cit*, Jenks, fn 31, p 20.
72 *Op cit*, Morrison, fn 6, p 183.
73 Segal, L, *Straight Sex: The Politics of Pleasure*, 1994, London: Virago.
74 *Op cit*, Morgan, fn 25.
75 *Op cit*, Fineman, fn 59.

Other to everyday child care practices, beyond the dominant primary man/child nexus of economic provider and socialising role model.

Secondly, this chapter has sought to trace aspects of the legacy of a historical bifurcation between ideas of safe and dangerous spaces, both within and beyond the family/familial, through reference to which the relationship between men and children has been understood and regulated. In undermining this dualism, and in surfacing sexed (as different) experiences of community, solidarity and ideas of family life, complex social changes have served to question and disturb taken for granted ideas about the nature of men's location within the social *per se*. This relationship between men and children can be seen as constituting one of the major political conversations of the late 20th century. Furthermore, as the meaning of the 'good father' is being reconfigured, so too are perceptions of men's dangerousness. What has increasingly surfaced as problematic, not least as a result of feminist arguments, has been the frequently problematic nature of the presence of men *in* the lives of children, whether in their capacity as biological or social fathers or as caregivers to children and welfare workers across institutions and organisations.[76]

Thirdly, I have sought in this chapter to reframe issues around the legal regulation of the relationship between men and children in a way which transcends the sphere of crime and criminality or child and family law. What is at issue involves wider shifts in cultural configurations of sex/gender which have themselves prompted a crisis of representation around the relationship between adults and children. It is in this context that debates about the contours of masculine dangerousness continue to trade in, and reproduce, some familiar ideologies of normality and criminality, sanity and madness, good and evil, psychopathology and sociopathology. Yet, as Hollway and Jefferson have suggested, what is needed in seeking to appreciate such developments is the presentation of a more complex psychical dimension to the construction of subjects as 'fearful' or 'anxious' parents, or indeed 'good fathers', in a context where social explanation can itself so easily become a 'psychic reality'.[77] Certainly, what is required is a richer, more nuanced account than that contained in representations of parental 'hysteria', social 'breakdown', family collapse or an 'evil' Other endemic in press accounts of fears and anxieties relating to childhood.

It may well be that the fear of harm to the child is a particularly 'apt discourse'[78] within the modernist quest for order, since the risks which are seen as threatening to the child are, at once, both knowable and potentially controllable, whilst also, importantly, presenting a blameless (innocent) victim.

---

76 Pringle, K, *Men, Masculinities and Social Welfare*, 1995, London: UCL.
77 *Op cit*, Hollway and Jefferson, fn 41.
78 *Op cit*, Hollway and Jefferson, fn 41.

Ultimately, however, and in order to 'reflexively reconfigure the relationship between the social and subjectivity',[79] these debates about the changing relationship between men and children are themselves serving to raise questions, not just about perceived failures to protect the public from the depredations of 'psychopathic' males, but about the boundaries of what is understood to constitute acceptable male behaviour, whether 'in' or 'outside' the family. In such a context, it is no wonder, perhaps, that considerations of 'how men are' would appear at once ubiquitous – all around culturally inescapable – and yet simultaneously ephemeral, marginal issues to the mainstream of 'proper' debate, the issues they raise about the nature of society fading, all too often, into air behind the resonant, catch all, but ultimately obfuscatory discourses of sex/gender 'war', 'masculine crisis' and the much heralded, but ever elusive, 'crisis of the family'.

---

79   Jefferson, T, 'Review' (1996) 36(2) Br J Crim 323.

CHAPTER 7

CONTACT AND DOMESTIC VIOLENCE: THE IDEOLOGICAL DIVIDE

Adrienne Barnett

INTRODUCTION

Within current child law in England and Wales, the 'bad father' seems to have practically disappeared. Contact with non-resident fathers is presumed to be in the child's best interests, however abusively the father may have behaved towards the mother. This means that more and more women and children are being coerced into maintaining contact with violent, abusive men for the sake of 'the welfare of the child'; if they try to resist, they are seen as unreasonable and selfish, and risk imprisonment or loss of residence of the children to the father.[1]

This chapter explores legal and professional discourses informing the issue of child contact proceedings where domestic violence is an issue, along with the possibilities for effective resistance by women to the child law processes by which they are currently regulated. In so doing, it is suggested that we need to acknowledge the complexities of the social system within and through which these processes take place, and the possibilities for, and limitations on, effective social change. In this respect, it is suggested that autopoietic theory can provide helpful though challenging insights.

Over the past decade, several commentators have written about the erasure of the 'bad father' from legal discourse and the predominance of the 'bad mother'.[2] This chapter suggests that, within current child law, the 'bad

---

1   See Kaye, M, 'Domestic violence, residence and contact' (1996) 8(4) CFLQ 285; Smart, C and Neale, B, 'Arguments against virtue – must contact be enforced?' (1997) 27 Fam Law 332; Wallbank, J, 'Castigating mothers: the judicial response to "willful" women in disputes over paternal contact in English law' (1998) 20 JSWFL 357; Smart, C and Neale, B, *Family Fragments*, 1999, Cambridge: Polity; Humphreys, C, 'Judicial alienation syndrome – failures to respond to post-separation violence' (1999) 29 Fam Law 313.

2   See, eg, Smart, C, 'Power and the politics of gender'; Fineman, M, 'The politics of custody and gender', both in Smart, C and Sevenhuijsen, S (eds), *Child Custody and the Politics of Gender*, 1989, London: Routledge; Smart, C, 'The legal and moral ordering of child custody' (1991) 18 JLS 485; Boyd, S, 'Some post-modernist challenges to feminist analyses of law, family and State: ideology and discourse in child custody law' (1991) 10 CJFL 79; Boyd, S, 'Is there an ideology of motherhood in (post)modern child custody law?' (1996) 5 SLS 495.

father' has slipped into the ideological space between contact and domestic violence, a space fashioned by discourses of law, child welfare science,[3] politics and social work. It is also suggested that the developing professional discourse amongst barristers and solicitors continues to mould the contours of that space.

From this process, the gendered subjectivities of 'safe family men' and 'implacably hostile mothers' have emerged and these subjectivities currently structure legal decision making in contact cases. Central to these discursive constructs is a particular notion of 'the welfare of the child', which lies at the heart of current attempts to reconstruct the nuclear family at a time when the masculine subjectivity of the 'safe family man' is being undercut by the newly emerging subjectivity of the abuser. The way in which 'the welfare of the child' is constructed within legal discourse means that it has become axiomatic and incontestable that children 'need' fathers for their psychological well being. In this way, 'the law has constructed the modern "good father" as a desirable presence in the family',[4] so that contact by children with violent men is not only a possibility, but is actively encouraged by law. It is this process that silences ways of talking about familial relations that challenge the increasingly hegemonic status of the importance of the father within the modern family.

The focus of this chapter will be on the way in which courts and professionals respond to contact cases where domestic violence is an issue, focusing on current research in this area, with specific reference to my recent small scale study of barristers' representation of women in such cases. It is hoped that this study will highlight the strategic importance, for a feminist analysis of child law, of retaining a focus on the interaction between legal, scientific and professional discourses, and on the complexities, limitations and possibilities for effective social change in the context of such discursive interactions. By disrupting the 'centralising powers' of 'the welfare of the child', it is hoped that women, as 'speaking discursing subjects' whose experiences have been diminished by the prioritising of scientific discourse, can gain a valid voice, knowledge and morality in the context of family proceedings.

---

3   By 'child welfare science' I mean information about children's welfare derived from the 'psy' discourses – psychiatry, psychology, psychoanalysis – that enters law's environment and which, arguably, can be described as a scientific discourse. See, further, King, M and Piper, C, *How the Law Thinks about Children*, 1995, Aldershot: Gower, especially pp 43–49.

4   Collier, R, 'Waiting till father gets home' (1995) 6 SLS 5, p 6. See Collier, Chapter 6, in this volume.

THEORETICAL PERSPECTIVES

In recent years, there has been an increasing consideration of the way forward for a feminist analysis of child law, particularly in the light of post-modern perspectives on law and society.[5] However, the complexities and difficulties involved in such an approach cannot be underestimated. What follows, therefore, is a brief exploration of some recent theoretical perspectives.

Deconstruction – pure nihilism or revolutionary potential?

There have been suggestions recently that feminist analyses of family law should refocus on law's ideology. Fegan, for example, suggests that we should oppose the 'unwarranted nihilism' of a 'purely deconstructive approach' and expose law's failure to deliver its own internal ideals, thereby resisting 'the entrenchment of gender biased ideologies in public consciousness'.[6] While it is fully accepted that, as Fegan suggests, feminist strategies of resistance to dominant ideology should challenge and deconstruct assumptions about law's neutrality and impartiality, it is suggested that, despite the helpful elements, there are a number of problems with this approach.

First, the idea of 'public consciousness' is problematic, suggesting as it does the notion of the social body as constituting a universality of wills. It is suggested that the problem in challenging child law 'is not changing people's consciousness ... but ... the political, economic, institutional regime of the production of truth'.[7]

Secondly, while it is undeniable that we need to expose 'law's role as a discourse of construction, which is self-legitimating in so far as its power to construct is sustained by its own ideological claims to truth',[8] we also need to consider the extent to which, and manner in which, law's power to construct is reliant on its legitimation of claims to truth of discourses external to law, such as scientific discourses. As Turkel notes, 'law must be analysed in terms of its internal relations of power and knowledge, as well as its relations to other discourses and sources of power'.[9]

---

5   See, eg, Smart, C, 'The quest for a feminist jurisprudence', in Smart, C, *Feminism and the Power of Law*, 1989, London: Routledge; *op cit*, Boyd, 1991, fn 2; Diduck, A, 'Legislating ideologies of motherhood' (1993) 2 SLS 462.

6   Fegan, E, '"Ideology after discourse": A reconceptualisation for feminist analyses of law' (1996) 23 JLS 173, p 190.

7   Foucault, M, *Power/Knowledge: Selected Interviews and Other Writings*, 1976, New York: Pantheon, p 133.

8   *Ibid*, Fegan, p 197.

9   Turkel, G, 'Michel Foucault: law, power and knowledge' (1990) 17 JLS 170.

Finally, the notion of a 'purely deconstructive' approach is particularly problematic. This fails to recognise the revolutionary potential of deconstruction as a practico-political project. As Hekman says: '... feminists cannot overcome the privileging of the male and the devaluing of the female until they reject the epistemology that created these categories.'[10] Thus, a problem with critiquing law on its own terms is that we may not displace the hierarchical dualisms of Enlightenment thought. So, even if law is shown not to be objective or neutral, the moral validity of objectivity and neutrality itself is not necessarily displaced.

A central aspect of the deconstruction of current legal and professional discourses is an examination of the processes by which 'scientific truth' is produced and understood (and, specifically, 'truth' about children's welfare). In particular, by deconstructing the notion of 'the welfare of the child' and locating it within its historical, social and ideological context, it can be seen to operate as a mechanism of power that serves particular interests. By exposing the contingent nature of this construct, it is hoped that we can create the space for oppositional meanings to emerge and for the 'shifting of subjectivities' which, as Boyd says, 'can, at certain junctures, be as crucial and as difficult as shifting economic structures'.[11]

Morality in/and family law

By deconstructing the notion of 'the welfare of the child', we will also be making visible the moral discourse underpinning that concept, a morality based on abstract claims to universal principles. While there is nothing 'wrong' with choosing children's welfare as the basis for making moral distinctions, what can do damage, as Bauman suggests,[12] is when a moral basis is elevated to a prescriptive ethic at the expense of other forms of moral decision making. In this way, 'other' ways of constituting morality are rendered invisible and, in the case of women who resist contact with violent men, reconstituted as individual pathologies or self-interest. Drawing on the work of JC Tronto, Carol Smart and Bren Neale[13] shows how a moral discourse that arises from practice and activity fails to find expression in current family law, which results in practices of care (usually undertaken by mothers) and violent behaviour by fathers being erased and reconstructed through images of 'implacably hostile mothers' and 'safe family men', which have rendered the possibility of care as a moral practice invisible. Smart and

---

10 Hekman, S, *Gender and Knowledge: Elements of a Post-Modern Feminism*, 1990, Cambridge: Polity, p 8.
11 *Op cit*, Boyd, 1991, fn 2, p 113.
12 Bauman, Z, *Post-Modern Ethics*, 1993, Oxford: Blackwell.
13 Tronto, JC, *Moral Boundaries*, 1993, London: Routledge; *op cit*, Smart and Neale, 1999, fn 1.

Neale also argue that a moral discourse of care would place the child in a set of relationships:

> The child would not be completely isolated from his/her carers as if his/her interests could be legislated upon independently of the web of relationships in which the child finds him or herself.[14]

However, by privileging a moral discourse of care, I am not seeking to assert it as a superior morality; rather, it should be seen as part of the process of disrupting current dominant feminine and masculine subjectivities, which structure legal decision making and professional practice in this area, and enabling different ways of articulating morality to be represented. In this way, we can see a moral discourse of care as a counter-discourse, a feminist construction of justice built not out of abstract principles, but from the ground up, out of concrete, specific practices, that resists the discipline of the moral self and exerts a morality that is not amenable to the existing rational order.[15]

Autopoietic theory

A key question is: what is the epistemic base of 'the welfare of the child' within legal discourse? Or, put differently, how can we usefully theorise the way in which 'the welfare of the child' has been constructed in/by current child law? In answering this question, I will draw on insights from autopoietic, or 'systems', theory. It is immediately recognised that the problems of undertaking a feminist critique of law from the perspective of autopoietic theory are immense and probably irreconcilable. This chapter does not seek to propound a theory of 'autopoietic feminism'. Indeed, the framework of this chapter owes rather more to Foucault than to Luhmann. However, it is suggested that autopoietic theory has immense utility in helping us confront, rather than avoid, the complexity of modern society.

The notion of society upon which autopoietic theory rests, derives from the work of the social theorist, Niklas Luhmann. He offers the idea of society as consisting of constructions arising out of communications emanating from social systems, rather than from individual interaction.[16] Luhmann defines an autopoietic system as one that 'produces and reproduces its own elements by the interaction of its elements'.[17] The differences between social systems reflect the principal organisation of modern society into different functions. Law's function (as a sub-system of modern society) is to process 'normative

---

14 *Op cit*, Smart and Neale, 1999, fn 1, p 193.

15 See *op cit*, Bauman, fn 12.

16 See Luhmann, N, 'Differentiation in society' (1977) 2(2) Canadian J Soc 29; Luhmann, N, *Ecological Communications*, 1989, Cambridge: Polity; King, M, 'The "truth" about autopoiesis' (1993) 20 JLS 1.

17 Luhmann, N, 'Law as a social system' (1989) 83 Northwestern UL Rev 136.

expectations that are capable of maintaining themselves in situations of conflict'.[18] According to Luhmann, each functional system processes society's expectations of it by means of a binary code and, for law, the binary code is legal/illegal. Law not only decides whether an event is lawful or unlawful, it also decides whether a conflict is a legal or non-legal one.

Each functional system is normatively closed to the external world. Before it can be recognised as existing for the system, information has to be reproduced in the system's own terms and can only then enter the system's programmes. All social function systems are dependent on other social function systems producing communications on which they are able to rely. For example, judges in family proceedings are increasingly reliant on information from the 'psy' and social science discourses in the form of reports from court welfare officers, social workers and psychologists, in order to produce legal decisions.

Because of their normative closure, direct and simple exchanges, or communications, between social systems are impossible. Information from a system's environment may enter the system only upon its transformation into a form that the system is able to recognise. What may sometimes appear to constitute direct communications between systems has been described as 'interference' – 'communications that apparently bridge both discourses [but which] are, in reality, separate pieces of information in each discourse and are coupled only by their synchronisation and co-evolution'.[19] Consequently, concepts originating from child psychology cannot be simply transferred unchanged into law, since each discourse produces its own 'reality', using its own processes.

Possibilities for change?

Another key question is whether, and to what extent, it may be possible to disrupt the current construction of 'the welfare of the child' and to shift the discursive hierarchy. In particular, with reference to autopoietic theory, what are the chances of planned changes or reforms succeeding, where direct communication between systems (both moral and social) is impossible?[20] From this perspective, it is simply not possible to 'steer' law in particular directions; in other words, the chances of changes occurring in pre-planned ways are highly contingent. Even if new laws enter the environments of other systems as authoritative political communications, those other systems will construe them in ways that make sense to that system alone. Law 'may interpret statutes in ways which restrict or even negate the intention of the

18 *Ibid*, p 140.
19 *Op cit*, King and Piper, fn 3, pp 33–34.
20 See *op cit*, Luhmann (1989), fn 16, especially pp 66, 88–89.

legislators or it may decide to what extent these intentions should be put into effect'.[21] We thus have to abandon notions of linear causation, which see legal norms capable of bringing about social change directly. The most that any system can achieve in changing society are 'irritations'[22] (such as demands for legislation, or new legal arguments); yet, as King points out, even this can be quite an achievement, though there is no guarantee that such irritations within a system's environment will produce change in a particular direction.

From a Foucauldian perspective, there is a hierarchical element to the dualistic codes of modern social systems; and the power relations that give rise to that hierarchy are constitutive of the social body. It may be possible to see the effects of those relations of power often (but not necessarily), in the form of ideological effects, as sustaining particular discursive constructs and subjectivities – of 'hostile mothers' and 'safe family men'. From this perspective, it is thus important to retain a notion of ideology[23] in deconstructing current family law, which explains how certain discourses 'remain subjugated and others seem to attain a more dominant status'.[24]

However, the only way in which we can act as if changes in the discursive hierarchy may benefit women is to enter the debate constructed within the feminist discourse, and thus lose the capacity for impartial sociological observation. It is, therefore, recognised that, in advancing explanations from a feminist post-structural perspective, I am abandoning my perspective as an impartial sociological observer and that this is an unavoidable outcome of moral or political observation of social systems.

In drawing on these apparently cheerless prospects for change, I am not suggesting that it is futile to even attempt to oppose the way in which women are currently regulated by child law. Far from it; the purpose is to try to work with as full an acknowledgment of the complexities of society as is possible, rather than trying to deny it, for, without doing so, we could spend our time endlessly attempting to change laws, scientific theories or political agendas, which may or may not benefit the women whose lives are so harshly regulated by current child law.

---

21 King, M, *A Better World for Children*, 1997, London: Routledge, p 166.

22 An 'irritation' is an event that occurs in one or more social system and causes that system to respond by reconstituting it in ways that the system can understand – see, further, *ibid*.

23 The conception of ideology that informs this chapter draws a distinction between discourse as process and ideology as effect, and sees ideology as the contingent, interpolated effects of the power produced by discursive claims to truth that arise out of and reproduce complex systems of domination. See *op cit*, Foucault, fn 7.

24 *Op cit*, Boyd, 1991, fn 2, p 112. See, also, *op cit*, Diduck, fn 5.

HISTORICAL AND POLITICAL BACKGROUND

Prior to the 1970s, while the legal position of both married and unmarried mothers had gradually improved, the father's position 'in' the family remained unchanged. This was primarily because of the continued dominance, since the 19th century, of the breadwinner ideology, which constructed paternal subjectivities by reference to their capacity for paid employment and maternal subjectivities by reference to their 'caring' functions.[25] Additionally, the breadwinner ideology has, until recently, tended to erase domestic violence from legal discourse on the family.[26] The breadwinner ideology went largely unchallenged until the early 1970s, when a range of cultural and economic developments combined to render the construction of the father as economic provider increasingly problematic.[27] These changes, which both led to and combined with legislation during the 1970s, improved the legal rights of married and unmarried mothers,[28] which in turn led to an increasing fear of autonomous motherhood and threw into question the breadwinner ideology.[29]

Additionally, from the end of the 1960s, there was renewed focus on domestic violence due to the work of feminists, resulting in social and policy changes, government monitoring of domestic violence, the setting up of women's refuges and legislation.[30] So, despite the continuing endorsement of the nuclear family in legal discourse, the law was simultaneously constructing the father as outside of, and inimical to, the mother and child unit.

A crucial shift in material and ideological conditions came in 1979, when the Conservative Government came to power with the aim of 'rolling back the frontiers of the State'. The ideology of the New Right has increasingly dominated the discursive field of child and family law ever since.[31] The New Right, reinforced by the fathers' rights movement, sought to reinstate and reinforce the traditional nuclear family, with its gendered subjectivities as it

---

25 See Williams, F, *Social Policy: A Critical Introduction*, 1989, Cambridge: Polity; *op cit*, Collier, fn 4.

26 Marcus, I, 'Reframing "domestic violence": terrorism in the home'; Meier, J, 'Introduction', both in Fineman, M and Mykitiuk, R (eds), *The Public Nature of Private Violence*, 1994, London: Routledge.

27 Eg, more women in the workforce; fewer years spent by women in pregnancy; mass unemployment; the shift from an industrial to a service economy; and the dramatic increase in lone parent and particularly single mother families.

28 See, eg, Guardianship of Minors Act 1971; Guardianship Act 1973; Inheritance (Provisions for Families and Dependents) Act 1975; Fatal Accidents Act 1976.

29 David, M, 'Moral and maternal: the family in the New Right', in Levitas, R (ed), *The Ideology of the New Right*, 1986, Bristol: Policy; *op cit*, Smart, 1989, fn 2.

30 Domestic Violence and Matrimonial Proceedings Act 1976.

31 *Ibid*, David; Clarke, J, Cochrane, A and Smart, C, *Ideologies of Welfare: From Dream to Disillusion*, 1992, London: Routledge.

represented the family form that could best be privatised. However, initial attempts to equalise the position of married and unmarried fathers using rights discourse were not wholly successful. Although the Law Commission initially considered abolishing the status of illegitimacy,[32] they subsequently took heed of arguments against according automatic rights to all fathers, based on the vulnerable position of mothers who 'may well be exposed to pressure, and even harassment, on the part of the natural father'.[33] Furthermore, since the early 1990s, there has been increasing recognition of male violence against women in the home, with government inquiries, inter-agency working groups and new legislation.[34]

It is through the ideological separation of contact and domestic violence that the reconstruction of the nuclear family is being effected, so that the 'dangerous subjectivity' of the abuser does not undercut the masculine subjectivity of the 'safe family man'. This is being achieved through the notion of 'the welfare of the child', which, in the 1940s and 1950s, had constructed the mother as vital to the child's welfare and, in the 1980s and 1990s, is doing the same for the father.

THE WELFARE OF THE CHILD

In family proceedings, judges have encountered a problem – how to decide disputes concerning residence and contact, without appearing arbitrary, unjust and uncertain. The overriding principle that 'the welfare of the child is paramount' is not one that is easily resolved by the application of law's legal/illegal code. According to Luhmann, all that checklists (such as the welfare checklist in s 1(3) of the Children Act 1989) do is 'distribute the self-validation of legal decisions over many stages'.[35] For this reason, child law has developed principles that have enabled judges to purport to base their decisions on 'true' information about children's welfare derived from child welfare science. Law cannot, however, apply science in scientific terms because it is not science, that is, it cannot reproduce the complexities and differing theoretical perspectives found within child welfare science.

What law does, however, is select information from child welfare research and portray that as a consensus within those discourses.[36] 'Legal, political or economic recognition of what is scientifically harmful to children will not,

---

32 Law Commission, *Illegitimacy*, No 74, 1979, London: HMSO.

33 Law Commission, *Illegitimacy (Second Report)*, Cmd 157, 1986, London: HMSO.

34 Family Law Act 1996, Pt IV.

35 *Op cit*, Luhmann 1989, fn 16, p 70.

36 See *op cit*, King and Piper, fn 3; Piper, C, 'Divorce reform and the image of the child' (1996) 23 JLS 364.

therefore, consist of direct translations from the scientific.'[37] The result of this selective construction is that, within the world constructed by law, the impression can be given that it is able to advance children's welfare by deciding that contact between children and non-resident parents is 'legal', and no contact 'illegal', whatever the eventual outcomes for particular children.

Psychological research on children's welfare, parental separation and divorce does not, however, support this law's simplified construction of 'the welfare of the child'. Behind the hegemonic status of the assumption that children 'need' contact with non-resident parents, lies a complex body of research, which frequently contests the apparent scientific consensus portrayed by legal discourse. Some studies that emerged during the early 1980s presented children as damaged by the divorce process, but less so if the father could be kept involved.[38] Judges, lawyers and politicians, along with court welfare officers and other child welfare professionals, interpreted these studies as meaning that contact with the natural father was necessary for children's emotional and psychological well being.[39] However, psychological and social science research and theoretical literature does not provide clear support for this interpretation. Elliott *et al* conclude, with respect to psychologists' research on children and divorce over the preceding decade, that 'the picture this research gives is a complex one with no simple answer of how children are affected. There are many different children and many kinds of divorce'.[40]

Research from the early 1980s about the importance of post-separation contact has long been superseded by more recent, methodologically sophisticated studies, which show 'no correlation between child welfare and the amount of contact with the father'.[41] In fact, researchers and clinicians now appear to emphasise the quality and stability of a child's care and

---

37 *Op cit*, King, fn 21, p 19.

38 Wallerstein, J and Kelly, J, *Surviving the Breakup*, 1980, New York: Basic; Richards, M and Dyson, M, *Separation, Divorce and the Development of Children*; Hetherington, E, Cox, M and Cox, R, 'The aftermath of divorce', both in Stevens, JH and Matthews, M (eds), *Mother-Child, Father-Child Relations*, 1979, Washington DC: National Association for the Education of Young Children.

39 See, eg, Walsh, E, 'The Wallerstein experience' (1991) 21 Fam Law 49; Jaffe, P, Wolfe, D and Wilson, S, *Children of Battered Women*, 1990, Newbury Park, Cal: Sage; Stone, N, 'Out of sight but not out of mind' (1988) 18 Fam Law 216; Johnson, A, 'Access – the basics' (1990) 20 Fam Law 483. See, also, Law Commission, *Review of Child Law: Guardianship and Custody*, No 172, 1988, London: HMSO; Lord Chancellor's Department, *Principles and Practice in Guidance and Regulations*, 1990, London: HMSO.

40 Elliott, J, Ochiltree, G, Richards, M, Sinclair, C and Tasker, F, 'Divorce and children: a British challenge to the Wallerstein view' (1990) 20 Fam Law 309. See, also, Elliott, J and Richards, M, 'Parental divorce and the life chances of children' (1991) 21 Fam Law 481; Amato, PR and Keith, B, 'Parental divorce and the well being of children: a meta-analysis' (1991) 110 Psychological Bulletin 26.

41 *Op cit*, Smart and Neale, 1997, fn 1, p 379. See, further, Buckley, A and Scholar, H, 'Long-distance love: practice issues in unmarried parent cases' (1993) 23 Fam Law 81; Hewitt, K, 'Divorce and parental disagreement' (1996) 26 Fam Law 368.

relationship with the primary carer. According to Kelly, 'the psychological adjustment of the custodial parent after divorce [is] emerging as a central factor in determining children's post-divorce adjustment'.[42]

It should be made clear that I am not asserting that this more recent research presents the 'correct' or a 'truer' picture of children's welfare on parental separation. On the contrary, what I am attempting to explore is the contingent nature of the concept of 'the welfare of the child'. By raising as a 'scientific truth' that continued contact between children and their non-custodial parents is 'good' for children, legal discourse is silencing other ways of talking about the interests and experiences of women and children, thereby denying the existence of other dangerous masculinities which can be highly problematic for women and children if they remain uncontested within families.

As far as the effects of domestic violence on children are concerned, research reveals that children are frequently witnesses to the violence perpetrated against their mothers.[43] Furthermore, a range of well documented physical, psychological and emotional problems, disorders and traumas are associated with children's experiences of living with domestic violence.[44]

Yet, this research and information, which has been available for over 20 years, has failed to find any expression within legal discourse informing the issues of residence and contact. Moreover, this ideological divide can be seen from the fact that, within the public law sphere, violence by the father against the mother is seen as emotionally abusive of the child, and is often cited as a reason for putting the child's name on the Child Protection Register. Yet, within the private law sphere, the father's 'dangerous masculinity' is rendered safe by the reconstruction of this research as individual, or family, dysfunction. It has principally been feminist analyses and studies, since the mid-1980s, that have attributed these effects on children directly to the 'effects

---

42 Kelly, J, 'Children's post-divorce adjustment' (1991) 21 Fam Law 52, p 54. See, also, Furstenberg, F and Cherlin, AJ, *Divided Families: What Happens to Children when Parents Part*, 1991, Cambridge, Mass: Harvard UP; Burghes, L, *Lone Parenthood and Family Disruption: The Outcomes for Children*, 1994, London: Family Policy Studies Centre; Hooper, C, 'Do families need fathers? The impact of divorce on children', in Mullender, A and Morley, M (eds), *Children Living with Domestic Violence*, 1994, London: Whiting & Birch. ·

43 Hughes, H, 'Psychological and behavioural correlates of family violence in child witnesses and victims' (1988) 58 Am J Ortho-Psychiatry 77. See, also, *op cit*, Kaye, fn 1.

44 Morley, R and Mullender, A, 'Domestic violence and children: what do we know from research?', in *ibid*, Mullender and Morley; *ibid*, Hughes; Moore, JG, 'Yo-yo children: victims of matrimonial violence' (1975) 54 Child Welfare 557; Rosenbaum, A, 'Children of marital violence: a closer look at the unintended victims' (1985) 55 Am J Ortho-Psychiatry 260; Smith, LJF, *Domestic Violence: An Overview of the Literature*, 1989, London: HMSO; Saunders, A, *It Hurts Me Too: Children's Experiences of Refuge Life*, 1995, Bristol: Women's Aid Federation England/Childline/National Institute for Social Work.

of the abuse itself or of directly witnessing it' and not to 'the effects of general, dysfunctioning family characteristics'.[45]

LEGAL DISCOURSE ON CHILD CONTACT

The enactment of the Children Act 1989 marked a decisive trend in law towards reinforcing the father's position in the post-separation family and, with it, important changes in the construction of maternal subjectivities. A harsher, more punitive stance towards mothers developed at the same time, as the interests of children and their primary carers were increasingly seen as separate.[46] Central to these processes is the concept of parental responsibility,[47] which underpins current family law and evokes a powerful ideology of permanent dual parenting as the norm to which all parents should aspire in the interests of their children.[48] What the concept of parental responsibility has done, however, is not 'make' parents take more responsibility for their children, but has created the ideological arena in which mothers' 'duty' to allow contact with absent fathers can be more strenuously imposed.[49] Underpinning parental responsibility is the image of safe, familial masculinity, which predominates in the field of child contact and makes it so difficult for mothers to raise other images of 'dangerous' masculinity.[50]

Prior to the enactment of the Children Act 1989, the case law had demonstrated an increasing endorsement of the child's perceived need for contact with its non-resident parent, using a complex interaction of rights and welfare discourse, together with forceful appeals to nature and common sense: 'A child, by the principles of law and nature, had the right to benefit from contact with his lawful or biological parent.'[51]

Since the inception of the Children Act in 1991, the welfare principle has been interpreted almost solely in terms of the child's perceived 'need' for contact with his or her non-resident parent. This position has been formulated into a general principle. According to Balcombe LJ, the question for the court

---

45 Silvern, L and Kaersvang, L, 'The traumatised children of violent marriages' (1989) 68 Child Welfare 421. See Stark, E and Flitcraft, A, 'Woman-battering, child abuse and social heredity: what is the relationship?', in Johnson, N (ed), *Marital Violence*, 1985, London: Routledge, for a critique of 'battered woman's syndrome'.

46 *Op cit*, Smart and Neale, 1997, fn 1.

47 Children Act 1989, s 3.

48 *Op cit*, Piper, fn 36.

49 See Diduck, Chapter 13, in this volume.

50 See Collier, Chapter 6, in this volume, for a discussion of the contested nature of the acceptable male in parenting.

51 *Re R (Minors) (Access)* [1992] Fam Law 67, p 67, *per* Waite J. See, also, *Re B (A Minor) (Access)* [1984] Fam LR 648, p 49, *per* Latey J.

is whether there are any 'cogent reasons ... why the child should be denied the opportunity of access to their natural father'.[52]

The 'implacably hostile' mother

A key factor in law's current construction of children's welfare (and a product of the 'gender free' discourse of parental responsibility) is the notion that it is 'possible to define children's interests independently when they are conceptually separated and set apart from parental interests'.[53] This enables the child to be conceptually detached, both from the relationships in which he or she lives, and from the partisan nature of the legal process itself, resulting in the re-inscription of the carer-child relationship as collections of individuals whose interests are often in conflict.

This has given rise to, and reinforced, the predominant feminine subjectivity in the area of child contact – the 'implacably hostile' mother who, through selfishness and unreasonableness, damages her child by refusing to allow contact with the father. The father's conduct has thus become increasingly invisible, and the problem is constructed as solely the mother, whose fears and concerns are reconstructed as obduracy and pathological self-interest.[54] It is also noteworthy that, of two reported cases identified between 1980 and 1997, where fathers with residence objected to contact by mothers, the mothers were refused contact by the courts and the fathers were not described as implacably hostile. The approach to 'hostile mothers' is being entrenched in professional discourse through articles by legal and child welfare professionals,[55] who even argue that the child should be removed from, and have no contact with, the mother, so that her 'pathology' can be treated.[56] The mother is thus 'irrational' if she disagrees with the professionals, and cannot speak legitimately about her child's interests.

The demonised figure of the implacably hostile mother enables courts to enforce contact orders against women more punitively, while still maintaining that the welfare of the child is being advanced. Before the Children Act 1989 was introduced, courts held that imprisoning mothers could harm children

---

52 *Re D (A Minor) (Contact: Mother's Hostility)* [1993] 2 Fam LR 1, pp 3–4. This 'general principle' has been affirmed in numerous cases; see, eg, *Re R (A Minor) (Contact)* [1993] 2 Fam LR 762; *Re H (Contact) (Principles)* [1994] 2 Fam LR 969; *Re M (Contact: Welfare Test)* [1995] 1 Fam LR 274.

53 *Op cit*, Fineman, fn 2, p 29.

54 *Op cit*, Boyd, 1996, fn 2.

55 See, eg, Ingam, T, 'Contact and the obdurate parent' (1996) 26 Fam Law 615; Mitchell, J, 'Contact orders and the obstructive parent – a third way?' (1998) 28 Fam Law 678.

56 Willbourne, C and Cull, L, 'The emerging problem of parental alienation' (1997) 27 Fam Law 807.

and do nothing to foster a relationship between father and child.[57] Over the past two to three years, however, courts appear to be of the view that it is no longer harmful to a child to imprison his or her mother, since she has made herself inimical to the child's interests by her hostility to contact.[58] There are thus grave consequences for women in opposing contact.

Domestic violence within child law

Until very recently, the courts had refused to recognise domestic violence as a reason to deny contact.[59] Many contact cases involving serious physical injury to the mother contain no mention of the father's violence, focusing instead on the mother's hostility and failing to consider her safety.[60] The courts often tend to minimise the violence, describing it as 'difficulties' between the parents,[61] or as 'mutual conflict'.[62]

It is even dangerous for women to raise allegations of violence by fathers, because they risk being constructed as implacably hostile and can be castigated for stirring up conflict.[63] The implication is that the mother is at fault if she fails to collude in her own silencing. Some judges even see the father's violence as caused by denial of contact.[64] It is thus very difficult for women to articulate abuse towards themselves by the father as a reason for resisting contact. As Smart notes: 'It is assumed that children need fathers so badly that mothers must be prepared to tolerate almost any behaviour.'[65]

This silence within legal and child welfare discourses on the issue of domestic violence is all the more striking when the incidence of violence

---

57 See *Churchyard v Churchyard* [1984] Fam LR 635; *Sheppard v Miller* [1982] 3 Fam LR 124; *Thomason v Thomason* [1985] Fam LR 214; *Re M (Minors) (Access: Contempt: Committal)* [1991] 1 Fam LR 355.

58 The landmark case on this point is *A v N (Committal: Refusal of Contact)* [1997] 1 Fam LR 533.

59 See, eg, *Re M (A Minor) (Contact: Conditions)* [1994] 1 Fam LR 272; *Re P (A Minor) (Contact)* [1994] 2 Fam LR 372; *Re F (Contact: Restraint Order)* [1995] 1 Fam LR 956; *Re K (Contact: Psychiatric Report)* [1995] 2 Fam LR 432; *Re S (Contact: Grandparents)* [1996] 1 Fam LR 158; *Re P (Contact: Supervision)* [1996] 2 Fam LR 314.

60 See, eg, *Re S (Minors) (Access Appeal)* [1990] Fam Law 336. See, further, Hester, M, and Radford, L, 'Contradictions and compromises. The impact of the Children Act on women and children's safety', in Hester, M, Kelly, L and Radford, J (eds), *Women, Violence and Male Power*, 1996, Milton Keynes: OU Press.

61 See *Re BC (A Minor) (Access)* [1985] Fam LR 639; *Re H (A Minor) (Contact)* [1994] 2 Fam LR 776; *Re F (Minors) (Contact: Appeal)* [1997] 1 FCR 523.

62 See *Re P (Contact: Supervision)* [1996] 2 Fam LR 314; *D v N (Contact Order: Conditions)* [1997] 2 Fam LR 797.

63 *Op cit*, Kaye, fn 1; Hester, M, Pearson, C and Radford, L, *Domestic Violence: A National Survey of Court Welfare and Voluntary Sector Mediation Practice*, 1997, Bristol: Policy.

64 See, eg, *D v D (Application for Contact)* [1994] 1 FCR 694.

65 *Op cit*, Smart, 1991, fn 2, p 497.

perpetrated against women with children, particularly after relationship breakdown, is considered. The British Crime Survey found that the two significant factors associated with risks of domestic violence were where women were separated or divorced and where they had children.[66] Mooney's study revealed that lone mothers were twice as likely as other women to have experienced violence from a partner or ex-partner within the last year.[67] Together, these findings strongly suggest that a large proportion of child contact disputes occur within a context of domestic violence.

It should be recognised, however, that, over the past year, a slight change can be detected in some judicial attitudes to the issue of contact and domestic violence. This started with the judgment of Staughton LJ and Hale J in *Re D (Contact: Reasons for Refusal)*,[68] in which the Court of Appeal upheld a decision of the trial judge to order no contact on the basis of the father's violence towards the mother. Since then, the High Court and Court of Appeal have recognised domestic violence as capable of constituting a 'cogent reason' for denying a father contact in a number of cases.[69] Nevertheless, two points arising out of these cases should be noted. First, the judges draw a clear distinction between 'reasonable' and 'unreasonable' hostility to contact – it is still the professionals, and not the mother, who have the 'rationality' to decide whether the mother's fear is justified. Secondly, despite these shifts in judicial attitude, the cases continue to unequivocally endorse the overriding importance of contact; thus, the 'pro-contact' presumption can still be seen in many recent cases, even those involving domestic violence.[70]

The professional discourse

The regulation of women within current family proceedings does not rest solely on the shoulders of judges. Professionals involved in contact proceedings, including solicitors and barristers who represent mothers, play an important part in disciplining women and sustaining the ideological divide between contact and domestic violence.

Solicitors specialising in family law appear to have increasingly absorbed welfare and 'psy' concepts into their thinking, resulting in 'the gradual

---

66 Mirrlees-Black, C, *Estimating the Extent of Domestic Violence: Findings from the 1992 BCS Research Bulletin No 37*, 1995, London: Whiting & Birch.

67 Mooney, J, 'Domestic violence in a London Borough', 1994, paper presented to the British Sociological Association Annual Conference. See, also, *op cit*, Smith, fn 44.

68 [1997] 2 FLR 48.

69 Eg, *Re H (Contact: Domestic Violence)* [1998] 2 Fam LR 42; *Re M (Contact: Violent Parent)* [1999] 2 Fam LR 321; *Re K (Contact: Mother's Anxiety)* [1999] 2 Fam LR 703; *M v M (Parental Responsibility)* [1999] 2 Fam LR 737. See, also, Victor Hall, J, 'Domestic violence and contact' (1997) 27 Fam Law 813.

70 Eg, *Re A (Contact: Domestic Violence)* [1998] 2 Fam LR 171; *F v F (Contact: Committal)* [1998] 2 Fam LR 237; *Re P (Contact: Discretion)* [1998] 2 Fam LR 696.

assimilation of welfare ideology into family law'[71] and the emergence of a developing discourse among legal professionals specialising in family law. The strength of this discourse is demonstrated by the way in which it has impinged on the role of barristers, who have a long tradition of independent practice and zealous protection of the layperson's interests. According to the *Code of Conduct of the Bar*: 'A practising barrister must promote and protect fearlessly, and by all proper and lawful means, his lay client's best interests.'[72] The extent to which barristers in contact cases fulfil this role may be a good measure of the strength of the professional discourse. In examining the practices and perceptions of barristers, I will be drawing on my small scale study of barristers' representation of women in contact disputes where domestic violence is an issue.[73]

In general terms, current research shows that familial ideologies have a pervasive influence on the practices and perceptions of professionals in contact proceedings.[74] This means that women who have been abused by fathers seeking contact may find it hard to articulate their experiences of domestic violence, or to get professional recognition of these experiences and its impact on them and their children. Consequently, they may be pressured into agreeing unsafe contact arrangements. The ideological divide between contact and domestic violence means that professionals have difficulty recognising domestic violence as a legitimate reason for mothers denying contact between fathers and children. Professionals' views of children's wishes and their client's concerns are filtered through images of 'hostile mothers' and 'safe family men', while abusive conduct by men is obscured by the pervasive assumption that the child's perceived need for contact takes precedence over all else.

Pressure on women to agree to contact

Most of the professionals interviewed by Marianne Hester and Jill Radford encouraged women to agree to some contact; women thus felt under pressure to agree to unsafe contact arrangements rather than be viewed as 'hostile' or

---

71 Neale, B and Smart, C, '"Good" and "bad" lawyers? Struggling in the shadow of the new law' (1997) 19 JSWFL 377. See Diduck, Chapter 13, in this volume.

72 General Council of the Bar, *Code of Conduct of the Bar of England and Wales*, 1991, London, para 203a.

73 A representative sample of 39 barristers specialising in family law completed my questionnaire, and a further small selected sample were interviewed. See Barnett, A 'Contact and domestic violence: the ideological divide', 1998, unpublished LLM dissertation, Brunel University; Barnett, A, 'Disclosure of domestic violence by women involved in child contact disputes' (1999) 29 Fam Law 104.

74 Hester, M and Radford, L, *Domestic Violence and Child Contact Arrangements in England and Denmark*, 1996, Bristol: Policy. Hester *et al* also conducted follow up research into court welfare officers and voluntary sector mediators (*op cit*, fn 63).

unreasonable by courts and court welfare officers.[75] Similarly, most barristers do not contest contact cases at a final hearing, particularly where a court welfare officer recommends some contact. Likewise, it is also very difficult to get contact stopped.[76] Many advise their clients of the child's 'need' for contact, while a significant minority would go further and cajole their clients into permitting some contact. None of the barristers felt that violence to the mother alone would enable her to successfully oppose contact.

If the mother is perceived as 'hostile' to contact, barristers' advice is generally stronger and more openly coercive:

Ms S: I would advise her that it will go against her in the end, that it will not be to her benefit in the end to be very awkward now as it will be seen as being vengeful and unco-operative, and that's not in her interests. I will also point out that judges have been known to change residence if they feel that a parent ... is absolutely obstructive about contact.

Similarly, solicitors frequently advise their clients forcefully on the 'presumption of contact' and back this up with the implied threat of committal.[77]

The most popular tactic with 'implacably hostile' clients was to take on the role of 'child psychologist' and persuade the mother to agree to contact, even if the father continued to be violent towards her, explaining that this was for the child's benefit. Although most barristers do not see themselves as openly coercive, this type of 'persuasion' can be particularly effective, because of the barristers' position of authority and their sincerely held belief in the advice that they give.

Thus, we can see how the notion of 'the welfare of the child' becomes reconstructed within the professional discourse as itself part of a strategy in the task of achieving ongoing contact by non-resident fathers with their children.

Lawyers' perceptions of the welfare of the child

Hester and Radford found that the 'presumption of contact' was very entrenched among all legal and child welfare professionals involved in contact cases.[78] Similarly, all but one barrister participating in my research felt that

---

75 Research conducted by Women's Aid found that nearly half of the refuges participating in their study said that women's solicitors had persuaded them to agree to unsafe arrangements for contact (Women's Aid Federation England, 'Women's aid and contact' (1997) 27 Fam Law 649).

76 Anderson, L, *Contact between Children and Violent Fathers*, 1997, London: Rights of Women.

77 *Op cit*, Neale and Smart, fn 71. In connection with solicitors and domestic violence, see Diduck, Chapter 13, in this volume.

78 See *op cit*, fn 73; *op cit*, Hester *et al*, fn 63.

children's welfare was best served by ongoing contact with non-resident fathers or, at least, did not query law's presumption in favour of contact, even those who had an appreciation of the mother's need for protection. Violence by the father did not, in itself, alter the beliefs of most barristers in the benefits of contact.

The gendered aspect of barristers' perceptions can be seen in the unwillingness of those I interviewed to envisage making the 'benefits' of contact available to children when the father is reluctant to take it up:

> **Ms S**: I don't see how the court could order a man to have contact with his children ... It would only make sense if the court could order a man to see his children and I don't think you can do that with a parent. And I think that, if somebody really does not want to see their children, well, that is something the child is going to have to come to terms with.

The 'kid gloves' approach taken by barristers with fathers contrasts starkly with the punitive approach taken by some of them to the enforcement of contact orders on unwilling mothers. Most barristers interviewed indicated that they could understand why a court might be justified in imprisoning an 'implacably hostile' mother:

> **Mr T**: Because it's sick and tired of mothers running implacable hostility cases and the message had to be sent to mothers that it's for the court to decide, and not for the mother to decide, about contact.

Additionally, most barristers assumed that mothers should have to make efforts to ensure not only that the father could have contact with the child, but that the child would want contact. The mother was also expected to assume the burden of making contact safe for herself and the child. Barristers were thus unable to see how much emotional and practical work goes into the way many women sustain contact.[79] Despite the almost unanimous assumption by barristers of the benefits of contact, the barristers interviewed indicated that they had fairly low opinions of the actual fathers they had encountered, and minimal expectations of them: 'A father who merely expressed an interest in seeing his child was usually seen to be a "good enough father".'[80]

Attempts by professionals to find out about domestic violence

Professionals interviewed by Hester and Radford generally made no effort to find out about the violence, nor about children's experiences of it, relying on it 'coming up' in discussions. Many solicitors withheld information about past

---

79 See, further, *op cit*, Smart and Neale, 1999, fn 1.
80 *Op cit*, Hester and Radford, fn 74, p 4.

abuse in their efforts to reach agreements.[81] Similarly, most barristers rely on information about domestic violence being mentioned in their brief or 'coming up' spontaneously when they speak to the client. Some would even avoid asking about such issues, for fear of 'putting ideas' into the client's head. A few barristers showed a marked reluctance to raise issues of domestic violence with the court, for fear of being thought confrontational, not wishing to be contaminated by the mother's hostility.[82]

Women's and children's safety

Very few of the contact arrangements made by mothers participating in Hester and Radford's study were ultimately safe, for mother and/or child; only three of the women participating in their study had not been assaulted when taking or collecting children from contact visits.[83] Despite this, most of the professionals interviewed by Hester and Radford (though to a lesser extent solicitors) 'saw women's experiences of violence and abuse as separate from the impact of the violence on the welfare of children'.[84] They rarely questioned how a man's use of violence might impinge on the quality of contact for the child. Similarly, most barristers felt that:

Mr A: ... it is only the child's welfare that is important. The mother's safety is relevant in so far as it is linked to the child's welfare.

A significant minority of barristers actually considered domestic violence to be totally separate from the question of contact and the father's violence as, therefore, wholly irrelevant.

Professionals' perceptions of children's wishes and views

Most professionals, especially solicitors and court welfare officers, tend to see children's claims that they do not want to see their father as resulting from the mother's influence, even where children have witnessed severe violence by the father against the mother. It is difficult for children to get their wishes acknowledged as genuine.[85] Although most barristers do not see the mother as directly malevolent, they cannot accept the child's views at face value, holding the mother responsible by filtering the child's views through their

---

81 Hester *et al* found that court welfare officers were making greater efforts to find out about domestic violence. However, mediators were still found to be minimising the existence and impact of domestic violence and did not have systematic screening policies: *op cit*, fn 63.

82 *Op cit*, Barnett, 1998, fn 73.

83 *Op cit*, Hester and Radford, fn 74. See, also, *op cit*, Women's Aid Federation England, fn 75.

84 *Op cit*, Hester and Radford, fn 74, p 5.

85 See *op cit*, Hester and Radford, fn 74; *op cit*, Anderson, fn 76.

own interpretations of child psychology. Yet, as Smart and Neale point out, 'the focus on manipulation obscures the extent to which children are themselves agents in the making of post-divorce childhood'.[86]

This response by professionals to children's wishes must be seen in the context of the Children Act 1989, which has placed a greater emphasis on children's wishes and feelings.[87] However, none of the barristers in my sample indicated that they would advise the mother that, if the child did not want to see the father and was considered mature enough, the court might possibly go along with his or her wish not to have contact. Barristers, therefore, rely on the law when it accords with their professional discourse of encouraging agreement, but disregard it when it does not. In this way, the law itself is reconstructed within the professional discourse as part of a strategy to achieve a contact agreement.

We can thus see that the perceptions and practices of legal professionals are both shaped by, and reinforce, the ideological separation within legal discourse, of contact and domestic violence. In this way, the 'principle of contact' is not affected by domestic violence. The result is that the mother's voice is further disqualified by legal professionals in contact cases, since her experience of abuse can only be expressed through the prism of the welfare of the child. She cannot, therefore, express a legitimate interest in her own protection without risking being constructed as selfish.

CONCLUSIONS

The perspective employed in this chapter is an attempt to theorise the issue of child contact proceedings outside of the 'child welfare' debate altogether, to examine ways in which society, including law, may acknowledge the legitimacy of factors other than the welfare of the child, that are at stake in contact decisions. Choosing to base decisions purely on the basis of a particular construction of 'the welfare of the child', instead of on any other factors, itself constitutes a moral choice and a moral position and enables that concept to function as a mechanism of power that sustains dominant relations.

It is clear that, so long as the current construction of 'the welfare of the child' lies at the heart of contact proceedings, the ideological divide between contact and domestic violence will be difficult to fragment. Violent or abusive behaviour by fathers seeking contact with children will always already be erased by images of safe family men and implacably hostile mothers, despite recent successes in bringing the issue of domestic violence to light in such cases. This is reinforced by the hegemonic status of law's claims to objectivity,

---

86 *Op cit*, Smart and Neale, 1999, fn 1, p 95.
87 Children Act 1989, s 1(3).

neutrality and certainty, which can be seen in barristers' and solicitors' unquestioning acceptance of law's selective construction of 'the welfare of the child'. The regulation of women within current family proceedings thus occurs as much by operation of the practices of professionals as by decisions of the courts.

Smart and Neale suggest, as a guiding principle, that outcomes in cases concerning parents and children should be derived from 'the reality of the lives of the people involved'; decisions should be related to a recognition of practical realities, such as who the primary carer has been, who the child has relationships with, and whether there is a climate of coercion and fear.[88] As discussed earlier, however, law cannot derive its decisions directly from the 'reality' of anyone's lives, but from its own reconstructions of aspects of those lives that enter law's environment. Although legal decisions may be observed in moral terms by moral campaigners within the legal system itself, King argues:

> The co-evolution of law and child welfare science has left virtually no space for such moral observation. It is the weight of scientific evidence which is seen as justifying the correctness of the decision, and not morality.[89]

Thus, within legal and professional discourses, disputes between parents about children are not seen as moral conflicts, 'only as emotional (and, hence, selfish) disputes which are, by definition, assumed to be void of moral content'.[90]

Even if practices based on care could be introduced into law's environment, there is no guarantee that law would consider them relevant to legal decision making or, if it did, make decisions based on those practices in a way that could be seen by moral campaigners to benefit the people whose lives are affected by legal decisions. Nevertheless, by disrupting law's construction of 'the welfare of the child', it may well be more difficult for judges to rely on child welfare science when making decisions in contact cases. This may then create the possibility for factors other than abstract principles of welfare – such as the moral, practical and emotional work involved in sustaining contact relationships – to enter law's environment and 'count' as determinants in contact cases. It could also create the possibility that law could withdraw altogether from decision making in this area. Under current ideological conditions, however, it is extremely unlikely that society would tolerate decisions in contact cases being made solely by the custodial parent; it is more likely that another institution, such as mediation, would step into the breach, which may well have similarly harsh consequences for mothers.

---

88 *Op cit*, Smart and Neale, 1999, fn 1.

89 *Op cit*, King, fn 21, p 45.

90 *Op cit*, Smart and Neale, 1999, fn 1, p 115.

It is therefore suggested that, if we wish to oppose the way in which women are regulated by current child law, it is essential that we change the ideological and discursive conditions within which decisions about parenting are made. It is hoped that engaging in the deconstructive process may create the space and opportunity for an alternative discourse to develop that can contribute to such change.

Postscript

Since writing this chapter, there have been significant developments relating to contact cases where domestic violence is an issue. In April 2000, the Lord Chancellor's Department published a Report[91] which recommends that 'Good Practice Guidelines' should be promulgated as soon as possible.[92] Additionally, on 19 June 2000, the Court of Appeal handed down a combined decision in respect of four cases involving contact and domestic violence[93] which decided that there should be no automatic assumption that contact with a violent parent is in the child's interests. There is no doubt that both the Report and the recent Court of Appeal decision are a direct response to the research that challenges the merits of enforcing contact between children and violent parents, and mark a sea change in judicial and governmental attitudes to this issue. Nevertheless, it remains to be seen how courts and legal professionals will respond to these developments while the 'presumption of contact' remains so entrenched and while courts are so reluctant to undertake fact-finding hearings in Children Act cases.

---

91 Lord Chancellor's Department, *A Report to the Lord Chancellor on the Question of Parental Contact in Cases where there is Domestic Violence*, 2000, London: HMSO.

92 Probably by way of a Practice Direction from the President of the Family Division and the Lord Chancellor.

93 *Re L (Contact: Domestic Violence); Re V (Contact: Domestic Violence); Re M (Contact: Domestic Violence); Re H (Contact: Domestic Violence)* [2000] FLR forthcoming – see (2000) 30 Fam Law 576.

CHAPTER 8

GOVERNING BAD GIRLS: CHANGING CONSTRUCTIONS OF FEMALE JUVENILE DELINQUENCY

Anne Worrall

INTRODUCTION

Two runaway schoolgirls took over a pensioner's home in Manchester, covered her walls in graffiti, bandaged her face so tightly that she choked, then pushed her body through the streets in a wheelie bin and dropped it into a canal.[1]

Four young women beat a 17 year old girl with gardening tools to warn her off a boy she was seeing. She suffered minor injuries. Police said, 'These girls are known for hanging around the B*** area'.[2]

She's too young to smoke. Too young to drink. Too young to vote. And far too young to see an 18 certificate film. She cannot marry and is under the legal age of consent for sex. But babyfaced Nicola Doherty, who celebrated her 15th birthday in January, is the mother of four day old twins![3]

These stories illustrate the three faces of what the media would have us believe to be the 'new breed' of girls who behave badly. In the first, we are presented with an example of 'girl power' at its most excessive and gruesome, reinforcing the fear that girls are turning to sadistic violence in apparently unprecedented numbers. In the second, an unpleasant incident of schoolgirl bullying (something which has, arguably, always existed) is reconstructed as worthy of a local newspaper's 'Crimestopper' spot, accompanied by an identikit picture of one of the suspects. In the third, readers are invited to regard under age pregnancy as an act of 'near criminality', and to contact the newspaper to say what they think about 'girls of 15 having babies ... Is it a disgrace or do they make good mums? Ring us today!'.[4]

In this chapter, I am concerned with making sense of changing attitudes towards 'bad girls' and, in particular, those girls[5] and young women under

---

1   Fowler, R (1999) *The Guardian*, 12 July.

2   'Crimestoppers' (1998) *The West Australian*, 17 July.

3   (1998) *The Sun*, 25 April.

4   In 1999, stories of 15 year old mums have been superseded by stories of 12 year old mums, but no one, as far as I am aware, is debating whether or not motherhood at 12 might be something to be celebrated.

5   I am using the term 'girls' in the remainder of this chapter, partly for the practical purpose of distinguishing young offenders under the age of 18 from slightly older young women, who are also referred to as young offenders by the prison system, and also out of respect for the move by some girls to reclaim their power as girls and give the word a new and non-traditional connotation. See Alder, C, 'Passionate and willful girls: confronting practices' (1998) 9(4) Women and Criminal Justice 81.

the age of 18 who commit offences and who are dealt with by the criminal justice system. I want to map out both the continuities and discontinuities with traditional constructions of 'troublesome' girls and suggest possible indicators of a shift in the paradigm that has dominated feminist critiques of juvenile justice, namely, the 'sexualisation' theory of adolescent female law breaking.

According to the 'sexualisation' theory, 'troublesome' girls have always provoked anxiety in those who work with them, and fear and suspicion in those who look on.[6] They have been socially constructed within a range of legal, welfare and political discourses as, on the one hand, deeply maladjusted misfits and, on the other (and more recently), dangerous folk devils, symbolic of post-modern, adolescent femininity.[7] Although professional responses to girls 'in trouble' have always been dominated by their welfare, the concern to protect has always been mingled with anxieties about the wildness and dangerousness of girls who are 'out of control'. 'Passionate and willful girls' [8] (sic) have always aroused as many respectable fears, as have hooligan boys.[9] In particular, bad girls who become pregnant, engage in prostitution or commit acts of violence run the risk of no longer being socially constructed as children or even as troubled young women, but rather as witting threats to the moral fabric of society.

The main arguments of this chapter are as follows:

(a) that the continuity of official concern about the welfare of troublesome girls, and the consequent 'protective' policies and practices of regulating adolescent *female* sexuality, has always been, to some extent, a proxy for concern about the government's (in)ability to regulate adolescent *male* sexuality. Stricter controls on girls are seen to be, simultaneously, the best way of protecting them and of preventing men from raping, sexually abusing and even killing them. They also ensure that young women make young men face up to their responsibilities and prevent the feral masculinity of the underclass becoming intergenerational.[10] Troublesome girls are not really *cared* about in their own right, but only in so far as they have a role to play as future mothers;

---

6   Hudson, A, 'Troublesome girls: towards alternative definitions and policies', in Cain, M (ed), *Growing Up Good: Policing the Behaviour of Girls in Europe*, 1989, London: Sage; Brown, HC and Pearce, J, 'Good practice in the face of anxiety: social work with girls and young women' (1992) 6(2) JSWP 159; Baines, M and Alder, C, 'Are girls more difficult to work with? Youth workers' perspectives in juvenile justice and related areas' (1996) 42(3) Crime and Delinquency 467.

7   Worrall, A, 'Troubled or troublesome? Justice for girls and young women', in Goldson, B (ed), *Youth Justice: Contemporary Policy and Practice*, 1999, Aldershot: Ashgate.

8   *Op cit*, Alder, fn 5.

9   Davies, A, '"These viragoes are no less cruel than the lads": young women, gangs and violence in late Victorian Manchester and Salford' (1999) 39(1) Br J Crim 72; Pearson, G, *Hooligan: A History of Respectable Fears*, 1983, London: Macmillan.

10   Murray, C, *Underclass: The Crisis Deepens*, 1994, London: IEA Health and Welfare Unit.

(b) that the continuity of official attempts to deal with troublesome girls through means other than formal criminal justice has resulted not only in formal welfare regulation, but also in three alternative discourses: informality, 'just deserts' and the reconstruction of troublesome girls as 'innocent' victims;

(c) that these attempts to foreclose the debate about female juvenile delinquency have between them created a lacuna, from which has emerged the 'bad girl' – the ungovernable, 'knowing-ignorant', 'nasty little madam' – who can *only* be dealt with by formal criminal justice.

FEMINIST CRITIQUES OF JUVENILE JUSTICE

There now exists a paradigmatic feminist critique of the social construction and treatment of 'troublesome girls'. The key features of that paradigm are that:

(a) the youth justice system both reflects and reinforces myths that bad boys are criminal, while bad girls are immoral;

(b) the symbolic core of bad girls' immoral behaviour is sexual precocity, which, it is argued, may lead to early pregnancy or prostitution;

(c) preoccupation with girls' sexual precocity reflects a traditional view of woman's social role and sexuality;

(d) these conventional assumptions result in discriminatory juvenile justice practices, with girls being dealt with more punitively (being more frequently incarcerated) than boys for behaviour that would not be regarded as criminal in adults;

(e) these discriminatory tendencies are exacerbated by class- and race-based fears, which means that working class and 'immigrant' girls are over-represented in the system.

I have presented this critique in the present tense, as though it related to contemporary youth justice in England and Wales, but I have borrowed from Paul Colomy and Martin Kretzmann's critique of the so called progressive era of juvenile justice in the US at the beginning of the last century.[11] In doing so, I hope to demonstrate that traditional constructions of bad girls have contained the same elements for well over a century and that they also transcend national boundaries in Western societies. This long standing belief that girls 'in trouble' require 'care', not punishment, has been tenacious. In particular, difficult and deviant behaviour by adolescent girls has been interpreted as a

---

11 Colomy, P and Kretzmann, M, 'The gendering of social control: sex delinquency and progressive juvenile justice in Denver, 1901–27', in McGillivray, A (ed), *Governing Childhood*, 1997, Aldershot: Dartmouth.

symptom of problematic sexuality requiring welfare regulation.[12] As Annie Hudson has argued:

> The majority of girls do not get drawn into the complex web of the personal social services because they have committed offences. It is more likely to be because of concerns about their perceived sexual behaviour and/or because they are seen to be 'at risk' of 'offending' against social codes of adolescent femininity.[13]

But Colomy and Kretzmann found evidence that, even at a time when preoccupation with girls' sexual precocity appeared at its highest, there was a diversity of approach within the juvenile courts and an acceptance by some that the problem was not so much the behaviour of the girls (which was a normal part of growing up), but the 'superstitious, intolerant and hypocritical' conventions[14] which sought to control girls and compel their parents to bring formal complaints against them. Colomy and Kretzmann's study of Denver Juvenile Court shows that complaints against girls were far more likely to be brought by families[15] than by public control agents, the reverse being the case for boys. The complaints for which boys most frequently appeared in court were 'taking things', 'truancy' and 'breaking in and taking things'. Girls appeared most frequently for 'running or staying away from home', staying 'out late at night or loitering' and being 'beyond [the] control of parents or guardian'.[16]

Consequently, enlightened juvenile judges attempted to deal with these complaints informally to protect girls from the likelihood of incarceration as a result of formal proceedings. One judge in particular – Lindsey J – engaged in semi-public conferencing sessions with girls and their families, using the court as a 'protective buffer between the girl and a punitive traditionalism'.[17]

Such attitudes towards difficult girls were by no means rare. Batsleer recounts the sympathetic relationship between Victorian youth worker, Maude Stanley, and her 'wild girls': 'Our work with many girls is to help them find out their own powers and to raise them more in their own estimation.'[18]

---

12 Carlen, P and Wardaugh, J, 'Locking up our daughters', in Carter, P, Jeffs, T and Smith, MK (eds), *Social Work and Social Welfare Year Book 3*, 1991, Milton Keynes: OU Press.

13 *Op cit*, Hudson, fn 6.

14 *Op cit*, Colomy and Kretzmann, fn 11, p 60.

15 Lest it be thought that the bringing of complaints by families is of only historical interest, see Reitsma-Street, M, 'Justice for Canadian girls: a 1990s update' (1999) Canadian J Crim, July 335, which demonstrates the important role played by parents in the increase in charges of failure to comply with court dispositions brought against girls.

16 *Op cit*, Colomy and Kretzmann, fn 11, p 69.

17 *Op cit*, Colomy and Kretzmann, fn 11, p 59.

18 Stanley, M, *Clubs for Working Girls*, 1890, London: Macmillan, cited in Batsleer, J, *Working With Girls and Young Women in Community Settings*, 1996, Aldershot: Ashgate, p 9.

Davies' work on gender discrimination in the sentencing of violent youth gangs (or 'scuttlers') at the end of the last century also shows an official ambivalence.[19] Although female 'scuttlers' were denounced publicly in terms that suggested that female violence was viewed more seriously than male violence, the sentencing of young women tended to be relatively lenient, especially if parental co-operation in chastisement was forthcoming.

It is this complex and ambiguous relationship between 'offending girls' and justice authorities which caused Kerry Carrington to challenge the received feminist wisdom embodied in the 'sexualisation' theory of adolescent female law breaking.[20] With reference to Australia, she argued that it is not possible to demonstrate empirically that girls are treated more harshly than boys or that they are over represented in statistics relating to welfare matters. More recent figures for England and Wales[21] support her contention that the drive to regulate the behaviour of bad girls may have more to do with the desire to control, albeit indirectly, the sexual behaviour of men and boys:[22]

> The concerns of the juvenile justice authorities, just with the regulation of adolescent female sexuality, has been vastly overstated in essentialist readings of female delinquency. Not only is the burden of this regulation spread unevenly throughout the adolescent female population, but the object of this regulation may, in fact, be undesirable forms of male sexuality. The strategic point for feminist intervention, as I see it, is to suggest how abusive and violent forms of male sexuality, such as incest, can be governed in ways other than through the discipline of the adolescent female body.[23]

In recognition of the problems highlighted by feminist critiques of traditional approaches to adolescent female delinquency, three alternative discourses have (re-)emerged in the late 20th century: informality (in the specific form of restorative justice), just deserts and a renewed appeal to the 'lost' innocence of childhood, as a result of victimisation (predominantly by men).

Restorative justice and the problem of informality

The concept of 'restorative justice' has emerged in criminal justice discourse as a result of dissatisfaction with the limitations of formal criminal justice in relation both to the treatment of offenders and the needs of victims. Although

---

19 *Op cit*, Davies, fn 9.

20 Carrington, K, *Offending Girls*, 1993, New South Wales: Allen & Unwin.

21 There is no evidence that girls are overrepresented in local authority secure accommodation, but, those who *are* in that accommodation are more likely than boys to be there for welfare (as opposed to criminal) reasons and are likely to be there for shorter stays than boys.

22 *Op cit*, Worrall, fn 7.

23 *Ibid*, Carrington, p 35.

it is an 'umbrella' term, covering a range of theories, policies and practices, the following is a widely recognised definition:

> Restorative justice is a process whereby parties with a stake in a specific offence resolve collectively how to deal with the aftermath of the offence and its implications for the future.[24]

Its key aims are to restore both the victim and the offender to full participation in the community and to repair the damage done to the relationships and self-esteem of those involved. It is a problem solving approach rather than a punitive one, which views crime in its social context. In practice, the implementation of restorative justice takes many forms but tends to consist of group conferences, which are co-ordinated and facilitated by either the police or an independent mediator (the difference being very significant, but not relevant to my arguments here). Jackson posits two models – one concerned with *family empowerment* in decision making, the other with bringing the victim and offender together within a *restorative* (and, in some cases, shaming) context.[25] Family group conferencing, as one particular manifestation of restorative justice,[26] has been adopted rather uncritically in the UK, in the misguided belief that it is based on tried and tested 'traditional' forms of indigenous justice in Canada, Australia and New Zealand.[27] The relationship between restorative justice and the formal system is problematic and varies from scheme to scheme.

As we have seen, adolescent female delinquency has always lent itself to informal interventions, and family group conferencing has been viewed by some as an appropriate mechanism for the control of girls' bad behaviour. Although many girls have suffered at the hands of formal criminal justice and welfare regulation, others have been subjected to attempts at informal control which buttress the social controls of the family, through negotiation, mediation and conferencing. Because adolescent girls are perceived to be articulate and emotional, they can more readily be persuaded to talk about

---

24 Marshall, T, *Restorative Justice: An Overview*, 1998, London: Restorative Justice Consortium, p 1.

25 Jackson, SE, 'Family group conferences in youth justice: the issues for implementation in England and Wales' (1998) 37(1) Howard J Crim Justice 34; Jackson, SE, 'Family group conferences and youth justice: a new panacea?', in *op cit*, Goldson, fn 7.

26 Family group conferencing (FGC) is particularly well developed in New Zealand and Australia as a means of dealing with young offenders. As well as allowing the victim of crime to be involved in the process of dealing with the offender, the key assumption underlying FGC is that 'families are competent to make decisions rather than the more traditional view that they are "pathological", "dysfunctional" or "deficient" in some way': see Hudson, J, Galaway, B, Morris, A and Maxwell, G, *Family Group Conferences: Perspectives on Policy and Practice*, 1996, Sydney: Federation. It is also a lot cheaper than formal intervention.

27 For a scathing critique of these cosy imperialist assumptions, see Blagg, H, 'A just measure of shame? Aboriginal youth and conferencing in Australia' (1997) 37(4) Br J Crim 481.

their feelings and can be more influenced by the articulacy and emotion of adults than can their monosyllabic brothers, whose inarticulacy is discomforting and unrewarding. This is not to argue that boys are not also subject to attempts at informal control, but it is far easier to take *them* up a mountain and assume that they will be influenced by its grandeur and their own unarticulated 'sense of achievement'. *They* are not required to indulge in *relationships*; *they* are not required to *talk*. In contrast, Australian research on the views of girls attending family group conferences claims that they found the experience empowering:

> Young women attending conferencing are extremely capable of expressing their feelings about the offence and their opinions about how it should be dealt with. In fact, as a general observation, this eloquence seems to be better developed in female offenders at conferences than in male offenders. For instance, it is more likely that girls will argue about an outcome and, of the girls interviewed, all held strong opinions about the fairness, or otherwise, of their conference.[28]

What such an apparently enlightened approach historically failed to take account of, however, was the risky nature of informal control in relation to bad girls. What we now know, though still fail to take account of, is the fact that many girls behave badly because their experience of informal control has been physically, sexually or emotionally abusive. Christine Alder, writing about bad girls in Australia, suggests that 'estimates of young women in the juvenile justice system who have been abused range from about 40–73%'.[29] The victimisation of girls in the home, at the hands of other participants in the conferencing process, may become an excluded discourse and entrenched attitudes about appropriate female adolescent behaviour may become reinforced rather than challenged.[30]

Additionally, Alder points out that the concept of 'shame', which is integral to restorative justice, has particular connotations and risks for young women.[31] I have argued in the past that women who commit crimes

---

28 Baines, M, 'Viewpoints on young women and family group conferences', in Alder, C and Baines, M (eds), *And When She Was Bad? Working with Young Women in Juvenile Justice and Related Areas*, 1996, Tasmania: National Clearinghouse for Youth Studies, p 44.

29 *Op cit*, Alder, fn 5. However, Alder herself recognises the danger of sexual abuse 'becoming a catch all explanation for a range of her behaviours in a form that pathologises young women and the problems they confront. Sexual abuse thereby becomes another of the "deficit discourses" that frame responses to female delinquency'. See Alder, C, 'Young women offenders and the challenge for restorative justice', unpublished paper presented to the American Society of Criminology Conference, Toronto, 1999.

30 There are parallels here with concerns expressed about Family Court welfare mediation: see Kaganas, F and Piper, C, 'Domestic violence and divorce mediation' (1994) 16 JSWFL 265; Kaganas, F and Piper, C, 'Divorce and domestic violence', in Day-Sclater, S and Piper, C (eds), *Undercurrents of Divorce*, 1999, Aldershot: Ashgate.

31 *Ibid*, Alder.

sometimes have difficulty in distinguishing between the strict legal concept of 'guilt' and their own subjective feelings of guilt (and, by implication, feelings of shame).[32] This all pervading sense of failure and lack of self-esteem is often cited as the underlying cause of the self-harming behaviour that is endemic in women's prisons (discussed more fully below), and Alder is right to counsel caution in relation to situations where remorse and self-blame are encouraged too enthusiastically.

Against this background of knowledge, in the name of restorative justice, the reification and the uncritical advocacy of informal mechanisms of conflict resolution, such as family group conferencing, may be dangerous for bad girls. The gender bias of the formal criminal justice system may be reproduced in informal practices but without even the minimal checks and balances afforded by the formal system. The informal is not necessarily benign or neutral.

The solution of just deserts[33]

In England and Wales, one possible solution to this gender bias was thought to be found in the return to a 'just deserts' or proportionate approach to juvenile justice. In the White Paper, *Crime, Justice and Protecting the Public*,[34] which preceded the Criminal Justice Act 1991, the Conservative Government suggested that the numbers of girls under the age of 18 sentenced to custody by the courts were so small that the abolition of detention in a young offender institution for this group might be feasible in a civilised society. The 150 or so girls in custody (compared to over 7,000 boys) could be dealt with quite adequately by the 'good, demanding and constructive community programmes for juvenile offenders who need intensive supervision'.[35] Those few who committed very serious crimes could still be dealt with by means of s 53 detention in local authority secure accommodation.[36]

The ascendancy of the 'just deserts' model of criminal justice, coupled with the inclusion of a supposedly anti-discriminatory clause in the 1991 Criminal Justice Act,[37] might have resulted in fewer girls being incarcerated. The

---

32 Worrall, A, *Offending Women: Female Lawbreakers and the Criminal Justice System*, 1990, London: Routledge, p 75.

33 Parts of this and the following sub-section have been reproduced from *op cit*, Worrall, fn 7.

34 Home Office, *Crime, Justice and Protecting the Public*, Cm 965, 1990, London: HMSO.

35 *Ibid*, p 45.

36 Detention under the Children and Young Persons Act 1933, s 53 provides for the long term detention of children and young persons under 18 for certain grave crimes such as murder, manslaughter and other serious crimes of violence.

37 Criminal Justice Act 1991, s 95 required the Home Secretary to monitor the administration of criminal justice to ensure the absence of discrimination on grounds of race, sex or other 'improper' grounds.

principle of proportionality in sentencing should have led to the fairer sentencing of women (since their offending behaviour is generally less serious than that of men), and this trend should have been buttressed by greater access for women to community sentences. But any such optimism was short lived. Nearly a decade later, custody in young offender institutions remains for girls and the reason, we are led to believe, is that girls are committing more crime, especially violent crime.

The 1990s have seen the emergence of several moral panics in relation to juvenile delinquency.[38] The first was 'rat boy', the elusive persistent offender who laughed at the system. The 'discovery' that a small number of children were committing a disproportionate amount of not so trivial crime, especially burglary and criminal damage, led to public outrage that, because of their age, these children could not be given custodial sentences.[39] The Government's response to this was to announce the introduction of secure training units for 12–14 year olds, the first of which opened in April 1998. But this concern was to prove merely a precursor to the second moral panic, which followed the murder of Jamie Bulger in 1993. After this appalling event, serious questions were asked about the retention of a system of justice for children which was based on a belief in the still developing understanding of right and wrong between the ages of 10 and 14 (the principle of *doli incapax*) and the consequent need to protect such children from the full weight of the criminal law. Increasingly, the media demanded that so called 'adult' offences should be dealt with by 'adult' sentences, regardless of the age and maturity of the offender. The vexing issues of the age of criminal responsibility and *doli incapax* became matters of public and parliamentary debate until the latter was finally abolished in the Crime and Disorder Act 1998. [40]

This level of media-fuelled public anxiety was based on the scantiest of empirical evidence. Hagell and Newburn,[41] for example, found far fewer persistent young offenders (and virtually none of them girls) than Michael Howard, the then Home Secretary, had claimed existed. Nevertheless, it was against this backdrop that the third moral panic emerged. Newspapers and magazines – and some academics – claimed to have discovered 'all girl gangs menacing the streets' and 'cocky, feminist, aggressive' super heroines

---

38 Worrall, A, *Punishment in the Community: The Future of Criminal Justice*, 1997, Harlow: Longman.

39 Hagell, A and Newburn, T, *Persistent Young Offenders*, 1994, London: Policy Studies Institute; Morton, J, *A Guide to the Criminal Justice and Public Order Act 1994*, 1994, London; Butterworths.

40 *Op cit*, Goldson, fn 7; Muncie, J, *Youth and Crime: A Critical Introduction*, 1999, London: Sage.

41 *Ibid*, Hagell and Newburn.

targeting vulnerable women and other girls.[42] Moreover, this 'new breed' of criminal girl apparently 'knows' that the criminal justice system is lenient on her. She 'knows' how to work the system, dressing smartly for court and playing up to the magistrates.

The causes of this supposed upsurge in young female crime are, however, contentious. On the one hand, Lisa Brinkworth argues that women's liberation has raised women's expectations but has not delivered in terms of careers and wealth.[43] Consequently, frustration and anger lead to street violence. On the other hand, women are supposedly sick of feeling unsafe in the home and are now fighting back. Either way, according to Brinkworth, the responsibility for all this lies with feminism. This is what happens when you loosen the controls on women. This is what happens when adolescent girls are allowed to think themselves equal, or superior to, boys. It is every mother and father's nightmare – their daughter's sexuality rampant and violent. Journalists are now warning us that 'psychologists have projected that, by the year 2008, the number of girls reverting to violence will outnumber boys if they carry on lashing out at this rate'.[44] This prediction is, it seems, based on a claim that the number of women sentenced for violence against the person 'has quadrupled from just a handful of cases in the 1970s'. The fact that the numbers (according to Rebecca Fowler's own, inaccurate, statistics) are now 460, compared with over 11,000 crimes of violence committed by men, does not cause her to reflect on her hypothesis.[45] In fact, although there has been an increase in violent crime committed by young people, the ratio of such offences has remained that of around one female to five males throughout the 1990s.[46] There is some evidence to support concern about an increase in crimes classified as 'robbery' committed by young women, but, as will be argued later, the nature of the *kind* of behaviour that is being classified in this way requires examination.

Whatever the promise the 'just deserts' approach might have held for young women in the early 1990s, it has, in practice, resulted in a greater criminalisation of girls' bad behaviour.

---

42   Archer, D, 'Riot Grrrl and Raisin Girl: femininity within the female gang', in Vagg, J and Newburn, T, *Emerging Themes in Criminology*, 1998, Loughborough: British Criminology Conferences Selected Proceedings, Vol 1; Brinkworth, L, 'Sugar and spice but not at all nice' (1994) *The Sunday Times*, 27 November.

43   Brinkworth, L, 'Angry young women' (1996) *Cosmopolitan*, February.

44   Fowler, R, 'When girl power packs a punch' (1999) *The Guardian*, 12 July.

45   I am not sure where Fowler's statistics come from. Official criminal statistics indicate that young women of 14–17 years accounted for about 1,800 offences of violence and robbery in 1996, compared with 11,000 young men: Home Office, *Criminal Statistics for England and Wales*, Cm 3764, 1996, London: HMSO. The figure of 460 seems to refer only to robbery committed by young women.

46   *Ibid.*

The problem of the appeal of innocence

A third discourse has been adopted by criminal justice and children's campaigning organisations, which seeks to reclaim the *welfare* needs of bad girls by reconstructing them as innocent victims. This is reflected in changing police practices towards very young prostitutes[47] and is also demonstrated in reports on child prostitution, such as those by The Children's Society and Barnardo's.[48] In the latter, Sara Swann argues powerfully for a model of understanding which reconstructs the 'young prostitute' as the 'abused girl', the 'pimp' as an 'abusing adult' and the 'punter' as a 'sex offender'. Her tightly structured argument identifies a common process of developing control by a young adult man over a young teenage girl, through four distinct stages of ensnaring, creating dependency, taking control and total dominance. Throughout this process, the girl is the helpless victim, misperceiving her abuser as her 'boyfriend' and deceived into a belief that this intense relationship is uniquely 'special'.

Re-imagining the so called prostitution triangle as an abuse triangle is a powerful challenge to the emergence of 'nasty little madams'. But there is a problem with this appeal to childhood innocence. Well intentioned as these rhetorical claims by campaigning groups might be, their methodological and definitional liberties lead to an exaggeration of a problem which is constructed as widespread and horrific.[49] Couched in 'deficit terms', such appeals emphasise the dependence and vulnerability of girls, rather than their strengths or competencies:

> Whether for compensatory, consolatory, controlling or more fundamental economic reasons, adult myth making about children and childhood reflects and maintains the relative powerlessness of children and ensures that they have little recognition as potential authors of their own biography.[50]

In an article on child sexual abuse, Jenny Kitzinger highlights the problem of engaging public sympathy for victims of abuse by appealing to the 'loss of innocence' argument.[51] The traditional dilemma in governing girls (all girls) is a concern to promote and protect their construction as 'innocent' and to

---

47 Edwards, S, 'The legal regulation of prostitution: a human rights issue', in Scambler, G and Scambler, A (eds), *Rethinking Prostitution: Purchasing Sex in the 1990s*, 1997, London: Routledge; Taylor-Browne, J, 'A crying shame: young people involved in prostitution' (1999) 11 Focus on Police Research and Development 24, pp 24–26.

48 Barnardo's, *Whose Daughter Next? Children Abused through Prostitution*, 1998, Ilford: Barnardo's; The Children's Society, *One Way Street? Retrospectives on Childhood Prostitution*, 1999, London: The Children's Society.

49 Shaw, I and Butler, I, 'Understanding young people and prostitution: a foundation for practice?' (1998) 28 Br J Social Work 177.

50 *Ibid*, p 180.

51 Kitzinger, J, 'Who are you kidding? Children, power and the struggle against child sexual abuse', in James, A and Prout, A (eds), *Constructing and Reconstructing Childhood*, 1997, London: Falmer.

prevent their construction as 'knowing-ignorant'.[52] The 'knowing-ignorant' girl is the girl who 'doesn't know what adults want her to know' (and knows a lot they don't want her to) while the 'innocent' girl is the girl who 'doesn't know what adults don't want her to know'. The 'knowing-ignorant' girl has forfeited her moral right to protection – she is 'damaged goods' and a 'walking invitation'.[53] By romanticising the 'innocence' of childhood, and the lost innocence of the sexually abused child (and, indeed, the *sexual* child), public sentimentality serves both to stigmatise the 'knowing-ignorant' girl and to deny access for all girls to the genuine knowledge and power which might reduce their vulnerability to abuse.

But Kitzinger argues further that this construction of abused children within 'adult-centric' discourses, which are concerned about children only to the extent that they impinge on the worlds of adults, fail to recognise the many and varied ways in which abused children *act to resist* their abusers: 'children are constantly acting to pre-empt, evade or modify sexual violence.'[54]

Many abused children successfully negotiate their own survival without the assistance of adults who disbelieve or fail to support them. But others, whose resistance and survival strategies fail, suffer the triple jeopardy of failing to survive, being blamed for their own victimisation and having their acts of resistance criminalised. This is how bad girls are created.

The latest government report on teenage pregnancy encapsulates all these dilemmas.[55] First, a moral panic is constructed. England has the highest rate of teenage pregnancy in Western Europe (but similar to rates in Australia, Canada and New Zealand and much lower than rates in the US) and, in the summer of 1999, the press seemed determined to 'discover' a new 12 year old mother almost every other day. In fact, rates of conception for those under the age of 16 have remained stubbornly consistent at around 8,000 per year. Although there has been an increase since 1993, this has only brought the numbers back to the levels they were in 1985 – the decline in numbers may have been reversed, but the overall numbers have not markedly increased. Secondly, some pregnant girls are constructed as 'innocent' – victims of abusing or feckless men who must be made to pay. But others are constructed as 'knowing-ignorant' girls who must be 'supported' in hostels – supervised and monitored. Yet the same report also makes clear that the use of contraception by UK teenagers is markedly lower than in other European countries. One of the main reasons for this is the confusion, which still exists,

---

52 Kitzinger does not use the phrase 'knowing-ignorant', but she refers to the 'knowing' child who is simultaneously described by adults as 'ignorant' of those protective 'truths' which adults try to impart and wish to see absorbed by children. The juxtaposition of 'knowing' and 'ignorant' seems to capture this adult ambivalence.

53 *Op cit*, Kitzinger, fn 51.

54 *Op cit*, Kitzinger, fn 51, p 173.

55 Social Exclusion Unit, *Teenage Pregnancy*, Cm 4342, 1999, London: Cabinet Office.

about the circumstances under which a young person under the age of 16 may be given contraceptive advice without parental consent.[56] This level of confusion and ignorance reflects adult ambivalence about the expression of adolescent sexuality and a reluctance to give teenagers (and particularly girls) control over their own bodies.[57]

'NASTY LITTLE MADAMS'

I have argued so far that alternative approaches to dealing with bad girls, which attempt to divert them from the formal criminal justice system, have proved no more successful than traditional welfare intervention. Instead, we have seen a number of indicators of a paradigm shift in the treatment of bad girls:

(a) More girls who offend are being dealt with by the criminal justice system rather than the looked after children (formerly care) system.

There has been a disproportionate increase in the number of girls being brought to court, placed on community service and combination orders and sentenced to young offender institutions since 1993.[58] In Canada and the US, there is evidence that the much criticised use of 'status offences' to justify the incarceration of girls on welfare grounds has now been replaced by 'failure to comply' charges. The latter, which may concern breaches of non-criminal court orders (curfews, residence and association conditions), allow the courts to reclassify status offenders as delinquent and incarcerate them in penal, rather than welfare, facilities.[59]

(b) More bad behaviour by girls is being redefined as criminal, particularly fighting.

The Howard League Report, *Lost Inside*, found that half of the girls imprisoned for 'violence' were there for fighting with other girls.[60] Beikoff has identified another pattern among Australian girls charged with assault.[61] The assault charge is frequently one of 'assaulting a police officer', accompanied by a charge of 'resisting arrest', arising out of a public order incident involving drunk and disorderly behaviour. She refers to this as the 'public space

---

56 See Thomson, Chapter 9, in this volume.

57 See Bridgeman, Chapter 11, in this volume, for a discussion of the participation of teenagers in decision making regarding their bodies.

58 Though this increase has to be set against the backdrop of dramatic reductions in juveniles of both sexes being processed during the 1980s (*op cit*, Worrall, fn 7).

59 *Op cit*, Reitsma-Street, fn 15.

60 Howard League, *Lost Inside: The Imprisonment of Teenage Girls*, 1997, London: Howard League for Penal Reform.

61 Beikoff, L, 'Queensland's juvenile justice system: equity, access and justice for young women?', in *op cit*, Alder and Baines, fn 28.

trifecta' and asks whether this has replaced the 'care and control' applications of the past.

(c) More immoral behaviour by girls is being constructed as 'near criminal', for example, so called 'early' pregnancy and lone parenthood.

'Underclass' theorists and right wing politicians from all parties increasingly present such conditions as 'lifestyle *choices*' with 'consequences'. Increasingly, young women are blamed for making these 'choices' and are held responsible for producing the next generation of unsocialised *male* juvenile delinquents. As Charles Murray says, 'the real problem with ... unmarried parenthood is that it offers no ethical alternative for socialising little boys'.[62]

As a consequence of these changing attitudes, there has been a shift away from the 'welfarisation' of troublesome girls towards their criminalisation. Talking to prison officers in women's prisons about the inappropriateness of imprisoning girls, the response one invariably receives these days is that they are *not* lost and bewildered souls, but 'nasty little madams'.

The plight of girls in prison was highlighted in 1997 by three events: a thematic review of women in prison by HM Chief Inspector of Prisons;[63] a report by the Howard League on the imprisonment of teenage girls;[64] and a High Court ruling that a teenage girl should not be held in an adult female prison.[65] There are no institutions in the female prison estate designated solely as Young Offender Institutions. There are two standard Prison Service justifications for mixing young and adult offenders in the female prison estate. First, there are too few young offenders to warrant separate institutions, which would, in any case, exacerbate the problem of women being imprisoned at unreasonable distances from their homes. Secondly (and conveniently!), adult women are regarded as having a stabilising influence on young women (though, strangely, adult men are seen as having a corrupting influence on young men). Setting aside the complaints of adult women that young women have a disruptive influence on *their* lives,[66] reports from the Chief Inspector and Howard League present a rather different picture of girls and young women being bullied, sexually assaulted and recruited as prostitutes and drugs couriers:

There are serious child protection issues in mixing young prisoners with others who may include Schedule 1 offenders (women convicted of offences of violence against children under the 1933 Children and Young Person Act)

---

62 *Op cit*, Murray, fn 10, p 26.

63 HM Inspector of Prisons, *Women in Prison: A Thematic Review*, 1997.

64 *Op cit*, Howard League, fn 60.

65 *R v Secretary of State for the Home Department and Others ex p Flood* [1997] Independent LR, 2 October, cited in *op cit*, Howard League, fn 60.

66 *Ibid*, HM Inspector of Prisons.

which covers a multitude of behaviours ... We noted, for example, women convicted of procuring being held alongside 15 and 16 year olds.[67]

The exposure of girls to an environment that is seriously damaging is explored in detail by the Howard League. In particular, the 'culture' of self-harm, or 'cutting up', which is endemic in most women's prisons, can socialise vulnerable girls into dangerous and disturbed ways of expressing their distress:

> For the vast majority of the young girls we interviewed it was the first time they had come across self-mutilation and we were told by staff that it was rare a 15, 16 or 17 year old would come in self-harming. The danger is that they will copy this behaviour, partly as a way of creating some control in their distressed and chaotic lives, and partly because it is part of the culture of prison life to which they now belong.[68]

The special needs of adolescent women are not being addressed. Prison officers reported to the Howard League that girls in prison had disproportionate experience of sexual abuse, poor or broken relationships with parents, local authority care (between one-third and a half of women in prison have been in care), drug or alcohol abuse, prostitution, school exclusion and truancy.[69]

If one has any lingering doubts about the 'special needs' of girls and young women in prison, one has only to consider the statistics of offences against prison discipline.[70] The rate of disciplinary offending is considerably higher in all young offender institutions than in adult prisons, but the rate for female young offenders is the highest. By far the most common offence is that of 'disobedience or disrespect'. However one chooses to explain this phenomenon (as being an indicator of either very badly behaved young women or overly controlling female prison officers), it is clear that young women have great difficulty in 'settling' in to prison life.

The holding of 18–20 year olds in female prisons, which are currently also designated as young offender institutions, is set to continue. Indeed, the Prison Service is proposing abolishing the terms 'young offender' and 'young offender institutions' for this age group (male and female) altogether.[71] This is the result of the reform of sentencing for 12–17 year olds introduced by the Crime and Disorder Act 1998.[72] It has become clear that holding girls under

---

67 *Op cit*, HM Inspector of Prisons, fn 63, p 26.

68 *Op cit*, Howard League, fn 60, p 33.

69 Hudson, B, 'Lost inside' (1997) 30 Criminal Justice Matters 24.

70 Home Office, *Statistics of Offences Against Prison Discipline and Punishment in England and Wales*, Cm 3715, 1997, London: HMSO.

71 Home Office, *Detention in a Young Offender Institution for 18–20 Year Olds: A Consultation Paper*, 1999, London: HMSO.

72 The Crime and Disorder Act 1998 introduces the detention and training order for under 18 year olds which will require the Prison Service to develop separate establishments and regimes for this younger age group.

the age of 18 alongside adult prisoners contravenes the United Nations Convention on the Rights of the Child and fails to protect them from harm under the Children Act 1989. The Howard League has called for legislation prohibiting the use of prison custody for all girls aged under the age of 18 and the placing of 'those girls who genuinely require secure conditions in local authority secure accommodation units'.[73] After several U-turns, the Government has now announced its intention to do just that in relation to 15 and 16 year olds,[74] though probably not for several years.

CONCLUSION – 'THERE'S 14 AND THEN THERE'S 14'

In the recent trial of Gary Glitter for the sexual abuse of a 14 year old girl, Butterfield J ensured a place for himself in the gallery of judges who have made 'unfortunate' misogynistic remarks about the victims of sexual assault. He is alleged to have commented:

> There's 14 and then there's 14. Some 14 year olds look like sophisticated young ladies. And some 14 year olds still look like little girls. You may wish to consider which category the girl [making the accusation against Glitter] was in.[75]

The implication of this remark is that the only criterion for judging whether a 14 year old girl should be regarded as a child or an adult is her appearance. Her physical maturity is assumed to correlate with her intellectual, emotional and social maturity. All this is then taken not only to justify neglecting her legal right to protection from harm by adults, but to turn an 'innocent' girl into a 'knowing-ignorant' girl – a victim into a predator.

If girls are to be regarded as social actors, genuinely shaping and influencing their own environments, they have to be freed from what Carrington refers to as 'deficit discourses', which 'locate the source of pathology in the defective individual or dysfunctional family, thus providing the rationale or administrative logic for punitive ... intervention'.[76] But such an approach runs the risk of reinforcing the construction of the 'passionate and willful' girls so feared by respectable Victorian and contemporary citizens alike.[77] The potent mixture of female sexuality and independence conjures an image of bad girlhood embedded in the collective conscience, simultaneously titillating and terrifying it.

---

73 *Op cit*, Howard League, fn 60, p 11.

74 Howard League, 'Prison ends for girls' (1999) 17(2) *Howard League Magazine*, p 3.

75 (1999) *The Observer*, 14 November.

76 Carrington, K, 'Offending girls: rethinking intervention regimes', in *op cit*, Alder and Baines, fn 28, p 10.

77 *Op cit*, Alder, fn 5.

Bad girls (that is, girls whose behaviour is depicted as unacceptably sexual, emotional, rebellious and aggressive) may arouse respectable fears, but they are also attractive to respectable citizens, for whom they represent the Lacanian 'Other'. Bad girls hold up a mirror to respectable men and women, reminding them of their own suppressed desires and allowing them to deny the contradictions in their own lives. Misrecognising themselves, they split off and project onto bad girls the 'badness' in themselves, in order to maintain the myth of unity in their own identity.

Despite media and government attempts to have us think otherwise, girls still do not, on the whole, behave badly. But, because so many girls – including the daughters of many magistrates, judges and other criminal justice professionals – are now behaving exceptionally well (when judged by conventional indicators of achievement), the few who do not are becoming increasingly visible. The repositories of collective misogynistic myths about adolescent female sexuality, such girls are constructed as either 'innocent' or 'knowing-ignorant'. What we need to find is a third way of constructing girls as knowledgeable, informed and confident decision makers about their own behaviour. One way forward may be to explore the ways in which young people acquire, develop and create social capital.[78] Rather than focusing on processes of 'normalisation', which seek to close the gap between the 'good girls' who succeed and the 'bad girls' who fail, it may be more fruitful to examine the social networks of trust, co-operation and reciprocity which girls acquire and create *for themselves* and to give greater credence to the value of these in providing girls with self-esteem and a sense of self-efficacy.

---

78 Morrow, V, 'Conceptualising social capital in relation to the well being of children and young people: a critical review' (1999) 47(4) Sociological Rev 744.

CHAPTER 9

LEGAL, PROTECTED AND TIMELY: YOUNG PEOPLE'S PERSPECTIVES ON THE HETEROSEXUAL AGE OF CONSENT

Rachel Thomson

INTRODUCTION

Interviewer: But do you think that legally you should be allowed to have sex at 14?

Lee: It's meant to be an adult thing, isn't it?

Gus: Like legally – well, if legally comes into it, well, probably 16. [Young men's group, 13–14 years, school 6.][1]

Although the average age of sexual debut in the UK is 17, a significant minority of young people in Britain experience heterosexual intercourse before the age of 16.[2] Despite such widespread flaunting of the law, and ongoing campaigns to bring the age of consent for gay men into line with that for heterosexuals, the notion of an age of consent for heterosexuals receives little public scrutiny. Moves to raise the age of consent in the Sexual Offences (Amendment) Bill 1998 where there may be an 'abuse of trust' (where the older party is in a position of authority, such as a teacher or social worker) reinforce rather than question the purpose of existing legislation. The law currently makes it illegal for a man to have sex with a girl under the age of 16, with a maximum penalty of two years' imprisonment, or life imprisonment if the girl is under 13. While there is no defence for the latter offence, if a girl is aged between 13 and 15 and the man is under 24, he is able to defend himself on the grounds that he reasonably believed her to be over 16. The number of reports of these offences to the police, as well as police cautions and prosecutions, have fallen over the last 10 years.[3]

---

1   Thomson, R, Henderson, S, Holland, J, McGrellis, S and Sharpe, S, *Youth Values: Identity, Diversity and Social Change*, End of Award Report No L129251020, 1999, London: Economic and Social Research Council, available at www.sbu.ac.uk/fhss/ssrc/youth.shtml. See below, fn 32, for explanation of codes.

2   Johnson, A, Wadsworth, J, Wellings, K and Field, J, *Sexual Attitudes and Lifestyles*, 1994, London: Blackwell Scientific.

3   HMSO, *Teenage Pregnancy – Report by the Social Exclusion Unit*, 1999, London: HMSO.

There is a growing body of work that seeks to explore the codification of childhood sexuality in the law,[4] yet there continues to be little published material on how children and young people perceive law or the part played by the law in their everyday lives. In this chapter, I discuss current policy constructions of teenage sex. Drawing on the findings of a recent study, I explore young people's perceptions of the age of heterosexual consent, considering their views of the purpose and efficacy of the law, as well as the ways in which the law may contribute less directly to their sexual cultures.

SEX AND CHILDREN

The child is central to modern sexuality. Children and teenagers are sexualised by the way that youthfulness is sold to adult consumers and ultimately sold back to the young as they enter into market relations as consumers of make-up, fashion, music and games. Celia Lury describes how, within modern consumer culture, the category 'youth' has been dissociated from chronological age, and become an attitude or characteristic that can be acquired, cultivated and consumed.[5] But, at the same time that youth becomes available to those who have the time, money or inclination to produce it, the markers of adulthood become increasingly dispersed, uncertain and contradictory,[6] which contributes to anxiety about adult/child relations.[7] Children are also sexualised by the attention that we pay to those who prey on them, with media coverage of paedophiles and abusers revealing a prurient fascination with the child as a passive yet sexual object, sexually innocent yet corruptible. Debbie Epstein and Richard Johnson have reflected on the contradictions of this particularly British 'naughty but nice' approach to sexuality which simultaneously represses and incites, suggesting that the moral traditionalism of much tabloid and political commentaries on sex education and the age of consent feeds off scandalous revelation.[8]

---

4   Harris, N (ed), *Children, Sex Education and the Law*, 1996, London: National Children's Bureau; Monk, D, 'Sex education and the problematisation of teenage pregnancy, a genealogy of law and governance' (1998) 7(2) SLS 241; Waites, M, 'The age of consent and sexual citizenship in the United Kingdom: a history', in Seymour, J and Bagguley, R (eds), *Relating Intimacies: Power and Resistance*, 1999, London: Macmillan.

5   Lury, C, *Consumer Culture*, 1996, Cambridge: Polity.

6   Chisholm, L and Hurrelman, K, 'Adolescence in modern Europe: pluralised transition patterns and their implications for personal risks' (1996) 18 J Adolescence 128.

7   Jenks, C, *Childhood*, 1996, London: Routledge.

8   Epstein, D and Johnson, R, *Schooling Sexualities*, 1998, Milton Keynes: OU Press, p 184.

In formal terms, legitimate adult sexuality is dependent on the exclusion of the child,[9] effected through legal ages of consent. Introduced in the Criminal Law Amendment Act 1885, the age of consent for heterosexual sexual intercourse was designed to protect young women from predatory men, prohibiting sexual intercourse with a woman aged under 16. In drawing a line at 16, the law can be seen as defining the condition of those either side, both the child (in need of protection) and the adult (as having the right to consent).[10] However, the age of consent for heterosexuals must also be understood as enshrining in law an asymmetrical and gendered notion of sex and sexual agency. By defining sex as an act of bodily penetration, these legal prescriptions ignore the potential for sexual agency on the part of the receptive party, while also creating male sexual agency as a force requiring control.

The term 'age of consent' is itself misleading. Matthew Waites describes the law as prohibiting rather than empowering, a negative prohibition placing limits upon the rights of men to sexual access. As such, 'the law represented a limit on male agency rather than a recognition of women's equal agency'.[11] Although Waites observes that in more recent years there has been a shift in the popular imagination, from seeing the age of consent in prohibitive terms to an assertion of a positive right to consent, other feminist commentators have observed that the 'discourse of consent' that such legal formulations incite continues to anchor and compound restrictively gendered sexual scripts.[12] Some of the omission of female sexual agency from British law has begun to be addressed (for example, the measure to acknowledge and prohibit rape within marriage contained in the Criminal Justice and Public Order Act 1994), yet the implementation of the heterosexual age of consent and judgments in rape cases such as that described by Lynn Jamieson,[13] which ignore the intentions of the female party, reinforces the problem that British law has in representing a meaningful right to consent.[14]

While the formal ages of consent remain at 16 for heterosexuals and 18 for gay men, in practice, the age at which young people first have sex in Britain has been falling, and a significant minority will have sexual intercourse before

---

9   Evans, D, *Sexual Citizenship: The Materialist Construction of Sexualities*, 1993, London: Routledge. See Bridgeman, Chapter 11, in this volume, for an account of law's 'ideal' child and his or her relationship with adulthood.

10   *Op cit*, Waites, fn 4.

11   *Op cit*, Waites, fn 4, p 97.

12   Holland, J, Ramazanoglu, C, Sharpe, S and Thomson, R, *The Male in the Head: Young People, Heterosexuality and Power*, 1998, London: Tufnell; Gavey, N, 'Technologies and effects of heterosexual coercion', in Wilkinson, S and Kitzinger, S (eds), *Heterosexuality: A Feminism and Psychology Reader*, 1993, London: Sage.

13   Jamieson, L, 'The social construction of consent revisited', in Adkins, L and Merchant, V (eds), *Sexualising the Social: Power and the Organisation of Sexuality*, 1996, London: Macmillan.

14   *Op cit*, Waites, fn 4.

they are legally entitled to do so.[15] While a range of alternative explanations have been offered for this fall, including earlier menarche among young women[16] and the provision of sex education in schools,[17] international comparisons suggest that the norms of teenage sexual practice are culturally specific, with a higher age of sexual debut and 'responsible' sexual health practices being associated with more liberal public policy responses to the sexuality of the young.[18] Within a social and economic context where material independence from parents or the State is delayed, it has also been argued that sexual agency becomes an increasingly important marker of adulthood and autonomy.[19] Reaching the age of consent for sex does not bestow formal rights of citizenship (for women and gay men the law can still be seen as seeking to provide 'protection' rather than bestowing rights.[20] However, becoming 'legal' could be understood as welcoming one into a form of intimate citizenship with arguably equal or greater personal and cultural resonance than other dimensions of citizenship, such as the right to vote, to drive or to drink.[21]

POLICY AGENDAS

While the sexual agency of the young is acknowledged and sometimes celebrated in popular media forms such as magazines and pop music,[22] it poses problems for governments, institutions and professionals. The most obvious site for official discomfort over the sexuality of minors can be found in the enduring controversies that surround the provision of sex education in schools. For over 10 years, politicians, civil servants, educationalists, health professionals and the media have been embroiled in a continuing process of prescription, reform and revision to the curriculum, official guidance and regulation.[23] During most of this period, the agenda has been dominated by

15 Op cit, Johnson et al, fn 2.

16 Coleman, J, 'Puberty: is it happening earlier?' (1997) Young Minds Magazine, p 34.

17 Op cit, Epstein and Johnson, fn 8.

18 Ingham, R, The Development of an Integrated Model of Sexual Conduct Amongst Young People, End of Award Report No H52427501495, 1997, London: Economic and Social Research Council.

19 Furlong, A and Cartmel, F, Young People and Social Change, 1997, Buckingham: OU Press.

20 Op cit, Waites, fn 4.

21 Plummer, K, Telling Sexual Stories: Power, Change and Social Worlds, 1995, London: Routledge; Weeks, J, Invented Moralities: Sexual Values in an Age of Uncertainty, 1995, Cambridge: Polity.

22 McRobbie, A, 'More! New sexualities in girls' and women's magazines', in Curran, J, Morely, D and Walkerdine, V (eds), Cultural Studies and Communication, 1996, London: Arnold; op cit, Lury, fn 5.

23 Meredith, P, Sex Education: Political Issues in Britain and Europe, 1989, London: Routledge; Thomson, R, 'Moral rhetoric and public health pragmatism: the recent politics of sex education' (1994) 48 Feminist Rev (Autumn) 40.

conservative forces which have succeeded in enshrining in law a requirement for sex education to be taught within a 'moral framework' to promote marriage, a prohibition on the 'promotion of homosexuality' and for there to be a parental right to withdraw children from sex education classes. In addition, media exposés of progressive professional practice alongside condemnation from politicians and ministers have contributed towards an 'intimidatory culture' in relation to both teaching about lesbian and gay sexualities and the giving of explicit safer sex and contraceptive advice in the classroom.[24]

Alongside these conservative measures, however, we find requirements to teach about sexually transmitted disease within the statutory curriculum and acknowledgment that medical professionals have the discretion to provide confidential contraceptive advice to under 16s. Thus, the moral authoritarianism that sought to repress the sexuality of the young has been tempered by a public health pragmatism that, in seeking to address some of the consequences of adolescent sexual activity, must also acknowledge its existence. Monk has written about this tension in terms of law constructing children differently in the fields of health and education: in health, the child is a patient, being independent and potentially sexual; while, in education, the child is a pupil, dependent and asexual.[25] He suggests that this tension reflects a limited political resolution by enabling 'conflicting practices, or expertise to operate simultaneously'.[26] But these competing veins of political discourse have also resulted in a highly prescribed arena of public policy giving rise to considerable professional caution. Teachers continue to be uncertain as to whether they are 'allowed' to teach about lesbian and gay sexuality in the face of s 28 of the Local Government Act 1988[27] and health, education and social services professionals question the legitimacy of their role in the provision of advice and practical support to sexually active young people under the age of 16.[28]

While the New Labour Government have brought a new language and different priorities to bear on the area, teenage sex and its consequences continue to be a troublesome arena for politicians and policy makers. At the turn of the millennium, a plethora of competing government initiatives seek both to define and solve 'the problem' of teenage sex. Some of these initiatives

---

24 *Op cit*, Epstein and Johnson, fn 8.

25 Monk, D, 'Sex education and HIV/AIDS: political conflict and legal resolution' (1998) 12 Children and Society 295.

26 *Ibid*, p 304.

27 Douglas, N, Warwick, I, Kemp, S and Whitty, G, *Playing it Safe: Responses of Secondary School Teachers to Lesbian, Gay and Bisexual Pupils, Bullying, HIV/AIDS Education and Section 28*, 1997, University of London: HERU, Institute of Education.

28 Bridgeman, J, 'Don't tell the children: the Department's guidance on the provision of information on contraception to individual pupils', in *op cit*, Harris, fn 4.

have been inherited by the present Government, others form a deliberate part of New Labour's articulation of a third way in social and economic policy. Under John Major's Conservative Government, the 'problem of teenage sex' was situated within a framework of declining morality. Under the direction of Nick Tate, the Qualifications and Curriculum Authority sought to develop curriculum guidelines on spiritual and moral development as part of the revision of the National Curriculum for the year 2000. With a change of government, the language of morality has been superseded by that of citizenship and personal development. Now, sex education must find a place within a non-compulsory curriculum for personal, social and health education (at Key Stages 4 and 5) and a compulsory curriculum for citizenship. Outside of education, the 'problem of teenage sex' has been enthusiastically taken up by the Home Office under Jack Straw, this time cast in terms of parenting and its place in reproducing cycles of deprivation.[29] The Department of Health has continued to be a key player promoting an agenda of positive sexual health through a National Sexual Health Strategy and a task force on teenage pregnancy.

In the name of 'joined-up government', the Social Exclusion Unit located in the Cabinet Office has sought to transcend or incorporate these different perspectives in an agenda that focuses on a two way relationship between deprivation and premature parenthood.[30] Their report on teenage pregnancy has been widely welcomed, although it has been criticised by some for giving mixed messages.[31] The report can be seen as a shrewd attempt to integrate the discourses of competing lobbies, simultaneously providing tabloid headlines about hostels for young mothers and the pursuit of feckless fathers via the Child Support Agency, while also addressing the different professional agendas. Within the report, the health card was played by recommending the promotion of confidential contraceptive services to young women under the age of 16; the family card by calling in the support of parents of teenagers as well as providing practical and moral support for teenage parents. By recommending the training of teachers to provide sex education and inspection of school provision by Ofsted, the education lobby were also effectively engaged. But despite these efforts at coherence, the main policy hot spots continue to be unresolved. The difficulties faced by the Government in repealing s 28 of the Local Government Act and their willingness to appease the religious and conservative lobbies suggest that the enduring tensions between moral authoritarianism and progressive and pragmatic reform remain unresolved within the ideological project of New Labour. The failure

29 Home Office, *Supporting Families: A Consultation Document*, 1998, London: HMSO.
30 *Op cit*, HMSO, fn 3.
31 Sex Education Forum, *Response to Social Exclusion Unit Consultation Document on Teenage Pregnancy*, 1999, London: National Children's Bureau.

to 'trade' a smooth passage for a repeal of s 28 in the House of Lords with an amendment to the Learning and Skills Bill, which would make it a statutory requirement to both promote marriage and 'understand difference', has left the policy agenda lying in tatters. Pragmatic and detailed draft guidance on sex education and a range of initiatives growing from the Social Exclusion Unit report on teenage pregnancy are now paralysed and dependent on a political resolution that appears to be beyond the means of the Government to secure.

FROM POLICY TO PRACTICES

While such public politics can be understood to frame and influence the sexual culture within which young people become sexual agents, there is no simple process of translation between the world of teenage sex and that of social policy and the law. In the rest of this chapter, I will try to shed light on this interface from the perspective of young people themselves. Drawing on data from a recent study, I explore how young people perceive the law in the area of teenage sexuality and the ways in which they themselves engage with the various discourses that shape the social policy agenda. By considering the 'view from below', I hope to shed fresh light on the 'gap' between law and policy and everyday life.

The study *Youth Values: Identity, Diversity and Social Change*[32] is an investigation of the moral landscapes of young people aged 11–16 growing up in five contrasting areas of the UK. The study sample includes approximately 1,800 young people from eight secondary schools. Four of these schools were located in geographically and socially distinct locations in different parts of England, and a further four within one city in Northern Ireland. Study participants were identified by selecting one or two mixed ability tutor groups in each school year and these groups subsequently completed questionnaires administered by researchers in a classroom setting. Respondents were invited

---

32 *Op cit*, Thomson *et al*, fn 1. The study was funded by the Economic and Social Research Council as part of the programme, Children Five to 16: Growing Up into the 21st Century (No L129251020). The five areas, which are located in eight schools, can be described as follows. In Northern Ireland: school 1, an inner city area with a predominantly working class and mixed religious catchment; school 2, a suburban area with a mixed class and religious catchment (integrated); school 3, an inner city area with a working class and religiously homogeneous catchment (Catholic); and school 4, an inner city area with a working class and religiously homogeneous catchment (Protestant). In England: school 5, a large housing estate with a working class and ethnically homogeneous catchment; school 6, an inner city area with a largely working class and ethnically diverse catchment; school 7, a commuter belt area with a largely middle class and ethnically homogeneous catchment; and school 8, a rural village with a mixed class and ethnically homogeneous catchment. All quotes are identified by speaker (names have been changed), composition of the group (mixed, young women and young men), school year age group and school.

to volunteer to participate in single and mixed sex focus groups and subsequently in individual interviews. Here, I draw primarily on focus group data and, in particular, on an analysis of young people's responses to the suggestion that the age of consent for heterosexual sex should be lowered to the age of 14.

Legal sex

Guidance from the Department for Education and Employment suggests that sex education in schools should ensure that children are aware of the law on sexual conduct.[33] The proposal that the age of consent for heterosexual sex be lowered from 16 to 14 caused some confusion among young people in the study. The characteristic response was for groups to work their way through a number of different positions before forming a view, and frequently contradicting themselves in the process. These contradictions can be seen to arise directly from those effected by the law and the inconsistency between the law and other competing values, discourses and regimes. The idea of values regimes is employed in order to describe the different terms of reference that young people employ when making judgments, distinctions and choices.[34]

Few young people accepted the authority of the legal prescription, observing that 'most people don't go by the law'. While many found themselves supporting the age of 16 or suggesting it be raised to 18, they were at pains to clarify that it was not the law *per se* that made sex legitimate but a range of other factors. For some, the imposition of public rules on an area of such private intimacy was challenged. As one young woman observed, 'it's like putting an age on loving. People don't believe in it, 'cos you can't control your feelings by a law can you?'.

One factor undermining the authority of the law in this area was the problem of policing. This was observed both in terms of the inappropriateness of the police engaging in the everyday romances of teenagers and in their knowledge and experience that transgressions of the law go without punishment:

---

33 Department for Education, *Education Act 1993: Sex Education in Schools*, Circular 5/94, 1994.

34 Building on the idea that values exist within specific discursive formations (see Tronto J, *Moral Boundaries: A Political Argument for an Ethic of Care*, 1993, London: Routledge), the notion of different values regimes is used to describe the criteria employed to make judgments within different discourses. Eg, some of the regimes that characterise young people's moral discourse identified in the study include aesthetic regimes (enabling distinctions to be made on the basis of beauty and unattractiveness), entertainment regimes (enabling distinctions on the basis of exciting and boring) and, most relevant to this discussion, health regimes (enabling distinctions on the basis of health and sickness) and regimes centred on agency (enabling distinction between choice and compulsion): *op cit*,Thomson *et al*, fn 1.

Carla:	You can't say it's illegal because you can't go round everywhere getting all people who've done it under 16 and putting them in prison. [Mixed group, 11–16 years, school 5.]
Angela:	It's not as if you're going to go to the police every time you've got a problem, you know, like yer boyfriend's asked you to go with you is that ok? [Young women's group, 12–13 years, school 5.]
Elliot:	Well, the law is the police and they're just nothing really.
Lee:	'Cos say you do it and you're under 16, the police find out like that boy and the girl that got pregnant, the police didn't do nothing, did they? [Young men's group, 13–14 years, school 6.]

While the idea of the police intervening to enforce the legal age of consent was ridiculed, a number of young people felt that parents might have a more legitimate role in policing this boundary:

Interviewer:	... who polices underage sex?
Keith:	They can't lock you up.
Jean:	The only people who might catch you is your parents
Francis:	They could lock you up. [Mixed group, 14–15 years, school 8.]

Although parents regularly exercise consent on behalf of their children in other areas,[35] the area of sexual agency was felt to lie beyond the scope of regular parent/child negotiations. Young people's responses suggested that sexual agency was a very personal and private realm in which they did not expect the State nor parents to be in a position to intervene, making the legal age of consent a difficult law to implement. As Keith observed, 'It's sort of like in law but it's not sort of there, is it? It's not sort of like a crime or drugs or whatever'.

Protected sex

Although young people ridiculed the idea of the State intervening in their intimate lives, they did not argue for the abolition of the age of consent. In fact, most thought that, if any change was to be made to the existing age limit of 16, it should be to raise the age to 18. In several cases, discussions of the age of consent gave rise to references to the sexual abuse of children by adults. However, it was in their discussions of sexual relations between the young that discussants were most animated. A number of young women described the difficulties associated with freely consenting to sex within a cultural context in which pressure from partners is the norm. Although it was recognised that young women may want to have sex, it was also considered

---

35 See Bridgeman, Chapter 11, in this volume.

that they might need to be protected from the consequences of having sex at such a young age:

Louise: I think if you lower the age to 14 they go, oh, yeah, that's great, you know, oh, yeah, 'cos I can be like everybody – I can be like my sister ... and everything but because they do it sometimes girls feel cheap and dirty about it afterwards 'cos they just thought, oh, great. But it's not as good as they thought it would be and because they've heard all this great stuff from magazines and this is great and that's great they think, oh, it's going to be absolutely brilliant. But sometimes it's not and they can get put down by that. But I think raising – no, lowering it to 14 is a really bad idea because girls are – they're just –

Lindsey: More stupid!

Louise: They're growing up – they're still growing and if anything I wouldn't really care if they raised it because I still think at 16 it's dangerous. [Young women's group, 13–14 years, school 7.]

Young men talked less easily about the negative consequences of sex, but they too acknowledged that there was pressure to lose their virginity:

Taylor: I think we should have it when we're 16 ... Because it's a suitable age – 14's not suitable.

Lee: I think you should do it when you're ready to do it.

Elliot: Absolutely, that's true.

Gus: Yeah, when you're ready.

Taylor: When you think you're ready – no one should force you to do it.

Gus: Yeah, there's a lot of peer pressure. Yeah, some people – some friends will tend to go 'you gotta do it man'.

Elliot: You're a VIRGIN! [Young men's group, 13–14 years, school 6.]

In most areas of young people's moral discourse, there was a tendency to accentuate personal agency and to downplay the influence of traditional and institutional forms of authority, a tendency that is consistent with wider social processes of individualisation where deeply rooted social changes are seen to transform social structures and identities, giving rise to increasingly tolerant, liberal and individualistic interpersonal and sexual values.[36] While young people were relatively respectful of most aspects of the law (and particularly that concerning the protection of property), they tended to be more critical and less observant of legal proscriptions on personal behaviour and individual freedoms. But, although they did not recognise the authority of the

---

36 Beck, U, *Risk Society: Towards a New Modernity*, 1992, London: Sage; *op cit*, Furlong and Cartmel, fn 19; Thomson, R, 'Dream on: the logic of sexual practice' (2000) 3(3) J Youth Studies 8.

law to determine their sexual practices, they did, grudgingly, accept that the law could lend support when under pressure:

Francis:	Whatever they change it to – if they change it to – it's not going to stop anybody, is it?
Andrew:	I don't think there's a need to sort of hide behind the law.
Keith:	I suppose there is for some people ...
Jean:	Yeah, it's your willpower isn't it?
Helena:	'Cos like if your boyfriend's much older than you and he wants to and you're like really young and you're not sure, then I think you just shouldn't need to hide behind the law because if he really loves you then you could say no and he'll respect it.
Jacqueline:	It is something to hide behind if they wanted, they've got the excuse, haven't they?
Keith:	If you're ready you're ready, aren't you?
Interviewer:	So do you think that the law actually –
Jacqueline:	It's a protective for them. [Mixed group, 14–15 years, school 8.]

So, despite their ambivalence about the authority of the law, young people were unhappy about dispensing with rules altogether. Girls in particular were not confident that their interest would be served if sexual negotiations were completely private. Although the idea of needing protection was not attractive to most young women, either because they wanted to see themselves as positive sexual agents and/or because it conflicted with romantic ideas of mutuality, most considered the law to be a necessary, albeit a rather ineffective, safety net which could be invoked if 'cornered'. The law then becomes a resource upon on which they can draw when they need support. Girls also recognised that the law was framed in such a way that it protected or possibly absolved them from legal responsibility:

Louise:	But say you're 14 and it's against the law until you're 16 and you had sex with a 17 year old and then people find out, then that 17 year old could get done. For rape or something. [Young women's group, 13–14 years, school 5.]

Although young men recognised that there was pressure on them to become sexually active (usually from friends or peers), they were unlikely to talk in terms of pressure from sexual partners. In their discussions of the age of consent, a number of the groups of young men commented on the asymmetry of the law and the presumption that only males can be agents or aggressors. In some cases, these discussions implied suspicion of the motives of women who, they suggest, may 'claim' rape to protect or advance their own interests:

Paul:	It's up to the girl though, innit? 'Cos if you have sex and they know it now, like rape or something.
Guy:	Not if they say that they want it.

Paul:	No, 'cos – then they get pregnant – they could say they didn't want it.
Jack:	Yeah, I know.
Liam:	They get money for it, can't they?
Paul:	Yeah, and you get arrested for it.
Jack:	You wouldn't get arrested if you –
Paul:	No, but, say, they don't know that you've said yeah – the girl said yes or –
Guy:	Why don't they take them to court and say, 'Oh, said, yeah, I wanted the sex, I wanted the baby, it was my choice'.
Jack:	Why? Because the man could have raped her.
Guy:	Well, if the girl said that she wanted it right then –
Jack:	And then like the boy said, 'She said yeah'. [Young men's group, 12–13 years, school 5.]

In this discussion, the young men attempt to square their emergent knowledge that both men and women can desire sex, and that both can also manipulate and pressure their partners, with a legal paradigm that assumes gendered agency. While this discussion demonstrates considerable confusion concerning the implementation of the law and the judicial process, it does suggest that the expression of gender difference contained in such legislation contributes to the cultural definition of a form of masculinity constructed in opposition to femininity.

In another case, young men criticise the sexism at the heart of the law on sexual consent, both noting its inconsistency with their knowledge of women's agency in other spheres and also questioning the suggestion that all men are potential rapists:

Elliot:	What I don't think's fair though is like there's some kind of law if the girl's under age and the boy's – he's got the age – yeah, like he's 17 or something and the girl's 15 then that happens – that – he could be accused of rape and that.
Gus:	Yeah, why is that?
Elliot:	Is it – 'cos look, right – a lot of people like will say like, oh, men are sexist when they say, oh, go and play your netball or something, right? But they're trying to make out that like – I don't know like.
Lee:	All men are.
Gus:	Huh?
Lee:	All men are – they make out all men are –
Elliot:	And then people will say like the men are the ones that rape – I don't know why – maybe 'cos like we are a bit stronger, I think that's a known fact even though there's these muscly women on

> TV, but, you know what – I don't know, I just think there's no
> need for that really. [Young men's group, 13–14 years, school 6.]

As it is constructed in terms of protection and male sexual agency, the law on heterosexual consent suggests a social context characterised by mutually exclusive and oppositional gender roles. While this is consistent with some aspects of young people's sexual experiences, it is inconsistent with other powerful cultural narratives that influence their sexual and gender identities. It is in young people's discussions of the other side of this legal boundary, the point at which they believe they are old enough or mature enough for a sexual relationship, that we can hear the expression of more positive notions of sexual consent.

Timely sex

The idea that sex should only happen when you are 'ready' for it was widespread and expressed by young men as well as young women. The definition of being 'ready' was complex and shifting, reflecting some of the underlying tensions in the construction of sexual agency and maturity. For example, the widely held view (in the study) that girls mature more quickly than boys existed in some tension with another popular belief that boys pressure girls to have sex before they are ready. In response to the suggestion that the age of consent be lowered to 14, one group of girls tried to work through this contradiction:

Luu: 'Cos – I'm not really sure because it can be because you know when girls sort of like mature very quickly in the age of 13 to 16 so girls should learn – they should have – put it down to 14; but then boys – they're sort of like – their minds just stay like children and like if you give them some questions about sex they all start giggling and laughing their heads off and then they start pointing at each other and go ...

Interviewer: Right, so you think it should be different for boys and girls then – the age of consent?

Luu: But I don't think the girls' age should be lowered to 14 – I think that's a bit young 'cos I mean you might be physically ready but you might not be emotionally ready for what's going to happen – like you might not be able to deal with things that come afterwards – like just say you was to have sex at like 14 and then like the guy would – 'cos guys are just like that – they might not talk to you the next day and they like go around and tell all their friends and everything and you're really regretting it – you would have wished that you'd have waited until you were 16 or something like that, then you'd be able to deal with it. [Young women's group, 13–14 years, school 6.]

In this example, a number of different dimensions of maturity are simultaneously deployed. Luu is confident of the relative physical and emotional advantage that girls hold over boys, based on her personal experience of smaller and emotionally incontinent male schoolmates. However, this advantage in maturity cannot be easily translated into notions of sexual agency when sexual experience confronts young women with so many physical and moral dangers.[37] It is hardly surprising, then, that young people were concerned to make sex morally and socially legitimate within their own terms. Rarely was this by arguing for sex to be located exclusively within marriage. Rather, the source of this legitimacy was located in a notion of agency, choice and control mediated by time – most clearly expressed in discussions of being 'ready' for sex. This idea of readiness was flexible enough to accommodate individual and gender differences. So, for one person, being ready might mean being informed and not under pressure, while for another it could mean being in a committed and stable relationship, confident and informed enough to practise safer sex.

Achieving readiness posed the most obvious challenges to young women for whom untimely or illegitimate sex has immediate consequences for an individual's reputation within the immediate moral community of the school or the peer group. Although boys also reported experiencing pressure to have sex, they did not face the danger of engaging in morally illegitimate sex in the same way as girls. For girls, sexual activity presented a contradiction, since it is a requirement of normative (hetero)sex that they control sexual encounters (by accepting or rejecting advances), but that they do so from a position of relative passivity. Young women were most likely to define readiness for sex in terms of the quality of a relationship. In particular, it was felt that a relationship should be developed enough so that a partner could be trusted not to talk to friends and undermine a young woman's reputation in her wider moral community:

Sandra: You should be – you can't just go doing it with any lad you see when you're 14 – if you love him or if you're in a relationship and you know it's going to last and he's not gonna go round school saying, 'oh, I've done this with her'. [Young women's group, 12–13 years, school 5.]

In a cultural context where sexual pressure is perceived to be the norm, where female sexual agency is difficult to articulate and where inequalities of power and experience characterise sexual relationships, it can be difficult to judge when a person is 'ready' for sex. In the following example, a young woman describes a test:

---

37 Thomson, R, McGrellis, S, Holland, J, Henderson, S and Sharpe, S, 'From Peter André's "six pack" to "I do knees": the body in young people's moral discourse', in Milburn-Backett, K and McKie, L (eds), *Gendered Bodies*, 2000, London: Macmillan.

Hannah:	Yeah, but if you wanted to have sex and you feel it's the right moment, the way to test them is to say no and see how they react – if they say – 'oh, that's all right' then you say, 'all right then, let's have sex' [laughs] – that's if you're ready for it though. [Young women's group, 13–14 years, school 6.]

In this comment, achieving readiness can be seen as negotiating the space to allow a choice to be made, which enables positive consent. The various criteria for readiness can be understood as the factors that make a sexual relationship personally and socially legitimate. Trust and freedom from pressure are crucial, as are the maintenance of self-respect and a respectable sexual reputation. To ensure that contraception is used with the mother's blessing gains further legitimacy:

Sandra:	My sister – she's in a close relationship with a lad but he's 16 and if – you have to discuss it with your – she's mature enough now to do it – she's gone on the pill and everything – but not for that reason – and if she wants – me mum says if she wants to do it now 'cos my mum likes the lad – and if she wants to do it me mum said that she can but use contraception and everything because. [Young women's group, 12–13 years, school 5.]

There is no clear distinction in young people's accounts of sexual practice between morally safe sex and sex that is safe in medical terms.[38] Young people were aware of an alternative values regime within which the acceptability of sexual practice could be judged on the basis of physical safety. The main source of such values for young people was the advice of agony aunts and uncles in the problem pages of young women's magazines. In the following example, young women counterpoise moral, legal and health discourses on teenage sex:

Donna:	Sometimes the problem pages are good for them to write in and be able to tell them what's wrong with and then they like write back.
Sonia:	Give them advice something about sex – I think they're encouraging people to go out and do it, yeah.
Interviewer:	Right, so you think it's pressure?
Sonia:	Their comments on the end –
Interviewer:	Like what?
Sonia:	Just go out and do what you want but if –
Donna:	As long as its safe.
Sonia:	It's just telling you –
Donna:	Yeah.

---

38   *Op cit*, Holland *et al*, fn 12.

Interviewer: And you think that's bad advice?

Sonia: Yeah.

Donna: Yeah.

Interviewer: You think they should be saying don't do it?

Donna: Some magazines say you shouldn't be having it under age anyway 'cos like I am 15 and then the comments on the bottom say you shouldn't be having sex now but some just say as long as you're taking – as long as you're being – having safe sex. [Young women's group, 14–15 years, school 5.]

This group of young women have an ambivalent response to being treated as subjects of a health discourse – independent and sexual. Although they read the values regime of the discourse of the problem pages as equating safe sex with good sex, they challenge the authority of the agony aunts and uncles, invoking the law in support of their respectable sexual identities.

Readiness to have sex was also associated with wider social roles. If sex is 'an adult thing', then it may be inconsistent with other non-adult roles, particularly that of the dependent and asexual identity of a school pupil.[39] This is consistent with the view expressed by many young people that sex and the consequences of sex were likely to interfere with their education and their ability to achieve other elements of adult autonomy:

Terese: 'Cos if you had it when you were 14 and everything then you might get pregnant and you couldn't cope because like if you was 14 then you'd have to go through all your HSEs and everything in school and your GCSEs and everything – and you couldn't do it 'cos like say you –

Louise: You'd have no time.

Terese: 'Cos if you had like a career ahead of you and you wanted to be like that thing for ages and ages and then you went and got pregnant at 14 then you wouldn't be able to do it. [Young women's group, 13–14 years, school 5.]

The link between early parenthood and early sex and between sex and social exclusion was a surprising common theme arising in young people's discussions of the heterosexual age of consent. Different dimensions of adult status are not only fragmented,[40] but they may stand in some tension with each other. So, while being sexually experienced could be seen to constitute maturity, it could also be seen as a sign of immaturity and something that may have a very practical effect on material opportunities. Similarly, early

---

39 *Op cit*, Monk, fn 25; *op cit*, Monk, fn 4.

40 Jones, G and Bell, R, *Balancing Acts: Youth, Parenting and Public Policy*, Report to Joseph Rowntree Foundation, November 1999.

parenthood may offer young people access to adult responsibilities and status in the short term while also tying them to social and economic dependence in the long term.[41]

CONCLUSIONS

Young people's discussions about the age of consent were characterised by inconsistency, contradiction, resistance and the movement between a range of discourses and values regimes. Some of the ideas with which they engage can be traced directly to the major policy discourses that shape public debates over teenage sex – for example, the 'public health pragmatism' of agony aunts' advice (safe sex is legitimate sex), the 'welfarism' of their concerns about early parenthood and social exclusion (finish your exams first!). Others can be linked to more popular cultural forms such as consumerism (if it feels good, do it) and the therapeutic culture (if it feels right for you, do it). These different discourses provide young people with different ways of talking and thinking about sex, and with a range of identities and locations to imagine and deploy.[42] Yet these different ways of talking and thinking about sex do not offer freedom to young people to create unique individual identities and desires. Rather, they are underpinned by powerful and enduring gender asymmetries that are effectively enforced and policed within young people's own moral communities.

The law plays an important part in these processes. It does more than provide young people with a way of talking, for they encounter it as a fact about sex, of which they must make some sense. At the heart of the current law on the heterosexual age of consent are very strong messages about gender and sexual agency, which stand in contradiction to the way in which young people think about themselves. The law presents sex as an instrumental act, seeking only to limit male agency, ignoring the existence of or the potential for agency on the part of the woman. Where young people think of themselves as equal, the law treats them as different and as gendered. Where young people would like to think of themselves as being in control, the law treats them as either out of control or as in the control of another. There is a clear tension here between legal and lay notions of consent, the former speaking in terms of protection, the latter in terms of rights. Yet this is not a tension that young people are easily able to resolve, for, despite the dominance of the rhetoric of

---

41 For a full discussion, see Thomson, R, 'Authority', in Rutherford, J (ed), *The Art of Life*, 2000, London: Lawrence & Wishart.

42 Thomson, R and Scott, S, *Learning About Sex*, 1991, London: Tufnell; *op cit*, Holland *et al*, fn 12.

individualism, the gendered power relations implicit in the asymmetry of the law are confirmed in the social relations that underpin their social worlds.[43]

Public discourses can be understood as resources that young people can employ in their intimate and local negotiations of sexual practice and identity. They can 'hide behind the law', 'demand safe sex', 'be mature and do it', 'be mature and wait'. What was clear from their discussions was that, although they expressed the desire to be respected and trusted, they also recognised the importance of publicly negotiated rules in the form of the law. And, while they may ignore these rules, they also engage with them in the creation of their sexual cultures. There was no clear consensus among young people as to whether the law should or could encroach into the privacy of their intimate relationships, reflecting enduring controversy that has traditionally characterised public debate over the law on sexual conduct. Their views on privacy were shaped most obviously by gender, with young men most dismissive of the attempts to control or define their behaviour and young women most aware of the potential benefits of such interventions into the private. However, similarities between the public policy agenda and the concerns of the young end here. It appears that for young people, it is less important that sex is legal or protected than for it to be 'timely', a delicate state of social and interpersonal acceptability. In order to judge readiness, it is necessary to consider the balance of interests and power of particular circumstances and relationships. While it is unlikely that the law concerning sexual conduct will be flexible or sensitive enough to capture such specificity, an understanding of consent informed by lay understandings could make a contribution to developing discussions of sexual citizenship,[44] as well as enriching policy and practice approaches to sexual health.

---

43 *Op cit*, Furlong and Cartmel, fn 19; *op cit*, Holland *et al*, fn 12.

44 *Op cit*, Evans, fn 9; *op cit*, Plummer, fn 21; *op cit*, Weeks, fn 21; Richardson, D, 'Sexuality and citizenship' (1998) 32(1) Sociology 83.

CHAPTER 10

EDUCATION LAW/EDUCATING GENDER

Daniel Monk

INTRODUCTION

Education law has evolved over the last 15 or so years into a distinct and widely accepted category of academic law and legal practice. No longer simply an aspect of public, welfare, tort or family law, it now has its own specialist practitioners, legal associations,[1] case reports,[2] law journals,[3] and textbooks and courses within the legal curriculum. It is possible to view this development as both a process of consolidation and as a response to the dramatic increase in education related litigation. While not denying these simple explanations I want to argue for a more critical engagement. My starting point is a refusal to accept that the categorisation of education law as a distinct discipline is purely functional or simply a matter of 'common sense' convenience. A central premise to this approach is an understanding of law as not simply functional but productive, which is to say that education law does not simply determine where, when and how a child, as a pre-given psychological subject, should be educated, but that it plays an important role in the construction of childhood subjectivities.[4] Adopting this approach, I attempt to demonstrate that exploring the boundaries to education law and refusing to accept the subject/object of education law as a pre-given entity provides insights into contemporary notions of childhood and educational practice.

Education law covers a wide range of issues, but this chapter focuses on only two aspects. The first section explores the boundary between nursery, or child care provision, and school based education or, to put it another way, the spatial boundaries between the 'infant' and the 'pupil'. The second explores

---

1   The Education Law Association (established in 1991).

2   Education Law Reports (first issue 1992).

3   Education and the Law (first issue 1988), Education, Public Law and the Individual (first issue 1996), Education Law (first issue 2000).

4   The concept of subjectivities in this context refers to the ways in which 'the human subject is produced in discursive practices that make up the social world (as opposed to a pre-given psychological subject who is made social or socialized)': Walkerdine, V, 'Children in cyberspace: a new frontier', in Lesnik-Oberstein, K (ed), *Children in Culture: Approaches to Childhood*, 1998, London: Macmillan, p 233.

the boundary between ideal or normal pupils and problem pupils. This section focuses on the law relating to school exclusions and special educational needs and examines the role of law in the current 'failing boys' debate. While the two sections of this chapter are distinct they both focus on controversial and politically contentious issues. Moreover, both issues reflect the shifting and contingent nature of the boundaries of education law.

SPATIAL BOUNDARIES

> Space is no longer seen merely as an environment in which interaction takes place, but is itself deeply implicated in the production of individual identities and social inequalities.[5]

Space plays a particularly crucial role both in cultural understandings of childhood and in the embodied lived experiences of children.[6] Indeed, the emergence of childhood as a distinct, and relatively modern, social category[7] was, and continues to be, intimately linked to the production and regulation of spatial boundaries which serve to demarcate the world of adults from that of children. Thus, images of children in factories and on battlefields and, indeed, crossing roads and roaming through shopping malls unattended by adults, have the ability to shock the sensibilities of many in Western societies,[8] not only because these environments are perceived as inappropriate and potentially damaging for children, but because they challenge the very essence of childhood. As Allison James, Chris Jenks and Alan Prout argue, 'Childhood ... is that status of personhood which is by definition often in the wrong place'.[9]

Law is heavily implicated in the governance of childhood spaces by instigating boundaries between adults and children. Thus, numerous provisions exist to exclude children from 'the wrong places', such as the workplace, the public house and places for 'adult entertainment'. By default, these provisions identify the very limited environments deemed appropriate for children – 'the right places'. The most important of these are the home, or domestic space, and the school. These two spaces are regulated, in varying degrees, by different branches of law: child law and education law

---

5   Schilling, C, 'Social space, gender inequalities and educational differentiation' (1991) 12(1) Br J Sociology of Education 23.

6   For a more detailed analysis of childhood and space, see James, A, Jenks, C and Prout, A, *Theorising Childhood*, 1998, Cambridge: Polity, pp 37–58.

7   Aries, P, *Centuries of Childhood*, Baldwick, R (trans), 1962, London: Jonathan Cape; Archard, D, *Children, Rights and Childhood*, 1993, London: Routledge.

8   See Buss, Chapter 14, in this volume, for a critique of the dominance of Western notions of childhood.

9   *Ibid*, James *et al*, p 39.

respectively. That the home and the school are regulated by distinct categories of law reflects not simply the fact they are concerned with different environments, but that, within these environments, children are constructed in different ways. Consequently, the boundary between education law and child law represents a boundary not simply between different environments (the home and the school) and between different professions (social workers and teachers), but between the identities and subjectivities inherent in the social categories of 'child' and 'pupil'. To put it another way, the object of child law is distinct from that of education law.[10]

Compulsory education begins at the age of five.[11] This is expressed in law not in terms of a child's right to education but by the placing of a duty on parents to ensure that their children receive efficient full time education.[12] Parents can comply with their duty by educating their children at home but this is highly unusual and increasingly difficult.[13] Furthermore, school attendance as the usual form of education is reinforced by the placing of a duty on local education authorities to provide sufficient school places for all children in their area over the age of five.[14] These provisions construct a crucial spatial and temporal boundary between children under five outside of school and those at school over the age of five. Prior to the enactment of the School Standards and Framework Act 1998, this boundary was far clearer. For, while local education authorities had the power to provide and maintain nursery schools for children under the age of five,[15] they were not under any duty to do so[16] and child care for this age group was regulated by the Children Act 1989. The School Standards and Framework Act 1998 imposed a new duty on local education authorities to ensure that sufficient nursery education is provided for children below compulsory school age who have attained the age of four.[17] This provision, which reflects increased political interest in early childhood, is significant in that it constructs the nursery as a space distinct from both the home and the school. These three spaces are now examined in more detail.

---

10 For an analysis of the contingent nature of the child as a legal object child, see O'Donovan, K, *Family Law Matters*, 1993, London: Pluto, pp 90–105.

11 Education Act 1996, s 8.

12 *Ibid*, s 7.

13 It has become even harder if, as Harris has argued, 'efficient education' is interpreted as meaning the provision of all aspects of the National Curriculum. See Harris, N, *Law and Education: Regulation, Consumerism and the Educational System*, 1993, London: Sweet & Maxwell, p 209. See, also, *H v UK* (1984) 38 DR 105, where the European Court of Human Rights rejected a parent's claims regarding assessment of home education.

14 Education Act 1996, s 14(1).

15 *Ibid*, s 17.

16 *Ibid*, s 14(4).

17 School Standards and Framework Act 1998, s 118; Education (Nursery Education and Early Years Development) (England) Regulations 1999 (SI 1999/1329), reg 2.

Home

Education law is silent about children under the age of four.[18] Consequently, it might initially appear odd to discuss the home and children under school age in a chapter concerned with education law. However, for critical perspectives on law, 'silences' such as this are significant as they reveal discursive constructions and understandings too often accepted unquestioningly as 'common sense'. In this context, the silence in education law reflects and legitimises a variety of complex perceptions that view formal learning and compulsory school attendance for young children as inappropriate, unnecessary and, as the debate regarding nursery schooling discussed below demonstrates, even potentially harmful. Furthermore, it similarly reflects and legitimises the closely aligned view that young children – regardless of their gender – should be cared for at home and, ideally, by their mother.

These views reflect ideologies of care and of privacy and draw on numerous discourses: 'common sense' and traditional conservative perceptions of the family and the mother-child bond as private and innately natural; neo-liberal constructions of the family as an economically self-sufficient unit; and psychological and psychoanalytical calculations concerning ideal child development in the early years. This last perspective imbues the mythical and deeply held beliefs regarding the mother-child bond with a scientific claim to truth.[19] This is significant, as it enables State intervention in early childhood to be problematised not simply through rights claims to parental or family privacy, but also on the basis that it is not in a child's best interests. As such, it represents an example of the way in which political discourses are able to draw upon neutral 'scientific' claims regarding child welfare to perpetuate and defend traditional images and roles for women and motherhood.[20]

The normative ideal of children spending their pre-school years at home and with their mothers constructs the domestic space as private, safe and feminine. 'Private' in that it is free of direct State intervention; 'safe' in that the young child is protected not simply from harm but also from adult/masculine cares and structured knowledge; and 'feminine' in that it is dependant upon essentialist constructions of women and mothers as empathetic, intuitive and nurturing.[21] In this way, domestic space constructs early childhood as innocent and as a nostalgic time of carefree play.

---

18 One exception to this is a provision relating to children with special educational needs under the age of five (Education Act 1996, s 312(2)(c)).

19 Mitchell, J and Goody, J, 'Family or familiarity', in Day-Sclater, S, Bainham, A and Richards, M (eds), *What is a Parent? A Socio-Legal Analysis*, 1999, Oxford: Hart.

20 Reece, H, 'The paramountcy principle – consensus or construct?' (1996) 49 CLP 267; Smart, C, *Feminism and the Power of Law*, 1989, London: Routledge.

21 Diduck, A, 'Justice and childhood: reflections on refashioned boundaries', in King, M (ed), *Moral Agendas for Children's Welfare*, 1999, London: Routledge.

The reality of family/domestic life is increasingly at odds with this normative 'ideal'. In particular, the ideal of the home as 'a safe haven' has been challenged as a result of the increased awareness of a variety of forms of abuse and dangers within the home. More generally, a particular challenge to the traditional ideal has been the large scale movement of mothers into paid employment outside of the home. Child law, and in particular provisions in the Children Act 1989 relating to day care, reflect a pragmatic social and political recognition of this fact. Of particular relevance in the context of this chapter is the way in which in these provisions implicitly uphold and legitimise the domestic space as the ideal. Again, silences in the law are informative and three in particular.

The first is the lack of a universal system of day care for children. Local authorities are only under a duty to provide day care services for children under the age of five if the child is defined as a 'child in need'.[22] While these services can be provided for all children,[23] the limited nature of this duty reinforces family – in particular mothers' – responsibilities in this area.

The second, and an example of the unregulated nature of domestic space, is the fact that child law does not place parents or carers under any duties regarding the educational development of children pre-school age.[24] This reinforces the construction of domestic space as 'feminine', in that it serves to emphasise emotional care rather than structured rational learning – an issue explored below in more detail in the context of the nursery.

The third 'silence' is the Government's recent refusal to establish a national nanny registration scheme. That this decision implicitly relied upon essentialist constructions regarding the relationship between women and children is clear from the fact that it was in part justified on the basis that such a scheme would raise the qualifications for child care jobs in the home and that, consequently, 'many competent people with *common sense* and high standards of *personal responsibility* would be driven out of these domestic posts'.[25] Similarly, in connection with day care and pre-school education, the Children Act 1989 permits people, in reality almost always women, with no professional training or qualifications to care for children, and, significantly, like domestic work, much of this work is unpaid.[26] Not only do these

---

22 Children Act 1989, s 18(1).

23 *Ibid*, s 18.

24 An example of this is the controversial case of *Sutton LBC v Davis* [1994] 1 FLR 737, where the High Court held that a local authority was wrong to refuse to officially register a childminder who, with the parents' permission, reserved the right to use corporal punishment.

25 Childright, 'National register of nannies ruled out' (1998) 148 Childright 20 (emphasis added).

26 This is implicit in provisions relating to the registration of childminders and in the *discretionary* power of local authorities to provide training for those involved with child care: Children Act 1989, s 18(3); see, also, Hevey, D and Curtis, A, 'Training to work in the early years', in Pugh, G (ed), *Contemporary Issues in the Early Years*, 1996, London: National Children's Bureau.

provisions once again clearly rely upon essentialist constructions of women but the names of many of these places, for example *'family* centres', *'parent-*toddler groups', similarly serve to construct them as quasi-domestic space.

The 'private' nature of the home has been commented on and effectively deconstructed by numerous critical and feminist commentators who have revealed its contingency and political and 'public' function.[27] However, what has perhaps been overlooked is the fact that it constructs identities not only for women and mothers, but also for children. There is notably little research into how the domestic space is experienced by children, a fact which serves to uphold the ideology of privacy and reflects the dominance of 'common sense' and intuitive constructions.[28] However, within the home and alternative domestic spaces, early childhood identities are constructed by common sense and professional discourses in terms of innocence and carefree play and emotional and physical, rather than intellectual, needs. What is significant in the context of this chapter is that these identities become challenged when children enter educational spaces.

Nursery

That the boundaries between the home and the school and between the pupil and the infant are highly contingent is particularly apparent in the recent developments regarding nursery education. The word 'nursery' itself is significantly ambiguous, as it refers to either a domestic space or a school space. This hybrid quality is reflected in law by the fact that nurseries are the object of both education law and child law. Prior to the School Standards and Framework Act 1998, while local education authorities could provide and maintain nurseries, they were regulated by the Children Act 1989 in the same way as other day care services. In three ways, recent developments have repositioned them firmly within the realm of education law. First, the School Standards and Framework Act, while not making attendance compulsory, has placed local *education* authorities under a duty to provide sufficient places in nurseries in the same way as they must for children of school age.[29] Secondly, regulation of nurseries, together with childminders and day care provision, is no longer to be carried out by local authority *social services* departments but by

---

27 Donzelot, J, *The Policing of Families*, 1980, London: Hutchinson; O'Donovan, K, *Sexual Divisions in Law*, 1985, London: Weidenfeld & Nicolson; Freeman, M, 'Towards a critical theory of family law' (1985) 38 CLP 153. See, also, Bridgeman, Chapter 11, in this volume.

28 *Op cit*, James *et al*, fn 6, p 54; James, A, 'Parents: a children's perspective', in *op cit*, Day-Sclater *et al*, fn 19.

29 School Standards and Framework Act 1998, s 118; Education (Nursery Education and Early Years Development) (England) Regulations 1999 (SI 1999/1329).

the Office for Standards in Education (Ofsted).[30] Thirdly, the Government has introduced plans for what amounts to a national curriculum for children aged three and four.[31] On a political level, these developments represent a re-opening of the debate regarding pre-school child care.[32] But the redrawing of legal boundaries represents more than a political commitment to extend day care service provision. For, while nurseries are excluded from the statutory definition of 'school',[33] these developments reconstruct nurseries as educational spaces and consequently remove them from the realm of the domestic. This represents a conceptual shift which has implications for social and cultural understandings of early childhood and, consequently, for the identities and subjectivities of young children.

This is particularly clear from the debate regarding the new curriculum for three and four year olds. These proposals, which require that children should start learning to read, write and count before the age of five, have been strongly opposed by the Association of Teachers and Lecturers, the Early Childhood Education Forum, the Pre-School Learning Alliance and, most embarrassingly for the Government, by 16 out of 18 of the head teachers of nursery schools which the Government had selected as representing beacons of good practice.[34] They argue that formalising education for the under fives marginalises the importance of play, that introducing learning targets will inevitably create 'failures at five' and that, put simply, the proposals will harm children[35] – to the extent that one expert was quoted as accusing the Government of 'destroying childhood'.[36] Much emphasis is placed on the fact that these views are those of early childhood 'experts' and that they are supported by 'the latest neuro-scientific research about how young children's

30 This policy was proposed in the *Consultation Paper on the Regulation of Early Years Education and Day Care*, 1998, London: DfEE/DoH and is contained in the Care Standards Bill 1999. For critical responses to this move, see Smithers, R, 'Ofsted to oversee childcare services' (1999) *The Guardian*, 3 August, p 4; Wallace, W, 'Double standards' (1999) *Nursery World*, 15 July; Mercer, A, 'Councils fear loss of care expertise' (1999) *Nursery World*, 26 August.

31 Quality and Curriculum Authority, *The Review of the Desirable Learning Outcomes for Children's Learning on Entering Compulsory Education*, 1999, London: QCA, superseded by *Early Learning Goals*, 1999, London: QCA/DfEE; Carvel, J, 'Curriculum plans for nurseries under attack' (1999) *The Guardian*, 6 May; Smithers, R, 'Is the playful approach best' (1999) *The Guardian*, 1 June; Carvel, J, 'Play is out, early learning is in' (1999) *The Guardian*, 23 June.

32 While the Children Act 1989 reflected a broad political consensus, the provisions regarding day care provision were highly controversial: Bainham, A, *Children: The Modern Law*, 1999, Bristol: Jordan, p 335.

33 Education Act 1996, s 4.

34 *Ibid*, Carvel, 23 June 1999; *ibid*, Smithers.

35 *Ibid*, Carvel, 23 June 1999; *ibid*, Smithers.

36 Lepkowska, D, 'The nursery sweatshop' (1999) *The Express*, 20 February.

brains develop'.[37] Yet the Government similarly claims that their proposals are driven by concerns about child welfare. They argue that the distinction between learning through work and learning through play is outdated; that the lack of provision in the pre-school years is a significant cause of disruptive behaviour and school failure in later years; and that their proposals will narrow the educational gap between children from privileged and underprivileged backgrounds.[38] Both sides in this debate claim to know the 'truth' about young children and this demonstrates both the contingency of child welfare and the extent to which political and economic issues regarding education and children are subsumed and expressed through the 'neutral' rhetoric of the interests of the child.[39]

Early childhood and pre-school age child care raise a wide number of highly complex and interrelated issues, and it is not possible to explore them here in detail.[40] In the context of this chapter, what is significant is the fact that the nursery represents a contested space between the domestic and the school, within which educational and developmental discourses construct early childhood identities in conflicting ways. On the one hand, we find an innocent, care free, playful infant protected from competitiveness and the harshness of the adult world. On the other hand, we find a rational, intellectually developing child protected from ignorance. Both these children can be understood as representing adult 'fictions', in that they represent not so much knowledge of children but, rather, objects or projections of adult concerns about childhood. The former represents a repository of adult nostalgia for childhood as a time of innocence, and the latter a repository for adult hopes and aspirations for the future.[41] It is this child of the future that we see more clearly in the context of the school space.

School

At the age of five – the age of compulsory education – children enter not simply the physical environment of the school but also the social category of

---

37 Op cit, Carvel, 6 May 1999, fn 31. For post-structural critiques of scientific approaches towards child development, see Stainton Rogers, R and Stainton Rogers, W, 'Word children', in Lesnik-Oberstein, K (ed), Children in Culture, Approaches to Childhood, 1998, London: Macmillan; Burman, E, Deconstructing Developmental Psychology, 1994, London: Routledge.

38 Op cit, Carvel, 23 June 1999, fn 31; op cit, Smithers, fn 31.

39 Op cit, Freeman, fn 27; op cit, Reece, fn 20.

40 Penn, H (ed), Early Childhood Services: Theory, Policy and Practice, 2000, Milton Keynes: OU Press; Smidt, S (ed), The Early Years: A Reader, 1999, London: Routledge; op cit, Pugh, fn 26; Vernon, J and Smith, C, Day Nurseries at a Crossroads, 1994, London: National Children's Bureau; Dahlberg, G, Moss, P and Pence, A, Beyond Quality in Early Childhood Education and Care: Postmodern Perspectives, 1999, London: Falmer.

41 Jenks, C, Childhood, 1996, London: Routledge, pp 97–99. See Collier, Chapter 6, in this volume.

pupilhood. In a strict definitional sense, children become 'pupils' when taught by another, but pupilhood refers more generally to the construction of childhood through discourses of education. It is, therefore, possible for children to be pupils outside of school. In this respect, current policies such as home-school contracts, increased emphasis on homework and 'improving' nursery provision can be understood as representing the latest of long standing attempts to encourage parents to relate to their children as 'pupils' both before and throughout the school years.[42] In a similar fashion, social workers have been criticised for overlooking the educational development of children in their care.[43] The difficulties encountered in extending pupilhood into spaces outside of school indicates the extent to which pupilhood is currently understood as a particularly space specific construction deeply associated and produced within the school space and hints at a tension between the construction of children within domestic space and the school.

Whereas the domestic space is largely unregulated and is constructed as a 'feminine' space for emotional and physical nurturing and carefree unhindered play, school represents the opposite, in that it is explicitly regulated and characterised by (masculine) rational thought, discipline and work. Consequently, whereas the home is characterised as private, the school represents a more public space. Three points can be made to demonstrate this.

First, located within school, all children, as pupils, are the legitimate and explicit object of public concern and detailed State regulated practices. This is not to say that within the family and the home children are not the object of public concern – they clearly are;[44] but what is significant is that the *ideology* of privacy, so powerful in relation to the child within domestic space and a central feature of child law, has far less impact on the pupil in school. Compulsory education is no longer seen as an infringement of parental rights but as an uncontroversial right of the child;[45] and attempts in the 1980s to give parents more rights over their children's education, while not insignificant, have in reality proved to be little more than political rhetoric.[46] Consequently,

---

42 Chazan, M, 'The home and the school', in Coleman, J (ed), *The School Years, Current Issues in the Socialisation of Young People*, 2nd edn, 1992, London: Routledge.

43 Blyth, E and Milner, J, *Social Work with Children: The Educational Perspective*, 1997, London: Longman; Firth, H and Horrocks, C, 'No home, no school, no future', in Blyth, E and Milner, J (eds), *Exclusion from School*, 1996, London: Routledge.

44 *Op cit*, Donzelot, fn 27; *op cit*, O'Donovan, fn 27; *op cit*, O'Donovan, fn 10; *op cit*, Freeman, fn 27.

45 Hodgson, D, *The Human Right to Education*, 1998, Aldershot: Ashgate. An exception to this is sex education, where parents' rights are still perceived by many as particularly important: Monk, D, 'Sex education and the problematisation of teenage pregnancies, a genealogy of law and governance' (1998) 7(2) SLS 241; Packer, C, 'Sex education: child's right, parents' choice or societal obligation?', in Heinze, E (ed), *Of Innocence and Autonomy, Children, Sex and Human Rights*, 2000, Aldershot: Dartmouth.

46 This is particularly the case with parental choice of school and in connection with the curriculum: *op cit*, Harris, fn 13.

and in contrast to the family, the legitimacy of State intervention in education, while not uninfluenced by parental failures, is not *dependent* upon establishing them. Rather, State intervention in education is generally unquestioned and perceived as unproblematic and 'a good thing' for all children; a perception reinforced by the upholding of children's right to education by international law.[47] While this can be understood as a progressive move towards recognising both children's developmental rights and children as individuals independent of their family, it is also an example of how the powerful and 'neutral' rhetoric of the interests of the child renders other interests less visible, for the provision and content of education has been, and continues to be, deeply interlinked with and motivated by social, political and economic interests quite distinct from the interests of individual.[48] Indeed, while child welfare reformers campaigned for universal and compulsory State education, it was, arguably, the need for an educated workforce and political concerns which brought it about.

Secondly, the school can be understood as a public space from the perspective of the child. School attendance enables and encourages a child to make relationships outside of the family. Compulsory schooling in this way legitimises the separation or breaking apart of the mother-child dyad. It is a significant indication of the dominance of scientific theories of child development and of rigid temporal boundaries that this separation is so unquestioningly accepted as harmful at one age but necessary and healthy at another.[49]

Finally, and again from a child's perspective, the school can be understood as a public space by reason of the fact that schooling is experienced as a form of adult-like work. Highly regulated and structured by detailed curricula and timetables and both formal and informal assessments, schoolwork conforms to almost every definition of work – apart from the fact that it is unpaid.[50] Furthermore, the clear spatial and temporal division between the classroom and the playground imposes and reinforces the distinction between work and play, and it is a distinction that children learn from an early age.[51] Significantly, schoolwork is not simply work from a child's perspective, for, as a form of employment training, it is intimately linked to the needs of the economy. However, characterising schoolwork as a form of adult-like labour is

---

47 *Op cit*, Hodgson, fn 45; Hamilton, C, 'Rights of the child: a right to education and a right in education', in Bridge, C (ed), *Family Law Towards the Millennium: Essays for PM Bromley*, 1997, London: Butterworths.

48 Finch, J, *Education as Social Policy*, 1984, London: Longman; *op cit*, Blyth and Milner, fn 43. See Reece, Chapter 5, in this volume.

49 *Op cit*, Stainton Rogers and Stainton Rogers, fn 37. This is one of the criticisms of home education.

50 *Op cit*, James *et al*, fn 6, p 119.

51 Sherman, A, 'Five year olds' perception of why we go to school' (1997) 11(2) Children and Society 117.

controversial and relatively new,[52] largely because of the dominance of progressive and children's rights narratives within which the introduction of compulsory education is historically closely linked to the imposition of restrictions on child labour.[53] From this perspective, school protects and 'saves' children from work.

Excluding schooling from the category of work challenges the construction of the school as a public space. Moreover, thinking beyond categorising the school space as public and the domestic space as private enables us to see similarities between constructions and understandings of school and domestic space and three examples demonstrate this point.

First, while pupils are 'made to work' and while the content of their work is informed by public/masculine political and economic considerations, they are not autonomous political and economic subjects. Consequently, while compulsory schooling prepares children for adulthood, at the same time it ensures that they are excluded from adulthood by effectively restricting their access to and participation in the 'public' sphere. Secondly, there is a notable similarity between domestic work and schoolwork. Both are frequently perceived and characterised as not being 'real work', with the result that women are similarly excluded from the public sphere.[54] Thirdly, conceptualising school as a public space is problematic, for school, like the home, is a 'child-appropriate' space within which children are protected/excluded from adult public spaces. The recent shootings in US schools and in Dunblane in the UK,[55] together with the increasing awareness of bullying,[56] consequently upset and challenge the construction of the school as a safe space in much the same way as stories of child abuse challenge the construction of the home as a safe haven.

The boundaries of the school ideally protect children from physical harm and exploitation in the workplace, but they also enable the censorship of material, which children are exposed to, in accordance with adult perceptions

---

52 *Op cit*, James *et al*, fn 6, p 119.

53 Piper, C, 'Moral campaigns for children's welfare in the 19th century', in *op cit*, King, fn 21.

54 That children are excluded from the adult (male) public sphere in ways similar to that experienced by women indicates how feminist perspectives can be used to challenge essentialist assumptions about childhood. The linking of 'women and children' in this way is, however, not unproblematic (see Lim and Roche, Chapter 12, in this volume). A significant distinction in this context is that, while the domestic work carried out by women, and mothers in particular, is upheld as an ideal within traditional discourses, the domestic work performed by children, while largely hidden from public attention (see Dearden, C and Becker, S, 'The needs and experiences of young carers in the UK' (1998) 148 Childright 15), is perceived as problematic, as it challenges idealised image of children as passive participants within the home and the family (see *op cit*, James, fn 28).

55 See Collier, Chapter 6, in this volume.

56 Tattum, DP and Lane, DA (eds), *Bullying in Schools*, 1989, Stoke on Trent: Trentham.

of what is 'appropriate' for their age. The debates and controversies surrounding sex education indicate that what is considered appropriate is often contested.[57] While similar attempts are made outside of the school – for example, the 'top shelf' in newsagents and the rating of films – the physical boundaries of the school enable a far greater degree of control. This is particularly evident with the advent of the internet or cyberspace, for, while it enables children to learn outside of the school, it is frequently perceived as a potentially dangerous space for children primarily because it is not regulated, but also because, in marked contrast to learning within school, it allows children a degree of autonomy.[58]

Distinguishing the home and the school in terms of the public/private dichotomy acknowledges the work-like nature of schooling, a separation of the child from the family and the legal and political uses of the ideology of privacy. However, it is important to recognise that it also obscures the similarities between the home and the school, oversimplifies children's experiences of both spaces and the power relations within them. For, as a conceptual tool, while it identifies gendered notions, there is a risk that it simultaneously reinforces them. Consequently, as Richard Collier argues, the 'public/private dichotomy, it might seem, is to be accepted, rejected and "transcended" all at the same time'.[59]

This chapter has so far focused on the home, the nursery and the school and identified the shifting and contingent nature of the boundaries between these spaces and how they operate as distinct sites of childhood governance. The next section explores the construction of an ideal pupil within the school. While the focus is therefore on childhood within the school, this is not to suggest that real children experience an absolute division between the home and the school in terms of their own individual perceptions of themselves, but, rather, the aim is to demonstrate how education law is implicated in the discursive production of specific school based childhood roles and identities which are subsequently imposed on real children.

LAW AND THE IDEAL PUPIL

Inside school, all children can be classified as pupils. However, pupilhood is not a monolithic category and children within schools are formally and informally distinguished and categorised in a variety of ways. For example, from the perspective of the school and of teachers within the classroom, pupils may be perceived as high or low achievers; good or disruptive; loud or quiet;

---

57 See Thomson, Chapter 9, in this volume.
58 *Op cit*, Walkerdine, fn 4.
59 Collier, R, *Masculinity, Law and the Family*, 1995, London: Routledge, p 60.

hardworking or lazy. Children's own perceptions of their relative 'success' or 'failure' as pupils is often quite distinct[60] and, consequently, fellow pupils are categorised, or labelled, as variously popular, unpopular, ugly, cool, brainy, thick and as swots and bullies, to name only a few. Education law also has a number of sub-categories of pupils, such as children with 'behavioural difficulties'[61] and 'special educational needs'[62] and children who are 'educated otherwise',[63] 'permanently excluded'[64] or 'fail to attend regularly'.[65] These legal categories or labels are significant for three reasons.

First, as statements of law, they are perceived and experienced as particularly authoritative and neutral 'statements of truth' which serve to legitimise the localised perceptions of teachers and school governors. For example, if, after all the legal procedures have been correctly followed,[66] a child is excluded or deemed to have a special educational need, then we 'know' that the child *really is* bad or disruptive or has a special need and that it is not simply the opinion of an individual teacher whose views may be influenced by a variety of other factors.

Secondly, what is notable about many of these legal categories is that they refer to children outside of school, whether for 'lawful' reasons, in the case of those excluded or educated at home, or 'unlawfully' in the case of those who fail to attend without a legitimate reason (truants).[67] Whether because of illness, exclusion or truancy, once outside of school, children become not simply objects of education law but objects of concern for a variety of other categories of law and State agencies such as police, health and social services. Children outside of school are problematised and marginalised by education law, thereby reinforcing the association of education and pupilhood with schooling and legitimising the conceptualisation of the school as the 'lawful' and 'right' place for children of school age. Indeed, as mentioned earlier, it is difficult and rare for education at home to be deemed 'sufficient' and is neither encouraged nor, for many parents, a feasible option. Moreover, where children are absent from school for long periods because of illness or because they have been excluded, the provision of education is generally considered

---

60 *Op cit*, James *et al*, fn 6; Epstein, D and Johnson, R, *Schooling Sexualities*, 1998, Milton Keynes: OU Press.

61 Education Act 1996, s 527A (as inserted by the Education Act 1997, s 9).

62 *Ibid*, s 316.

63 *Ibid*, s 19.

64 *Ibid*, s 156.

65 *Ibid*, s 444.

66 In reviewing special educational needs proceedings, and even more so with exclusions, while the courts are reluctant to challenge the merits of a particular decision, they are rigorous in upholding the procedures: Monk, D, 'School exclusions and the Education Act 1997' (1997) 9(4) Education and the Law 227.

67 See Barnett, Chapter 7, in this volume, for an analysis of law's binary coding of reality as 'lawful'/'unlawful'.

inadequate and the statutory duties regarding the education of these children are frequently overlooked.[68] Consequently, for children of school age outside of school, their absence is not simply a physical absence from school, but can be understood, and is experienced, as a removal from the social category of pupilhood.

The third feature of the legal categories or labels is the fact they all, to varying degrees and for various reasons, represent problem pupils, that is to say, pupils who do not conform to the norm or ideal. Consequently, they do not simply uphold and legitimise the spatial boundaries of the school but, by default, inform us of the ideal attributes and capabilities of pupils within the school space. This is particularly clear in the context of the 'excluded child' and the 'child with special educational needs'. Exclusion proceedings in an explicit way determine acceptable behaviour within a particular school. Similarly, the statutory definitions and proceedings relating to special educational needs are based and rely on a notion of 'normal' educational development.[69] Consequently, these constructions of problem or 'other' pupils represent not simply a functional aspect of the legal regulation of educational practices but, rather, can be understood in a broader sense as representing boundaries for a complex, shifting, discursively produced notion of ideal or normal pupilhood. This approach is particularly significant for the insights it can provide into the recent 'globalised moral panic' about boys' educational achievements.[70]

'FAILING BOYS' AND EDUCATION LAW

In a formal sense, full legal equality has been achieved in education; girls now have the same rights to education as boys and the requirements of the National Curriculum apply to both sexes equally. To this extent, it can be argued that education law, like child and family law, has reached a position of gender neutrality.

While this is a positive development, and the result of feminist engagement with education that can be traced back to the early pioneers such as Frances Mary Buss (1827–94) and Dorothea Beale (1831–1906), more recent feminist engagements with education have, as in so many other areas, moved

68 In the context of exclusions, see Blyth, E and Milner, J (eds), *Exclusion from School, Inter-Professional Issues for Policy and Practice*, 1996, London: Routledge, Pt II. In the context of children absent because of illness, see National Association for the Education of Sick Children Research Report, *Losing the Thread*, 1997, London: National Association for the Education of Sick Children.

69 Monk, D, 'Failing children: responding to children with behavioural difficulties', in *op cit*, King, fn 21.

70 Bright, M, 'Girls really are better than boys – official' (1998) *The Observer*, 4 January; see, generally, Epstein, D, Elwood, J and Hey, V (eds), *Failing Boys? Issues in Gender and Achievement*, 1999, Milton Keynes: OU Press.

beyond the liberal/equal rights paradigm. These more recent engagements have been particularly significant in demystifying the recent panic about 'failing boys', as they question the equating of girls' 'success' with simply attaining or overtaking boys achievements, question the institutionalised masculinity inherent in educational objectives and, more generally, 'disturb the naturalness and self-evident character of the "child", "boys" and "girls" as pre-given objects of study'.[71]

Consequently, while the gender neutral nature of education law is positive, it is at the same time, as Shelley Day-Sclater and Candida Yates argue in relation to the gender neutral approach to parenting in family law, 'fraught with tensions and difficulties because it signifies a denial of the conflictual social realities and power-dynamics of gender difference'.[72] Moreover, the appearance of formal equality in education law obscures the highly gendered nature of educational practices and the experience of schooling. Indeed, it can be argued that school represents a particularly significant site for the construction of gender; which is to say that children learn not simply the subjects on the formal curriculum but what it means to be a 'boy' or a 'girl'.[73] Single sex schools and dress codes are examples of explicit and formal gender distinctions but they are expressed and perpetuated in a plethora of more informal and less explicit ways, for example, the use of space in schools[74] and the behaviour of teachers.[75] Education law is itself implicated in the construction and perpetuation of gendered roles and in the production of the recent panic about boys, and this is particularly clear in the context of school exclusions and special educational needs.

Boys are currently four to five times more likely than girls to be excluded from school[76] and, similarly, 'incontestably dominate special needs

---

71 Tyler, D, 'At risk of maladjustment: the problem of child mental health', in Peterson, A and Bunton, R (eds), *Foucault: Health and Medicine*, 1997, London: Routledge, p 78; Miles, S and Middleton, C, 'Girls' education in the balance: the ERA and inequality', in Flude, M and Hammer, M (eds), *The Education Reform Act 1988: Its Origins and Implications*, 1990, London: Falmer.

72 Day-Sclater, S and Yates, C, 'The psycho-politics of post-divorce parenting', in *op cit*, Day-Sclater *et al*, fn 19, p 288.

73 Collier, R, *Masculinities, Crime and Criminology*, 1998, London: Sage, p 81; Skeggs, B, 'Challenging masculinity and using sexuality' (1991) 12 Br J Sociology of Education 127; *Op cit*, Epstein and Johnson, fn 60.

74 *Op cit*, Schilling, fn 5.

75 Blyth and Milner (*op cit*, 1997, fn 43, p 18) provide a useful summary of the research in this area and argue that 'the single biggest determinant of teacher behaviour is the pupil's gender'. Significantly, this different treatment is just as prevalent pre-school: Hilton, G, '"Boys will be boys" – won't they? The attitudes of playgroup workers to gender and play experiences' (1991) 3(3) Gender and Education 311, pp 311–13.

76 Blyth, E and Milner, J, 'Exclusions: trends and issues', in *op cit*, Blyth and Milner, fn 43, p 5; Brodie, I, 'Exclusion from school' (1995) *Highlight* No 136, London: National Children's Bureau.

provision'.[77] These statistics can be, and are, perceived as incontrovertible evidence of the 'fact' that boys' behaviour is increasingly problematic and that they are 'failing' both socially and educationally. However, this interpretation assumes and requires that we accept that the legal processes and definitions that regulate these educational practices are neutral and authoritative; which is to say that they simply 'reflect reality'. A closer examination challenges this and demonstrates that, rather than simply *proving* that boys are failing, they play an important role in the *construction* and production of the current 'crisis'.

Critical analyses of school exclusions and special educational needs challenge the assumption that the predominance of boys reflects a change in boys' behaviour and consequently suggest that we look beyond explanations such as the perceived increase in irresponsible parenting, the lack of male teachers, misguided progressive teaching methods and increased violence on television. Such explanations, frequently expressed in popular discourses, reflect distinct ideological or political perspectives and consequently justify conflicting responses. Moreover, they seek to explain boys' failure by reasons extrinsic to boys. This is a common feature in many of the discourses regarding failing boys. Significantly, the opposite is true of girls; their failures are attributed to their intrinsic nature and their success to external reasons such as improved teaching.[78] This discrepancy in part explains why girls' educational failures are not, and never were, perceived as a 'crisis', but, rather, are accepted as part of the 'natural' order of things.

Looking beyond these explanations, critical perspectives focus on the dominant political discourses in education and the associated radical changes in the organisation of the educational system. In particular, the Conservative Government's neo-liberal market-based system which 'creates winners and losers'[79] and New Labour's discourses of 'school effectiveness' and 'school failure', which emphasise assessment on the basis of narrowly defined academic achievement, similarly problematise underachieving pupils. Within these prevailing 'managerialist and technicist approaches of New Labour/Old Tory',[80] pupils are constructed in a particularly individualistic way, which significantly excludes radical and feminist educational discourses of the 1970s locating pupils in a broader social context, incorporating critical insights into

77 Hey, V, Leonard, D, Daniels, H and Smith, M, 'Boys' under-achievement, special needs practices and questions of equity', in *op cit*, Epstein *et al*, fn 70, p 128.

78 Cohen, M, '"A habit of healthy idleness": boys' under-achievement in historical perspective', in *op cit*, Epstein *et al*, fn 70, p 20.

79 Berridge, D and Brodie, I, 'An "exclusive" education' (1997) Community Care, 30 January–5 February, p 4; Searle, C, 'The signal of failure: school exclusions and the market system of education', in *op cit*, Blyth and Milner, fn 43.

80 Epstein, D, Elwood, J, Hey, V and Maw, J, 'Schoolboy frictions: feminism and "failing boys"', in *op cit*, Epstein *et al*, fn 70, p 14.

the power relations in schools and challenging the purely vocational and economic purposes of education.[81]

Law is heavily implicated in marginalisation of alternative and more critical discourses. This is particularly clear in the construction of the 'excluded child' and 'child with special educational needs'. These legal objects are distinct and, in many ways, contradictory; in particular, unlike the child with special educational needs, the excluded child is held responsible for his actions.[82] However, as legal objects they simplify, individualise and depoliticise the complex issues inherent in both educational practices. Moreover, as gender neutral objects, they render invisible the highly gendered perceptions and practices that construct certain attributes, behaviours and achievements as falling short of the norm or ideal pupil.

In exclusion proceedings, the focus is almost exclusively on the inappropriate behaviour of the child in question. These proceedings adopt a quasi-criminal framework, within which the head teacher is the lawmaker and the excluded pupil is in effect the criminal.[83] The central question in these proceedings is whether or not a child has behaved in a particular way; the extent to which the behaviour breaches the school's disciplinary rules; and the effect of such behaviour on the other pupils. This narrow, individualised focus deems irrelevant familial and social factors outside of the school, the possibly uninspiring and rigid nature of the curriculum, and the effect of changing demands on schools in terms of pupil achievements, institutionalised in league tables. Moreover, while exclusion proceedings problematise behaviours – in particular, 'masculine' violence, loudness and general class disruptiveness – they deem irrelevant an understanding of how such behaviours and identities are produced within schools; which is to say that exclusion proceedings and the behaviour of boys do not simply reflect a 'crisis in masculinity' but are a product of educational and teaching practices and school based cultures.

Special educational needs proceedings are significantly distinct from exclusions. For, while similarly highly legalistic and individualised, they are informed not by the moral or disciplinary culture of individuals schools but, rather, by scientific discourses and, in particular, developmental psychology. This increasingly dominant discourse has been the object of much critical sociological analysis, which challenges its scientific, and consequently 'neutral', determination of 'normality' and its 'within the person' theory of

---

81 Jackson, D, 'Breaking out of the binary trap: boys' under-achievement, schooling and gender relations', p 128; Reed, LR, '"Zero tolerance": gender performance and school failure', both in *op cit*, Epstein *et al*, fn 70.

82 *Op cit*, Monk, fn 69.

83 *Op cit*, Monk, fn 69.

causation.[84] These critical approaches challenge the assumption that boys' dominance of special needs provision simply reflects their academic underachievement. For example, in a recent study of special needs provision in a range of different schools, Valerie Hey *et al* found that the only school where the gender ratio in special needs provision favoured girls was a school where there was a clear policy to distinguish educational needs from behavioural needs.[85] This suggests that, in most schools, it is the 'acting out' behaviour of boys which triggers concern and a 'diagnosis' of an educational behaviour disorder, a category of special educational need. Yet, while the management of gendered behaviour by schools and teachers is therefore central to the subsequent identification of special educational needs, this gendered understanding is rendered invisible, as it is excluded from the gender neutral and individualised discourses of law and developmental psychology within which special needs provision is currently constructed.

An important, but frequently overlooked, consequence of the gender discrepancy in exclusions and special educational needs is that, by reaffirming and upholding the perception that it is boys, rather than girls, who are failing, they make girls invisible. In particular, as Hey *et al* argue, ways of 'acting out' distress associated with girls, such as withdrawal, anorexia, flirtatiousness, over-compliance with sexual abuse and relational and verbal bullying, as opposed to masculine violence, are overlooked, as they do not disrupt the classroom and the narrowly defined purposes of education.[86] More generally, the invisibility of girls in school has a negative impact on the provision of time and resources for girls' education, and on the perceived need and urgency for continued research into the experiences and disadvantages of girls in schools.[87]

Inherent within critical approaches, which endeavour to render gender visible, is a recognition of the fact that exclusions and special educational needs are not simply responses to 'reality' but, rather, involve, and indeed are contingent upon, shifting constructions of the good or ideal pupil, as well as the purpose of education against which the appropriateness of a child's behaviour can be evaluated and judged. Consequently, it is not so much that boys' behaviour is deteriorating[88] but, rather, that what is required of pupils is

---

84 *Op cit*, Stainton Rogers and Stainton Rogers, fn 37; *op cit*, Burman, fn 37; Barton, L and Oliver, M, 'Special needs: personal trouble or public issue?', in Cosin, B and Hales, M (eds), *Families, Education and Social Differences*, 1997, London: Routledge; Barton, L and Tomlinson, S, *Special Education and Social Interests*, 1984, London: Croom Helm; Walkerdine, V, 'Beyond developmentalism' (1993) 3(4) Theory and Psychology 451.

85 *Op cit*, Hey *et al*, fn 77, p 141.

86 Significantly, girls are removed from schools, albeit 'voluntarily' as opposed to through formal exclusion, if they become pregnant; and this reaffirms a perception that, whereas 'bad boys' get involved with crime, 'bad girls' get involved with boys.

87 *Op cit*, Epstein *et al*, fn 80.

88 Cohen (*op cit*, fn 78) argues that they have always underachieved.

changing and that this shift *currently* problematises behaviour associated with masculinity. Tyler suggests that, while a decade ago parents wanting the best for their daughters were urged to treat them more like boys, the emphasis is now the other way round and boys are being asked to be more caring, nurturing and, most significantly, more able to manage themselves – which is to say, to be more like girls as these characteristics reflect the changes in the employment market that require people to be more flexible, adaptable and self-regulating.[89]

However, Tyler and other critical writers warn against relying too heavily on 'shifting of the goal posts' explanations, for, while they highlight gender differences, they are problematic to the extent that they simultaneously reinforce an overly essentialist understanding of the differences between boys and girls whereby human and gendered attributes become permanently fixed to sexed bodies. For example, the academic success of girls is sometimes explained by the change in methods of assessment from exams to assessed work, which 'girls' are considered to be better at than 'boys'.[90] Similarly, the dominance of special needs provision by boys is sometimes explained by the fact that special needs is assessed on the basis of reading abilities and 'girls' are perceived as preferring the quiet solitary activity of reading more than 'boys'. This approach also reinforces an unhelpful gendered binaryism towards educational achievement, which overlooks the arguably far more significant distinctions of class and race. Being sensitive to these issues requires us to be aware of 'the complexity of what it means to speak of boys in the first place'.[91] Collier suggests that what is central to this approach is an openness to understanding that 'schools are not gender neutral, pre-given institutions but are themselves sites for the active production of gendered/sexualised identities and not simply agencies which reflect dominant power relations'.[92]

These critical understandings have implications for a critical reading of education law. In particular, they highlight law's silences and its boundaries. Education law is silent about gender and individualises deeply political and cultural struggles. It also encourages us to focus on the problem pupils – their moral badness in the context of exclusions and their disabilities in the context of special educational needs – and to ignore the external structural and institutional local and national practises that produce them. In this way, law acts as an important legitimising agency in the increasing political pathologising and disciplining of children that do not conform to the ideal.

---

89 *Op cit*, Tyler, fn 71.
90 Judd, J, 'Boys take risks and get better A-levels than girls' (1999) *The Independent*, 3 May.
91 *Op cit*, Collier, fn 73, p 80.
92 *Op cit*, Collier, fn 73, p 80.

CONCLUSION

As this is a book about child law, by way of conclusion I want to comment briefly about the relationship between child law and education law. Child law, as a distinct legal category, is itself relatively new. Its development as a category distinct from family law encourages a perception of children as individuals and not simply family members; a shift in thinking which owes much to the children's rights movement and to feminist critiques of the public/private dichotomy which 'opened up' the domestic private space. In keeping with the child-centred approach and the 'working together' rhetoric which encourages inter-agency co-operation, child law textbooks and journals often include a chapter and occasional articles on education law. In a similar vein, numerous child lawyers have commented on the lack of children's rights within education law.[93] Yet, despite these attempts to bridge the gap between them, there remains a large gulf between these categories. A critical engagement with education law can provide an insight into this gap. This chapter has demonstrated that, by reflecting and upholding a conceptual distinction between domestic space and the school space, law is implicated in the construction of distinct 'pupil', 'infant' and 'child' identities and that the object of education law is not simply the child within the school but a complex construction of legal and educational discourse. Highlighting law's productive role in the shifting of the boundaries between school and home, and pupil and infant, is not to suggest that these boundaries are 'problems' to be overcome by, for example, converging the language and definitions within education law and child law, but, rather, that they enable an understanding of them as an inevitable consequence of the adult world's complex relationship with childhood. Consequently, it challenges us not to attempt to make or enable 'pupils' to be more like 'children' (or, indeed, both more like 'adults'), but to explore exactly what those terms mean and, by so doing, to attempt to distinguish the fears and projections of adults from the needs and experiences of real children.

---

93 Monk, D, 'Education law/child law: conflict and coherence', paper delivered at the Social Legal Studies Conference, Loughborough, April 1999.

CHAPTER 11

EMBODYING OUR HOPES AND FEARS?

Jo Bridgeman[1]

INTRODUCTION

The female body has long been the object of legal intervention. The law has, for example, established a medicalised framework for abortion decision making; given legitimacy to the provision of medical treatment to pregnant women and anorexics without their consent; sanctioned the making of judgments about fitness for motherhood through access to fertility treatment services; permitted the scrutiny in court of the sexual history of rape victims; confined the activities of the prostitute and surrogate to private, unprotected arrangements; and failed to accommodate the female criminal providing explanations for her actions within her own body. Undertaking critiques of the ways in which the law discriminates against the female, regulates the female body and constructs an ideal against which real women are measured have been, and continue to be, preoccupations within feminist legal analysis, providing valuable insights into the relationship between the law and its female subject.

Whilst many of the issues which have been exposed to feminist analysis affect both the adult and the child female, children's bodies are additionally subjected to specific legal regulation in both its legislative and judicial forms. Setting boundaries around the appropriate lifestyle for children and permissible uses and modification of their bodies, the legal issue has been the circumstances in which children[2] are to be permitted to make decisions affecting their bodies. In relation to some activities – including buying

---

1   I would like to thank the participants at the Feminist Legal Studies Seminar, University of Kent and the Feminist Legal Research Unit Seminar, University of Liverpool for their comments on and discussion of papers which form the basis of this chapter.

2   In this chapter, I use the terms 'child', 'teenager' and 'adult'. The cases discussed are all concerned with children in their teens. These children could also be described as 'adolescents' (which carries connotations of 'problem' individuals), 'mature minors' (adopting a term used in some of the cases) or even the term employed by Johnson J in *Re S (A Minor) (Medical Treatment)* [1994] 2 FLR 1065 – 'in-betweens'. I am aware that using these terms replicates and risks reinforcing the distinctions implying that there are clear divisions, which do not exist either in law or in children's lives.

cigarettes,[3] purchasing and consuming alcohol in a pub,[4] having a tattoo[5] and engaging in sexual activity[6] – a status approach is adopted. That is, it is stated categorically within legislation that children are prohibited from engaging in the activity until they reach a specified age.[7] Where the common law has been invoked to determine whether children can make decisions for themselves affecting their bodies, for example, in relation to the provision of contraceptive advice and treatment[8] and medical treatment,[9] the courts have looked to the capacity of the child concerned. A child can consent as long as he or she has 'sufficient understanding and intelligence to enable him or her to understand

---

3   Children cannot buy cigarettes until they are 16 years old, although the law does not prohibit children of any age from smoking in private (Children and Young Persons Act 1933, s 7, as amended by the Children and Young Persons (Protection from Tobacco) Act 1991).

4   Until they reach the age of 18, children are prohibited from purchasing and consuming alcohol in a public house: Licensing Act 1964, s 169(1) and (2), although beer, cider and perry can be consumed by someone aged 16 or over with a meal in restaurants or an area of a pub set aside for meals and children are allowed to drink alcohol at home or in other private places from the age of five: Licensing Act 1964, s 169; Children and Young Persons Act 1933, s 5.

5   Ie, have 'inserted into the skin any colouring material designed to leave a permanent mark' (Tattooing of Minors Act 1969, s 3) (unless performed for medical reasons by a qualified medical practitioner (s 1)). Jonathan Montgomery argues that, following the cases of *R v Dilks* (1964) 4 Med, Sci & the Law 209 and *Burrell v Harmer* [1967] Crim LR 169, the 1969 Act 'turn[ed] the moral principle that minors are insufficiently mature to understand the wider significance of tattooing into legal reality': Montgomery, J, 'Children as property?' (1988) 51 MLR 323, p 339.

6   For girls engaging in heterosexual activity, the age is 16 (Sexual Offences Act 1956, ss 5 and 6), although no offence is committed by a girl participating in sex before this age because the aim of the legislation is to protect girls (*R v Tyrell* [1894] 1 QB 710), whereas homosexuality is criminalised unless both participants are over the age of 18 (the Government intends to introduce legislation to lower the age to 16), in private and with no other persons present (Sexual Offences Act 1956, ss 12, 13, 16 and Sexual Offences Act 1967, s 1, as amended by the Criminal Justice and Public Order Act 1994). Legislation does not address the participation of boys in heterosexual intercourse or lesbian sexual activity, although, if their partner is over 16, she may be guilty of indecent assault (Sexual Offences Act 1956, ss 14 and 15). See Thomson, Chapter 9, in this volume, for children's views about the heterosexual age of consent.

7   For a useful outline of legal provisions governing the ages at which children are permitted to engage in different activities, see Children's Legal Centre, 'At what age can I ...?' (1999) Information Sheet, University of Essex.

8   *Gillick v West Norfolk and Wisbech AHA* [1985] 3 WLR 830. The Family Law Reform Act 1969, s 8, creates a presumption that children over the age of 16 will have the capacity to give a valid consent to surgical, dental or medical treatment. This provision does not address whether children under the age of 16 can give a valid consent, nor the ability of children of any age to refuse their consent.

9   *Re E (A Minor) (Wardship: Medical Treatment)* [1993] 1 FLR 386; *Re R (A Minor) (Wardship: Medical Treatment)* [1991] 4 All ER 177; *Re W (A Minor) (Medical Treatment: Court's Jurisdiction)* [1992] 3 WLR 758; *South Glamorgan CC v W and B* [1993] 1 FLR 574; *Re K, W and H (Minors) (Medical Treatment)* [1993] 1 FLR 854; *Re S (A Minor) (Medical Treatment)* [1994] 2 FLR 1065; *Re L (Medical Treatment: Gillick Competency)* [1998] 2 FLR 810; *Re M (Medical Treatment: Consent)* [1999] 2 FLR 1097.

fully what is proposed'.[10] The level of understanding and intelligence which a child must possess depends upon the circumstances[11] and whether the specific child has the required capacity is a question of fact. Legislation does not comprehensively address all issues relating to the lifestyle of children or permissible uses and modification of their bodies. In the absence of statutory regulation, the requirements of the common law must be fulfilled, although it is uncertain whether the common law extends to body piercing[12] – a common form of self-expression amongst children – or to cosmetic surgery or organ donation.[13]

In the absence of reported case law on many of these issues, this chapter focuses upon cases concerning decisions made by teenagers affecting their bodies in the form of medical treatment. Before turning to the cases, I

---

10 *Gillick v West Norfolk and Wisbech AHA* [1985] 3 WLR 830, p 858, *per* Lord Scarman. The doctrinal limitations of the law mean that the question of consent arises in relation to whether a criminal or civil battery is committed, and not in relation to the important issue of the participation of the individual in decisions affecting his or her body. Applicable in areas beyond decisions relating to the body, eg, the right to apply for permission of the court to commence proceedings for residency, contact or a specific issue order (Children Act 1989, s 10(8)).

11 Although, as Montgomery argues, comparing the approaches taken by Lord Scarman and Lord Fraser, it is not clear from the judgments in *Gillick* what this entails (*op cit*, fn 5). He argues that the law is concerned with 'physical intrusions, not moral judgments' (p 338), so that, for a child to give consent, all that should have to be understood is the physical act.

12 Lois Bibbings and Peter Alldridge argue that, in the case of adults, as long as the body is pierced by a reputable practitioner, a valid consent can be given to what would otherwise amount to a criminal and civil battery (Bibbings, L and Alldridge, P, 'Sexual expression, body alteration and the defence of consent' (1993) 20 JLS 356). The same approach may be thought appropriate where consent is given by a child who has 'sufficient understanding and intelligence'. The Law Commission took the view in its Consultation Paper, *Consent and Offences Against the Person*, No 134, 1994, para 11.22, that, 'in some cases, such as ear-piercing and perhaps tattooing [of adults], one is driven to think that they are assumed to be lawful only because no one would ever be minded to suggest otherwise'. Following further consideration, the Law Commission proposed that body piercing would be lawful as long as it did not amount to 'seriously disabling injury', but that the Department of Health should give consideration to licensing body piercing (Law Commission, *Consent in the Criminal Law*, No 139, 1995, London: HMSO, para 9.22). However, the Law Commission sought views as to whether an age limit of 18 should be applied to piercing below the neck, branding and scarification for cultural or cosmetic purposes (or whether the age limit for tattoos should be removed) (para 9.24). *The Guardian* reported concern within the nursing profession about body piercing of children and the decision of the annual congress of the Royal College of Nursing to advocate regulation of piercing. The reported concerns included that the bodies of children as young as six were being pierced, an example of a 13 year old who had her naval pierced without parental consent and the infections and disfigurement which some have suffered after being pierced (Brindle, D, 'Warning over body piercing' (2000) *The Guardian*, 5 April).

13 The Family Law Reform Act 1969, s 8(2), applies to 'any procedure undertaken for the purposes of diagnosis' and 'any procedure ... which is ancillary to any treatment', which does not include the donation of blood or organs. The lawfulness of the donation of organs by children has not been judicially determined, although it is clear from the debate in the BMJ that children do act as donors (Delany, L, 'Protecting children from forced altruism' (1996) 312 BMJ 240).

commence with consideration of a move within feminism to theorise the body, believing that these cases present the opportunity to 'mediate ... the mind/body polarization'.[14] I aim, therefore, to consider the whole person – his or her embodied self. I argue that the judiciary, in these cases, constructs the Ideal Child who stands in opposition to the adult norm. The teenagers, whose refusal to consent to proposed medical treatment is at issue, are measured against these two ideals and found to be childlike. This conclusion permits the judiciary to decide for them in their 'best interests' and giving effect to the adult desire to protect. The aim of this chapter is not to make reform proposals but to challenge the understanding of children, which determines the approach of the law to decision making by children about their bodies.

MIND AND MATTER

The legal subject has traditionally been conceived of as an isolated, separate, disembodied, autonomous individual. Fundamental to this understanding of the legal subject is a Cartesian split between mind and body. The law is primarily concerned with the mind of its subject – with questions of capacity, intention, consent – whilst, at the same time, extending to regulate the body.[15] In the context of the present discussion, that means specifying the lifestyle for and use of the body, or determining whether the individual possesses the qualities entitling him or her to make decisions including where that involves intruding upon the body. A clear example of the latter is the judicial consideration as to whether a particular teenager possesses the capacity to make for him or herself a decision relating to their body arising, most often, from a medical condition. The judicial framing of the debate in these terms has inevitably led to academic consideration of the judgments which adopt the same focus.[16] Within this body of work, there are instructive and interesting expositions on the meaning of autonomy and a range of opinion as to whether

---

14   Grosz, E, *Volatile Bodies: Toward a Corporeal Feminism*, 1994, Bloomington: Indiana UP, p 85, quoted in Murphy, T, 'Feminism on flesh' (1997) 8 Law and Critique 37, p 54.

15   Stychin, C, 'Body talk: rethinking autonomy, commodification and the embodied legal self', in Sheldon, S and Thomson, M (eds), *Feminist Perspectives on Health Care Law*, 1998, London: Cavendish Publishing, p 214.

16   Bridgeman, J, 'Old enough to know best?' (1993) 13 LS 69; Eekelaar, J, 'White coats or flak jackets? Doctors, children and the courts – again' (1993) 109 LQR 182; Thornton, R, 'Minors and medical treatment – who decides?' [1994] CLJ 34; Mulholland, M, '*Re W (A Minor)*: autonomy, consent and the anorexic teenager' (1993) 9 Professional Negligence 21; Lowe, N and Juss, S, 'Medical treatment – pragmatism and the search for principle' (1993) 56 MLR 865; Brazier, M and Bridge, C, 'Coercion or caring: analysing adolescent autonomy' (1996) 16 LS 84; Bridge, C, 'Religious beliefs and teenage refusal of medical treatment' (1999) 62 MLR 585; Huxtable, R, '*Re M (Medical Treatment: Consent)*: time to remove the "flax jacket"?' (2000) 12 CFLQ 83.

the court reached the correct conclusion on the facts, that is, whether the decision of the teenager should have been respected. Yet, an approach to these cases which draws upon feminist legal theory provides, I argue, interesting insights and raises questions about the participation of children in making decisions regarding their bodies.

First, feminist legal theory has exposed the abstract individualism of the legal subject, demonstrating the way in which the law, like other discourses, is not premised upon a single ideal, but rather constructs a number of ideals against which the individual is measured.[17] As Carol Smart has argued in 'The woman of legal discourse', the law constructs (the Ideal) Woman in opposition to (the Ideal) Man and also 'types of women'. The Ideal Woman is then available as a contrast to 'types of women', such as the prostitute, surrogate, female criminal, single mother. Real women are judged against these constructs, to their benefit or detriment depending upon the circumstances. Secondly, feminist analysis has provided a critique of the mind/body split which is replicated in other binary pairs such as culture/nature, rational/emotional, male/female. In all instances, one, the former, is valued over the other, the latter, but the existence of the dominant side is dependent upon the existence of its other. As feminists have demonstrated, women have long been associated with the devalued side – emotions, nature, the body.[18] Thirdly, one focus of contemporary feminist theory found within the work of, for example, Judith Butler, Elizabeth Grosz and Moira Gatens is analysis of the body.[19] The body, it is argued, has been accepted as a natural, biological given and, consequently, with the obvious exception of the biological sciences, have not been exposed to scrutiny. Feminist theory which has analysed the social construction of gender has provided many important insights, but, in doing so, has replicated and perpetuated this oversight by accepting the body as natural. Feminism has reproduced the mind/body dichotomy because underlying the analysis of the social construction of gender is an acceptance, almost as it were by omission, of the body as a biological given.[20] In the words of Judith Butler: 'The presumption of a binary gender system implicitly retains the belief in a mimetic relation of gender to sex whereby gender mirrors sex or is otherwise restricted by it.'[21] The consequence has been a failure to appreciate the extent

---

17 Smart, C, 'The woman of legal discourse' (1992) 1 SLS 29.

18 *Op cit*, Stychin, fn 15, p 215; Gatens, M, *Imaginary Bodies: Ethics, Power and Corporeality*, 1996, London: Routledge, p 61; Bordo, S, *Unbearable Weight: Feminism, Western Culture and the Body*, 1993, Los Angeles: California UP, p 5; Butler, J, *Gender Trouble: Feminism and the Subversion of Identity*, 1990, London: Routledge, p 12.

19 *Ibid*, Butler; *ibid*, Gatens; *op cit*, Grosz, fn 14. See, also, Davis, K, *Embodied Practices: Feminist Perspectives on the Body*, 1997, London: Sage.

20 *Op cit*, Murphy, fn 14, pp 37–41.

21 *Ibid*, Butler, p 6.

to which attitudes towards, treatment of and the value accorded to the body are historically and culturally specific.[22] Judith Butler, for example, argues that sex (the body), as much as gender (the mind), is socially constructed, that 'the ostensibly natural facts of sex [are] discursively produced by various scientific discourses in the service of other political and social interests'.[23] They argue that, as well as the social construction of gender, feminists must analyse the ways in which the meanings given to (and our understandings of) the body and, in their focus, the sexed body, are socially constructed.

Moira Gatens provides an analysis not of the 'physiological, anatomical, or biological understandings of the human body' but of the imaginary body.[24] That is, 'images, symbols, metaphors and representations which help construct various forms of subjectivity'.[25] She argues that it is through these culturally (and thus historically) specific symbols that the body in a particular culture at a particular time is given meaning and through them that we learn the appropriate use of, and value given to, the body.[26] But further, it is not only our understandings of the body, the value accorded to the body which is thus created, but its material reality.[27] Legal texts – statutory provisions and judgments – form part of this imaginary. As Carl Stychin points out, to this extent, the law can be understood as productive; creating our understandings of the body, and in a way which gives effect to dominant interests.[28] By way of example, Ngaire Naffine considers criminal laws concerning 'how people should relate to one another as physical beings'.[29] Whilst the body is understood within criminal law as 'bounded', a comparison of the law relating to assault, which provides exceptions for sports such as boxing and rugby, with sexual offences leads her to conclude that 'there has been ... a highly selective casting of boundaries around persons'.[30]

The feminist theory outlined provides insights into, and an analytical framework for consideration of, the cases concerning the decisions made by teenagers relating to their bodies. First, the cases can be analysed as constructive of the Ideal Child. In the same way that the law constructs the Ideal Woman, identifying her mental and physical characteristics, so the law

---

22 *Op cit*, Gatens, fn 18, p viii.

23 *Op cit*, Butler, fn 18, p 7.

24 *Op cit*, Gatens, fn 18, p viii.

25 *Op cit*, Gatens, fn 18, p viii.

26 *Op cit*, Gatens, fn 18, p viii.

27 *Op cit*, Gatens, fn 18, p 68: '... to claim a history for the body involves taking seriously the ways in which diet, environment and the typical activities of a body may vary historically and create its capacities, its desires and its actual material form.'

28 *Op cit*, Stychin, fn 15, p 215. See, also, Naffine, N, 'The body bag', in Naffine, N and Owens, R, *Sexing the Subject of Law*, 1997, London: Sweet & Maxwell.

29 *Ibid*, Naffine, p 84.

30 *Ibid*, Naffine, p 93.

identifies the characteristics of the mind and body of the child. Secondly, in the same way that the female is defined in contradistinction to the male, the child is constructed as other to the (male) adult norm. The identification of the qualities, nature, abilities and materiality of the child gives definition to the qualities, nature, abilities and materiality of the adult:

> Social consciousness depicts the child in relation to a conception of the adult just as a sense of adulthood is constructed on the positing of the child. This leads to the suggestion that parallel to a 'gender agenda' we can also imagine a 'generational agenda' being at work – a particular social order that organises children's relations to the world in a systematic way, allocates them positions from which to act and a view and knowledge about themselves and their social relations.[31]

In the same way that women, lacking the qualities of the male adult norm – rationality, independence, autonomy – are 'other' to the normal adult, so is the child – whether male or female.[32] Perspectives of childhood have been dominated by a view of children as physically immature. And, consequential upon their physical immaturity follows the view of children as mentally immature. Childhood is understood as a period of development during which, from a state of physical and mental immaturity, the child develops the physical maturity and qualities of adulthood. And, during childhood, children are socialised, learning ways of behaviour that are appropriate for adulthood.[33] This developmental concept has influenced a variety of fields ranging from theories of education, to practical advice for parents, to legal concepts such as the welfare principle and the best interests of the child. The developmental concept describes childhood and has become an entrenched way of understanding children. In addition, it has an impact upon the lives of real children as they conform both to expectations[34] and to, in this instance, the requirements of the law. As adults, be they parents, carers, lawyers or judges, and children accept and respond to the developmental concept, it is reinforced by ways of understanding children and in ways of being children.[35]

Three points need to be made. First, in arguing that childhood is constructed by discourses, in this instance, law, and that this legal construction

---

31 Alanen, L, 'Gender and generation: feminism and the "child question"', in Qvortrup, J, Bardy, M, Sgritta, G and Wintersberger, H (eds), *Childhood Matters: Social Theory, Practice and Politics*, 1994, Aldershot: Avebury, p 37.

32 Oakley, A, 'Woman and children first and last: parallels and differences between children's and women's studies', in Mayall, B (ed), *Children's Childhoods: Observed and Experienced*, 1994, London: Falmer, p 15.

33 Prout, A and James, A, 'A new paradigm for the sociology of childhood? Provenance, promise and problems', in Prout, A and James, A (eds), *Constructing and Reconstructing Childhood*, 1997, London: Falmer, p 12.

34 *Ibid*, p 23.

35 *Ibid*, Alanen, p 40.

has an impact upon the material reality of children's lives, I am not saying that children are nothing but constructed by discourses. Whilst the developmental concept of childhood does have an effect upon the lives of children, children are at the same time living, determining, choosing individuals. Secondly, I am not arguing that there is no difference between adults and children. Clearly, there are but this prior differentiation ignores that there are also similarities and that there are differences amongst adults. Nor, thirdly, am I seeking to argue that children do not spend time learning. Clearly, they do. What I am suggesting is that the child is constructed as different from the adult because the child has still to learn, ignoring the fact that for adults there is still much to be learnt. I now turn to consider how this perspective of the child might inform the judiciary in cases concerning decisions made by teenagers regarding their bodies.

LAW'S CHILDREN

Caring for children includes equipping them with the skills to enable them to take care of themselves, amongst other things, to manage the body by routine maintenance.[36] Through a process of negotiation with their parents and depending upon such factors as parental views about their respective roles and the degree of responsibility taken by the individual, teenagers will have gained the experience to be able to undertake for themselves the tasks of basic personal hygiene. In addition, to varying degrees, they will make decisions about, for example, what to eat, when to sleep, the amount of exercise that they will take. Some will also smoke cigarettes, drink alcohol and have sex.[37] Many will express themselves by changing their bodies in temporary ways through the use of make-up, choice of hairstyle or clothing, or semi-permanently, by piercing their nose, ears or naval.

Having gained experience of health and pain, many teenagers will also be able to identify when medical help is required and enter into negotiations with professionals to obtain it.[38] Where it is routine medical care involving examination by, for example, general practitioners, opticians or dentists, teenagers can describe their symptoms or the assistance they require, listen to

---

36 The death, in the US, of 13 year old Christine Corrigan from heart failure caused by obesity demonstrates the sad consequences which may follow from leaving children to take responsibility for themselves. The prosecution of her mother, Marlene Corrigan, for child neglect shows the danger, for adults, that others may take a different view of whether the child should have been taking that responsibility (see Bridgeman, J, 'Criminalising the one who really cared' (1998) 6 FLS 245).

37 See Thomson, Chapter 9, in this volume; Johnson, A, Wadsworth, J, Wellings, K and Field, J, *Sexual Attitudes and Lifestyles*, 1994, London: Blackwell Scientific.

38 Alderson, P, 'Everyday and medical life choices: decision making among eight to 15 year old school students' (1992) 18 Child: Care, Health and Development 81.

advice, discuss the options available and give or refuse the necessary consent. As is apparent from the case law, everyday arguments over situations such as going to the dentist, eating greens or returning home with a pierced belly button do not become translated into legal disputes. But neither have examples of far more serious interventions, such as cosmetic surgery or organ donation. The court has been asked to adjudicate in cases where there is *both* a disagreement between adult (whether professional or parent) and teenager *and* the adult perceives that the decision of the teenager is one which presents a serious threat to health or life.[39] The obvious exception to this characterisation of events are the cases such as *Gillick*, where sex (read morality) rather than death presents the ground of contention.[40] The current state of the law is that teenagers aged 16 and 17 are presumed to be able to give a valid consent to surgical, dental or medical treatment and teenagers who are under 16 years old can give a valid consent if they have a full understanding of what is proposed. However, where the teenager is refusing consent, there is a willingness on the part of the court to determine that understanding is lacking and, anyway, a valid consent can be given by the court or any party with parental authority.

Child development

It was suggested above that the perception of childhood as a period of development of the mental qualities and bodily capacities of adulthood has been influential in a variety of disciplines, including law. The developmental approach to childhood is adopted by the judiciary in their consideration of the decisions made by teenagers about their health and their bodies. The employment of the developmental concept can be seen in the judgments of the House of Lords in *Gillick v West Norfolk and Wisbech AHA*.[41] The issue in this case, as is well known, was the legality of the provision of contraceptive advice and treatment to girls under the age of 16. That necessitated consideration of the criminal offences contrary to ss 5 and 6 of the Sexual Offences Act 1956 and in what, if any, circumstances a girl under the age of 16 could give a valid consent to the provision of contraceptive advice and treatment. The majority rejected the approach adopted by the Court of Appeal that there was a specified age, that being 16, as inappropriate. Whilst

---

39   *Re E (A Minor) (Wardship: Medical Treatment)* [1993] 1 FLR 386; *Re R (A Minor) (Wardship: Medical Treatment)* [1991] 4 All ER 177; *Re W (A Minor) (Medical Treatment: Court's Jurisdiction)* [1992] 3 WLR 758; *South Glamorgan CC v W and B* [1993] 1 FLR 574; *Re S (A Minor) (Medical Treatment)* [1994] 2 FLR 1065; *Re L (Medical Treatment: Gillick Competency)* [1998] 2 FLR 810; *Re M (Medical Treatment: Consent)* [1999] 2 FLR 1097.

40   *Gillick v West Norfolk and Wisbech AHA* [1985] 3 WLR 830; *Re P (A Minor)* [1986] 1 FLR 272; and *Re B (Wardship: Abortion)* [1991] 2 FLR 426 concerned the termination of pregnancy.

41   [1985] 3 WLR 830.

providing certainty, this would have left the child under the control of her parents until she reached the age of 16 at which point she would, effectively, be abandoned to her rights. The reality, Lord Fraser suggested, was that:

> In practice most wise parents relax their control gradually as the child develops and encourage him or her to become increasingly independent. Moreover, the degree of parental control actually exercised over a particular child does in practice vary considerably according to his understanding and intelligence ...[42]

With a modernising inclination, the majority dismissed earlier cases involving authoritarian fathers, explicable as representative of Victorian family life and not applicable given modes of parenting in 1980s Britain.[43] Lord Scarman identified as changing social circumstances which the 'law ignores ... at its peril' the provision of contraception through medical services, increased independence of the young and the status of women.[44] His Lordship suggested that:

> If the law should impose upon the process of 'growing up' fixed limits where nature knows only a continuous process, the price would be artificiality and a lack of realism in an area where the law must be sensitive to human development and social change.[45]

In contrast to the status approach, there is inevitably some uncertainty arising from the developmental approach. But Lord Scarman was of the opinion that this was necessary for the law to accommodate the social reality that many girls are able to decide for themselves about many issues whilst under the age of 16.[46]

Lords Fraser and Scarman thus envisaged a model of parenting in which, as the child develops physically and mentally, he or she is given more independence and control, and is allowed to make decisions for him or herself commensurate with his or her capacities. Dissenting, Lord Templeman also adopted a developmental view of childhood. Consenting to have tonsils or appendix removed was one thing:

> But any decision on the part of a girl to practise sex and contraception requires not only knowledge of the facts of life and of the dangers of pregnancy and disease, but also an understanding of the emotional and other consequences to her family, her male partner and to herself. I doubt whether a girl under the age of 16 is capable of a balanced judgment to embark on frequent, regular or casual sexual intercourse fortified by the illusion that medical science can protect her in mind and body and ignoring the danger of leaping from

---

42 *Gillick v West Norfolk and Wisbech AHA* [1985] 3 WLR 830, p 842, *per* Lord Fraser.

43 *Ibid*, pp 841–43, *per* Lord Fraser, p 856, *per* Lord Scarman, approving of the opinion of Lord Denning in *Hewer v Bryant* [1969] 3 All ER 578 on the earlier case of *Re Agar-Ellis, Agar-Ellis v Lascelles* (1883) 24 Ch D 317.

44 *Gillick v West Norfolk and Wisbech AHA* [1985] 3 WLR 830, p 852, *per* Lord Scarman.

45 *Ibid*, p 855, *per* Lord Scarman.

46 *Ibid*, p 860, *per* Lord Scarman.

childhood to adulthood without the difficult formative transitional experiences of adolescence.[47]

The developmental approach can, therefore, be enabling but it can also be used to limit the extent of decision making by a teenager over his or her life.

Lord Donaldson employed the developmental concept in *Re W*, positioning the teenager between the two extremes of childhood and adulthood:

> This is not, however, to say that the wishes of 16 and 17 year olds are to be treated as no different from those of 14 and 15 year olds. Far from it. Adolescence is a period of progressive transition from childhood to adulthood and, as experience of life is acquired and intelligence and understanding grow, so will the scope of the decision making which should be left to the minor, for it is only by making decisions and experiencing the consequences that decision making skills will be acquired. As I put it in the course of argument, and as I sincerely believe, 'good parenting involves giving minors as much rope as they can handle without an unacceptable risk that they will hang themselves'.[48]

The process of development involves acquiring the qualities, nature, behaviour and physical maturity of normal adulthood. That is, the process is one of development towards appropriate adulthood from a starting position of expectations (on the part of adults) of the other, the child. The individual can then be judged with reference to either (abiding by norms of) adulthood or (conformity to expectations of) childhood.

Treated like a child

The developmental concept may be premised upon increasingly vesting children with responsibility over their bodies and for their actions. However, it may also be employed to the opposite effect – enabling a conclusion that the child has not developed sufficiently to be able to make decisions for him or herself. I now turn to consider the cases concerned with the decisions of teenagers regarding their bodies. I argue that, in these cases, the judiciary construct the child to stand in opposition to the male adult norm. In order to justify giving consent to treatment contrary to the decision of the teenager, facts are selected and interpreted to support a conclusion that the individual teenager is childlike. I draw upon feminist analysis of the female as 'other' to the male norm to provide a structure through which to explore the construction of the child as 'other' to the adult and the selection and

---

47 *Gillick v West Norfolk and Wisbech AHA* [1985] 3 WLR 830, p 869, *per* Lord Templeman, which compares with the absolutist view taken by Lord Brandon. The law should, his Lordship said (p 866), reinforce the message: 'Wait till you are 16.'

48 *Re W (A Minor) (Medical Treatment: Court's Jurisdiction)* [1992] 3 WLR 758, p 770C–D, *per* Lord Donaldson MR. See, also, p 776B, *per* Balcombe LJ.

interpretation of facts in these cases. That is, I consider the judicial construction of the child as confined to the private sphere, dependent upon his or her family, irrational and self-destructive.

The private world of the child

As the judiciary portray it in these cases, the locus of the child is the private, domestic realm: the realm of the family.[49] This private world provides a protected environment in which children are allowed to be children: a place in which childhood is played out. But, because they have not been exposed to the public world, children lack experience and understanding of matters of importance. The court looks to the lives of these teenagers and finds there a concern with childish pursuits disrupted by their medical condition. Setting out the facts, Ward J stated that, prior to the onset of leukaemia, E had excelled at athletics and had enjoyed watching football but was no longer 'big and strong'.[50] In his judgment, Johnson J recounted with approval the account given by the official solicitor that M had enjoyed swimming and playing netball but, within a few weeks, had been transformed from a healthy active girl and was now, due to her heart condition, close to death.[51] L is graphically brought to life by Sir Stephen Brown P as a popular, well regarded, reliable family girl, a 'model of a young person ... not attracted by some of the more undisciplined pursuits of youth'.[52] The impression given is that L has been protected from the harsh realities of the public world and sheltered in a state of innocence within the family. Sir Stephen Brown explained that this meant that she lacked experience of life:

> She has led what has been expressed to have been a sheltered life, not an unrealistically sheltered life, but nevertheless a sheltered life ... It is, therefore, a limited experience of life which she has – inevitably so – but that is in no sense

---

49   The distinction is between the public sphere – the world of government, business, professions, education – and the private sphere – the domestic world of the family (see O'Donovan, K, *Sexual Divisions in Law*, 1985, London: Weidenfeld & Nicolson, p 3). Feminist theory has demonstrated how this division has been premised upon the allocation of women to the private and men to the public. Eg, Eisenstein, Z, *The Radical Future of Liberal Feminism*, 1981, London: Longman, p 5: 'Although the meaning of "public" and "private" changes in concrete ways, the assignment of public space to men and private space to women is continuous in Western history.' This allocation was considered appropriate, given beliefs about the different natures of men (rational, self-interested, educated) and women (emotional, dependent).

50   *Re E (A Minor) (Wardship: Medical Treatment)* [1993] 1 FLR 386, p 387, *per* Ward J: 'He is a boy of ordinary average intelligence, a boy of considerable athletic prowess – big and strong and, until the catastrophic events of the last few weeks, fit and healthy. He proudly proclaimed that he had scarcely ever been ill in his life. He was on holiday when he first felt certain pains in his stomach. They grew progressively worse and on a Saturday when he was watching his favourite football team the pain was so severe that medical intervention was clearly necessary.'

51   *Re M (Medical Treatment: Consent)* [1999] 2 FLR 1097, p 1100.

52   *Re L (Medical Treatment: Gillick Competency)* [1998] 2 FLR 810, p 812.

a criticism of her or her upbringing. It is indeed refreshing to hear of children being brought up with the sensible disciplines of a well conducted family. But it does necessarily limit her understanding of matters which are as grave as her own present situation.[53]

As with women, it is the nature of children which dictates their suitability for confinement to the private realm, as children are perceived to be dominated by their emotions, lacking the rationality for participation in the public sphere (the realm of men). Children – boys and girls – are located within the private, domestic realm where they play as a means to, and whilst they, develop the physical and mental capacities required for participation in the public sphere. At the same time, until they develop the required characteristics, children need the protection afforded by the private realm for they are not equipped to deal with the demands of the public sphere. Failure to enjoy a protected childhood is given as an explanation for W's physical condition and for S's response to her illness. The account which Lord Donaldson gives of W's childhood begins, 'Fate has dealt harshly with W'[54] and continues to document the death of her father from a brain tumour when she was five, her mother's death from cancer three years later, bullying and the deaths of a foster parent and her grandfather as causes of the anorexia from which she suffers. S had been born with, and received treatment since birth for, beta minor thalassaemia major. At the age of 15, she refused to continue to receive blood transfusions necessary for the treatment of her condition. The court endorsed the views of Dr S, consultant child psychiatrist, that S's home situation was 'puzzling' for its lack of affection and of Dr J, consultant paediatrician, that her mother's view (formed since adopting the beliefs of a Jehovah's Witness) that she would rather S die than have further blood transfusions was 'rather more than tactless'.[55]

A feminist critique of the public and private realms demonstrates, amongst other things, that they are not self-contained in the way presented. Not only is the idea that the private realm is a protected haven untainted by the public sphere and vice versa unsustainable but, further, we are not either confined to the private or out enjoying the public but shift between the two. Defining the lives of these teenagers in these terms ignores the experiences, including of illness and death, which they will have gained through, amongst other things, their contact with adults, teachers, their peers and exposure to a wide range of issues through the media and schooling.

---

53 *Re L (Medical Treatment: Gillick Competency)* [1998] 2 FLR 810, p 812.
54 *Re W (A Minor) (Medical Treatment: Court's Jurisdiction)* [1992] 3 WLR 758, p 761.
55 *Re S (A Minor) (Medical Treatment)* [1994] 2 FLR 1065, pp 1073–74.

Dependent

The child is understood as physically, and thus emotionally, dependent upon his or her parents: lacking the skills to care for him or herself or to make decisions for him or herself. In contrast with the independent, self-interested individual which is accepted as the adult norm, the teenagers in these cases are shown to be dependent, looking to parents for advice and guidance and influenced by the wish to respect their parents. M showed consideration for her family when she acknowledged that her decision to refuse to undergo a heart transplant operation would affect them: 'I feel selfish. If I had the transplant I wouldn't be happy. If I were to die my family would be sad.'[56] The judiciary are particularly concerned about dependency where religious beliefs are material to the decision. E, a few months short of his 16th birthday, was refusing blood transfusions for the treatment of leukaemia. He, like his parents, fervently believed in the tenets of the Jehovah's Witnesses' faith. Ward J would not go so far as to say that E had been subjected to undue influence, but viewed him as a child who was dependent upon his family: 'He is a boy who seeks and needs the love and respect of his parents whom he would wish to honour as the Bible exhorts him to honour them.'[57]

The teenager is presented as dependent upon their family, unable to make decisions for themselves, but heavily influenced by a desire to respect their parents. This is in contrast to mature decision making which is independent and self-interested. Susan Stefan notes the study by Steven Miles and Allison August of US cases concerning the right to die. This study found that the sex of the patient led to distinct responses to their decisions. Whilst the decisions of the males were seen as considered and rational, those of the women were dismissed as 'unreflective, emotional or immature'.[58] The authors suggest that the views of the women were dismissed because they 'employ[ed] care-centred or communal moral reasoning to make decisions rather than affirming generalizable moral rules' or because they explained their decisions in terms of emotions or experiences.[59] To the extent that women, and the teenagers in these cases, can be seen to be influenced by their emotions or family relationships in making a decision, or express themselves in terms of physical or emotional dependency, they fail to apply the criteria accepted as the norm for independent, self-interested decision making.

---

56 *Re M (Medical Treatment: Consent)* [1999] 2 FLR 1097, p 1100.

57 *Re E (A Minor) (Wardship: Medical Treatment)* [1993] 1 FLR 386, p 393.

58 Miles, S and August, A, 'Courts, gender and the "right to die"' (1990) 18 Med & Health Care 85, discussed in Stefan, S, 'Silencing the different voice: competence, feminist theory and law' (1993) 47 Miami UL Rev 763, p 771.

59 *Ibid*, Stefan, p 773, discussing Miles and August (*ibid*).

Irrational

The judiciary present the decisions of the teenagers refusing treatment as irrational and, although this is not sufficient to lead to a conclusion that they lack competence, it does contribute to the portrayal of the teenagers as childlike. It is interesting to note that Lord Donaldson in *Re W* was not only clearly of the opinion that W's refusal to transfer to a different centre for treatment of anorexia was irrational but, further, his personal belief was that 'religious or other beliefs which bar any medical treatment or medical treatment of particular kinds are irrational'.[60] However, in those cases where religious beliefs were material to the decision, the general rationality of holding those beliefs was not questioned whilst the belief of the individual was. In all cases, the court expressed doubts about the reasoning underlying the belief. Sir Stephen Brown accepted the evidence of Dr Cameron, consultant child psychiatrist, that L's refusal was based on a 'very sincerely, strongly held religious belief' but one which 'does not in fact lend itself in her mind to discussion', unlike 'the constructive formulation of an opinion which occurs with adult experience'.[61] S's explanation for her refusal was considered inadequate by the court. Johnson J quoted Dr S, consultant child psychiatrist: 'There were a lot of things that concerned me, the patness of her replies, some of her phrases. She and her mother were using exactly similar phraseology. S was not able to explain her thoughts except that, "it was said in the Bible".'[62] The extent to which S was willing and able to articulate in acceptable terms the reasons for her refusal led to conclusions about her understanding. E's sincerely and long held beliefs were dismissed as attributable to the enthusiasm of youth:

> I have to take account of the fact that teenagers often express views with vehemence and conviction – all the vehemence and conviction of youth! Those of us who have passed beyond callow youth can all remember the convictions we have loudly proclaimed which now we find somewhat embarrassing.[63]

The values of the teenagers are acknowledged but are dismissed as irrational, unreasonable beliefs.

Self-destruction

Carol Smart, highlighting some of the ways in which the law has regulated the female body, argues that women have often been treated in law as if they were nothing but their bodies, bodily functions or bits of bodies.[64] The graphic descriptions of disease, illness, injury provided by the judiciary bring to the

---

60 *Re W (A Minor) (Medical Treatment: Court's Jurisdiction)* [1992] 3 WLR 758, p 769.
61 *Re L (Medical Treatment: Gillick Competency)* [1998] 2 FLR 810, p 812.
62 *Re S (A Minor) (Medical Treatment)* [1994] 2 FLR 1065, p 1074.
63 *Re E (A Minor) (Wardship: Medical Treatment)* [1993] 1 FLR 386, p 393.
64 Smart, C, *Feminism and the Power of Law*, 1989, London: Routledge, p 96.

forefront the physical conditions of the teenagers. Their decisions are explained as dictated by their physical conditions with their bodies in, and out of, control. The self-destructive course upon which their bodies have set them demands protective intervention.

W suffered from anorexia, an illness which, Lord Donaldson explained, like pneumonia or appendicitis, is not the fault of the sufferer, although it does result in addictive behaviour for which the anorexic, unlike the drug user, is not to be blamed.[65] W had restricted her eating beyond acceptable limits so that whilst she was 5 ft 7, she weighed only 5 stone 7 lb. Those caring for W were concerned that her reproductive capacity was in danger of being irreversibly damaged and beyond that her life was at risk.[66] Lord Donaldson considered that W was in the grip of anorexia to the extent that her physical condition affected her judgment:

> ... it is a feature of anorexia nervosa that it is capable of destroying the ability to make an informed choice. It creates a compulsion to refuse treatment or only to accept treatment which is likely to be ineffective. This attitude is part and parcel of the disease and, the more advanced the illness, the more compelling it may become.[67]

M explained that she did not want someone else's heart because that would make her feel different, nor did she want to have to take medication for the rest of her life. This was interpreted as an inability to cope with the physical condition of her body and the effect it had had upon her life, rather than as a decision arising from her sense of who she was: her identity. S had beta minor thalassaemia major, a condition in which the body does not produce red blood cells, treated by a blood transfusion every four weeks and a daily injection to counter the inability to excrete iron. S was described as of small stature, at 15 being 4 ft 6 and of slight build, because she had not injected herself daily.[68] She attended court, but was frail, pale and weak. Johnson J accepted the view that S's refusal of further treatment could be attributed to treatment fatigue: that she was fed up with constant medical treatment. This was supported by evidence that she likened her body to a pin cushion and as a response to the taunts from her peers, who called her 'ironing board'.[69] Dr J, consultant paediatrician, referred to patients of his with diabetes who, as teenagers, get fed up with the need for ongoing treatment but that: 'I find that if I can hold a situation for a year or so, by the age of 17 or so their added maturity leads to a change in attitude.'[70] Court orders were made to prevent the self-destruction of W, M, S, E and L.

---

65 *Re W (A Minor) (Medical Treatment: Court's Jurisdiction)* [1992] 3 WLR 758, p 761.
66 *Ibid*, p 768.
67 *Ibid*, p 769.
68 *Re S (A Minor) (Medical Treatment)* [1994] 2 FLR 1065, p 1066.
69 *Ibid*, p 1073.
70 *Ibid*, p 1072.

The teenagers in these cases are located within the private sphere of the family, with experiences confined to childish preoccupations, but sheltered and protected from the realities of the public world. They are dependent – practically, physically, emotionally – upon their families and are influenced not solely by self-interest but by a respect for their parents. The values governing their decision are well meant but not fully understood or, alternatively, grasped with childish enthusiasm. Their decisions are affected by the physical deterioration of their bodies which have set them upon a course of self-destruction. Facts are selected and interpreted to support the conclusion that each is childlike, and this is the case irrespective of the sex/gender of the teenager. What permits this conclusion is the distance between the identified physical and mental characteristics of the individual and the adult male norm, not whether the individual teenager is male or female. Unable to care for themselves, adult protection is justified.

The desire to protect may explain the failure by medical professionals and parents, acknowledged without comment by the judiciary, to fully inform the teenagers of the consequences of their decision. Paradoxically, this gap in their understanding presents a further justification for providing treatment:

> I am quite satisfied that [E] does not have sufficient comprehension of the pain he has yet to suffer, of the fear that he will be undergoing, of the distress not only occasioned by that fear but also – and importantly – the distress he will inevitably suffer as he, a loving son, helplessly watches his parents' and his family's distress. They are a close family, and they are a brave family, but I find that he has no realisation of the full implications which lie before him as to the process of dying. He may have some concept of the fact that he will die, but as to the manner of his death and to the extent of his and his family's suffering I find he has not the ability to turn his mind to it nor the will to do so.[71]

Likewise, Sir Stephen Brown stated that L failed to understand the distress which she and those caring for her would undergo as she died a 'horrible' death from the gangrene which would set in if she did not undergo surgery for her extensive burns. But L was not going to be in a position to understand, for the simple reason that nobody had told her.[72]

---

71 *Re E (A Minor) (Wardship: Medical Treatment)* [1993] 1 FLR 386, p 391.
72 *Re L (Medical Treatment: Gillick Competency)* [1998] 2 FLR 810, pp 811–12; see, also, *op cit*, fn 39, *Re S (A Minor) (Medical Treatment)* [1994] 2 FLR 1065, p 1076.

In their marshalling of the facts, in the interpretation given to them, in their reconfiguration of teenage experience, the judiciary are clearly motivated by a well meaning desire to protect.[73] However, as Ann Oakley says:

> ... judgments about the welfare of ... children are based not on asking them what they want or need, but on what other people consider to be the case. It is a philosophy of exclusion and control dressed up as protection, and dependent upon the notion that those who are protected must be so because they are deemed incapable of looking after themselves.[74]

The price of protection may be 'exclusion and control' but, further, what the court is sanctioning in the name of protection is intrusive, invasive and potentially very harmful. In theoretical terms, permitting treatment of teenagers contrary to their expressed wishes amounts to a violation of the boundaries of their bodies.[75] In practical terms, implicit within the conclusion that treatment may be provided contrary to the wishes of the individual is the use of force to achieve this. In the cases of W and S, the court was able to rely upon evidence that a court order would be complied with,[76] and Ward J was of the opinion that: '... although [E] will protest, at the end of the day, he will respect the decision of this court.'[77] But, in M's case, both the physical and emotional effects of the decision were acknowledged:

> There are risks attached to the operation itself and there are risks continuing thereafter, both in terms of rejection in the medical sense and rejection by M of the continuing medical treatment. There is the risk too that she will carry with her for the rest of her life resentment about what has been done to her.[78]

---

73 This is not confined to judgments concerning the bodies of children; see, also, *Re R (A Minor) (Wardship: Medical Treatment)* [1991] 4 All ER 177; *South Glamorgan CC v W and B* [1993] 1 FLR 574; *Re K, W and H (Minors) (Consent to Treatment)* [1993] 1 FLR 854. Discussed by Montgomery, J, 'Parents and children in dispute: who has the final word?' (1992) 4 JCL 85; Bainham, A, 'The judge and the competent minor' (1992) 108 LQR 194; Lyon, C, 'What's happened to the child's "right" to refuse? *South Glamorgan County Council v W and B'* (1994) 6 JCL 84; Bates, P, 'Children in secure psychiatric units: *Re K, W and H* – "out of sight, out of mind"?' (1994) 6 JCL 131. There is a comparable body of law facilitating the provision of treatment to refusing pregnant women and anorexics: *Riverside Mental Health NHS Trust v Fox* [1994] 1 FLR 614; *South West Hertfordshire HA v KB* [1994] 2 FCR 1051; *Tameside and Glossop Acute Services Trust v CH* [1996] 1 FLR 762; *St George's Healthcare NHS Trust v S, R v Collins and Others ex p S* [1998] 3 All ER 673; *Norfolk v Norwich Healthcare (NHS) Trust v W* [1996] 2 FLR 613; *Re L (Patient: Non-Consensual Treatment)* [1997] 2 FLR 837; *Re MB* [1997] Fam Law 542; *Rochdale Healthcare NHS Trust v C* [1997] 1 FLR 274. Discussed by Widdett, C and Thomson, M, 'Justifying treatment and other stories' (1997) 5 FLS 77; Morris, A, 'Once upon a time in a hospital ... the cautionary tale of *St George's Healthcare NHS Trust v S, R v Collins and Others ex p S* [1998] 3 All ER 673' (1999) 7 FLS 75; Lim, H, 'Caesareans and cyborgs' (1999) 7 FLS 133.

74 *Op cit*, Oakley, fn 32, p 16.

75 *Op cit*, Naffine, fn 28.

76 *Re W (A Minor) (Medical Treatment: Court's Jurisdiction)* [1992] 3 WLR 758, p 768; *Re S (A Minor) (Medical Treatment)* [1994] 2 FLR 1065, p 1067.

77 *Re E (A Minor) (Wardship: Medical Treatment)* [1993] 1 FLR 386, p 394.

78 *Re M (Medical Treatment: Consent)* [1999] 2 FLR 1097, p 1100.

However, the reality of the harm of coerced medical treatment is downplayed in the interests of giving effect to the adult desire to protect.

DECIDING WITH CHILDREN

My aim in this conclusion is not to advocate comprehensive proposals for reform but, having employed feminist legal theory to explore one specific issue within the case law, to reflect upon the participation of children in making decisions affecting their bodies.[79] The boundaries set by the law establishing the appropriate lifestyle for children and permissible uses and modification of their bodies are premised upon an understanding of childhood as a period of development from a state of dependency to normal adulthood. It is clear that the construction of the child adopted and employed in the cases is constituted without any consideration of the realities of the lives of the teenagers in question. Ann Oakley has observed that adults need to challenge our own desire to protect and the view that what children need most of all is our protection by, she suggests, listening to children.[80] The views of children have long been ignored, dismissed, excluded, as children are silenced by an enduring belief that they are too immature, capricious and open to the influence of others to have anything of value to contribute. There is, consequently, little known about children's experiences of health, illness and disease.

One account of children's experiences of illness is provided by Myra Bluebond-Langner's study of terminally ill children with leukaemia.[81] The adults caring for them had not told the children that they were terminally ill or of the progression of their illness but the children developed an awareness and understanding from watching those around them. They could see other children suffering from the same illness (against whom they were able to compare their own bodies) and could detect changes in the way the adults caring for them were towards them. A shroud of secrecy, motivated by a desire to protect, effectively precluded giving support to the children through what they were experiencing. In turn, to protect their parents, the children kept from them their awareness of their condition. Withholding information creates a lost opportunity for sharing feelings, something which David Bearison found was important to children in his interviews with children with cancer.[82]

---

79 Alderson, P and Montgomery, J, in *Healthcare Choices: Making Decisions with Children*, 1996, London: IPPR, suggest legislation establishing a Code of Practice governing healthcare decisions made with children.

80 *Op cit*, Oakley, fn 32, p 20.

81 Bluebond-Langner, M, *The Private Worlds of Dying Children*, 1978, Princeton: Princeton UP.

82 Bearison, D, *'They Never Want to Tell You': Children Talk about Cancer*, 1991, Cambridge, Mass: Harvard UP.

Priscilla Alderson listened in her study of children aged eight to 15 years facing orthopaedic surgery.[83] Listening to the views of children about their need for, the benefits of, and understanding about, surgery, Priscilla Alderson identified amongst the children she spoke with a range of ability, experience and approaches to decision making, that is, whether they wished to decide themselves, to decide together or for another to make the decision for them. She noted that, where children did decide, they invariably did so responsibly and cautiously. Her interviews with children led her to conclude that decisions should be made with and not for children.[84]

Research with children may reveal, as does that outlined above, a very different picture of children's abilities to cope with information, to understand and participate in decisions than is extended to the child constructed by legal discourse. These studies provide insights into the experiences, feelings and opinions of children with experience of illness, disease and disabling conditions. Only by listening to children's experiences on a wide range of issues, including health, illness, alcohol, cigarettes, body image and modification, will it be possible to dismantle the child constructed by law and for a legal framework to be developed which is sensitive to the realities of children's lives and responsive to the needs and wishes of the individual child.

The responsibility which this imposes upon adults is to listen to feelings, fears, anxieties, expectations and experiences and not to silence, to inform in comprehensible terminology and not attempt to conceal the truth, to involve and not to exclude.[85] Where the adults who care for them share with children decision making about these issues, we may even protect them more effectively.

83 Alderson, P, *Children's Consent to Surgery*, 1993, Oxford: OUP. See also, Alderson, P, 'Researching children's rights to integrity', in *op cit*, Mayall, fn 32.

84 *Ibid*, 1993, p 194.

85 See Lim and Roche, Chapter 12 and Diduck, Chapter 13, in this volume.

FEMINISM AND CHILDREN'S RIGHTS

Hilary Lim and Jeremy Roche

INTRODUCTION

In this chapter, we explore the relationship between feminism and children's rights. We argue that, despite the paucity of feminist writing on children's rights, the emphasis within modern children's rights scholarship on the symbolic and transformative power of rights is not only historically resonant but constitutes a point of common interest for feminism and children's rights. By way of introduction, we consider the fragmentary character of feminist and children's rights discourses and the hitherto partial engagement of feminists with the children's rights question. We then go on to explore the interconnectedness of the woman question with the child question and, having looked at some of the feminist contributions to the children's rights literature, speculate how those feminists working around issues of difference might engage with this literature. Finally, we consider the idea of vulnerability, in order to open up a rethinking of notions of competence and adult-child relations, thus permitting a sketching out of the value of possible future feminist engagements with children's rights.

RIGHTS SCEPTICISM

One difficulty for the encounter between feminism and children's rights arises from feminists' 'complex and ambiguous relationship' to all legal rights.[1] As Kiss emphasises in her recent exploration of 'feminist doubts about rights', they arise from 'so many otherwise disparate viewpoints'.[2] Feminist critiques of rights analyses include the charge that they are abstract, impersonal, atomistic and induce conflict. Others suggest that rights talk 'obscures male dominance' while its strategic implementation 'reinforces a patriarchal status quo and, in effect, abandons women to their rights'.[3] This long standing

---

1   See Olsen, F, 'Children's rights: some feminist approaches to the United Nations Convention on the Rights of the Child' (1992) 6 IJLF 192.

2   Kiss, E, 'Alchemy or fool's gold? Assessing feminist doubts about rights', in Shanley, ML and Narayan, U (eds), *Reconstructing Political Theory*, 1997, Cambridge: Polity, p 2.

3   *Ibid*, p 2.

feminist debate about women's problematic relations with law and the notion of liberal rights also has an international dimension. As Olsen indicates, 'feminist human rights lawyers have found ways to use the norms of international human rights' to enhance women's lives, but, at the same time, 'the human rights system not only tolerates but in significant ways perpetuates the international subordination of women'.[4] Perhaps the most sustained arguments against the social purchase or symbolic meaning of the language of rights come from those who 'embrace an ethic of care', prompted by the work of Gilligan, with which they seek 'to supplement or even supplant'[5] the ethic of rights:

> Its proponents argue that dominant modern approaches to ethics ignore or underplay the relevance of intimate human relationships and of emotional responses like compassion as a source of theorising about moral life ... As a result, personal connections, and the care, attentiveness and responsibility that is the first virtue of central human relationships, like those between parents (especially, given traditional gender roles, mothers) and children, have not received the theoretical attention they deserve. The result has been an excessively rationalistic and legalistic model of moral life.[6]

For Sevenhuijsen, for example, a feminist 'ethics of care' is about recognising mutual dependency 'without attaching a negative value to it'. She argues for the recognition of vulnerability to be 'incorporated into the concept of a "normal" subject in politics'.[7]

These are well worn arguments in the ongoing debate about whether 'rights are right for women'.[8] However, the problems associated with rights at a general level are linked with and overlay the further difficulty for many feminists arising from the idea of personal connection, particularly between women and children.

THE INTERCONNECTEDNESS OF WOMEN AND CHILDREN

Writing in 1971, Firestone could argue that:

> Women and children are always mentioned in the same breath ... The special tie women have with children is recognised by everyone. I submit, however, that the nature of this bond is no more than shared oppression. And that,

---

4   *Op cit*, Olsen, fn 1, p 193.

5   Gilligan, C, *In a Different Voice: Psychological Theory and Women's Development*, 1982, Cambridge, Mass: Harvard UP.

6   *Op cit*, Kiss, fn 2, p 9.

7   Sevenhuijsen, S, *Citizenship and the Ethics of Care Feminist Considerations on Justice, Morality and Politics*, 1998, London: Routledge, p 146. We return to this later.

8   Bridgeman, J and Millns, S, *Feminist Perspectives on Law*, 1998, London: Sweet & Maxwell, p 17.

moreover, this oppression is intertwined and mutually reinforcing in such complex ways that we will be unable to speak of the liberation of women without also discussing the liberation of children, and vice versa.[9]

Of course, this is not to say that the social positioning and experience of women and children are identical, but 'rights for women and children are ... [still] seen', at least by some feminists, 'as complementary'.[10]

A key theme in much feminist writing has been the analysis and exploration of the fictional unity of family life, being seen as a cover for male supremacy.[11] It can no longer be argued that the family is a simple unity of interest, or that power within the family is exercised in a benign, fair or efficient way. Such feminist critiques of injustice did not stop at the family. The critique of the public/private divide was/is central to feminist scholarship. Woman's place in the home, tending the hearth and looking after the children, was seen as being at the root of her disadvantaged position within the public sphere. The struggle for citizenship on the part of women has entailed a struggle to redefine the boundary between the public and the private and the rights that women enjoy in both spheres. Thus, the link between women and children, which may be represented as complementary, is at the same time imbued with conflict, denied or strangely absent. Indeed, it is indicative of the partial engagement that Alanen asks how feminist theories *might* engage with questions relating to the child. Having explored the linkages between feminism and the 'child question', she writes:

> Feminist theory has not disrupted the sociological inheritance of marginalising children; in discussing gender issues related to children, it has, unfortunately, remained just as functionalist and adult centred in its analyses as mainstream/malestream social science.[12]

It is striking in researching this area that there is a dearth of Western feminist work focusing upon children's rights. Thus, perhaps it is no accident that Olsen, in her exploration of four feminist perspectives on children's rights – legal reformist, law as patriarchy, feminist critical legal theory and post-modern feminism – is concerned also with predicting how these feminist theories might approach children's rights in general, and the United Nations Convention on the Rights of the Child (UNCRC)[13] in particular, rather than

---

9   Firestone, S, *The Dialectic of Sex*, 1970, New York: Bantam, p 81. See, also, Griffin, S, *Made From this Earth*, 1982, London: The Women's Press.

10 *Op cit*, Olsen, fn 1, p 196.

11 O'Donovan, K, *Family Law Matters*, 1993, London: Pluto.

12 Alanen, L, 'Gender and generation: feminism and the "child question"', in Qvortrup, J, Bardy, M, Sgritta, G and Wintersberger, H (eds), *Childhood Matters: Social Theory, Practice and Politics*, 1994, Aldershot: Avebury, p 34.

13 The UNCRC was adopted by the General Assembly on 20 November 1989 and came into force more quickly than any other human rights treaty. It has been ratified by 191 States Parties and only two countries in the world – the US and Somalia – have not ratified it. It combines protection of both civil-political rights and economic, social and cultural rights in one instrument. For further consideration of the Convention, see Buss, Chapter 14, in this volume.

engaging with existing feminist writings on children's rights. Moreover, such writing is more concerned with children's rights discourse, and the women/children paradigm, from the adult woman's point of view than from that of the child.

This partial relationship is perhaps easiest to isolate at the level of the discussion about international human rights treaties, particularly the UNCRC and the Convention on the Elimination of All Forms of Discrimination against Women (CEDAW),[14] where there is a concentration in Western feminism upon discrimination against girl children. This focus may be a reflection of the way in which children are viewed in some women's campaigns in the South as 'intrinsically linked' because they have both 'been the hidden objects of human rights violations'.[15]

It must, of course, be acknowledged that 'women's organisations and groups within Asia, as elsewhere, in general [have] tended to delink children's issues from women's issues' because of the perception that the family and childbearing may 'undermine the efforts of women to obtain equity and justice in their societies'.[16] There is a concern about the reinforcement of a stereotyped assumption 'that mothers are the primary caretakers of children',[17] not least because of its 'implications for the childless woman, or the motherless child, who both have rights'.[18]

Price-Cohen provides a concrete example of the way that the partial engagement between feminism and children's rights manifests itself, exploring also some of these concerns.[19] Her analysis, therefore, provides an interesting entry point to this debate about international human rights treaties and children's rights. She describes two meetings held under the auspices of the International League for Human Rights and UNICEF in 1996 'aimed at

---

14 CEDAW was adopted by the UN General Assembly in December 1979 and entered into force on September 1981. It was implemented very quickly in comparison to similar human rights documents. The primary purpose of CEDAW is to address inequalities between the sexes and progressively eliminate discrimination against women. It imposes obligations on States Parties and individual actors such that States Parties are obliged to take positive action to regulate private conduct in order to eliminate discrimination against women.

15 Agosin, M, *Surviving Beyond Fear: Women, Children and Human Rights in Latin America*, 1993, New York: White Pine, p 23.

16 Gooneskere, SK, *Children, Law and Justice*, 1998, New Delhi: Sage, p 27.

17 Armstrong, A, Chuulu, M, Himonga, C, Letuka, P, Mokobi, K, Ncube, W, Nhlapo, T, Rwezaura, B and Vilakazi, P, 'Towards a cultural understanding of the interplay between children's and women's rights: an Eastern and Southern Africa perspective' (1995) 3 IJCR 333.

18 *Ibid*, p 334. Moreover, some Western feminisms have dwelt upon the cultural practices of Others, utilising the language of children's rights while failing to interrogate their own. Issues such as female circumcision, child labour and forced marriage are more likely to feature than corporal punishment.

19 Price-Cohen, C, 'The United Nations Convention on the Rights of the Child: a feminist landmark' (1997) 3 William and Mary J Women and the Law 29.

creating a dialogue', the absence of which Price-Cohen found odd, considering the interrelationship between the treaties, between proponents of both CEDAW and the UNCRC.[20] Moreover, a number of supporters of CEDAW were 'uneasy about becoming associated with a children's treaty':

> Some participants suggested that, when women and children are linked together, it usually places both groups in a subservient position that is based on their alleged similar need for care and protection. Many participants worried that this linkage with children might diminish the status of women by characterising them as incompetent and incapable of being independent human beings who are worthy of respect.[21]

Price-Cohen is unusual amongst those adopting a gender perspective because she attempts to uphold the UNCRC as an inherently feminist text, worthy of sustained attention. Writing from what Olsen would probably describe as a legal reformist stance, she seeks to downplay or defuse a perceived problem of the CEDAW/UNCRC dialogue and feminist analyses of the UNCRC. This problem relates to the 'focus on the relationship between women and children', by concentrating upon the girl child and the girl child's rights. She conceives of the two Conventions as sequential, with the UNCRC as a precursor to CEDAW, the former giving rights to girls which can be exercised prior 'to the time that they can exercise their rights as women'.[22]

In particular, Price-Cohen is impressed by what is sometimes called the 'gender neutral' language of the Convention, although she prefers the description 'gender equal' or 'gender inclusive'. For her, this 'remarkable' feature of the text, together with its future-oriented rights, mean that the rights of the girl child are of benefit to women and the Convention should be regarded as 'a perfect example of feminist principles'.[23] Gooneskere is more ready to acknowledge the potential for conflict between women's rights and children's rights within the South Asian context, but is in broad agreement with this argument. She concludes that it is 'vital that fixed perceptions of 'paternalism' and 'protection' in likening women with children should not be allowed to undervalue the importance of making the concern with the girl child a central issue in campaigns and strategies to realise women's rights'.[24] Her view is a more enthusiastic one than Olsen's mildly grudging statement that, despite her criticisms of the Convention, 'it is better for it to be ratified and enforced than for it not to be'.[25]

---

20 *Op cit*, Price-Cohen, fn 19, p 68.

21 *Op cit*, Price-Cohen, fn 19, pp 70–71.

22 *Op cit*, Price-Cohen, fn 19, p 74. However, see Chinkin, C, 'Torture of the girl-child', in van Bueren, G (ed), *Childhood Abused*, 1998, Dartmouth: Ashgate.

23 *Ibid.*

24 *Op cit*, Gooneskere, fn 16, p 170.

25 *Op cit*, Olsen, fn 1, p 217.

In contrast, Backstrom points to aspects of both the text and the implementation of the UNCRC which undermine its ability to alleviate the problems of the girl child. She seeks to demonstrate that the development of an approach which integrates the provisions of CEDAW and the UNCRC would better protect girl children. However, Backstrom is in agreement with Price-Cohen when she argues that 'there exists a traditional link between women's and children's rights ... [although] it has not been developed to any significant degree'[26] and that, while they may be connected, there is 'a tendency to disassociate women's and children's rights because they are viewed as undermining each other'.[27] She suggests that women's rights advocates wish to separate women and children 'in order to emphasise the woman's right to equality despite her reproductive capabilities and traditional care-giving role'.[28] Similarly, Olsen points out that, while a society which tries to protect children from abuse and neglect is likely to create a climate which is beneficial to women as their primary caretakers, it is also the case that 'legal protection of children can be and has been used as a basis for controlling women'.[29]

In short, to some writing from feminist perspectives, both the Convention and children's rights discourse represent 'a threat to the autonomy of adult women',[30] who are in danger of being tainted with children's dependency and either being infantilised by the connection or suppressed in the name of the child. Perhaps there are also elements here, as Price-Cohen indicates, of a disturbing and more generally pervasive 'adult/child syndrome in which children are considered to be pre-human'.[31] Yet, much of contemporary children's rights literature is concerned to disrupt this pre-human, object status of children. We thus need to consider the different meanings associated with children's rights.

THE DISCOURSE OF CHILDREN'S RIGHTS

A number of very different theoretical perspectives have been deployed in the children's rights literature, but perhaps the most fundamental divide is between welfare and liberty rights. Running through this discussion, we find a widespread 'assumption in the development of children's rights that

---

26 Backstrom, KM, 'The international human rights of the child: do they protect the female child?' (1996–97) 30 George Washington J Int Law and Economics 541.

27 *Ibid*, p 572.

28 *Ibid*, p 572, fn 285.

29 *Op cit*, Olsen, fn 1, p 193.

30 *Op cit*, Price-Cohen, fn 19, p 72.

31 *Op cit*, Price-Cohen, fn 19, pp 77–78.

children cannot have the same rights and responsibilities as adults because they are not autonomous' and their rights must be considered within 'a context of control and dependence'.[32] Some arguments for children's rights are, therefore, in essence, arguments for the promotion of their welfare and their better protection. This 'welfare rights' narrative was dominant until the emergence of the modern children's rights movement in the 1970s. Much work, historical as well as contemporary, details the many 'child rescue' campaigns of the 19th and 20th centuries,[33] in which women (and men) campaigned to save the child from conditions of social neglect, poverty and abuse. Within such campaigns the child appears as requiring rescue – from neglectful parents, degrading social conditions and male violence – within a story of gradual progress.

One of the problems with the welfare rights narrative is that such language can be (and has been) deployed almost anywhere. After all, it is also 'in the name of the child' that anti-abortionists are active and that women, both here and in the US, have found themselves subject to coercive medical intervention during or just prior to going into labour. Adults pursue their own agendas via this discourse; to save the child is a powerful cry. More recently, the progressive appearance of the welfare project has been questioned. Forced emigration of children to Canada and Australia in the early 20th century and the Aboriginal assimilation strategies in Australia[34] have been revealed, not as rescue missions of moral and social reclamation, but as colonialism, institutional abuse, class violence and racism. Furthermore, in the well worn, but perhaps not well understood, words of Butler Sloss LJ, the child should not simply be an object of concern. If nothing else, the Cleveland scandal carried within it two strong messages: children themselves were not listened to by those professionals who claimed to be acting in pursuit of their welfare; and children found the protection process itself abusive – especially repeat intimate medical examinations.

Children's liberty rights occupy a different territory. Liberty rights can be taken as a reference to that bundle of rights associated with autonomy in liberal society. A good example of these is supplied by the UNCRC, in which Arts 12–16 cover core liberal concerns around participation, freedom of expression and thought, freedom of association and privacy. Within liberal thinking, these 'rights' are seen as indispensable to respect for the individual and any meaningful participation in society. So, in one sense, the call to liberty rights for children could be read as a call for citizenship and an increased

---

32 *Op cit*, Backstrom, fn 26, p 560.

33 Platt, A, *The Child Savers: The Invention of Delinquency*, 1969, Chicago: Chicago UP; Behlmer, G, *Child Welfare and Moral Reform in England 1870–1908*, 1983, Stanford: Stanford UP.

34 McGillivray, A, 'Therapies of freedom: the colonisation of aboriginal childhood', in McGillivray, A (ed), *Governing Childhood*, 1997, Aldershot: Dartmouth.

recognition of the importance of fostering the participation of children within the communities in which they live their lives.[35] Some arguments about liberty rights may almost be described as 'abolitionist', in that they argue for the extension of adult rights to all children because the adult-child distinction is spurious, thereby beckoning the end of childhood.[36] For those writing from such a position, the argument is that children lose out as a result of the rigid separation of child from adult.[37] The 'remedy' is to abolish all legal distinction between child and adult, with children exercising rights as and when they are in a position to practically do so.[38]

The notion of such rights sets alarm bells ringing over great distances. Ghazi expressed a popular opinion when she warned that:

> Parents who turn up their noses when their children bury themselves in *Viz*, *Smash Hits* or *Just 17* may be making a mistake. The magazines may soon contain advertisements for a booklet entitled *Your Say in Court*, which could have a significant effect on family relationships. Aimed at 10–16 year olds, it provides a step by step guide on how to 'divorce' parents.[39]

Here are children's rights, not as moral rescue, but as a sign of the catastrophic collapse of familial authority. The notion of children having rights, which are exclusive to the rational, competent adult, is presented as absurd: a Trojan horse built by zealots to undermine the family.[40]

The liberationist position, which appears to revision the child and argue that 'children should have the same legal and political rights held by adults because children are competent', simply makes an easy target for 'opponents of children's rights to claim that children do not have capacity'.[41] O'Neill's argument that the thrust of children's rights language is misconceived and that the struggle for the rights of the child cannot be compared with that of other groups, such as women, may be extreme, particularly in her statement that the main remedy for the child's sense of powerlessness is 'to grow up', but she is articulating a common view.[42] Just such an assumption underpins much of the debate surrounding the UNCRC and yet, at the same time, the notion of 'dependency' has been the subject of feminist attention.

---

35 Roche, J, 'Children: rights, participation and citizenship' (1999) 6 Childhood 475.
36 Holt, J, *Escape from Childhood*, 1975, Harmondsworth: Penguin.
37 Farson, R, *Birthrights*, 1974, London: Collier Macmillan.
38 Freeman, MDA, *The Moral Status of Children*, 1997, The Hague: Kluwer.
39 Ghazi, P (1993) *The Observer*, 25 July.
40 Such a development could be seen as supporting the development of a more rational authority within the family. See Matthews, GB, *The Philosophy of Childhood*, 1994, Cambridge, Mass: Harvard UP.
41 Federle, KH, 'Rights flow downhill' (1994) 2 IJCR 343, p 349.
42 O'Neill, O, 'Children's rights and children's lives', in Alston, P, Parker, S and Seymour, J (eds), *Children, Rights and the Law*, 1992, Oxford: OUP, pp 43–51.

Dependency, power and powerlessness

Freeman has rightly pointed out that 'an important contribution of feminist moral theory has been to question the firmly embedded assumption that moral agency and citizenship rights require as a pre-condition that a person be independent, totally autonomous'.[43] Referring to the work of Gilligan and Friedman, he argues that 'dependency is a basic human condition' and that 'it is also possible, as is argued within feminism, to accord respect and participation rights in decision making to those who are dependent'.[44] Freeman's position on dependency and children's rights is one with which we would concur, and we would point also to those feminist writers who have felt compelled to respond to O'Neill's arguments. Olsen, for instance, while 'generally sympathetic' to some of O'Neill's approach, suggests that, while she 'is correct that children are dependent in many ways that adults are not dependent ..., this difference is not itself a problem for children'.[45] However, this does not mean that adults are never dependent or vulnerable. These are not conditions unique to children.

Some feminists are beginning to ask questions about how women over the course of their lives undergo qualitatively significant changes such that the unitary notion of woman is again questioned.[46] Similarly, one can disaggregate the category child. Even O'Neill concedes that rights rhetoric may be relevant to older children, 'well on the way to majority and to the ending of the forms of disability and dependence that are peculiar to children'.[47] However, younger children assume responsibilities and act in a mature way in a range of environments and, in doing so, handle and negotiate a range of complex demands and emotions.[48] A life course perspective not only allows us to consider how we change over time and the nature of the transitions we experience: it also calls into question the artificiality and rigidity of the adult-child divide. As McGillivray suggests, 'human autonomy must be seen as a process, not an end alone'.[49] Perhaps a part of the exploration of dependency should be to disrupt its correlation with the child. If we challenge the allegation that 'young human beings are ... incapable of

---

43 Freeman, MDA, 'The sociology of childhood and children's rights' (1998) 6 IJCR 433, p 440.

44 *Ibid*, p 441.

45 *Op cit*, Olsen, fn 1, p 206.

46 Pratt, G and Hanson, S, 'Women and work across the life course', in Katz, C and Monk, J (eds), *Full Circles: Geographies of Women Over the Life Course*, 1996, London: Routledge.

47 *Op cit*, O'Neill, fn 42, p 39.

48 De Winter, M, *Children as Fellow Citizens: Participation and Commitment*, 1997, Abingdon: Radcliffe Medical.

49 *Op cit*, McGillivray, fn 34, p 220, summarising an argument put by Nedelsky, J, 'Reconceiving autonomy: sources, thoughts and possibilities' (1989) 7 Yale J Law and Feminism 1.

judgment',[50] we also undermine the process of infantilisation with its detrimental effects, particularly upon women.

Capacity and rights theory

Like Alanen, Olsen and Price-Cohen, in their different ways, we are trying to suggest how some feminisms might move on from this partial approach and relate to children's rights. One aspect of this discussion is life course perspectives and a deconstruction of prevailing notions of dependency. However, there is a further aspect arising from race critiques of feminist and critical legal theory. Freeman argues that feminism has not only questioned the depiction of the independent and totally autonomous rights holder, but also seems to offer possible answers to those who deny children rights on the grounds of incompetence. He refers to the work of Federle, who contends that 'we must reconstruct our rights talk if we are to reconceive rights for children'[51] and find a language which shifts 'the dialogue of rights beyond arguments about competence'[52] to accommodate notions of power.

Through a series of articles, Federle develops her view that, 'when discussing the concept of children's rights, the debate invariably returns to the capacity of children',[53] which results only in the promotion of children's powerlessness. Her main concern is not to explore dependency and incapacity in order to challenge their association with children, but to remove the significance of competency as an organising concept from all rights talk.

In the first article, Federle uses feminist legal methods to challenge rights theory. However, from the outset, she warns that 'women ... must recognise that power seduces regardless of gender' and finds in deep ecology, rather than feminist doctrine, the possibility for transforming the children's rights debate.[54] Her argument is that much feminist writing which replaces traditional rights discourse with a focus upon relationships and interdependence maintains a concern with questions of children's incompetencies.[55] The main focus for Federle's critique of feminist writing is Minow's 'interpretive' legal scholarship.[56] While Minow is conscious of the theoretical importance of connection, she retains a commitment to rights

---

50 Lugones, M, 'Hablando cara a cara/speaking face to face: an exploration of ethnocentric racism', in Anzaldua, G (ed), Making Face, Making Soul/Haciendo Caras, 1990, San Francisco: Aunt Lute.

51 Op cit, Federle, fn 41, p 345.

52 Federle, K, 'On the road to reconceiving rights for children: a post-feminist analysis of the capacity principle' (1993) 42 De Paul L Rev 983.

53 Ibid, p 985.

54 Ibid.

55 Ibid, p 1017.

56 Minow, M, 'Interpreting rights: an essay for Robert Cover' (1987) 96 Yale LJ 1860.

language and does not seek to replace an ethics of rights with an ethics of care. Minow's approach to children's rights is that, while the rhetoric may 'mislead, seduce, falsely console or wrongly inflame',[57] it should not be abandoned but reclaimed and reinvented. The main opposition to extending children's rights is, in Minow's opinion, organised around two main objections. First, that rights claims by children induce conflict between them and adults where there should be connection or shared interests. Secondly, that children need protection, since they do not have the necessary competence to properly make a rights claim. However, Minow contends that rights talk may encompass notions of mutual connection and need, irrespective of the capacity of children.

Minow's attention is caught by the part of 'interpretivism' which concentrates upon 'the ways that texts help to create communities, to establish a shared discourse, and to provide contexts for linking past with future, and creativity with tradition'.[58] Rights, here, become a part of articulating and reinforcing community, rather than rampant individualism. Rights are not the end, but what move the individual or group on to 'negotiate new relationships'.[59] With reference to children's rights, Minow finds the prevailing discourse, which talks simply of autonomy rather than need, as 'terribly lacking, especially the central need for relationships with adults who are themselves enabled to create settings where children can thrive'. It is not whether the child's right to self-determination should prevail over adult concerns about the child's welfare; rather, the child acquires the right to be part of the conversation about their life. At the moment, when a claim to a separate, individual interest is made, you find also the moment of interdependence. In addition, these parameters shift and change through human negotiations. Rights discourse here becomes one means or one tool 'with which to articulate challenge and hold to account relationships of power'.[60]

Federle summarises this argument as it pertains to the children's rights debate thus:

> This type of rights discourse neither creates conflict nor disrupts community since the very act of claiming is, in itself, a communal affirmation. Rights claims, however, do not grant equality but merely equality of attention: in this way, rights claims challenge existing hierarchies by making the community hear different voices. Community and claiming are part of a slow historical process that will invigorate the debate about children's rights and will,

---

57 *Op cit*, Minow, fn 56, p 1910.
58 *Op cit*, Minow, fn 56, p 1865.
59 *Op cit*, Minow, fn 56, p 1876.
60 *Op cit*, Minow, fn 56, p 1888.

someday, lead to a better life for children through the articulation of ideal relationships between children and adults in the larger community.[61]

However, Federle finds Minow's account to be problematic in two respects, both of which are derived from the emphasis placed upon relationships within this version of rights as communal language. First, she makes a distinction between the nature of connectedness amongst adults and their relations with children, the latter having 'no real choice in the creation or continuation of the relationship precisely because they are thought to "need" these relationships' as a consequence of immaturity and incapacity. 'Claiming rights, then, is merely another way to catalogue children's dependencies and to portray idyllic, rather than ideal, relationships.'[62] Secondly, 'feminist concerns about the importance of connection and social relationships actually mask the power (perhaps the only power) that women have',[63] foreclosing 'an honest assessment of the power we have over our children'.[64] In summary, therefore, feminism offers more than it can deliver, and 'tying rights to relationships is nothing more than a "sophisticated" version of the argument that children should not have rights because of their incompetencies'.[65]

Rights and the language of power

While we might disagree with aspects of Federle's reading of Minow's approach to children's rights, this is not our main interest. The immediate focus of Federle's argument is that rights should be reconceptualised upon the premise of 'power or, more precisely, powerlessness' because, she suggests:

> ... rights tied to power create zones of mutual respect for power that limit the kinds of things we may do to one another [sic]. This has a transformative aspect as well, for the empowering effects of rights would reduce the victimisation of children because we would no longer see them as powerless beings ... Paternalistic justifications, therefore, would be unacceptable because they are premised upon notions of powerlessness.[66]

It is the deep ecology movement, described by Federle as 'vigorously anti-hierarchical', which provides her with encouragement for this reconstruction of rights discourse. In contrast to feminism, specifically eco-feminism, which 'falls back on notions of relationships and ... principles of caring and loving ...

---

61 *Op cit*, Federle, fn 41, pp 355–56. Minow appears to share with Federle a belief both in the possibilities of rights language for children and in the irrelevance of notions of competency or capacity to the acquisition of rights.

62 *Op cit*, Federle, fn 52, p 1019.

63 *Op cit*, Federle, fn 52, p 1020.

64 *Op cit*, Freeman, fn 43, p 441.

65 *Op cit*, Freeman, fn 43.

66 *Op cit*, Federle, fn 41, p 366.

[with] hierarchical consequences',[67] deep ecology is non-anthropocentric and 'rejects a human centred, rights based framework in favour of a holistic gestalt, of person in nature'.[68] It permits questions of capacity or status to be discarded as rights talk is transformed 'by seeing ourselves, not in terms of relationships, but as existing within each other'.[69] She argues that it is 'the transformative aspect of deep ecology that ... has the most to offer to the debate about the rights of children'.[70]

We have two difficulties with this thesis. The first relates to Federle's reliance upon something beyond anthropocentrism, while the second problem is with her understandings of power and powerlessness. It is by no means unattractive to envisage 'a universe larger than humanity, a single organism in which harm to a part damages the whole',[71] but we are wary of theories based upon notions of unity and universalism. Within feminism, for instance, the manifold assaults upon the possibility of a feminism which claims to speak for a universal category of woman has effectively shattered grand theoretical claims. This is not to say that white Western feminism has taken fully on board, for instance, the very powerful critique that it is tainted with ethnocentrism. It has not. However, those challenges upon feminism as an institutionalised discourse, although frequently interrupted and fragmentary themselves, have demanded recognition of the limits to its theorised space. In our view, difference and division cannot be dismissed. Immediate struggles must remain in focus and be reflected in rights talk.

Perhaps it is a misreading of Federle to suggest that her references to deep ecology are somewhat utopian, particularly given her argument that a rights theory should do more than envision 'what should be rather than what is', because 'it lacks the force, even the persuasiveness, to effect true change'.[72] This point is supported by Federle's discussion of African American experiences prior to the Civil War, which 'taught ... that rights must be able to challenge existing hierarchies if they are to have value'.[73] However, she continues: '... a rights theory premised upon powerlessness creates an ethic

---

67 *Op cit*, Federle, fn 41, p 363.

68 *Op cit*, Federle, fn 41, p 362, fn 117.

69 *Op cit*, Federle, fn 41, p 364.

70 *Op cit*, Federle, fn 41, p 363. Federle credits Arne Naess with coining the phrase deep ecology (fn 116): 'According to Naess, deep ecology has seven basic principles: acceptance of man as merely one of many organisms in the environment; the equal right of all organisms to live and blossom; the enhancing potential of diversity and symbiosis; the need for an anti-class posture; the dangers of pollution and resource depletion; the value of ecological complexity; and the liberating influences of decentralisation and local autonomy on environmental policy.' See Naess, A, 'The shallow and the deep, long range ecology movement: a summary' (1973) 16 Inquiry 95. She also refers to Devall, B, 'The deep ecology movement' (1980) 20 Nat Resources J 299.

71 *Op cit*, Federle, fn 41, p 363.

72 *Op cit*, Federle, fn 41, p 366.

73 *Op cit*, Federle, fn 41, p 360.

grounded in our own sense of the world as it is.' For Federle, power which she regards as 'fundamental to the human condition', such that 'it is inconceivable to imagine a world without' it, 'does not require us to bridge a cultural gap'.[74] It is with this stage of her argument that we encounter our second difficulty – her theory of power and, more particularly, powerlessness is as silencing as the denial of difference.

Traditional rights theory, which is married to the notion of self-determination and children's incapacity, is, according to Federle, necessarily paternalistic in the way in which interventions on behalf of children are justified in the name of protection. Such an approach, she argues, implicitly acknowledges children's powerlessness, as does the claim that 'rights flow from certain interests', which inevitably relate to children's needs and vulnerabilities. Rights divorced from questions of capacity are, on the other hand, empowering. However, this version of power, as a possession or commodity, seems a little negative, skeletal and narrow. Whatever the problems with Foucault's analysis of power, his theory demands an appreciation of power in all its complexity.[75] Most importantly, there is no space in Federle's discussion for resistance; children are either powerless or, in her new rights theory, powerful. This is, perhaps, hardly surprising given her desire to banish the issue of competency from rights language, but that very process may remove their resistance from view. The slippage in Federle's argument, where at one stage she writes that 'to have a right is to have power, to obtain a right is to be powerless', but elsewhere in the context of the new rights theory speaks of 'giving children rights',[76] may be indicative.

We have emphasised already in the context of a discussion of life course perspectives that children, even young children, do act. The concept of empowerment is not just a matter for children's rights discourse; children themselves are challenging and disrupting boundaries. Older children have expressed their anger, for instance, about the conduct of politics in Northern Ireland,[77] the divorce process[78] and racism in schools. Younger children have recently passed judgment on 'loving smacks' – 'A smack is parents trying to hit you but instead of calling it a hit they call it a smack'[79] – as well as the quality of child care.[80] Part of the children's rights project means taking

---

74 Op cit, Federle, fn 41, p 366.

75 Said, E, 'Foucault and the imagination of power', in Couzens-Hoy, D (ed), Foucault: A Critical Reader, 1986, London: Basil Blackwell, pp 149–56.

76 Op cit, Federle, fn 41, pp 365–66.

77 Democratic Dialogue, Politics: The Next Generation (Report 6), 1997, Belfast: Democratic Dialogue.

78 Lyon, C, Surrey, E and Timms, J, Effective Support Services for Children and Young People when Parental Relationships Break Down, 1999, Liverpool: Calouste Gulbenkian Foundation/NYAS/Liverpool University.

79 Willow, C and Hyde, T, 'The myth of the loving smack' (1999) 154 Childright 18, p 19.

80 Moorhead, J, 'Out of the mouths of babes' (1999) The Guardian, 2 June, pp 9–10.

children seriously in the here and now. The danger may be that, in searching for this transformative version of rights to reduce the victimisation of children, such challenges and disruptions are hidden, 'for the notion of the "victim" is stealthily pervasive in feminist discourse'[81] and the category of child *all* pervasive. The feminist race critique, referred to by Minow but not Federle, has contributed to another reassessment of rights as transformative, albeit in a different sense, at the same time as questioning alternatives based around notions of need, intimacy and connectedness.

TRANSFORMATIVE RIGHTS AND RESISTANCE

The race critique of the trashing of liberal legalism and rights thinking perpetrated by the Critical Legal Studies (CLS) movement in the late 1980s continues to have resonance. A number of theorists depict rights as transformative, 'an attempt to turn society's 'institutional logic' against itself'.[82] The writing of Williams, in which she likens this process to alchemy, has become a particular point of debate within feminist discussions around rights and the ethics of care. It is worth revisiting some of the detail of this argument, which is perhaps in danger of being forgotten in the repeated references to the alchemy simile.

Williams challenges those who prefer the language of needs to the language of rights and contends that black people have been expressing their needs – in poetry, literature, jazz and the blues – since time immemorial. This has been an aesthetic success, but a dismal failure in political terms: 'Shorn from the hypnotic rhythmicity which blacks are said to bring to their woe ... stark statistical statements of need are heard as "strident", "discordant", and "unharmonious".'[83] The word 'need' out of a white man's mouth is, and has been heard, in one way; out of a black person's mouth, it is heard with a different tone. Williams compares the political failure of 'needs' with the relative success of 'rights' and argues that, although African Americans never fully believed in rights, they have also, in the manner of alchemists, 'believed in them so much and so hard that [they] gave them life where there was none before'.[84]

---

81 Ibrahim, H, 'Ontological victimhood: "other" bodies in madness and exile – toward a Third World feminist epistemology', in Nnaemeka, O (ed), *The Politics of (M)othering*, 1997, London: Routledge, p 152.

82 Crenshaw, KW, 'Race, reform and retrenchment: transformation and legitimation in anti-discrimination law' (1988) 101 Harv L Rev 1331, p 1366.

83 Williams, P, 'Alchemical notes: reconstructing ideals from deconstructed rights' (1987) 22 Harv Civil Rights-Civil Liberties Rev 401, p 413.

84 *Ibid*, p 430.

The CLS movement shared with some feminists a 'masculine image of the typical rights bearer as an isolated self insisting on its boundaries'.[85] A minority amongst proponents of CLS scholarship also envisaged something 'beyond' liberal legalism, in which 'authentic connectedness' and community would prevail. It is a world in which rights would be unnecessary because needs would be met. There is a strong correlation between notions of 'unalienated relatedness' and the ideas of Gilligan and Karst concerning women's moral values or 'different voice'. Associated with such images is a critique of rights as boundaries which serve to legitimate 'aggressive selfishness' and deny 'community', both within feminism and the CLS movement. Kiss has argued that the 'chief practical flaw' in such a feminist critique 'is that it overlooks the importance of the boundary marking features of rights for vulnerable people, including women'.[86] Similarly, Williams argues that what appears alienating and disempowering to a white person may be empowering to a black person. The distance of boundaried rights can make a lot of sense to those who have too often been at the bottom in subordinating relationships. Delgado put this succinctly when he said, 'We will settle for safety, even if this means that some of the barriers must remain up'.[87]

Interconnectedness, disconnectedness and difference

In illustrating the importance of black feminist writing to any exploration of rights discourse, it is valuable to return briefly to the issue of connectedness. This remains very much an issue for feminism, especially with respect to a whole series of issues surrounding pregnancy, including abortion, surgery upon foetuses in the womb and enforced Caesarians. The theme of connection in this feminist work is, in part, an attempt to grapple with certain parts of the range of ideas proffered in the name of children's rights; a concentration upon the bond between women and children which does more than point to a shared oppression.

Williams, writing from the perspective of an African American woman in a context where a myriad of State regulation has sought to control and even imprison pregnant women in the name of 'child saving', expresses the connection as 'flesh-and-blood-bonded'. In the face of such legislation, emphasising the political utility of interconnectedness, she argues that: '... it seems only logical ... [that] pregnant women would try to assert themselves through their foetuses; that they would attempt to rejoin what has been

---

85 *Op cit*, Kiss, fn 2, p 4.

86 *Op cit*, Gilligan, fn 5; Karst, K, 'Women's constitution' (1994) Duke LJ 447.

87 Delgado, R, 'Critical legal studies and the realities of race – does the fundamental contradiction have a corollary?' (1988) 23 Harv Civil Rights-Civil Liberties Rev 407, p 412.

conceptually pulled asunder'.[88] Wells, discussing the 'frantic challenge to our moral antennae' presented by enforced caesareans, suggests connectedness as a means to thinking about the 'special state' of pregnancy which is not offered by arguments of either foetal rights or autonomy.[89]

In the area of reproductive politics, as elsewhere, however, the notion of interconnectedness has to be read in the context of disconnections/differences between women. Writers, including Gilligan, who have challenged the link between autonomy and rights as 'derived from a specifically male experience of social relations which values competition and solitary achievement'[90] have also been subject to sustained critique for their tendency to universalise the experience of some white women. Experiences of oppression and, therefore, connections between women and children vary greatly. For instance, black women living in North America and Europe have pointed out that the family is by no means the source of daily oppression, for either adult women or their children, which it represents in much of white feminism. It may be a refuge or place of creativity, rather than a hidden prison. Similarly, 'childrearing is just that place where the split between Third World and white feminist discourses takes place' and 'Third World women writers have often asserted that women are not victimised by motherhood, but motherhood provides a tenacious resistance against the victimising world'.[91]

Feminism has become feminisms, multilayered writings from the inside and the outside, and this glimpse, albeit fleeting, of the specificity of some women's lives not only raises obvious questions about feminist claims to a grand theory, but also points to very different versions of connection between women and children, physically, psychically and spiritually, whether as a joint oppression or as a political tool.

The primacy of resistance struggle

Here, we try to ask how feminists researching difference would engage with children's rights, drawing again upon the work of Williams, together with another African American woman, bell hooks. Both are critical of much white Western feminist writing, although feminism is relevant to their theoretical

---

88   Williams, P, *The Alchemy of Race and Rights*, 1991, London: Virago, pp 184–85.

89   Wells, C, 'On the outside looking in: perspectives on enforced caesareans', in Sheldon, S and Thomson, M (eds), *Feminist Perspectives on Health Care Law*, 1998, London: Cavendish Publishing, pp 254–55. See, also, Fraser-Delgado, C, 'Mother tongues and childless women: the construction of "Kenyan" "womanhood"', in *op cit*, Nnaemeka, fn 81, p 133; Lim, H, 'Caesareans and cyborgs' (1999) 7 FLS 133.

90   *Op cit*, Freeman, fn 43, p 441.

91   *Op cit*, Ibrahim, fn 81, pp 154–55.

perspectives.[92] As we have already mentioned, while Williams does not deny the negative in rights and rights rhetoric, to reject rights is, for Williams, to reject something 'deeply enmeshed in the psyche of the oppressed', which cannot be lost 'without trauma':

> Instead, society must give them away. Give them to trees. Give them to cows. Give them to history. Give them to rivers and rocks. Give to all society's objects and untouchables the rights of privacy, integrity and self-assertion; give them distance and respect ... and wash away the shourds of inanimate-object status.[93]

Absent from Williams' list of society's objects are, of course, children. We choose to think that they are included, for, elsewhere, she speaks of 'more generously extending rights to all one's fellow creatures, whether human or beast', and remarks that Hillary Clinton's representation by the American media as 'this loose unmanaged female'[94] was, in part, because of her 'uppity audacity' in writing law review articles 'which suggest that children have rights too, that children as well as their mothers ought to be liberated'.[95]

However, Williams does not just remind us of the power of rights; she fearlessly explores dependency and its racial imagery. Fraser and Gordon suggest that the 1980s saw a 'rise of new psychological meanings of dependency with very strong feminine associations'[96] and clear racial markings. White women were depicted in 'burgeoning cultural-feminist, post-feminist and anti-feminist'[97]writings as either dependency addicts, hooked on their subordination, or the creators of others' co-dependency. Black women, on the other hand, were first regarded as the independent, 'regal hard working mother'[98] and then the imagery switched to the 'new icon of welfare dependency', the single black teenage mother:

> This image has usurped the symbolic space previously occupied by the housewife, the pauper, the native and the slave, while absorbing and condensing their connotations. Black, female, a pauper, not a worker, a housewife and mother, yet practically a child herself – the new stereotype partakes of virtually every quality that has been coded historically as antithetical to independence.[99]

---

92 As a white man and a white woman, we have to take great care that we are not appropriating another culture; but, at the same time, we have to recognise that '"diversity" and "difference" are vague, ambiguous terms, defined differently by white feminists and feminists of colour'. We must try not to change those differences with a 'white, racialised, scrutinising and alienating gaze' (*op cit*, Anzaldua, fn 50, p xxi).

93 *Op cit*, Williams, fn 88, p 165.

94 Williams, P, *The Rooster's Egg*, 1995, Cambridge, Mass: Harvard UP, p 151.

95 *Op cit*, Williams, fn 88, pp 161–62.

96 Fraser, N and Gordon, L, 'Decoding "dependency": inscriptions of power in a keyword of the US Welfare State', in *op cit*, Shanley and Narayan, fn 2, p 37.

97 *Ibid*, p 37.

98 *Ibid*, Williams, p 175.

99 *Ibid*, Fraser and Gordon, p 39.

Williams takes apart the prevailing stereotype of this particular cultural panic and forcefully concludes that 'it is time to stop demonising single mothers or anyone else who makes family where there was none before'. She writes of children's 'happy irrationality and complete dependence' as 'perpetual reminders that we are all members of a larger community' such that children are not the sole responsibility of their mother, or, indeed, father, but of civic communities 'across fences, across religion, across class and across town'.[100] In her emphasis upon interdependence, there is necessarily a reminder of our dependence, not just of children, but of all of us at different times.

Williams is also remembering a different kind of dependency, free from the fear raised by the portrayal in current Western socio-legal relations of the 'highly stigmatised' figures of deviants and incompetents posited against the ideal of 'independent male breadwinners'.[101] Whilst young children are largely absent from this catalogue of deviance, it is in Williams' easy inclusion and understanding of the full range manifestations of defencelessness, shared by children, the old, the infirm, the illiterate and so on, that we can affirm that dependency is not the exclusive preserve of the child and the potential power of rights rhetoric. Elsewhere, she has argued that, for 'slaves, sharecroppers, prisoners, mental patients ... the experience of poverty and need is fraught with the terrible realisation that they are dependent "on the uncertain and fitful protection of a world conscience", which has forgotten them as individuals'. The 'goal is to find a political mechanism that can confront the denial of need' and rights signify not independence, but the right to interdependence, 'the respectful behaviour, the collective responsibility, properly owed by a society to one of its own'.[102] In this context, it does not seem suspect, as O'Neill suggests, to draw an analogy with children's dependence and to say that children also need their rights.

One of the strengths of feminism has always been the personal narrative, and we were struck by the part that this played in a collection subtitled *Creative and Critical Perspectives by Feminists of Color*. As in Williams' writing, there is the exploration of powerlessness and, in particular, the vulnerability of childhood. bell hooks remembers a childhood in the southern black community where '"back talk" and "talking back" meant speaking as an equal to an authority figure', which led to punishments 'intended to suppress all possibility that I would create my own speech ... the backhand lick, the slap across the face that would catch you unaware, or the feel of switches stinging your arms or legs'.[103] She reflects on the work of Alice Miller that 'it is not clear why childhood wounds become for some folk an opportunity to grow, to

---

100 *Op cit*, Williams, fn 94, pp 180–81.
101 *Op cit*, Fraser and Gordon, fn 96, p 42.
102 *Op cit*, Williams, fn 94, p 153.
103 hooks, b, *Talking Back*, 1989, London: Sheba, p 5.

move forward rather than backward in the process of self-realisation'.[104] Remembering both a resistance to the attempts to break her spirit which nurtured her defiant speech and 'the deepseated fears and anxieties' which meant that she 'would not ride a bike, play hardball, or hold the gray kitten', she contemplates the voices of those 'wounded and/or oppressed individuals' whose voices are not heard:

> I write these words to bear witness to the primacy of resistance struggle in any situation of domination (even within family life); to the strength and power that emerges from sustained resistance and the profound conviction that these forces can be healing, can protect us from dehumanisation and despair.[105]

It was this resistance that, in her own words, led bell hooks 'to emerge as an independent thinker and writer'. Ibrahim has drawn her own conclusions about mothers from this discussion, but, in the following, the word 'mothers' could be easily replaced by 'children':

> It is this small power, as bell hooks would say, of 'talking back' with legitimate tools of resistance that gives mothers, even as victims, their survival credence. It is through this talking back that language has the potential, as Cixous tells us, to be 'born over and over again', that even a 'victim' ... can 'give birth' to the hidden self in her.[106]

CONCLUSION

We have argued that the complexities of dependency and interconnection are important to both feminist discourses and children's rights debates. For us, it is the reinstatement of the importance of capacity and participation that is central. As noted earlier, for some theorists, the appropriate response to the recognition of our interdependencies and vulnerability is to argue for an ethics of care.[107] How dependency and responsibility are dealt with is central to an ethics of care. Within this argument, the solution to dependency and vulnerability is not more legal rights but a rethinking of caring relationships. Sevenhuijsen observes:

> Clearer ideas about what constitutes necessary care can be gained by granting those who are the 'object' of care cognitive authority over their needs and giving them the opportunity to express these in a heterogeneous public sphere which allows open and honest debate.[108]

---

104 *Op cit*, hooks, fn 103, p 7.
105 *Op cit*, hooks, fn 103, p 8.
106 *Op cit*, Ibrahim, fn 81, p 155.
107 *Op cit*, Sevenhuijsen, fn 7.
108 *Op cit*, Sevenhuijsen, fn 7, p 146.

We agree with feminist critics of rights theory that 'a political theory inattentive to relationships of care and connection between and among people cannot adequately address many themes and issues facing families'.[109] We would also contend that rights based views 'require public articulation of the kinds of freedoms that deserve protection and the qualities of human dignity that warrant societal support' and that 'rights articulate relationships among people'.[110]

At another level, the social positioning of the child as the most vulnerable serves to consolidate in the adult imagination a particular reading of the adult-child relationship. In this, the adult is rational, competent and knowledgeable, while the child is not. But it is more than this. It is as if in 'our' imagination the child becomes the repository for all 'our' adult anxieties about vulnerability – ultimately, 'we' know that children need protecting from themselves and that they do not need the burden of decision making being put on them. However, at times, it may be harder for children not to take up the burden. Perhaps we should be asking why children become involved and in whose name they are acting.[111] While we might tolerate, or even applaud, the image of the visible child in some instances, for example, the high level of children's participation in the struggle against apartheid, or in the American civil rights movement, we do not always feel the same way about this image in other spaces. We can only be sure, 'what children want', what burdens children might want to shoulder and share, if we create conditions under which children are able to find out what they think about their own predicaments.[112] This is not something which the legal system has been designed to facilitate.[113] Whatever these conditions look and feel like, it seems that a prerequisite would be a commitment to enabling the child to speak, to be heard, to participate in the decision about his or her own life in whatever forum.[114] However, the idea of family privacy and children's dependency has been used to justify the denial of liberty rights, just as patriarchal presumptions about women's place secured their disadvantage.

---

109 Minow, M and Shanley, M, 'Revisioning the family: relational rights and responsibilities', in *op cit*, Shanley and Narayan, fn 2, p 99.

110 Minow and Shanley (*ibid*, p 99) conclude, that, in the context of family matters, rights based theories should draw on the insights of those who study caretaking – 'enriching rights based theories with strong attention to relationships and their preconditions'.

111 Adams, R, *Protests by Pupils*, 1991, London: Falmer; Coles, R, *Children of Crisis*, 1967, New York: Little, Brown.

112 See Cooper, A, 'With justice in mind: complexity, child welfare and the law', in King, M (ed), *Moral Agendas for Children's Welfare*, 1999, London: Routledge, p 156.

113 Levine, D, in 'To assert children's legal rights or promote children's needs: how to attain both goals' (1996) 64 Fordham L Rev 2023, p 2024, argues that, while children are often competent to direct their representation, this does not mean that lawyers alone are best suited to represent them.

114 See Diduck, Chapter 13 and Bridgeman, Chapter 11, in this volume.

Almost 30 years ago, Firestone argued that it was up to 'feminist revolutionaries' to 'speak on behalf of children'.[115] Should we not enable children to speak for themselves or, at the very least, have access to adults who can advocate for them? The furore over children 'going to law' in order to resolve what are seen as 'private matters' is revealing. In the American case of *Gregory K*, [116] part of the controversy centred on the question of authority. Giving children the right to 'go to law' (and all that that entails, including the possibility of a negotiated outcome) was seen as tantamount to undermining authority within the family. It seemed to endorse the observation that children's rights marked the end for the idea of family privacy (as did the struggle for women rights). If this action had been taken by State officials, there would not have been the same outcry – what sparked off the controversy was the idea that the child him or herself could initiate this process of review. It is arguable that giving children such a right opens up the possibility of a different kind of authority within the home, one that is more rational and democratic.[117] It is the process of review that contains within it the seed of a more rational authority and one which is more respectful of the interests of all the family members. As Diduck argues, 'there is a degree of human dignity that autonomy and legal rights provide for people'.[118] To be able to make a claim, to be able to demand attention to one's self-defined needs, is central to respect for human dignity.

We might avoid some of the cruelties that characterise adult-child relations, cruelties that (often) arise out of the ways in which we define children as passive and dependant. This attempt to reassert the value of the language of children's rights is ultimately concerned with questions of inclusion and respect. This is not to uncritically celebrate the processes and practices of the law, nor is it to insist that the language of children's rights holds the key to the resolution of the ills of childhood. Rather, it is to suggest that we all, feminists included, need to engage seriously with the range of issues raised by children themselves and children's rights scholarship.[119] There are points of potential conflict, but there are also many points of common concern. The trend of recent years, in which children have 'gained'

---

115 *Op cit*, Firestone, fn 9, p 101.

116 Gregory K's father had agreed to sign away his parental rights, and so the case focused on his mother, with whom he had lived for only eight months during the past eight years. This 12 year old boy was very clear as to what he wanted to do and why – to be adopted by his foster parents because he did not trust his mother.

117 This case raises similar issues as the leave to apply for 's 8 order' cases in England and Wales under the Children Act 1989.

118 Diduck, A, 'Justice and childhood: reflections on refashioned boundaries', in *op cit*, King, fn 112, p 133.

119 Oakley, A, 'Women and children first and last: parallels and differences between children's and women's studies', in Mayall, B (ed), *Children's Childhoods: Observed and Experienced*, 1994, London: Falmer, p 13.

rights, will continue and, despite some 'warnings' to the contrary, this can be seen as a positive development – particularly if it permits us to rethink adult-child relations, our interdependencies and our vulnerabilities.

CHAPTER 13

SOLICITORS AND LEGAL SUBJECTS

Alison Diduck[1]

INTRODUCING THE FRAMEWORK

I am interested in the constitution of legal subjects: the ongoing process by which a multiplicity of contributions, including law(s), legal language, or legal discourse, if you will, actually constitute social, material and legal subjects and relations. In particular, I am interested in the changing nature and contestability of those subjects. Often, in work of this kind, the legal discourse examined consists of legislative and judicial pronouncements which are said to play an important part in constituting the subjects who come to law and are not merely demonstrations of law regulating those subjects.[2] Importantly, the participation of the subject, him or herself, is also a crucial part of the process, so that, in child and family law, for example, the process of legal 'meaning making' is the constant negotiation and renegotiation of judicial utterances, legal arguments and interpretations of the parties' 'stories', which result in the mother, father or child, of English law:

> Legal thought and legal relations influence self-understanding and understanding of one's relations to others. We are not merely pushed and pulled by laws that exert power over us from the 'outside'. Rather, we come, in uncertain and contingent ways, to see ourselves as law sees us; we participate in the construction of law's 'meanings' and its representations of us even as we

---

1 The initial ideas for this chapter were presented to the Critical Lawyers' Group in Damwoude, The Netherlands, and I would like to thank the members of that group for their feedback. I am also grateful for feedback provided by the editors and contributors to this volume, for Bela Chatterjee's research assistance and for the helpful comments upon early drafts offered by David Seymour, Felicity Kaganas, Michael King and Christine Piper. I must also express my thanks to the solicitors who participated in this study.

2 See, eg, Collier, R, *Masculinity, Law and the Family*, 1995, London: Routledge; Diduck, A, 'The unmodified family: the Child Support Act and the construction of legal subjects' (1995) 22 JLS 527; James, AL and James, A, 'Pump up the volume: listening to children in separation and divorce' (1999) 6 Childhood 189; Neale, B and Smart, C, 'Agents of dependants? Struggling to listen to children in family law and family research', *Working Paper 3*, 1998, Leeds: University of Leeds Centre for Research on Family, Kinship and Childhood; Smart, C, 'Disruptive bodies and unruly sex: the regulation of reproduction and sexuality in the 19th century', in Smart, C (ed), *Regulating Motherhood: Historical Essays on Marriage, Motherhood and Sex*, 1992, London: Routledge. See, also, Bridgeman, Chapter 11, in this volume.

internalise them, so much so that our own purposes and understandings can no longer be extricated from them.[3]

It is from this theoretical perspective that I am interested in law's contribution to meaning making and the degree to which it facilitates, or inhibits, the agency of the subject in the process. At this juncture, however, I am interested in the contribution of a different part of legal discourse: that 'law' created at the advice giving stage, during which the solicitor-client relationship is negotiated, and after which the client-litigant-legal subject emerges, either to engage with formal law in the courts or to be diverted from it to alternative forms of dispute resolution. During this 'subjectification' process, the agency of the client-subject is negotiated with the solicitor and each brings to those negotiations feelings, perceptions and other information from a range of discourses.

Others[4] have explored how solicitors reconstruct clients' problems into legal problems, noting that, sometimes, the fit must be forced and sometimes cannot be made at all. Austin Sarat and William Felstiner examine the way in which power is negotiated and meaning is made in the solicitor-client relationship by, among other things, solicitors sustaining an 'ideology of separate spheres'[5] – the lawyer's rational sphere of the legal and the client's emotional or moral sphere of the social: 'Lawyers attempt to draw rigid boundaries demarcating the legal as the domain of reason and instrumental logic and the social as the domain of emotion and intuition.'[6] They suggest, however, that, although the client and the lawyer bring to their negotiations these 'worlds' that they experience as separate and distinct, the worlds 'are, in fact, highly interactive and interdependent':[7]

> Law exists and takes on meaning in and through the everyday world of social relations, while everyday life is, in turn, constructed and made meaningful by legal ideas and practices. What seem to the participants like independent domains on a collision course are inseparable and mutually constitutive.[8]

In other words, Sarat and Felstiner found that the meaning of 'law', of 'cases' or of legal professionalism is 'produced, deployed or contested'[9] in lawyers' offices through the separate spheres ideology, even while the boundaries between the spheres were constantly blurred. They observe that:

---

3   Sarat, A and Felstiner, WLF, *Divorce Lawyers and their Clients*, 1995, Oxford: OUP, p 12.

4   See, eg, Smart, C, *The Ties That Bind*, 1984, London: Routledge; King, M, '"Being sensible": images and practices of the new family lawyers' (1999) 19 J Social Policy 249. The contribution of the legal profession to the construction of the legal subject is also discussed by Barnett, Chapter 7, in this volume.

5   *Ibid*, Sarat and Felstiner, p 6.

6   *Ibid*, Sarat and Felstiner.

7   *Ibid*, Sarat and Felstiner.

8   *Ibid*, Sarat and Felstiner.

9   *Ibid*, Sarat and Felstiner, p 7.

... the lawyer-client interactions we have observed involve on-going, changing efforts to negotiate shared understandings of people and events and agreement on realistic goals and expectations, a division of responsibilities, legally acceptable and efficacious ways of presenting oneself and responding to others, and definitions of satisfactory resolutions of divorce. The negotiation of meaning in each of these areas is rarely neat and orderly ... The subjects of these negotiations cross the boundaries between law and society and intermix the social world of the client, the legal world of divorce and the nature of professional services.[10]

Recently, British scholars have also examined how extra-legal discourses, those from Sarat and Felstiner's 'other sphere', can infiltrate 'law talk' in the family and child law context to be reinterpreted as legal principles to change or to fashion the boundary of the legally realistic outcome.[11] Indeed, many suggest that this ability is part of what makes a 'good' specialist family lawyer.[12]

I wish to draw upon these insights in legal meaning making to explore the subjectification process in the context of 'private' child law. In this context, solicitors at first, or early, interviews with divorcing parents must give and receive basic information and then assess the merits of their clients' cases. Their assessment requires them understanding and sometimes manipulating the light in which the client will be seen, or the subject identity the client will adopt. It also means that clients' non-legal concepts, like deserving or non-deserving, must be accommodated or transformed by legal concepts like best interests. The negotiation of meaning in this way between solicitor and client obviously happens within the framework of legal rules, but it also happens within the framework of 'rules' other than legal ones, in which case the 'extra-legal', or social, assumes increasing importance. In this way, the child of divorce, or the divorcing father or mother, is constituted in solicitor-client negotiations which occur within the frameworks of legal rules (for example, parental responsibility), psychological rules (for example, harm) and emotional rules (for example, fear or love), all of which seem to have evolved into rules encompassing a presumed social consensus about the 'common sense' of divorce. The privileging of common sense in the political and legal discourse of the family assists the transition from the irrational emotional or psychological, for example, to the rational 'reasonable' or 'sensible'. It becomes a part of the legal discourse between the solicitor and client and

---

10 *Op cit*, Sarat and Felstiner, fn 3, p 144.

11 See, eg, Piper, C, 'How do you define a family lawyer?' (1999) 19 LS 93; Bailey-Harris, R, Davis, G, Barron, J and Pearce, J, *Monitoring Private Law Applications under the Children Act: A Research Report to the Nuffield Foundation*, 1998, Bristol: University of Bristol; *op cit*, King, fn 4; *op cit*, Neale and Smart, fn 2.

12 Neale, B and Smart, C, '"Good" and "bad" lawyers? Struggling in the shadow of the new law' (1997) 19 JSWFL 377; *ibid*, Piper.

affects the way in which they negotiate the meaning of the responsible parent and vulnerable child[13] and the good solicitor of divorce.

Of course, common sense itself contains understandings from many discourses, including the psychological, the emotional and the political, and scientific 'truth' plays a large part in endowing common sense with its rhetorical and legal power. In other, more subtle ways, however, the 'truth' of common sense is self-perpetuating. Both of these points are illustrated by the following example of a headline proclaiming the results of a long term study on teenage development. *The Daily Mail* told us:

> Now the figures that prove what common sense always told us:
> CONFIRMED – DIVORCE DAMAGES CHILDREN.[14]

Furthermore, common sense can be rhetorically contrasted with 'ideology' (as in, for example, the Government's 1993 White Paper on adoption which states that child placements should be considered according to common sense rather than ideology),[15] and it may also be characterised as part of an almost anti-intellectualist agenda. 'Experts' are castigated as ideologically or academically driven, while nostalgic laments are heard for all that which our forebears saw as natural and normal. What this perspective misses, however, is the notion that ideology itself often makes its appearance as common sense. The process of meaning making is a struggle and that which at any one time becomes 'taken for granted' is constantly being negotiated and renegotiated.[16] Those understandings which, at one time, are perceived as common sense, or as 'a part of the air that we breathe', are often ideological, even while their incorporation into the arena of meaning making is said by others to be an antidote to ideology. Understanding recourse to common sense as being, at least partly, ideologically motivated in this way may shed further light upon the meaning making process in law.

Sarat and Felstiner's separate spheres model is particularly apposite to understanding family lawyering. Familial relations are idealised within law and the liberal polity as relations of affection, emotion and reciprocity. They exist in the realm of the social. In this way, they can be understood as distinct from legal relations, which are characterised by self-interest and rationality and, thus, are removed from the social. More than in other legal matters, then, in family law, 'feelings' and other elements from the social sphere play a part in relations, including decision making and meaning making.[17] Historically,

---

13 *Op cit*, King, fn 4.

14 (1996) *The Daily Mail*, 22 April, p 1.

15 Department of Health, Welsh Office, Home Office, Lord Chancellor's Department, *Adoption: The Future*, Cm 2288, 1993, London: HMSO, p 8, para 4.28.

16 *Op cit*, Smart, fn 2, p 31.

17 *Op cit*, Piper fn 11; *op cit*, Bailey-Harris *et al*, fn 11.

law responded with statutes placing the legally discernable best interests of children at the forefront of the decision making process, and solicitors, in turn, adapted their roles to promote this rational legal principle at the expense of the irrational and the social.[18] They imposed onto intensely personal, emotionally volatile, *familial* questions, notions of arm's length objectivity, rationality and, more recently, liberal equality and the common sense of 'reasonableness'. With the possible exception of the construction of the good father,[19] it was neither legally sufficient nor, usually, legally relevant that a parent and child loved each other, perhaps because this feeling of affection was already assumed. Decisions were replete with courts re-interpreting, in the rational/legal context, evidence of a mother's or father's *feelings* according to supposedly objective tests against which best interests or 'welfare' was measured.[20]

Recent trends in family law have promoted informality of decision making such that the parties are encouraged to negotiate or mediate privately matters ancillary to their divorce, including the care of children. Sometimes, they are encouraged to do so with the help of professionals such as mediators or solicitors. It seems that the balancing of 'the family's' legal and social spheres, or of law and love, so difficult for so long, has now been accepted as futile, and the formal law of the courts appears to have bowed out of the family picture virtually entirely. The irrational and messy business of 'the family' is now thought best to be left to mediation and counselling, with their responsibility, unlike law's, to deal with 'feelings'.

It seems to me that, as a result of these trends in private child and family law, law's part in the negotiation of meaning is becoming more covert. While it always came from the solicitor's office, as well as from the pages of the Family Law Reports, it was the voices of judges and legislators which seemed to dominate the legal discourse. Now that the place of formal law in familial relationships is again questioned, the interests negotiated and the amount of extra-legal talk, including from the subject him or herself, in the solicitor's office, contribute more clearly to the subject making process. The issues I raise, then, are the degree to which solicitor-client legal discourse crosses Sarat and Felstiner's social/legal boundary and whether, or how, that crossing is acknowledged.

The Centre for the Study of Law, the Child and the Family at Brunel University completed interviews with 36 solicitors, with a substantial family law caseload, in order to discover what 'information' solicitors think new divorce clients with children need, particularly in relation to arrangements

---

18 *Op cit*, Neale and Smart, fn 2; *op cit*, King, fn 4.

19 Smart, C, 'The legal and moral ordering of child custody' (1991) 18 JLS 485; Kaganas, F, 'Responsible or feckless fathers? *Re S (Parental Responsibility)*' (1996) 8 CFLQ 165.

20 *Op cit*, King, fn 4.

concerning children, and to discover what factors determine the advice solicitors give to divorcing clients in relation to disputes about arrangements for children. The Centre was particularly interested in ascertaining the influence upon this advice of the legal concepts of non-intervention (the court shall not make an order unless it is better than making no order) and parental responsibility (as opposed to parental rights) introduced in the Children Act 1989. Michael King[21] and Christine Piper[22] have drawn upon the research with this same sample in their recent work on family lawyering. My focus on the research is upon how the advice and information sharing contributes to the constitution of the legal subjects of divorce.

SOLICITORS, NON-INTERVENTION AND PARENTAL RESPONSIBILITY

Together, the principles of parental responsibility and non-intervention demonstrate the Government's policy of reinforcing family autonomy and the privacy of family decision making. Piper[23] highlights the political implications of this imperative and how a policy of 'parents know best' for their children is a double edged sword. At the first meeting with a solicitor, it can empower parents by appearing to assume that their perceptions of their children's welfare and their parenting have some validity. The principle of parents know best empowers parents at least to the degree that they can enter the divorce process on the understanding that the law cares about, or will hear, their perceptions. In practice, this interpretation of the principle is often confirmed to parents by representatives of law. For example, research conducted by Rebecca Bailey-Harris *et al* at Bristol University[24] found that the 'no order principle', in particular, was frequently invoked by judges with statements like 'parents know better for their children than the court can'.[25] Crucially, however, this trust that law appears to place in parents' understanding of their children was then linked to the need for parental agreement so that the message became 'parents only know best if they agree'. This reframed message was, in turn, reinforced in certain ways to parents in the Bristol study, who were told by judges, for example, that their 'agreement was more likely to 'stick' than a court order'.[26]

---

21 See references in *op cit*, fn 4.
22 See references in *op cit*, fn 11.
23 See references in *op cit*, fn 11.
24 *Op cit*, Bailey-Harris *et al*, fn 11.
25 See references in *op cit*, fn 11.
26 See references in *op cit*, fn 11.

Virtually all of the solicitors in the Brunel study stated that the no order principle affects the advice they give to clients at the first interview. The influence, however, ranged from promoting parents' autonomy and affirming their agency in constructing themselves as the good mothers and fathers of divorce, to requiring parental agreement at any cost and thus negating the client's perceptions unless they were agreed by the other parent. The range of responses is demonstrated by the following:

Mr P: The no order principle influences my advice in so far as one is trying to persuade parents that they have to accept the responsibility. That's one of the most fundamental spin-offs of the Children Act – that parents must fundamentally be responsible for resolving the issues.

Mr C: The no order principle influences my advice in as much as telling clients who want their piece of paper that courts are looking towards not making any orders because now it's up to the individual parents to try to negotiate an amicable settlement.

Mr O: I would try to emphasise to the clients that it is their responsibility to do what is in the interests of the children and they've got to bloody well bang their heads together and try to reach agreement, and that's the whole philosophy of the Act, and cases shouldn't go to court.

On the one hand, therefore, the combination of parental responsibility and the no order principle promotes parental agency in determining their relationships with their children, their children's welfare and consequently their own legal subjectivity as parents, but, on the other, it does so only as long as the parents agree. More than that, to what they must agree is very circumscribed – they must agree to contact: usually mother-residence, father-contact.

THE WELFARE OF CHILDREN

Solicitors usually provide information to their clients about the welfare principle and its paramountcy in the legislation. They also must make some effort to determine how the welfare of the child in question can best be met. Often, however, it was apparent that, for many of our solicitors, the particularities of an individual child's welfare disappeared into the 'common sense' of dominant welfare rhetoric. This process has implications for the constitution of both the client and the child subject.

When questioned about how they advised clients about the welfare of the child, the majority of our solicitors said that it meant adopting a child focus. While it was not entirely clear what this meant, many went on to explain that the parties must be told to put aside their own feelings and adopt the child's point of view. Some then added that they would not presume to know, or give advice about, the particular child's point of view, but many more equated unquestioningly the child's welfare with continued contact with the non-residential parent. To those solicitors, safeguarding welfare appears to mean adopting the child's perspective which, in turn, appears to see contact as a given. In this way, a child's point of view, a child's welfare and contact become conflated:

> **Ms N**: You go on to say that it's in the interests of the child to have contact with both parents because, otherwise, they could have a potential identity crisis. I go on to explain that, especially with difficult clients – I call them difficult clients – clients who don't want contact – and want to say no contact with the father – but, generally speaking, I think there are more often than not – I would say 80% of – divorcing couples want their children to maintain contact with the other parent.

> **Ms Q**: So, as far as my position on the welfare of the child, it would be to promote the contact, to promote the general financing and to find out what was happening with respect to that and to try and, hopefully, to sort out that residence isn't in dispute.

Parents meeting with their solicitors for the first time, then, are greeted with mixed messages. They almost certainly have ideas about their own parenting and how they, as mothers or fathers, can provide for the welfare of their children. These ideas are based upon their own experience, as well as on other information including their understanding of the law, notions of common sense and the feelings, including guilt, these may or may not induce. Smart and Neale found that many of the parents in their study incorporated the 'common sense' that divorce harms children, and approached their divorces with this presumption of harm, but that they responded in different ways to the guilt that the presumption induced.[27] In these cases, it may be seen as important that parents are told that the law assumes they know best about what these responses should be. But the way in which solicitors interpret this to clients is not that courts will defer to a parent's superior knowledge and understanding of the welfare of their children, but rather as a direction to agree to contact. In our study, Mr M made it clear that he retained the last word with clients: 'I won't run applications which I think are silly just because clients ask me to, or even if they'll pay me to do it.'

Solicitors seem also to have internalised the presumption of harm, as exemplified by Ms N's ideas of the child's potential 'identity crisis'. They also seem to rely upon the common sense of the presumption as they characterise their clients as 'reasonable' or 'difficult'. A parent's voice is heard and validated in these cases, and his or her agency in constructing him or herself as a reasonable and, therefore, good father or mother, is confirmed only when they say the 'right' things to their solicitors about the common sense of harm, agreement and contact. If they do not, or if they are successful in resisting

---

27 Smart, C and Neale, B, *Family Fragments*, 1999, Cambridge: Polity, pp 87–88.

admonitions to be 'reasonable', they become, at least in the solicitor's eyes, and perhaps in their own, the difficult client-parent. Further, in line with domestic and international policy to recognise the rights or autonomy of children, and in the spirit of respect for childrens' personalities,[28] the Children Act 1989 requires decision makers to take account of their ascertainable wishes and feelings.[29] Considering their wishes and feelings accords children an active role in decision making and in the constitution of themselves as legal subjects. It appears to ascribe value to their perspectives and respect to their opinions and their agency. As it was with their parents, however, this agency is at least partly illusory. It is contingent upon the particular 'wishes and feelings' they express, as the 'received' notion of welfare can override even the most articulate child's expressions. The court is empowered to diverge from the child's wishes if its view of welfare so demands.

Related to this is the issue of how received notions of children and childhood, that is, who children are supposed to be and how they are supposed to feel, often obscure their individual realities. Liz Trinder[30] examined how 'a range of adult professionals constituted the very children whose voices they seek to represent'[31] and interviewed a number of court welfare officers about their engagements with children. She found that:

> ... the various adult perspectives on hearing 'the child's voice' were based on idealised and stabilised conceptions of childhoods, with no distinction between 'children' as living beings and 'childhood' as a shifting set of ideas.[32]

This research found that even court welfare officers, those professionals trained to engage with children and charged with the responsibility of assessing their welfare, failed to recognise children's agency in constituting themselves as subjects of a legal process.

The majority of our solicitors agreed that the ascertainable wishes and feelings of the child were a priority in determining what advice to give parents if a s 8 matter was in dispute. One approach they could have adopted to ascertain these wishes and feelings would have been to ask those who are said to know their children best – the parents. Our solicitors, however, almost without exception, felt this approach was of little use. They assumed that

---

28 Sawyer, C, 'One step forward, two steps back – the European Convention on the Exercise of Children's Rights' (1999) 11 CFLQ 151.

29 The Children Act 1989, s 1(3), contains a list of factors colloquially known as the welfare 'checklist', to which courts must have regard when considering a s 8 or Pt IV application. Paragraph (a) states that the child's ascertainable wishes and feelings must be considered 'in the light of his [or her] age and understanding'. See, in this regard, ibid, Sawyer.

30 Trinder, L, 'Competing constructions of childhood: children's rights and children's wishes in divorce' (1997) 19 JSWFL 219.

31 Ibid, p 291.

32 Ibid, p 301.

what parents said about their children's wishes was biased or self-interested, and thus accorded it little weight:

Mr M: Well, I never see the children so all I'm getting is what the parents tell me [laughs]. I'm not in a position to know what the children think ... a parent sits and tells me what the children think. I mean that a parent has a vested interest.

Mr S: Of course, to some extent, if it's from the client there's always going to be an element of bias.

Ms N: The difficulty is, if I'm acting for a mother, and mother says, 'my child does not want to see father' or whatever, I can only get the views of the child through the mother ... so I will make a note of the views or the alleged view.

Ms Q: All you can do is record your client's view of the children's wishes and feelings which doesn't really help you a great deal at all.

Another approach for them would have been to ask the children directly about their wishes and feelings, but our solicitors did not favour this approach either. They gave a number of reasons for this, stating, for example, that the child is not their client, or that they are not experts and, therefore, are not best placed to interview children. Again, however, many relied upon received wisdom or 'psychology' in reaching the decision not to interview children, arguing that it puts too much pressure on children to be involved in the decision making process. They seemed, like those in the study by Mervyn Murch *et al*,[33] to be conflating a consideration of wishes and feelings with a direction requiring children to make residence and contact choices. Many said that it was 'harmful' for children to be present at interviews, and others said that it was not 'sensible'. Limiting children's involvement in the legal procedure went further than this though. Received wisdom was also called in to aid in deciding whether children ought to be told what was going on, but there appeared to be no consensus in what that 'wisdom' was:

Mr L: I never cease to be amazed by how much emotional baggage parents put on their children. A child of five is being told exactly what's happening in divorce proceedings and I try to get across to them as parents that's not a thing to do.

Mr M: I mean, I think the received wisdom is that children benefit from being told at an early stage and that if they are made aware that there is this happening – again, that's not something I tell to clients you must do – I just tell them it's the received wisdom.

---

33 Murch, M, Douglas, G, Scanlan, L, Perry, A, Lisles, C, Bader, K and Borkowski, M, *Safeguarding Children's Welfare in Uncontentious Divorce: A Study of s 41 of the Matrimonial Causes Act 1973*, Research Series, No 7, 1999, London: HMSO.

Mr O sums up the solicitors' attitudes with respect to the degree to which they believe children ought to be involved in the decision making process. He takes on board the discourse of settlement and co-operation and the presumption of harm:

> **Mr O:** ... one would do what one can at an early stage to persuade them to consider mediation or discussion, avoiding confrontation, avoiding arguments, etc, in the presence of the children, avoiding – when the children are old enough – putting any pressure on them to make a decision and choose between the parents ... so that, *together* [emphasis in original], *they tell the children what is to happen* [emphasis added].

For him, the importance of familial co-operation in decision making does not extend to the children. They will still be told, after the event, what is to happen. This style lies in contrast with Neale and Smart's[34] research with children who have experienced divorce. They found that, while some children did not wish to be involved, others did, and that what was important to children was the opportunity to be heard:

> The issue over whether children should be involved in difficult choices is a hotly contested one in family law, with lack of consensus over whether this is harmful or beneficial. Children's own discourse suggests a third way of viewing this issue, one which accords children the competence to judge their own family dynamics and quality of relationships and to decide what kind and level of participation is necessary or appropriate in their own particular case.[35]

Trinder reached a similar conclusion:

> ... children's desire to participate or not appeared to be highly individual ... Nor did the degree of agency or rationality associate easily with a desire to participate in the decision making. Some children had very rational reasons for wanting to influence decisions, but others made a rational decision that they were better off acting like children by not participating in adult decisions, or choosing non-participation. The ability to participate is different from the desire to participate.[36]

By and large, our solicitors said they relied upon the court welfare officer to determine children's welfare, including children's wishes. This reliance seems unfortunate, given Trinder's[37] findings regarding the approaches taken with children by court welfare officers, and also given Neale and Smart's[38] report that the children in their study did not feel empowered by court welfare officers or that their confidences would be respected by a court welfare officer.

---

34 *Op cit*, Neale and Smart, fn 2.
35 *Op cit*, Neale and Smart, fn 2, p 29.
36 *Op cit*, Trinder, fn 30, pp 302–03.
37 *Op cit*, Trinder, fn 30.
38 See references in *op cit*, fn 2.

Of course, children's welfare and children's wishes are not the same thing. Welfare also takes into account factors including those on the welfare checklist, or other matters, such as the quality of children's relationships with extended family or parents' new partners, or children's school attendance and performance. A surprising number of our solicitors, however, said either that they did not routinely ask about these factors or that they only asked about them because the information was necessary to complete the Statement of Arrangements required by s 41 of the Matrimonial Causes Act 1973.[39]

Rather than viewing these factors as integral parts of a child's life and life experiences, a number of our solicitors also said that, if they did ask about them, it was for a specific purpose only. For example, grandparent contact was usually only asked about 'if it was relevant' or if the client identified it as a problem. Relevance was usually restricted to contact disputes between the parents. Ms K sums up the general feeling:

> That only really comes up when you've got problems with both parents at work ... sometimes they're used as a help if there's difficult contact ... a go between.

Information about new relationships was usually deemed relevant only for financial reasons and, less frequently, for contact issues:

Mr E: That's useful purely for financial reasons.

Ms M: Well that's – can sometimes pose problems so far as contact is concerned ... [*prompt*] How? ... you're not going to have contact, you're going to bring the child into contact with that new person – that's a very regular occurrence.

Ms N: I think two things – one is the child – sometimes, if a new spouse is introduced to the child immediately, the other party may have reservations about that ... it helps me to know why, for instance, the mother, if I'm acting for the father, why the mother is being *so* difficult in co-operating with contact – if I *know* there is a new relationship ... and also for financial reasons [emphasis in original].

Information about where the children go to school was usually deemed not relevant or only relevant for financial reasons:

Ms B: I don't think it is particularly useful ... but, as you know, it appears on the statement of arrangements.

---

39 The significance of the Statement of Arrangements in safeguarding the welfare of children has been considered in a recent study commissioned by the Lord Chancellor's Department: *op cit*, Murch *et al*, fn 33. The general findings indicate that both district judges and solicitors are sceptical about the utility of the Statement in meeting its objective and that parents would be happy for 'someone' to talk to their children directly about their wishes and feelings. Even the Statement of Arrangements, then, may be inadequate to safeguard the welfare of children in uncontentious divorces.

Ms D: Of no use whatsoever, I don't think I've ever had – funnily enough – a client tell me that his or her children were going to fee paying schools. That would be significant. But, as long as it's a local State school, it's not significant.

Of course, many did say information about all of these factors was relevant – they made comments such as 'it helps to get the whole picture' – but many more seemed to pigeonhole the required information into different categories which determined its legal relevance rather than seeing it as an important part of the picture of *this* client and the welfare of *this* child. This pigeonholing was most stark in the case of domestic violence. A small but surprising number of solicitors said that they would only ask about domestic violence if it was relevant to the ground for divorce:

Ms B: I mean, if a client came in and said, 'I'd like a divorce, my husband and I have been living apart for five years', I mean, it's clearly not going to be relevant.

Others said that they do not usually ask at all: either they would expect the client to have mentioned it if it were important or they would just sense it if it were important:

Mr M: I wouldn't raise it unless they did. Because, if it's relevant, they would have raised it in my experience – then I know there are frightening statistics with domestic violence. It's either relevant to the process or it's not, in my view.

Mr N: I don't ask the questions unless I start getting a smell. After 30 years or more doing this job I can nearly always smell [inaudible] ...

Additionally, virtually all interviewees interpreted our question as being whether they would ask the woman about domestic violence. The examples given in their answers were about asking 'her'. It seemed to be inconceivable, or inappropriate, to ask the man. For example:

Ms G: If the wife did not raise the issue – or say she couldn't stay in the house – there would be no reason to ask. If dad was the client, there would be no reason to ask, unless it was in the petition.

Where domestic violence was deemed relevant to children, it was usually specifically with reference to contact, and a small minority indicated that it might be important in getting an idea of the welfare of the child generally. This trend seems unfortunate, given the research suggesting the damaging effects on children of witnessing directly or indirectly violence in the home.[40] It is also unfortunate, given that virtually all of our solicitors said that they

---

40 See, eg, Hester, M and Radford, L, *Domestic Violence and Child Contact Arrangements in England and Denmark*, 1996, Bristol: Policy; Parkinson, P and Humphreys, C, 'Children who witness domestic violence – the implications for child protection' (1998) 10 CFLQ 147.

would refer clients to mediation for contact issues, although not all of them said that they would express this as a preference to their clients. In general, these findings seem to support Piper's contention that 'policy and practice are underpinned by fragmented, partial, and compartmentalised images of children which can only disadvantage real children'.[41] The 'real' flesh-and-blood child's experiences with school, violence or extended family are not seen as parts of a whole picture of their life or welfare, but are compartmentalised into categories of legal relevance or irrelevance.

Given the lack of general information solicitors seem to obtain about a particular child's welfare, how can they give their best advice to clients? It seems that welfare for these solicitors is 'what's good for children' according to policy, common sense or their interpretations of psychological research. It seems to have very little to do with 'what's good for *these* children'. Little effort is made to find out about *these* children. The individual subjectivity of the child is obscured in solicitors' offices by the general, abstract 'child' of divorce.

Despite the rhetoric, including their own, the 'child of divorce', for solicitors, still seems to be the object of their parents' divorce: a passive, potential trauma victim.[42] He or she is not an autonomous subject, is not ascribed agency to participate in proceedings, but is to be the object of a negotiated or mediated agreement. This view is confirmed by mediators and district judges who also decline to see children,[43] and by court welfare officers who, according to Trinder,[44] continue to rely upon an abstracted 'childhood' in constituting their child subjects, even after they ascertain directly or indirectly the child's views. At every turn, from the legislation, to the solicitors, to the mediators, the rhetoric is of a child focus, but it is difficult to see that focus in action. Solicitors do not speak to the child, they do not ask for specific information about this particular child and they do not assume that the child is already the parent's focus, despite findings indicating that parents do consider carefully the welfare of their children on divorce.[45] Rather, they assume, based upon a number of diverse discourses, that the child of divorce is too vulnerable or irrational to express a view, and that the parent of divorce is too overcome by self-interest to be 'sensible' about her child.

---

41 Piper, C, 'Divorce reform and the image of the child' (1996) 23 JLS 364, p 374.
42 *Ibid.*
43 *Op cit*, Murch *et al*, fn 33.
44 *Op cit*, Trinder, fn 30.
45 *Op cit*, Murch *et al*, fn 33, p 248.

MOTHER, FATHER AND CHILD SUBJECTS

A feminist approach to understanding what is happening in the solicitor's office adopts a constructivist perspective[46] and accepts very little as given. It means that dominant understandings are allowed to be changeable. Crucially, it holds that part of the changeability lies in what the previously silenced can contribute to the meaning making project. A feminist approach would, therefore, ascribe agency to the parties to the divorce and to the children of divorce and would mean that the rhetoric of child focus is taken seriously.

In a feminist model, children's voices would be important in constructing them as flesh-and-blood participants in the divorce process, rather than as silent and abstract 'child victims'. In these two respects, the denial of agency and the denial of individual subjectivity, legal discourse now denies a child's full subjectivity.

Certainly, this result can be due not only to solicitors' practice, but also to the legislation: the Children Act 1989 does not require children's autonomy to be considered and, indeed, by prioritising their welfare over their rights, it may operate to stifle it. Day-Sclater argues, moreover, that the welfare discourse itself may be at least partially responsible for this.[47] The welfare discourse, which gives legal meaning to decisions about children, positions children as vulnerable and dependent upon adults for their protection, and, by its very nature, excludes the possibility of autonomy, independence and agency for children. Consequently, children's views are not regularly sought, and when they are, they are likely to be heard through the welfare discourse. She argues that what is necessary is a redefined view of subjectivity, one that encompasses 'the irrational, the ambivalent and the vulnerable in all of us, without resorting to notions of pathology'.[48]

This feminist redrawing of boundaries appears, on the one hand, as a paradox, as dependence/independence, agency/passivity and welfare/autonomy appear to represent irreconcilable dichotomies. Part of the feminist project, however, is to reveal both the assumptions and the constitutive power behind binary oppositions so as to render them reducible and changeable.[49] A feminist analysis would therefore reveal the important role that irrationality, emotions and self-perception play in the rational world of the legal and, in crossing the autonomy/dependency divide, would destabilise the power dynamic within that opposition. The child subject would be constituted after acknowledging that individual children will experience dependence and

46 Lacey, N, *Unspeakable Subjects*, 1998, Oxford: Hart, p 3.

47 Day-Sclater, S, 'Children and divorce: hidden agendas?', 1998, unpublished conference paper, University of Hull.

48 *Ibid.*

49 O'Donovan, K, 'With sense, consent, or just a con? Legal subjects in the discourse of autonomy', in Naffine, N and Owens, R, *Sexing the Subject of Law*, 1997, London: Sweet & Maxwell.

autonomy differently and may wish to express these experiences differently. In other words, a feminist approach would challenge the taken for granted status not only of children's vulnerability, victimisation and dependence, but also that their welfare excludes their autonomy and agency. It would allow children themselves to give voice to the degree and nature of participation they require and would dismantle altogether the abstract child of divorce.[50]

The adult subjects of divorce must also be scrutinised from this feminist perspective. A re-vision of welfare which accommodates independence, agency and rights as well as dependence, vulnerability and care would require a re-vision of justice to one which accommodated the 'welfare' of its adult legal subjects as much as their rights. Whether we phrase it as Day-Sclater does: '... recognising the irrational, the ambivalent and the vulnerable in all of us,'[51] or whether we adopt a process which safeguards a subject's relationships as well as their independence, or which privileges substantive equality as well as an ethic of care,[52] it means that we are challenging oppositions and redrawing boundaries around the adult as well as the child subject of law.[53]

I noted earlier that parents' voices are validated by solicitors' legal discourse if they said the 'right' things in interviews. Given what the right things are, it seems to me that the subjectification process in legal discourse owes as much to gender as it does to generation. If it is accepted, as one of our solicitors stated directly, and others implied, that the 'normal situation' for children after divorce is to reside with their mother and have contact with their father, a parent who sees him or herself as promoting the welfare of their children by suggesting an alternative arrangement is seen as promoting an abnormal or unreasonable position. Our solicitors spoke, for example, of dealing with mothers who wished to deny contact by 'getting them to see sense', even it meant 'banging heads together'. Much *et al* found that solicitors used a number of different tactics to coerce agreement on contact, including threats to report recalcitrant parents to the Legal Aid Board and 'using the court as the excuse':

> I base what I tell clients, not on my own views, well, sometimes my own views, but my own views coincide largely with what I think the court's views are, which is just as well, really. So I don't have to say, 'Look you silly woman, see sense'. I can say, 'Well, at the end of the day the court will say: "blah, blah,

---

50 For further consideration of a focus upon the participation of children, see Bridgeman, Chapter 11 and Lim and Roche, Chapter 12, in this volume.

51 *Op cit*, Day-Sclater, fn 47.

52 On a 'justice' which adopts an 'ethic of care' rather than principles of equality, see *op cit*, Smart and Neale, fn 27. My position is that the two are not mutually exclusive.

53 See, also, my argument on this in 'Justice and childhood: reflections on refashioned boundaries', in King, M (ed), *Moral Agendas for Children's Welfare*, 1999, London: Routledge.

blah"'. So I don't come into conflict with her myself. I blame the court, which is great.[54]

Neither our solicitors nor those in the study by Murch *et al* seemed to question the common sense of mother-residence/father-contact, nor to reflect upon the implications of the 'normal situation' they promoted, which, in effect, attempts to recreate a version of the idealised, but gendered, nuclear family, with the mother as primary carer of children and the father as occasional carer, but unquestioned bearer of 'equal rights'. Indeed, when questioned about how they advised clients about the meaning of parental responsibility, many of our solicitors focused upon the equality of rights and responsibilities which they said parental responsibility confers upon parents:

Mr P: ... both stand equal with regard to the child, both have joint parenting responsibility for the child or children, neither of you are seen particularly by the court to be in a more advantageous position than the other. You both have duties and obligations towards this child.

Ms O: I tend to advise them that, really, it's a wide term that covers all the rights and duties they have as parents from a practical point of view. It means that father, for instance, assuming he's not the carer, has the ability to get copies of school reports. I tend to try to take it down to a specific level that's going to be appropriate to them rather than just talk about duties and responsibilities. But, basically, to convey the impression that they both are still involved and they can't take, or shouldn't take, unilateral action on important matters.

Ms M: Assuming that the children are living with the mother, I'll tell the father that, although they're living with the mother, ... he has the power, or he has the rights and duties similar to those of the mother, as far as the children are concerned, to determine where they attend school; whether at 16 they're allowed to marry; [and] important issues such as medical treatment. So, they are still involved to a great extent in the children's upbringing.

Mothers, then, enter negotiations with their solicitors as assumed carers who must respect the (contact) rights of non-residential fathers. If they assert resistance to this identity, they would be seen as unreasonable/irrational parents who need to be brought into line by solicitors. (Except in cases of domestic violence, when mothers are deemed to be rational and to speak up if it is relevant.) There is some evidence to suggest that even mothers who accept this 'norm' may already be conditioned to accept that their own perceptions or needs are less important than those of their children or their husbands. Although our solicitors did not remark upon this directly, Smart and Neale found that, in general, mothers' relationships with solicitors were more

---

54 *Op cit*, Murch *et al*, fn 33, p 178.

dependent than fathers' and that mothers 'did not construe themselves as legal subjects, rather, they identified a series of needs – not necessarily their own – that had to be met'.[55] Our solicitors' practice demonstrates a tacit, if unintended, encouragement of this denial of women's subjectivity.

Our study provided no direct information about the number of fathers who begin consultations with their solicitors seeking residence orders. Our solicitors did seem to suggest, however, that, if they did, they were not to be taken seriously. Either they were to be shown the pragmatic impracticalities of a 'working man' taking full time responsibility for children, or they were suspected of harbouring ignoble motivations behind their requests:

Ms D: Probably most arguments over residence are really arguments over contact or specific issue orders ...

Mr I: One tries to get the client to see the reality of the position: this is really about how can the children be brought up if dad is working split shifts six days a week ... and it isn't good enough to say 'his mum will do for the children' – just explain to them the realities about who has been primary carer and all the usual arguments about status quo ... I think residence applications are usually about something different to residence ... a genuine residence dispute will be about something else – some other issue underlying it.

Mr L: Sometimes, you look for what the client wants and must say that the chances of, for example, a dad working full time getting a residence order, if mum is almost beyond criticism, is so remote it's perhaps a strategy on dad's part to make these noises, but he's not going to get anywhere with it.

Fathers would tend to be listened to in their requests for contact, however, as these would be construed as 'reasonable', reflecting as they do the 'normal' nuclear family model in which fathers are only occasional carers, but bearers of rights. Fathers' perceptions of themselves as agentic legal subjects and good fathers in these cases tends to be validated by solicitors' discourse of rights and reasonableness. This position is also borne out by Smart and Neale's research, in which they found that fathers tended to articulate their wishes from a position of rights and usually perceived themselves to be in control of the legal process.[56] We could interpret these observations as suggesting that fathers, more frequently than mothers, perceived themselves as having a say in the legal process and in using law to support their self-identification as good fathers.

The subjects, then, of divorce practice belie the rhetoric of divorce policy. The policy promotes parental autonomy and child focus, but the practice

55 *Op cit*, Smart and Neale, fn 27, p 163.
56 *Op cit*, Smart and Neale, fn 27, pp 158–70.

seems to bear out little, if any, parental autonomy, except the rather spurious autonomy of agreeing the details of an idealised nuclear family arrangement already assumed to be in your children's welfare. I am not suggesting here that the law adopts any conscious partiality in favour of fathers, or that fathers in any way consciously manipulate the law in their favour. Rather, I am observing that legal discourse, managed in the solicitor's office, has the perhaps unintended consequence of confirming a father's subjectivity as a rights bearing, but non-residential, good father, and a mother's as the primary carer but protector of others' rights. In the same way, the child is reduced to the child 'victim' of divorce. Rarely is there evidence of solicitors' respect for expressions of individuality and agency, unless they accord with the law's notion of reasonableness. Further, generation and gender matter in the way in which legal discourse will hear, and be influenced by, the subject's agency to the extent that they matter in the nuclear family model 'prescribed' by reasonableness and common sense.

What about the 'messy' business of families: the irrationality of feelings like love or fear and the 'social' context that includes connections with grandparents or schools? Law, even that articulated at the stage of solicitor-client negotiations, appears still to disavow any association with this social sphere, as solicitors persist in recasting that messy business into the rational of the 'legal' and the reasonable. At a simple level, this may, unwittingly, be advantaging fathers who more frequently speak in the register of rights and the legal over mothers and children who more frequently speak in the register of connection, harm or care. But, more generally, it may operate to create a legal discourse which is 'happier' for a client whose own perceptions and wishes lie within the bounds of the supposedly legal sphere, as opposed to the social one. It is thus easier for a solicitor operating within an 'ideology of separate spheres' to disregard the 'social' perspective of a parent where it seems to be incongruent with the 'legal' perspective which maintains clear norms of reasonableness and boundaries for legal relevance.

Interestingly, however, where the social can be translated, or is thought to be translatable, we have seen that the transition is fairly easy. In our study, for example, solicitors appeared to slip easily between the legal and the moral, the rational and the irrational – the legal and the social – but without any apparent consciousness of doing so. They accepted, for example, the 'common sense' of harm or their ability to 'smell' or to 'sense' a legal issue even while they recast this information into a legal register. Indeed, common sense and folk wisdom are frequently elevated to the level of 'legal principle',[57] demonstrating that the boundaries between the social and the legal have, as Sarat and Felstiner conclude, already been irretrievably crossed. A feminist approach to understanding this process would suggest that what is necessary

---

57   *Op cit*, Bailey-Harris *et al*, fn 11, pp 41–44.

now is for law and its agents to recognise and to accept the spuriousness of its dichotomies and oppositions and, in particular, to appreciate the role that all aspects of our subjectivity have upon the constitution of our legal selves and upon legal discourse. A feminist/constructivist approach to lawyering would refuse to receive information through a separate spheres model and would accept that legal subjectivity is constituted through many and diverse discourses, is changeable and relies, unreservedly, upon the subject him or herself.

CHAPTER 14

'HOW THE UN STOLE CHILDHOOD': THE CHRISTIAN RIGHT AND THE INTERNATIONAL RIGHTS OF THE CHILD

Doris E Buss[1]

INTRODUCTION

In 1989, the United Nations (UN) General Assembly adopted the Convention on the Rights of the Child. Within one year, the Convention was ratified by the necessary minimum of 20 countries and entered into force in 1990. By 1999, the remarkable speed with which the Convention entered into force, together with its near universal acceptance,[2] established the Convention as something of an international human rights success story. Unlike other more controversial human rights agreements, such as the Convention on the Elimination of all Forms of Discrimination against Women, the Convention on the Rights of the Child is generally accepted as a positive and important development.

Despite this wide support for the Convention, conservative Christian organisations – the Christian Right[3] – have taken a fairly critical stance on the Convention and children's rights in general.[4] Recently, that critical stance hardened into a focused opposition to proposed international recognition of reproductive rights for adolescents. At the UN five year review of the

---

1   The research for this paper was funded and assisted by grants from Keele University, the Nuffield Foundation, the Leverhulme Foundation and the University of British Columbia's Centre for Research in Women's Studies and Gender Relations. An earlier version of this chapter was presented at the University of British Columbia, Faculty of Law, Centre for Feminist Legal Studies, and I benefited from the insightful comments of faculty and students there.

2   As of December 1999, only two States had not ratified the Convention: the US and Somalia.

3   By 'conservative Christian', I am referring to the primarily American, Protestant and Catholic organisations whose conservative politics are informed by a fundamentalist or orthodox theology. For a more detailed discussion of the theological aspects of some of the conservative Christian positions, see Herman, D, *The Antigay Agenda: Orthodox Vision and the Christian Right*, 1997, Chicago: Chicago UP; Brouwer, S, Gifford, P and Rose, SD, *Exporting the American Gospel: Global Christian Fundamentalism*, 1996, New York: Routledge, pp 13–46.

4   See, eg, Eagle Forum, 'The new world order wants your children' (1993) 26(8) Phyllis Schlafly Report, available at www.eagleforum.org. The title of this chapter is itself taken from a press release from the American conservative Christian organisation, Concerned Women for America (CWA), *The End of Innocence: How the UN Stole Childhood*, 15 July 1999, available at www.cwfa.org.

International Conference on Population and Development (see below), Christian Right organisations launched an effective campaign to prevent international recognition of adolescent sexual and reproductive health rights. This successful Christian Right intervention demonstrates the growing presence – and acumen – of the Christian Right at the UN. In recent years, Christian Right organisations have begun to look to the international realm as an important area of activism, largely because of perceived feminist and socialist dominance at the UN.

Children's rights are a banner issue for the Christian Right's domestic politics, and the prospect of international adolescent sexual rights attracted a lot of attention within Christian Right circles. For the Christian Right, the recognition of children's rights has implications for parental authority over children, governmental involvement in the private world of the family and the maintenance of the traditional family form in an increasingly secular and globalised world order. The debate over adolescent sexual rights, however, raises those issues in a highly emotive context that also includes concerns about the 'radical agenda' of feminists and gays and lesbians, who are seen as subverting the social order.[5] The decision by some Christian Right organisations to become active internationally reflects a concern that the international realm is an increasingly important arena in which social relations are considered and, potentially, recast. The debate around adolescent sexual rights is part of a larger struggle by the Christian Right to contest international developments seen as anathema to a conservative Christian orthodoxy.[6]

In this chapter, I examine the debate over adolescent sexual rights, and particularly Christian Right opposition to those rights, first, to consider the nature of Christian Right international activism and, secondly, to explore some of the contradictions and tensions inherent in the Convention on the Rights of the Child. The debate around adolescent sexual rights can be seen as part of the 'discursive struggle over the meaning of childhood and the meaning of harm'.[7] Inherent in the articulation of adolescent rights is a particular definition of childhood development and childhood need. Advocates of children's human rights, in this context, see rights as playing a central role in the empowerment and protection of children, while those from the Christian Right see rights as undermining the family and thus harming the child.

My aim in this chapter is not to refute Christian Right conceptions of international human rights, nor to lend legitimacy to the Christian Right

---

5 Lucier, JP, 'Unconvential rights: children and the United Nations' (1992) 5(3) Family Policy 1, p 2.

6 These, and other themes, are explored further in Buss, D and Herman, D, *Globalizing Family Values: The Christian Right's International Campaign Against Feminism and Gay Rights,* forthcoming, Chicago: Chicago UP.

7 Smart, C, 'A history of ambivalence and conflict in the discursive construction of the "child victim" of sexual abuse' (1999) 8 SLS 391, p 407.

position. Rather, I want to consider how the Christian Right's arguments may rely upon and exploit existing contradictions or weaknesses in the Convention on the Rights of the Child. By focusing on the nature of Christian Right international activism, I hope to better understand not only Christian Right positions, but also the various ways in which human rights narratives are deployed at the international level. Christian Right international activism needs to be seen in the context of an international realm in which the language of human rights is becoming a vehicle for the contestation of social relations. Christian Right opposition, when viewed in this context, can be instructive about some of the limitations and potential pitfalls inherent in using human rights guarantees to effect change.

In the first section of this chapter, I outline the debate over adolescent sexual rights that took place at the UN in 1999, locating the debate in the context of an increasingly active international civil society. In the second section, I look more closely at Christian Right opposition to children's rights in general and adolescent sexual rights in particular. In the third section, I consider some tensions and possible contradictions in the definitions of 'child' and 'childhood' incorporated into the Convention on the Rights of the Child. This section involves an examination of Western constructions of the gendered and raced child of international rights campaigns, and the difficulties posed by attempts to advocate on behalf of the 'girl child'. In the final section, I consider how some aspects of the Convention also prove problematic for attempts to recognise adolescent sexual and reproductive rights.

SEXUAL AND REPRODUCTIVE RIGHTS

Starting in 1999, the UN hosted a series of meetings to review international implementation of the 1994 Cairo Conference on Population and Development. Known as Cairo +5 (or ICPD +5), this review process took place in various stages, culminating in a UN General Assembly Resolution adopting an extensive 106 paragraph agreement entitled 'Key actions for the further implementation of the Programme of Action of the International Conference on Population and Development'.[8] The debate over adolescent sexual rights occurred during the negotiations of that review document. As with the original Cairo Programme of Action, the Cairo +5 report is a statement of international policy affecting the objectives, scope and funding of various population and development programmes. As such, it is not a treaty, binding State behaviour, but, rather, a statement of international priorities and policies with consequent resource implications. While a technical, five year review of a

---

8 *Report of the Ad Hoc Committee of the Whole of the 21st Special Session of the General Assembly*, New York, 1 July 1999 (UN Doc A/S-21/5/Add.1) (referred to here as ICPD +5 Key Actions).

population agreement may seem an unlikely context for a debate over children's rights, the introduction of a reproductive and sexual rights framework at the original Cairo Conference provided an opening within which adolescent sexual and reproductive rights could be negotiated.

Christian Right groups see the Cairo process as particularly problematic. For these groups, international population policy is a deeply flawed international intervention in the affairs of developing countries, and reflects the influence of groups and organisations promoting abortion. The adoption of reproductive and sexual rights at the original Cairo conference generated further opposition because this was seen as not only promoting abortion, but also representing a concerted attack on the traditional family form. The detailed inclusion of adolescent sexual rights within the Cairo +5 process provided further evidence for the Christian Right of the nefarious motives of feminist non-governmental organisations (NGOs) and UN departments, such as the UN Population Fund. To an extent, the debate over adolescent sexual rights at Cairo +5 is a product of these earlier controversial negotiations over the scope and meaning of women's rights, particularly reproductive rights.

The Cairo Conference on Population and Development

In 1994, the UN hosted the third major international gathering to consider funding and provision of international programmes addressing population growth, primarily in the Third World. Intended to provide a 20 year blueprint for international population policy, the Cairo Conference was a departure from its two predecessors, not just in the scope of its review, but also in the extensive involvement of NGOs, particularly women's groups. Since the 1980s, there had been a growing demand from feminist and women's groups to rethink international population policy in a way that shifted the focus from demographic targets to women's 'reproductive health'. Largely as a result of feminist campaigning, the Cairo Programme of Action[9] adopted a human rights framework within which population policy had to be considered and implemented. This meant, in effect, that the Cairo agreement rejected earlier approaches to population policy that focused on demographic targets, often resulting in coercive 'family planning'. In its place, the Cairo Programme introduced a more holistic approach, emphasising the interrelationship between population, women's empowerment, environmental security and

---

9   Programme of Action of the International Conference on Population and Development, Cairo, Egypt, 5–13 September 1994, in *Report of the International Conference on Population and Development*, UN Doc. A/CONF.171/13/Rev.1.

development. While it is important not to overstate this shift, it represented a potential sea change in international population policy.[10]

The call for women's rights, particularly to reproductive freedom, was seen by many as evidence of a radical feminist agenda to undermine the traditional family. The Vatican, through its status as a Permanent Observer to the UN,[11] launched a major initiative to oppose the draft Cairo Programme of Action. The result was that the Cairo Conference was paralysed for several days as the Vatican squared off against governments from Canada, the US, and the European Union over language relating to reproductive health, reproductive freedom, and abortion. While compromise language on abortion was eventually reached, the Cairo debate signalled an important shift in international gatherings. Women's groups, who demonstrated a fairly sophisticated level of organisation, were able to place women's human rights firmly on the international agenda. Christian Right organisations and the Vatican began to mobilise in response to this perceived radical feminist dominance at the UN, and subsequent conferences were characterised by repeat battles over abortion, references to sexual orientation, women's rights and, more recently, children's rights.[12]

Cairo +5 and youth sex and reproductive rights

The Cairo five year review process took place in three major stages: first, The Hague Forum in February 1999, which produced a non-binding report examining progress in implementing the Cairo Programme of Action; secondly, a Preparatory Committee (PrepCom) meeting in New York, in March 1999, which prepared a draft report for consideration and adoption by the UN General Assembly at the third stage of the process – the UN General Assembly meeting in July 1999.

While The Hague Forum, which included separate NGO, youth and parliamentarian representatives, was seen by some as providing a 'blunt and

10   Copelon, R and Petchesky, R, 'Toward an interdependent approach to reproductive and sexual rights as human rights: reflections on the ICPD and beyond', in Schuler, MA (ed), *From Basic Needs to Basic Rights: Women's Claim to Human Rights*, 1995, Washington; Institute for Women, Law and Development, p 343; McIntosh, CA and Finkle, JL, 'The Cairo Conference on Population and Development: a new paradigm?' (1995) 21 Population and Development Rev 233; Sen, G, 'The world programme of action: a new paradigm for population' (1995) 37 Environment 10, pp 10-5, 34-37.

11   The Vatican is a Permanent Observer to the UN, which entitles it to rights of attendance and representation that are somewhat less than those given to a full State member, but much more than it would have as an NGO (see Kunz, J, 'The status of the Holy See in international law' (1952) 49 AJIL 308). Although the correct term for the Vatican in its UN capacity is the 'Holy See', I use 'the Vatican' for clarity and continuity.

12   For a discussion of the Vatican's position at the Beijing Conference, see Buss, D, 'Robes, relics and rights: the Vatican and the Beijing Conference on Women' (1998) 7(3) SLS 339.

hard hitting' report,[13] it was the Youth Forum that produced the most interesting final document. The Youth Forum, which included youth delegates from around the world,[14] produced a fairly radical and innovative document calling for, among other things, sexual and reproductive health services for youth, sexual education, including education on 'sexual expression and orientation' in all levels of schooling, and a specific budget allocation for youth sexual and reproductive health services, which were defined as including 'abortion and emergency contraception'.[15]

While some of the Youth Forum recommendations were incorporated into The Hague Forum report,[16] very few survived to the final agreement adopted by the UN General Assembly. The PrepCom meetings in New York became the focus of a concerted and highly mobilised Christian Right campaign to oppose abortion, women's human rights and adolescent sexual and reproductive rights. Reflecting the active participation of youth delegates at The Hague, the PrepCom document under negotiation contained several references to adolescent needs and included a separate section on adolescent sexual and reproductive health. All of the references to adolescents were controversial, but the primary focus of debate concerned the following:

(1) adolescent access to medical services, including contraceptives, without parental involvement;

(2) sex education in schools;

(3) references to protecting adolescents from 'unsafe abortion'.[17]

The final text adopted by the UN General Assembly included compromise language in all references to adolescent rights and needs. For example, adolescent rights are balanced with language concerning the 'appropriateness'

---

13 Center for Reproductive Law and Policy, *ICPD +5, Gains for Women Despite Opposition*, undated, New York, p 3, available at www.crlp.org.

14 The Youth Forum was organised by the World Population Foundation in collaboration with the UN Population Fund. The close alliance between these institutions and youth delegates has been criticised by Christian Right organisations as leading to a distorted and pro-family planning bias in the Youth Forum Report (see Catholic Family Human Rights Institute, 'Pro-Life youth organise to counter radical groups at UN conferences' (1999) 2(45) Friday Fax, 17 September). However, a number of delegates to the Youth Forum issued reservations to the inclusion of 'sexual orientation' and 'abortion' on the basis of their 'religious and ethical values and cultural backgrounds' (*Report of the Youth Forum ICPD +5*, The Hague, Netherlands, 6–7 February 1999, Appendix, available at www.ngoforum.org/files/youth/final) ('Youth Forum Report').

15 *Ibid*, Youth Forum Report.

16 *Report of the International Forum for the Operational Review and Appraisal of the Implementation of the Programme of Action of the International Conference on Population and Development*, The Netherlands, 8–12 February 1999 ('Hague Forum Report').

17 For a discussion of the final negotiations and the controversy surrounding abortion, see 'Summary of the 21st Special Session of the General Assembly (ICPD +5)' (1999) 6(61) Earth Negotiations Bulletin, 5 July.

of service provision (para 73(a)), respect for cultural values and religious beliefs (para 73(a)), the active involvement of parents (para 21(b)) and the 'central role of families, parents and other legal guardians in educating their children' (para 73(d)).[18] In addition, the final document does not include language specifically protecting adolescents from unsafe abortions, nor does it include a designated funding allocation for programmes directed at adolescents.

THE CHRISTIAN RIGHT AND CHILDREN'S RIGHTS

While Christian Right organisations appear relatively satisfied with the final text adopted by the General Assembly,[19] the debate over adolescent sexual rights clearly signals a disturbing trend in international law for Christian Right activists for a number of reasons. First, adolescent sexual rights, as an extension of children's rights more generally, are viewed as problematic in many respects, but principally because they are seen as undermining parental authority over children. Secondly, adolescent sexual rights are seen as 'sexualising' children, robbing them of their childhood. Thirdly, these attempts to 'sexualise' children are considered to be part of a larger, nefarious agenda by radical feminists and gays and lesbians to undermine the traditional family form.

Parental authority and children's rights

Within some Christian Right literature, there is an attempt to distinguish between children's rights as applied in the US and those for the 'developing world'. Many Christian Right organisations limit their critique of the Convention on the Rights of Child to its potential impact in the US. The Family Research Council, for example, argues that, in countries where abuses such as 'sexual and industrial child slavery' are already illegal, children's rights only contribute to the multiplying 'violations of parents' rights'.[20] The Convention, when applied to the US, is seen as threatening because it represents an externally imposed standard that interferes with US sovereignty and children's rights in general enable the State (or the UN) to intervene in families.

---

18 *Op cit*, ICPD +5 Key Actions, fn 8, paras 21, 73.

19 CWA, *21st Special Assembly of the United Nations General Assembly: Cairo +5 Conference*, 2 July 1999, p 3, available at www.cwfa.org.

20 Family Research Council, *Update: United Nations Convention on the Rights of the Child*, 22 February 1995.

Not all Christian Right organisations are unanimous in this view. During the Cairo +5 negotiations, some Christian Right groups, as well as the Vatican, argued that the Convention and the original Cairo Programme of Action set an acceptable international standard for parental involvement in adolescent access to reproductive health services. The different position taken by some Christian Right organisations reflects, in part, a Protestant and Catholic divide in approach to international human rights. Conservative Protestant organisations, such as Concerned Women for America or the Eagle Forum, historically have had a strong isolationist stance and oppose any international developments that involve the US. In contrast, Catholic organisations tend to be supportive in principle of 'fundamental' human rights and oppose only those rights they see as 'new' or inconsistent with foundational human rights documents, such as the Universal Declaration on Human Rights.

Christian Right groups are unanimous, however, in their view that adolescent sexual rights, as a 'new' development in the area of children's rights, represent an attempt to undermine parental authority. For example, Austin Ruse, director of the Catholic Family Human Rights Institute, argues that 'The Cairo process is a blatant attempt to separate parents from their children on issues of sexual health and education'.[21] The prospect of sex education in schools is seen, in this regard, as particularly threatening. The Vatican issued a detailed statement of interpretation of the Cairo +5 document which defined 'the education of "young people"' as 'primarily and fundamentally the right, duty, and responsibility of parents'.[22]

The reference to parental rights in this context encapsulates the Christian Right's central argument against children's rights, which is that children do not need protection within the traditional nuclear family. The distinction drawn by some Christian Right groups between children's rights for the developing world and the US is an extension of this view. Protecting children from outside forces (the factory or the sexual predator) is acceptable. Protecting them from their parents is more controversial, precisely because it suggests that the traditional family form can be problematic. To the extent that children's rights empower children against adult, including parental authority, they are seen as threatening. Rights that empower children are problematic because they might be used against parents. In much of the Christian Right literature critiquing either the Convention on the Rights of the Child or the recent Cairo +5 process, the focus is on the chaos that would ensue if either of these documents were implemented in the US. Chaos in this context is defined

---

21 Quoted in *op cit*, CWA, fn 4, p 1.

22 'Official Position of the Holy See on the Key Actions for the Further Implementation of the Programme of Action of the International Conference on Population and Development', 2 July 1999, in *Statement of the Holy See at the Concluding Session of the 21st Special Session of the General Assembly for the Overall Review and Appraisal of the Implementation of the Programme of Action of the International Conference on Population and Development*, para 7, available at www.unfpa.org/icpd/icpdmain.htm.

through various examples of the wilful child: 'Does this mean that a child can assert his right to say anything he wants to his parents at the dinner table? Does this mean that the government will assist the child to join a cult or select a different church from the one his parents attend?'[23]

Sexualising children

For the Christian Right, adolescent sexual rights are not about addressing a health or rights issue for adolescents: 'It's about an agenda to sexualize your children.'[24] CWA, for example, argues that the promotion of adolescent sexual rights is part of (rather than a reflection of) a trend in which children are becoming sexually active at a younger and younger age: CWA makes a link between arguments for adolescent sexual rights and incidences in the US of groups of 'kids' engaging in sexual activity.[25] The implication is that children are susceptible to sexual corruption. Children, on this view, are seen as latently sexual, but are kept innocent through laws, parents, social norms and so on, which isolate them from the realm of the sexual.[26]

Sex education in schools is seen by the Christian Right as part of this campaign to sexualise children. According to Christian Right organisations, provisions in the draft Cairo +5 document relating to sex education were more than just a call for access to information. They constituted a demand that 'adolescents as young as 10 receive graphic information through programs that encourage sexual activity'.[27] For the Christian Right, sex education in schools is literally interpreted as 'sex training', teaching children how to be sexually active, rather than offering children protection from sexually transmitted diseases or teenage pregnancies. Consequently, for the Christian Right, sex education endangers children and places the most vulnerable members of society, girl children, at particular risk.[28]

The UN agenda against children

Within the Christian Right, there is a feeling that the UN is largely ineffectual and has become dominated by 'special interests'; radical feminists, gays and lesbians, and communists.[29] For the most part, Christian Right organisations

---

23 *Op cit*, Eagle Forum, fn 4.

24 *Op cit*, CWA, fn 19.

25 See *op cit*, CWA, fn 4; Wright, W, 'Exporting teen sex: UNFPA's radical agenda', 27 August 1999, available at www.cwfa.org.

26 Evans, DT, 'Falling angels? The material construction of children as sexual citizens' (1994) 2 IJCR 1, pp 5–7.

27 *Ibid*, Wright, p 1.

28 See, eg, *op cit*, CWA, fn 4.

identify 'radical feminists' and the UN Population Fund as the principal motivators behind this 'campaign against children'. The 'homosexual' threat appears to come from radical feminists, identified as 'lesbians'.[30]

For some Christian Right activists, the campaign for children's rights is a product of a larger trend, in which the international realm is becoming increasingly important to radical elements, such as feminists. According to this view, radical groups who failed at the domestic political level[31] have taken their campaigns to the less democratic international sphere.[32] To an extent, this shift is seen as consistent with a larger international focus in which organisations such as the UN, the World Trade Organisation and so on are strengthened and domestic, particularly US, influence is lessened. Claims for children's rights are an example of international actors – feminists, the UN – interfering in the domestic politics of the US and the private lives of families. More importantly, children's rights are seen as the vehicle by which these international actors seek to co-opt populations into their globalising projects: 'Not only does the UN want control over every aspect of our lives and every corner of the globe, they also want control over future generations. And the UN targets youth to advance their agenda.'[33]

At Cairo +5, the Christian Right framed these various objections to children's rights within two main critiques of the provisions relating to adolescents. First, the Christian Right noted that the term 'adolescent' is defined by the UN to include children aged 10–19 years old.[34] This definition of 'adolescent', which is also used by the World Health Organisation, was seen as evidence of the global agenda of radical feminists to target children. Christian Right publications suggest that while 'adolescent' may appear to be a relatively neutral term applying to 'teens', it disingenuously also includes 'children as young as 10 years'. In this way, argues Kay Balmforth, Executive Director for NGO Family Voice, the term 'adolescent' is indicative of a global agenda to target 'younger and younger children'.[35]

Secondly, this sexualisation of 'younger and younger children', according to the Christian Right, is robbing them of their childhood by undermining their innocence: 'Rather than exposing our children to such sexualization, we

29 Interviews by author with Eagle Forum, Catholic Family Human Rights Institute and CWA, October 1999.
30 Interview by author with CWA, October 1999.
31 See Thomson, Chapter 9, in this volume.
32 Interviews by author with Eagle Forum, Catholic Family Human Rights Institute and CWA, October 1999.
33 CWA, *Stealing their Childhood: The UN Agenda Against Generation Y*, 25 February 1999, p 2, available at www.cwfa.org.
34 CWA, *United Nations Cairo +5 Preparatory Conference*, 26 March 1999, available at www.cwfa.org.
35 Quoted in a Catholic Family Human Rights Institute press release, *Controversy Surrounds Cairo +5 PrepCom Pro-Life Push Promised*, undated.

should protect our young children and prosecute those who steal their innocence.'[36] The provision of sex education or reproductive health services does not protect children, according to the Christian Right; instead, it exposes them to more harm: 'the UN's actions and suggestions serve only to make the world's girls more vulnerable.'[37]

Thus, while Christian Right opposition to adolescent sexual rights is, on one level, consistent with a resistance to children's rights more generally, it is framed in terms that appear to affirm a particular model of children's rights. In the language of the Christian Right, what is needed is further or better protection of children. At Cairo +5, this protectionist argument conflicted with what are arguably attempts to give greater expression to children's autonomy through the recognition of adolescent sexual rights. The Christian Right's 'protectionist' position, while opposed to the so called 'empowerment' approach of sexual rights, finds support within the terms of the Convention on the Rights of the Child. It is in this respect that the Christian Right's intervention at Cairo is most significant.

While the Convention on the Rights of the Child has been hailed as the most universally endorsed human rights agreement, the Christian Right's opposition to adolescent sexual rights, I argue, exposes and exploits a lack of international consensus on the meaning and limits of children's rights. First, Christian Right arguments concerning childhood innocence resonate with dominant Western ideologies of childhood, which have been incorporated into the Convention. As I will argue below, Christian Right emphasis on childhood innocence highlights the centrality of this 'characteristic' to the definition of childhood and the consequent difficulty of introducing autonomy for children. Secondly, the Christian Right's arguments about the meaning of 'adolescence' as a social category exposes an uncertainty about the definition of childhood and particularly childhood's end. This becomes problematic, I argue, when attempts are made within a human rights context to reflect the 'evolving capacities' of children.

INTERNATIONAL RIGHTS OF THE CHILD

The debate over adolescent sexual rights, although occurring during the negotiation of a population and development agreement, builds on, and potentially extends, international agreement on children's rights. In 1989, the international community agreed the Convention on the Rights of the Child, which superseded two earlier declarations[38] on children's rights (1924 and

---

36 *Op cit*, CWA, fn 34.
37 *Op cit*, CWA, fn 34.

1959).[39] The Convention differs from its predecessors in many respects, but, for my purposes, most significantly in the range and scope of recognised rights. Geraldine Van Bueren divides the 41 substantive articles into four categories: '... the participation of children in decisions affecting their own destiny; the protection of children against discrimination and all forms of neglect and exploitation; the prevention of harm to children; and the provision of assistance for their basic needs.'[40]

While the provisions relating to basic needs include fairly predictable references to health services (Art 24), social security (Art 26), education (Arts 28 and 29) and the rights to an adequate standard of living (Arts 24 and 27), a more anomalous 'right to leisure' (Art 31) is also provided. The Convention calls for the protection of children from discrimination (Art 2), all forms of neglect and exploitation (Art 3) and sexual exploitation and sexual abuse (Art 34). Reflecting the reality of more 'global' threats, the Convention also includes protection from trafficking (Art 38), participation in armed conflict (Art 38), use of drugs (Art 33) and economic exploitation through work (Art 32). A number of provisions deal with children's relationship with their family through adoption, removal and so on (Arts 9, 10, 11, 19, 20 and 21). The most controversial provisions in the Convention concern the participation rights of the child, such as rights to freedom of expression (Arts 12 and 13), freedom of thought, conscience and religion (Art 14) and freedom of association (Art 15).

The Convention, generally applauded by children's rights advocates and scholars,[41] is seen as providing an innovative approach to children's rights for three main reasons. First, by stipulating that the best interests of the child must be a 'primary consideration' in dealing with children (Art 3); secondly, by recognising children's rights to self expression and freedom of thought (Arts 12–15); and, thirdly, by recognising that the 'responsibilities, rights and duties of parents' should be exercised 'in a manner consistent with the evolving capacities of the child' (Art 5; see, also, Art 14). Together, these aspects suggest a Convention that is much more child-centred than the two earlier declarations and has been described as initiating a 'sudden and dramatic change' in thinking about child protection issues, such as children's work.[42]

---

38 Declarations are resolutions of the UN General Assembly and are not as authoritative in international law as treaties or Conventions.

39 van Bueren, G, *The International Law on the Rights of the Child*, 1995, The Hague: Martinus Nijhoff, pp 7–12.

40 *Ibid*, p 15.

41 Myers, E, 'Considering child labour: the changing terms, issues and actors at the international level' (1999) 6 Childhood 13; *ibid*, Van Bueren, p 45; Alston, P, 'The best interests principle: towards a reconciliation of culture and human rights', in Alston, P (ed), *The Best Interests of the Child: Reconciling Culture and Human Rights*, 1994, Oxford: Clarendon.

42 *Ibid*, Myers, p 14.

The introduction of adolescent sexual rights in the Cairo +5 process can be seen as an important step in operationalising some of the potentially transformative provisions of the Convention. First, the Youth Forum itself and its call for greater participation of adolescents in the provision of adolescent health services reflect a commitment to the autonomy rights of children. The premise of the Youth Forum, and its resulting recommendations, appears to be the need to empower, rather than simply protect, children. Secondly, this call for empowerment explicitly recognises that some categories of children – specifically, the girl child – are more at risk than others. The Youth Forum Report addresses gender inequality and calls for programmes and service provision to address the different health needs of women and men.[43] Thirdly, the articulation of sexual rights for adolescents introduces an intermediate category between childhood and adulthood – adolescence – which attracts its own range of rights, in this case, sexual rights. In this way, sexual rights can be seen as an attempt to recognise and give meaning to the 'evolving capacities' of children.

In the following discussion, I examine the terms of the Convention in light of the Cairo +5 debate over adolescent sexuality. Despite the many positive aspirations of the Convention, as outlined above, I argue that the Convention both reinforces and reflects a Western construction of childhood defined in terms of innocence and vulnerability. Children's rights, in this model, function to protect that innocence. The result is a normative definition of childhood that is in tension with those aspects of the Convention that provide for autonomy rights and evolving capacities of the child.

Western childhoods and Third World children

One of the criticisms made against the Convention is that it is part of the 'globalisation of Western ideas of childhood'.[44] Within Western narratives, four themes are said to shape the definition of childhood:

(1) that the child is set apart temporally as different, through the calculation of age;

(2) that the child is deemed to have a special nature, determined by nature;

(3) that the child is innocent; and

(4) therefore is vulnerably dependent.[45]

---

43 See, eg, *op cit*, Youth Forum Report, fn 14, provisions in the sexual and reproductive health chapter, paras 4 and 5.

44 Jenks, C, *Childhood*, 1996, London: Routledge, p 123; Burman, E, 'Innocents abroad: Western fantasies of childhood and the iconography of emergencies' (1994) 18 Disasters 238, p 242.

45 Hockey, J and James, A, *Growing Up and Growing Old: Ageing and Dependency in the Life Course*, 1996, London: Sage, as cited in *ibid*, Jenks.

Henry Jenkins argues that childhood within Western thought is envisioned as a 'utopian space, separate from adult cares and worries, free from sexuality, outside of social divisions, closer to nature and the primitive world'.[46] This ideal of childhood fits comfortably within dominant Western constructions of the private world of the family.[47] In this ideal, the family functions to protect children not just from physical harm, but also from knowledge or experience that would dispel the innocence of childhood. Jenks argues that childhood is most often associated with innocence, through which the child is confirmed in its 'cultural identity as a passive and unknowing dependent, and therefore as a member of a social group utterly disempowered – but for good, altruistic reasons'.[48] Narratives of childhood innocence define vulnerability as an essential characteristic of 'childhood'.

The Convention on the Rights of the Child both incorporates and perpetuates this particular Western ideal of childhood. Olsen argues that the Convention reinforces 'and presuppose[s] a very conventional notion of the family as the centre of affective life'.[49] The reification of the traditional nuclear family serves to reinforce both dominant ideologies about the safety of the family and a particular conception of childhood vulnerability that is at the heart of children's rights. According to Mower, the Convention 'breaks new ground' by granting children rights on the basis of their status as 'a particularly vulnerable member of society'.[50]

The rights included in the Convention are directed at securing for children a childhood spent within the 'safe' confines of the nuclear family. For example, the Convention includes rights to protect children from a variety of threats from the State, global forces and, to a lesser extent, their parents. But the Convention also gives children rights to leisure, education and freedom from exploitation through paid work. This list of rights reflects a particular, largely Western, model, where childhood is defined as that utopian time of play and fun, where the stages of child development are marked by progression through school.

Burman argues that the Convention can be seen as part of the larger international child protection project which, despite aspirations to a more inclusive model of childhood, perpetuates and imposes Western norms. Together with the vast array of children's aid agencies, she argues that the

---

46 Jenkins, H, 'Introduction: childhood innocence and other modern myths', in Jenkins, H (ed), *The Children's Culture Reader*, 1998, New York: New York UP.

47 Olsen, F, 'The family and the market: a study of ideology and legal reform' (1983) 96(7) Harv L Rev 1497. See Lim and Roche, Chapter 12, in this volume.

48 *Op cit*, Jenks, fn 44, p 124.

49 Olsen, F, 'Children's rights: some feminist approaches to the United Nations Convention on the Rights of the Child' (1992) 6 IJLF 192, p 195.

50 Mower, AG, *The Convention on the Rights of the Child: International Law Support for Children*, 1997, Westport: Greenwood, p 3.

Convention exports 'idealised models of western childhood ... for mandatory consumption by the rest of the world'.[51] In this way, 'childhood becomes an entity, the deprivation of which constitutes a violation of human rights'.[52] While this idealised vision of childhood is out of reach for many of the world's children, it remains a powerful ideology that shapes and constrains the conception of children's rights within the Convention and elsewhere.

The ideology of childhood innocence both justifies rights for children, in the name of granting them a 'true' childhood, and, paradoxically, justifies the limitation of those rights. The Christian Right, for example, employ the language of childhood innocence to oppose adolescent sexual rights. Conference bulletins published by CWA used headlines such as 'The end of innocence: how the UN stole childhood'[53] or 'Stealing their childhood: the UN agenda against Generation Y'.[54] In this language, the Christian Right is evoking a protectionist stance to children similar to that found in the Convention. Both the Christian Right and the Convention rely on a vision of childhood that is both entity and abstraction. This Childhood is an idealised aspiration that functions concretely to police the boundaries of acceptable conduct of children and adults.

Childhood, as it is used in the Convention, becomes more than a description of a transient phase. It is a 'permanent social category',[55] based on which, rights and benefits are extended. In this conception, 'childhood' is a 'totalizing concept ... [that] concretely describes a community that at some time has everybody as its member'.[56] It is difficult in this narrative of childhood innocence/vulnerability to consider the ways in which childhood is a fragmented and varied experience.[57]

Although much sociological and anthropological work has been done on the varied social and cultural meanings assigned to childhood,[58] the Convention does not recognise the ways in which the experience of 'childhood' can vary along gender, class or racial lines. With the exception of limited provisions concerning children with disabilities (Art 23), refugee

---

51 *Op cit*, Burman, fn 44, p 242. See, also, *op cit*, Jenks, fn 44, p 123.

52 *Op cit*, Burman, fn 44.

53 *Op cit*, CWA, fn 4.

54 *Op cit*, CWA, fn 33.

55 Qvortrup, J, *Childhood as a Social Phenomenon: Lessons from an International Project*, 1993, Vienna: European Centre for Social Welfare, Policy and Research, as cited in Knutsson, KE, 'Children and the future: worthy causes or worthy citizens?' (1996) 1 Development 12, p 13. See, also, *op cit*, Jenks, fn 44, p 6.

56 *Op cit*, Jenks, fn 44, p 6.

57 *Op cit*, Jenks, fn 44, p 122; *op cit*, Burman, fn 44, p 240.

58 Boydon, J, 'Social and cultural meanings of childhood' (1996) 1 Development 18, p 18; *op cit*, Jenks, fn 44; Stephens, S, 'Introduction: children and the politics of culture in "late capitalism"', in Stephens, S (ed), *Children and the Politics of Culture*, 1995, Princeton: Princeton UP.

children (Art 22) and cultural rights of minority and indigenous children (Art 30), the Convention assumes a universal experience of childhood, and hence a shared interest in particular human rights guarantees.

This construction of childhood as an undifferentiated social category is clearly problematic in a world divided by economic, social and gender inequality. Not only is 'childhood' defined differently within and among cultures, but the experience of 'childhood' varies with economic and social factors. In addition, childhood 'risk' and vulnerability are variable. The definition of childhood in terms of a generalised state of innocence and vulnerability serves to construct both a universal childhood 'need' – for rights, protection and so on – and a particular population of children in need, namely non-Western children.

Earlier, I discussed a distinction within Christian Right thought between children's rights as applied to the Third World and those applied to the US. For some Christian Right organisations, an international body of rights for Third World children was understandable, if not wholly supportable, but was seen as completely inappropriate for the US. This split vision concerning international human rights is not isolated to the Christian Right. While human rights instruments are meant to be universally applicable, there is a sense in which rights are more immediately of concern to a Third World defined in terms of poverty and human rights abuses. It is difficult, if not impossible, to imagine international human rights without reference to dominant images of suffering and destitution in the Third World. The result is a tendency to elide international human rights with the chaos, destruction, corruption and desperation that defines the Third World for the West.

In the context of children's rights, the failure to make explicit the different experiences of childhood reinforces a gendered and racialised construction of the 'child' who is in need of protection. As Burman has demonstrated, media representations, including aid appeals, construct the Third World in feminised and infantilised terms.[59] Aid appeals often focus on children – usually young girls – who are in desperate need of assistance from the economic North.[60] This narrative, which echoes colonial paternalism, positions the masculine, adult North as the rescuer – through the 'donation' of money, food, knowledge – of the 'failed' and needy South.[61]

This poses a problem for women's rights activists who have sought to address the human rights needs of the girl child. While much of feminist activism at the level of international law and policy has focused on making

---

59 See *op cit*, Burman, fn 44, pp 241–43.
60 See *op cit*, Burman, fn 44, pp 245, 247.
61 See *op cit*, Burman, fn 44, p 241.

women visible in the male dominated international realm,[62] the girl child is problematically both visible and invisible. She is visible in terms of her representation of Third World need in a way that serves to reinforce the separateness of the Third World. But, she is invisible in terms of her particular needs defined by gender, race and economic inequality. Thus, the feminist project of 'including' the girl child in human rights protection becomes a difficult balancing act of making the needs of the girl child visible while challenging her symbolic representation as the 'poster child' of Third World 'Otherness'.

COMPLICATING CHILDHOOD: THE DILEMMA OF 'THE GIRL CHILD'

In 1995, at the Fourth World Conference on Women in Beijing, China, a concerted effort was made to highlight the particular vulnerabilities of the 'girl child', which had largely been ignored within international child protection, including human rights, initiatives.[63] The final agreement from that Conference, the Beijing Platform for Action,[64] contains a separate chapter on the girl child (Chapter L), which includes strategic objectives in the areas of discrimination against the girl child (Strategic objective L.1), cultural attitudes and practices (Strategic objective L.2), including health and nutrition, and labour discrimination (Strategic objectives L.5 and L.6), the rights of the girl child, (Strategic objective L.3), violence against the girl child (Strategic objective L.7) and the role of the family in improving the status of the girl child (Strategic objective L.9).

In many respects, the inclusion of these provisions within the Beijing Platform for Action represents a significant step in addressing some of the weaknesses in the international rights of the child. First, the Beijing Platform exposes the glaring omission of the girl child from the Convention. By explicitly articulating the ways in which the girl child is particularly vulnerable to human rights abuses, the Beijing Platform draws attention to the varied experience of childhood, and the inadequacies of 'childhood' as a social category for the purposes of human rights guarantees. Secondly, the Beijing Platform highlights the many ways in which girl children are susceptible to

---

62   Buss, D, 'Going global: feminist international law theory and the public/private divide', in Boyd, SB (ed), *Challenging the Public/Private Divide: Feminism, Law, and Public Policy*, 1997, Toronto: Toronto UP, p 360; Charlesworth, H, Chinkin, C and Wright, S, 'Feminist approaches to international law' (1991) 85 AJIL 613.

63   An exception to this is the Cairo Programme of Action, which refers to the sexual and reproductive rights and needs of girl children and, in a more limited context, adolescents.

64   Available at www.un.org.

discriminatory treatment even within the supposedly 'safe' confines of the nuclear family.

While the inclusion of this language is, at one level, important in highlighting the human rights needs of the girl child and the inadequacies of the Convention in addressing those needs, at another level, it is consistent with the gendered and raced conception of the 'needy' Third World discussed above. The human rights abuses of young girls – 'female genital mutilation', 'child brides', 'young mothers' – are, in many respects, the slogans for the modern human rights movement.[65] Thus, the recognition of human rights abuses suffered by the girl child within the family, for example, will not necessarily constitute a challenge to the dominance of 'safe family' ideology in the Convention. Rather, it might be marginalised as a peculiarly Third World concern and indicative of the many ways in which Third World children are deprived of a 'natural' childhood,[66] supposedly enjoyed by children in the West.

I am not suggesting by this that any attempt to address the rights of the girl child is necessarily doomed to failure. Rather, my point is that international recognition of the rights of the girl child may not necessarily challenge her historic marginalisation if that recognition reinforces problematic conceptions of Third World need. Alongside of the rights of the girl child must be a specific recognition of the inequality that shapes the meaning and experience of childhood. Relying on an unspecified 'childhood' as a category for rights protection, whether in the Convention on the Rights of the Child or elsewhere, is problematic precisely because the false universality of 'childhood' masks the particularity of Childhood. The result is that, while the Convention contains many promising aspects, it is also problematically vague and imprecise, yielding contradictory and confused definitions of 'childhood' and 'childhood need'. The interventions of the Christian Right at Cairo +5, while clearly motivated by a particular political or religious agenda, are important in exposing how that confusion can prevent attempts to give meaningful expression to children's rights.

Adolescence and the evolving capacities of 'the child'

As discussed above, the Christian Right characterised the promotion of adolescent sexual rights as the sexualisation of young children and as constituting an attack on childhood innocence. This language is quite

---

65 Eg, as Green and Lim have demonstrated, 'female genital mutilation' has become a standard feature in British human rights law classes: 'What is this thing about female circumcision? Legal education and human rights' (1998) 7 SLS 365.

66 *Op cit*, Burman, fn 44, p 242.

powerful, not only in its invocation of fears about the safety of vulnerable children, but also in its resonance with assumptions about the innocence of children. The types of rights included in the draft agreement at Cairo +5 were directed at 'children' who were sexually active. The sexual 'child', however, poses a problem for a conception of children's rights premised on an idealised childhood innocence. Sexual knowledge or behaviour blurs the 'heavily invested boundary' between childhood and adulthood.[67] This is not to suggest that, within dominant Western narratives, children are not seen as sexual.[68] Rather, it is sexual activity and sexual knowledge that remove the child from the realm of the innocent and, consequently, from the definition of 'child'. For example, in international population policy there is a tendency to refer to young mothers not as 'children' or 'adolescents', but as 'women'.[69] The implication here is that, despite the often very young age of some 'mothers', childbirth (and presumably sexual relations) transforms them into 'young' adults, regardless of other personality or social factors that might otherwise define them as children.[70]

By framing their objections to adolescent sexual rights in terms of the vulnerability of the child, Christian Right organisations highlight this fundamental tension in the concept of the sexual child. It could be argued that the use of the term 'adolescent' is important in this context because it distances the 'child' of human rights protection from the sexual activity of 'adolescence'. While this is true, Christian Right interventions once again are illustrative of some of the difficulties with this approach.

The Christian Right argue that the proponents of adolescent sexual rights used a confusing array of terms, such as 'youth' and 'adolescent', to obscure the sexualisation of 'the child'. Indeed, the terms employed by the UN and related organisations are not straightforward. In a 1998 agreed statement, the World Health Organisation, the UN Children's Fund and the UN Population Fund provided the following categorisation of young women and men:

Adolescent:	10 to 19 years.
Youth:	15 to 24 years.
Young people:	10 to 24 years.[71]

---

67 *Op cit*, Burman, fn 44, p 241.

68 *Op cit*, Evans, fn 26, p 5.

69 Center for Reproductive Law and Policy, *Implementing Adolescent Reproductive Rights through the Convention on the Rights of the Child*, undated, p 1, available at www.crlp.org.

70 See, eg, Cairo Programme of Action, para 7.41, which, although referring to the problems of very young girls having children, invariably refers to these girls as either 'young mothers' or 'women'. The implication is that, no matter how young these 'mothers' are, the very fact of their motherhood makes their childhood untenable.

71 UN Population Fund, *State of World Population*, 1997, p 37, as cited in *ibid*, Center for Reproductive Law and Policy, p 2.

These terms are deployed in different contexts presumably to convey different stages and contexts of child development. For example, in the Cairo Programme of Action, a sub-section of Chapter VI (Population Growth and Structure) is entitled 'Children and youth', and refers variably to the needs of children, youth, adolescents and young women. It is clear in this section that each category – child, youth, adolescent and young woman – has a distinct meaning and represents a different stage in 'child' development, though the exact contours of those stages are not clear.

In addition to the obvious difficulties in decoding the meaning of 'adolescent', 'youth' and 'young person', the use of these terms points to a larger tension in the area of adolescent sexual rights: how to give effect to the evolving capacities of the child. The introduction of various terms like 'adolescent' and 'youth' is clearly meant to identify separate stages of development that mark 'young people' as having moved beyond 'childhood' without necessarily having entered adulthood.[72] The transition through childhood to adulthood is culturally determined and generally defined in terms of either biological events – puberty, for example – or a set age limit.[73] The introduction of 'adolescence' and 'youth' suggests the possibility of an evolutionary approach, recognising that capacity may evolve alongside biological change. The difficulty with this, however, is that adolescence, like childhood, is defined by a predetermined age range, which undermines attempts to give expression to evolving capacities and universalises an experience of adolescence based on Western assumptions and priorities.

The first Article of the Convention on the Rights of the Child defines a child as 'every human being below the age of 18 years' unless domestic law provides for a lower age of majority. An exception to this is found in Art 38(2), which provides that children as young as 15 years can be drafted into military service. Both of these provisions rely on a chronological marker as determining the end of childhood and the start of adulthood. As discussed above, these age absolutes are potentially limited by the inclusion of language recognising the 'evolving capacities' of children (see Arts 5 and 14), but it is not clear how, if at all, the evolving capacities of children will be balanced against the chronological markers of childhood and adulthood. In the face of absolute age definitions, it is difficult to implement a workable recognition of evolving capacities that takes seriously changing abilities of young people, but which can still incorporate these 'able' young people into an often problematic 'childhood' of innocence of vulnerability.

---

72 Wyn, J and White, R, *Rethinking Youth*, 1997, London: Sage, p 11.
73 Stainton Rogers, R and Stainton Rogers, W, *Stories of Childhood: Shifting Agendas of Childhood Concern*, 1992, New York: Harvester Wheatsheaf, p 142. See Bridgeman, Chapter 11, in this volume, for discussion of this boundary.

This difficulty is highlighted by Christian Right arguments that insist on placing the 'child' at the centre of the adolescent sexual rights debate. In doing so, the Christian Right both reinforce the definition of child in terms of chronological age and play to ideologies of childhood innocence that make 'sexual rights' untenable.

The definition of 'adolescence' in terms of upper and lower age limits (that is, 10–19 years) incorporates a similarly problematic approach, positioning biology, and not some other characteristic, as definitive. As Wyn and White have argued, adolescence 'assumes the existence of essential characteristics in young people because of their age, focusing on the assumed link between physical growth and social identity'.[74] This generalisation functions to erase differences between youth, positioning the 'masculine, white, middle class experience as the norm'.[75] Problematically, in the context of international children's rights, 'adolescence' also ignores the role of other institutions and relations of power which shape the experience and meaning of youth:[76]

> On a global scale, social and economic changes, which affect remote, small scale and large urban communities alike, have a significant impact on the meaning and experience of 'growing up'. Although the impact of these changes is far reaching, it does not mean that the outcomes for young people are all the same – the social processes which affect the experience of growing up serve to differentiate groups of young people from each other, sharpening and reinforcing deeper social divisions rather than breaking them down.[77]

In the context of the Cairo +5 process, the categories of 'adolescence' and 'youth' contribute to a problematic generalisation of youth experience. For example, at Cairo +5, adolescent sexual rights were advocated largely without reference to the varied experience of youth and the implications that this might have for their sexual and reproductive needs. While the Youth Forum Report contains some specific recognition of gender relations and their impact on the health needs of young women, it is silent about other economic, political and social inequalities that impact upon children in different ways. The result is that the Report contains a set of relatively generic recommendations that are disturbingly silent about issues of concern to large numbers of youth. For example, HIV/AIDS infection in young people, particularly in South East Asia and Sub-Saharan Africa, is becoming a devastating problem.[78] According to a background paper prepared for the Youth Forum: 'Young people under age 25 account for half of all HIV infections. Every minute, five young people under age 25 are infected with

---

74 *Op cit*, Wyn and White, fn 72, p 12.
75 *Op cit*, Wyn and White, fn 72, p 13.
76 *Op cit*, Wyn and White, fn 72.
77 *Op cit*, Wyn and White, fn 72, pp 17–18.
78 See, eg, Youth Forum Background Paper, *Sexual and Reproductive Health of Young People*, 28 January 1999, p 1.

HIV, predominantly in South East Asia and Sub-Saharan Africa, with 2.6 million young people infected every year.'[79] Despite the significance of HIV/AIDS to large groups of children, no mention of this is made in the Youth Forum Report,[80] nor is there any recognition of the particular vulnerability of young women to infection.[81]

As with childhood, the generalisation of 'adolescence' as a universally shared experience both erases the different experiences that shape the process of 'growing up' and normalises Western assumptions about this experience. Just as 'childhood' echoes with Western ideologies of the child, so too do 'adolescent' and 'youth'. 'Youth', in the Anglo-American context, was initially associated with male threat to the stability of society.[82] While 'youth' has evolved over time to include other gendered contexts and meanings – for example, 'young mothers' – it is still depicted as a time of problematic transition. Griffin's work demonstrates that, in the West, adolescence has been defined as a sexualised and criminalised stage in youth development. It is characterised in terms of 'storm and stress'; a period of 'unprecedented emotional and hormonal turmoil which is heavily sexualised, so that young people are assumed to be particularly prone to "promiscuous" sexual behaviour'.[83]

This characterisation of adolescence as a period of extreme transition is accepted, and repeated as fact, by groups active in international reproductive initiatives. For example, the Center for Reproductive Law and Policy, an American feminist NGO, defines adolescence as 'a period of rapid physical, emotional, social, and sexual maturing'.[84] By framing their objection to adolescent sexual rights in terms of protecting children – particularly girl children – from sexual predators, the Christian Right's position plays to this conception of a fraught, sexualised youth. In the Christian Right's characterisation, the move to adolescent sexual rights will place young girls at risk from a dangerous, masculinised and highly sexed youth.[85]

---

79 *Op cit*, Youth Forum, fn 78, p 3.

80 The final agreement from the Cairo +5 process, however, does recommend that governments 'should enact legislation and adopt measures' to address the needs of vulnerable populations living with HIV/AIDS, 'including women and young people': *op cit*, ICPD +5 Key Actions, fn 8, para 67.

81 In parts of the developing world, HIV/AIDS infection among young women is increasing faster than among young men: UNAIDS, *1998 World AIDS Campaign Briefing Paper*, 1998, p 3, as cited in *op cit*, Center for Reproductive Law and Policy, fn 69, p 20.

82 *Op cit*, Wyn and White, fn 72, p 18.

83 Griffin, A, *Representations of Youth: The Study of Youth and Adolescence in Britain and America*, 1993, Cambridge: Polity, p 168.

84 Center for Reproductive Law and Policy, *Adolescent Reproductive Rights: Laws and Policies to Improve their Lives*, 1999, p 1, available at www.crlp.org.

85 *Op cit*, CWA, fn 34, p 2.

This concern of the Christian Right, however, is not entirely misplaced. While young girls may be sexually active, and in some cases this may be their choice, the problems of incest, child brides and child prostitution mean that evidence of sexual activity cannot be equated with sexual autonomy. While adolescent sexual rights may be one way of giving autonomy to girl children otherwise subject to sexual abuse, the Christian Right raise a legitimate concern that such an approach may normalise the sexualisation of young girls, as child brides, prostitutes and so on.[86] This is particularly of concern where children's rights are articulated without reference to the particular needs and vulnerabilities of groups of children, making it difficult to nuance the application of autonomy rights to account for power imbalances among children and between children and adults.

CONCLUSION

In this analysis of the Christian Right, my attempt has not been to legitimise their positions or read into them a potentially progressive spin. Rather, my objective in this chapter has been twofold. First, to better understand the nature of Christian Right opposition to women's and children's rights. The Christian Right are increasingly becoming a significant presence at the UN, seeking to counter human rights gains in the area of women's and children's rights, and to resist other social policy initiatives. For scholars and activists interested in international law and policy, the presence of the Christian Right is an important development in the evolution of the so called 'international civil society'. Secondly, the Christian Right intervention at Cairo +5 appears to have had an impact on the final agreement. Rather than dismiss the Christian Right as extremist groups of religious fundamentalists, it is helpful to consider why and how the Christian Right were able to impact on the development of international law and policy.

In the area of children's rights, the Christian Right's intervention is illustrative of some of the tensions and contradictions that make implementing children's rights difficult. In particular, the Christian Right's opposition to adolescent sexual rights highlights the need to make explicit the varied experiences of childhood. Without addressing inequality and the impact that this has on children, generalised rights guarantees may be detrimentally vague and open to contradictory interpretation. The example of

---

86 This is not to suggest that feminist and women's groups are not also concerned about the impact of international policy on the sexual exploitation of young girls. Many of the feminist NGOs active at Cairo and during the follow up process have been instrumental in both highlighting the marginalisation of the girl child and implementing programmes to redress imbalances between girls and boys in health and education.

children's rights suggests that one of the central challenges for international human rights is to find a way to balance the universality of rights guarantees with the particularity of inequality.

BIBLIOGRAPHY

Abdalla, H, Shenfield, F and Latarche, E, 'Statutory information for the children born of occyte donation in the UK: what will they be told in 2008?' (1998) 13 Human Reproduction 1106

Adair, VA and Purdie, A, 'Donor insemination programmes with personal donor: issues of secrecy' (1996) 11 Human Reproduction 2558

Adams, R, *Protests by Pupils*, 1991, London: Falmer

Adkins, L and Merchant, V (eds), *Sexualising the Social: Power and the Organisation of Sexuality*, 1996, London: Macmillan

Agosin, M, *Surviving Beyond Fear: Women, Children and Human Rights in Latin America*, 1993, New York: White Pine

Ahuja, KK, Mostyn, BJ and Simons, EG, 'Egg sharing and egg donation: attitudes of British egg donors and recipients' (1997) 12 Human Reproduction 2845

Alder, C and Baines, M (eds), *And When She Was Bad? Working with Young Women in Juvenile Justice and Related Areas*, 1996, Tasmania: National Clearinghouse for Youth Studies

Alder, C, 'Passionate and willful girls: confronting practices' (1998) 9(4) Women and Criminal Justice 81

Alderson, P and Goodwin, M, 'Contradictions within concepts of children's competence' (1993) 1 IJCR 303

Alderson, P and Montgomery, J, *Healthcare Choices: Making Decisions with Children*, 1996, London: IPPR

Alderson, P, 'Everyday and medical life choices: decision making among eight to 15 year old school students' (1992) 18 Child: Care, Health and Development 81

Alderson, P, *Children's Consent to Surgery*, 1993, Oxford: OUP

Alldrige, P and Brants, C (eds), *Personal Autonomy, the Private Sphere and the Criminal Law: A Comparative Study*, forthcoming, Oxford: Hart

Alston, P (ed), *The Best Interests of the Child: Reconciling Culture and Human Rights*, 1994, Oxford: Clarendon

Alston, P, Parker, S and Seymour, J (eds), *Children, Rights and the Law*, 1991, Oxford: OUP

Amato, PR and Keith, B, 'Parental divorce and the well being of children: a meta-analysis' (1991) 110 Psychological Bulletin 26

Anderson, L, *Contact between Children and Violent Fathers*, 1997, London: Rights of Women

Anzaldua, G (ed), *Making Face, Making Soul/Haciendo Caras*, 1990, San Francisco: Aunt Lute

Archard, D, *Children, Rights and Childhood*, 1993, London: Routledge

Aries, P, *Centuries of Childhood*, Baldwick, R (trans), 1962, London: Jonathan Cape

Aries, P, *The History of Childhood*, 1973, London: Jonathan Cape

Armstrong, A, Chuulu, M, Himonga, C, Letuka, P, Mokobi, K, Ncube, W, Nhlapo, T, Rwezaura, B and Vilakazi, P, 'Towards a cultural understanding of the interplay between children's and women's rights: an Eastern and Southern Africa perspective' (1995) 3 IJCR 333

Ashe, M and Cahn, NR, 'Child abuse: a problem for feminist theory' (1993) 2 Texas J Women and the Law 75

Backstrom, KM, 'The international human rights of the child: do they protect the female child?' (1996–97) 30 George Washington J Int Law and Economics 541

Bailey-Harris, R, Davis, G, Barron, J and Pearce, J, *Monitoring Private Law Applications under the Children Act: A Research Report to the Nuffield Foundation*, 1998, Bristol: University of Bristol

Baines, M and Alder, C, 'Are girls more difficult to work with? Youth workers' perspectives in juvenile justice and related areas' (1996) 42(3) Crime and Delinquency 467

Bainham, A, 'The judge and the competent minor' (1992) 108 LQR 194

Bainham, A, *Children: The Modern Law*, 1998, Bristol: Jordan

Bainham, A, Day-Sclater, S and Richards, M (eds), *What is a Parent? A Socio-Legal Analysis*, 1999, Oxford: Hart

Bainham, A, Pearl, D and Pickford, R (eds), *Frontiers of Family Law*, 1995, Chichester: Wiley

Baker, A and Duncan, S, 'Child sexual abuse: a study of its prevalence in Great Britain' (1985) 9 Child Abuse and Neglect 457

Balen, AH, 'Ovarian hyperstimulation syndrome' (1999) 14 Human Reproduction 1138

Banning, A, 'Mother-son incest: confronting a prejudice' (1989) 13 Child Abuse and Neglect 563

Barker, DL and Allen, S (eds), *Sexual Divisions and Society: Process and Change*, 1976, London: Tavistock

Barnardo's, *Whose Daughter Next? Children Abused through Prostitution*, 1998, Ilford: Barnardo's

Barnett, A, 'Disclosure of domestic violence by women involved in child contact disputes' (1999) 29 Fam Law 104

Bartlett, KT, 'Feminism and family law' (1999) 33 FLQ 475

Barton, L and Tomlinson, S, *Special Education and Social Interests*, 1984, London: Croom Helm

Bates, P, 'Children in secure psychiatric units: *Re K, W and H* – "out of sight, out of mind"?' (1994) 6 JCL 131

Batsleer, J, *Working With Girls and Young Women in Community Settings,* 1996, Aldershot: Ashgate

Bauman, Z, *Post-Modern Ethics*, 1993, Oxford: Blackwell

Bearison, D, *'They Never Want to Tell You': Children Talk about Cancer*, 1991, Cambridge, Mass: Harvard UP

Beck, RCE, 'The innocent spouse problem' (1990) 43 Vanderbilt L Rev 317

Beck, U, *The Risk Society: Towards a New Modernity*, 1992, London: Sage

Behlmer, G, *Child Welfare and Moral Reform in England 1870–1908*, 1983, Stanford: Stanford UP

Bender, L, 'A lawyer's primer on feminist theory and tort' (1988) 38 JLE 3

Benhabib, S and Cornell, D (eds), *Feminism as Critique*, 1987, Cambridge: Polity

Berlant, L, *The Queen of America Goes to Washington City: Essays on Sex and Citizenship*, 1997, North Carolina: Duke UP

Berridge, D and Brodie, I, 'An "exclusive" education' (1997) Community Care, 30 January–5 February, p 4

Berry, C, *The Idea of a Democratic Community*, 1989, Hemel Hempstead: Harvester

Bibbings, L and Alldridge, P, 'Sexual expression, body alteration and the defence of consent' (1993) 20 JLS 356

Birks, P (ed), *Frontiers of Liability*, 1994, Oxford: OUP

Blagg, H, 'A just measure of shame? Aboriginal youth and conferencing in Australia' (1997) 37(4) Br J Crim 481

Bluebond-Langner, M, *The Private Worlds of Dying Children*, 1978, Princeton: Princeton UP

Blyth, E and Milner, J (eds), *Exclusion from School, Inter-Professional Issues for Policy and Practice*, 1996, London: Routledge

Blyth, E and Milner, J, *Social Work with Children: The Educational Perspective*, 1997, London: Longman

Blyth, E, Crawshaw, M and Speirs, J (eds), *Truth and the Child 10 Years On: Information Exchange in Donor Assisted Conception*, 1998, Birmingham: British Association of Social Workers

Blyth, E, *Infertility and Assisted Conception: Practice Issues for Counsellors*, 1995, Birmingham: British Association of Social Workers

Bonnet, C, *Geste d'Amour*, 1991, Paris: Editions Odile Jacob

Bonnet, E, 'La loi de l'accouchement secret' (1995) Les Dossiers de l'Obstetrique, Mai, p 20

Bordo, S, *Unbearable Weight: Feminism, Western Culture and the Body*, 1993, Los Angeles: California UP

Boswell, J, *The Kindness of Strangers: The Abandonment of Children in Western Europe from Late Antiquity to the Renaissance*, 1988, London: Pantheon

Bottomley, A, *Feminist Perspectives on the Foundational Subjects of Law*, 1996, London: Cavendish Publishing

Bowlby, J, *Child Care and the Growth of Love*, 1953, Harmondsworth: Penguin

Boyd, S, 'Is there an ideology of motherhood in (post)modern child custody law?' (1996) 5 SLS 495

Boyd, S, 'Some post-modernist challenges to feminist analyses of law, family and State: ideology and discourse in child custody law' (1991) 10 CJFL 79

Boyd, SB (ed), *Challenging the Public/Private Divide: Feminism, Law, and Public Policy*, 1997, Toronto: Toronto UP

Boydon, J, 'Social and cultural meanings of childhood' (1996) 1 Development 18

Bradley, D, *Family Law and Political Culture*, 1996, London: Sweet & Maxwell

Brannen, J and O'Brien, M (eds), *Childhood and Parenthood*, 1995, London: Institute of Education

Brannen, J and O'Brien, M (eds), *Children in Families: Research and Policy*, 1996, London: Falmer

Brasse, G, 'Examination of the child' (1993) 23 Fam Law 12

Brazier, M and Bridge, C, 'Coercion or caring: analysing adolescent autonomy' (1996) 16 LS 84

Brewaeys, A, Golombok, S, Naaktgeboren, N, de Bruyn, JK and van Hall, EV, 'Donor insemination: Dutch parents' opinions about confidentiality and donor anonymity and the emotional adjustment of their children' (1997) 12 Human Reproduction 1591

Bridge, C (ed), *Family Law Towards the Millennium: Essays for PM Bromley*, 1997, London: Butterworths

Bridge, C, 'Religious beliefs and teenage refusal of medical treatment' (1999) 62 MLR 585

Bridgeman, J and Millns, S, *Feminist Perspectives on Law*, 1998, London: Sweet & Maxwell

Bridgeman, J, 'Criminalising the one who really cared' (1998) 6 FLS 245

Bridgeman, J, 'Old enough to know best?' (1993) 13 LS 69

Brinkworth, L, 'Angry young women' (1996) *Cosmopolitan*, February

Brodie, I, 'Exclusion from school' (1995) *Highlight* No 136, London: National Children's Bureau

Brophy, J, 'Parental rights and children's welfare: some problems of feminists' strategy in the 1920s' (1982) 10 IJSL 149

Brouwer, S, Gifford, P and Rose, SD, *Exporting the American Gospel: Global Christian Fundamentalism*, 1996, New York: Routledge

Brown, HC and Pearce, J, 'Good practice in the face of anxiety: social work with girls and young women' (1992) 6(2) JSWP 159

Bruch, H, *Eating Disorders*, 1974, London: Routledge and Kegan Paul

Buckley, A and Scholar, H, 'Long-distance love: practice issues in unmarried parent cases' (1993) 23 Fam Law 81

Bullivant, A and Bullivant, B, *Helping Children at Home*, 1996, Northampton: Home and School Council

Burgess, A and Ruxton, S, *Men and Their Children: Proposals for Public Policy*, 1996, London: Institute for Public Policy Research

Burghes, L, *Lone Parenthood and Family Disruption: The Outcomes for Children*, 1994, London: Family Policy Studies Centre

Burman, E, 'Innocents abroad: Western fantasies of childhood and the iconography of emergencies' (1994) 18 Disasters 238

Burman, E, *Deconstructing Developmental Psychology*, 1994, London: Routledge

Buss, D and Herman, D, *Globalizing Family Values: The Christian Right's International Campaign Against Feminism and Gay Rights*, forthcoming, Chicago: Chicago UP

Buss, D, 'Robes, relics and rights: the Vatican and the Beijing Conference on Women' (1998) 7(3) SLS 339

Butler, J, *Gender Trouble: Feminism and the Subversion of Identity*, 1990, London: Routledge

Cain, M (ed), *Growing Up Good: Policing the Behaviour of Girls in Europe*, 1989, London: Sage

Campbell, B, *Goliath: Britain's Dangerous Places*, 1993, London: Virago

Campbell, B, *Unofficial Secrets: Child Sexual Abuse – the Cleveland Case*, 1988, London: Virago

Carrington, K, *Offending Girls*, 1993, New South Wales: Allen & Unwin

Carter, A, *The Vintage Book of Fairy Tales*, 1990, London: Virago

Carter, P, Jeffs, T and Smith, MK (eds), *Social Work and Social Welfare Year Book 3*, 1991, Milton Keynes: OU Press

Catholic Family Human Rights Institute, 'Pro-Life youth organise to counter radical groups at UN conferences' (1999) 2(45) Friday Fax, 17 September

Center for Reproductive Law and Policy, *Adolescent Reproductive Rights: Laws and Policies to Improve their Lives*, 1999, available at www.crlp.org

Center for Reproductive Law and Policy, *ICPD +5, Gains for Women Despite Opposition*, undated, New York, available at www.crlp.org

Center for Reproductive Law and Policy, *Implementing Adolescent Reproductive Rights through the Convention on the Rights of the Child*, undated, available at www.crlp.org

Charlesworth, H, Chinkin, C and Wright, S, 'Feminist approaches to international law' (1991) 85 AJIL 613

Children's Legal Centre, 'At what age can I ...?' (1999) Information Sheet, University of Essex

Children's Society, *One Way Street? Retrospectives on Childhood Prostitution*, 1999, London: The Children's Society

Childright, 'National register of nannies ruled out' (1998) 148 Childright 20

Chisholm, L and Hurrelman, K, 'Adolescence in modern Europe: pluralised transition patterns and their implications for personal risks' (1996) 18 J Adolescence 128

Clarke, J, Cochrane, A and Smart, C, *Ideologies of Welfare: From Dream to Disillusion*, 1992, London: Routledge

Coleman, J (ed), *The School Years, Current Issues in the Socialisation of Young People*, 2nd edn, 1992, London: Routledge

Coleman, J, 'Puberty: is it happening earlier?' (1997) *Young Minds Magazine*, p 34

Coles, R, *Children of Crisis*, 1967, New York: Little, Brown

Collier, R, 'After Dunblane: crime, corporeality and the (hetero)sexing of the bodies of men' (1997) 24(2) JLS 177

Collier, R, 'The dashing of a "liberal dream"? The information meeting, the "new family" and the limits of law' (1999) 11(3) CFLQ 257

Collier, R, 'Waiting till father gets home' (1995) 4 SLS 5

Collier, R, *Masculinities, Crime and Criminology*, 1998, London: Sage

Collier, R, *Masculinity, Law and the Family*, 1995, London: Routledge

Conaghan, J, 'The invisibility of women in labour law: gender-neutrality in model-building' (1986) 14 IJSL 377

Concerned Women for America, *21st Special Assembly of the United Nations General Assembly: Cairo +5 Conference*, 2 July 1999, available at www.cwfa.org

Concerned Women for America, *Stealing their Childhood: The UN Agenda Against Generation Y*, 25 February 1999, available at www.cwfa.org

Concerned Women for America, *The End of Innocence: How the UN Stole Childhood*, 15 July 1999, available at www.cwfa.org

Concerned Women for America, *United Nations Cairo +5 Preparatory Conference*, 26 March 1999, available at www.cwfa.org

Corby, B, *Child Abuse: Towards a Knowledge Base*, 1993, Buckingham: OU Press

Cosin, B and Hales, M (eds), *Families, Education and Social Differences*, 1997, London: Routledge

Couzens-Hoy, D (ed), *Foucault: A Critical Reader*, 1986, London: Basil Blackwell

Creighton, S and Noyes, P, *Child Abuse Trends in England and Wales 1983–1987*, 1989, London: NSPCC

Crenshaw, KW, 'Race, reform and retrenchment: transformation and legitimation in anti-discrimination law' (1988) 101 Harv L Rev 1331

Crook, JA, *Law and Life of Rome*, 1967, London: Thames and Hudson

Cunningham, H, *Childhood and Children in Western Society*, 1995, London: Longman

Curran, J, Morely, D and Walkerdine, V (eds), *Cultural Studies and Communication*, 1996, London: Arnold

Dahlberg, G, Moss, P and Pence, A, *Beyond Quality in Early Childhood Education and Care: Postmodern Perspectives*, 1999, London: Falmer

Davies, A, '"These viragoes are no less cruel than the lads": young women, gangs and violence in late Victorian Manchester and Salford' (1999) 39(1) Br J Crim 72

Davis, K, *Embodied Practices: Feminist Perspectives on the Body*, 1997, London: Sage

Day-Sclater, S and Piper, C (eds), *Undercurrents of Divorce*, 1999, Aldershot: Ashgate

Day-Sclater, S, Bainham, A and Richards, M (eds), *What is a Parent? A Socio-Legal Analysis*, 1999, Oxford: Hart

De Winter, M, *Children as Fellow Citizens: Participation and Commitment*, 1997, Abingdon: Radcliffe Medical

Dearden, C and Becker, S, 'Protecting young carers: legislative tensions and opportunities in Britain' (1997) 19 JSWFL 123

Dearden, C and Becker, S, 'The needs and experiences of young carers in the UK' (1998) 148 Childright 15

Delany, L, 'Protecting children from forced altruism' (1996) 312 BMJ 240

Delgado, R, 'Critical legal studies and the realities of race – does the fundamental contradiction have a corollary?' (1988) 23 Harv Civil Rights-Civil Liberties Rev 407

Democratic Dialogue, *Politics: The Next Generation (Report 6)*, 1997, Belfast: Democratic Dialogue

Department for Education, *Consultation Paper on the Regulation of Early Years Education and Day Care*, 1998, London: DfEE/DoH

Department for Education, *Education Act 1993: Sex Education in Schools*, Circular 5/94, 1994

Department of Health, Welsh Office, Home Office, Lord Chancellor's Department, *Adoption: The Future*, Cm 2288, 1993, London: HMSO

Devall, B, 'The deep ecology movement' (1980) 20 Nat Resources J 299

Dewar, J, 'The normal chaos of family law' (1998) 61 MLR 467

Dewar, J, *Law and the Family*, 2nd edn, 1992, London: Butterworths

Diduck, A, 'In search of the feminist good mother' (1998) 7(1) SLS 129

Diduck, A, 'Legislating ideologies of motherhood' (1993) 2 SLS 462

Diduck, A, 'The unmodified family: the Child Support Act and the construction of legal subjects' (1995) 22 JLS 527

Donzelot, J, *The Policing of Families*, 1980, London: Hutchinson

Douglas, G and Sebba, L (eds), *Children's Rights and Traditional Values*, 1998, Aldershot: Dartmouth

Douglas, G, 'The retreat from *Gillick*' (1992) 55 MLR 569

Douglas, N, Warwick, I, Kemp, S and Whitty, G, *Playing it Safe: Responses of Secondary School Teachers to Lesbian, Gay and Bisexual Pupils, Bullying, HIV/AIDS Education and Section 28*, 1997, University of London: HERU, Institute of Education

Dreifuss-Netter, F, *'L'accouchement sous X': Liber amicorum à la memoire de Daniele Huet-Weiler*, 1994, Paris: PUS/LGDJ

Eagle Forum, 'The new world order wants your children' (1993) 26(8) Phyllis Schlafly Report, available at www.eagleforum.org

Eekelaar, J, 'The emergence of children's rights' (1986) 6 OJLS 161

Eekelaar, J, 'White coats or flak jackets? Doctors, children and the courts – again' (1993) 109 LQR 182

Eekelaar, J, *Regulating Divorce*, 1991, Oxford: Clarendon

Eisenstein, Z, *The Radical Future of Liberal Feminism*, 1981, London: Longman

Eisler, R, *The Chalice and The Blade*, San Francisco: Harper

Elliott, J and Richards, M, 'Parental divorce and the life chances of children' (1991) 21 Fam Law 481

Elliott, J, Ochiltree, G, Richards, M, Sinclair, C and Tasker, F, 'Divorce and children: a British challenge to the Wallerstein view' (1990) 20 Fam Law 309

Ellwood, D, *Poor Support: Poverty in the American Family*, 1988, New York: Basic

Elshtain, J and Buell, J, 'Families in trouble' (1991) 38 Dissent 262

Elshtain, J, 'Feminism, family, and community' (1982) 29 Dissent 442

Engle, K, 'Female subjects of public international law: human rights and the exotic other female' (1992) 26 New England L Rev 1509

Epstein, D and Johnson, R, *Schooling Sexualities*, 1998, Milton Keynes: OU Press

Epstein, D, Elwood, J and Hey, V (eds), *Failing Boys? Issues in Gender and Achievement*, 1999, Milton Keynes: OU Press

Etzioni, A, *The New Golden Rule: Community and Morality in a Democratic Society*, 1998, New York: Basic

Etzioni, A, *The Spirit of Community: Rights, Responsibilities and the Communitarian Agenda*, 1993, New York: Random House

Evans, D (ed), *Creating the Child*, 1996, The Hague: Kluwer

Evans, D, *Sexual Citizenship: The Materialist Construction of Sexualities*, 1993, London: Routledge

Evans, DT, 'Falling angels? The material construction of children as sexual citizens' (1994) 2 IJCR 1

Ezra, DB, 'Sticks and stones can break my bones but cigarette smoke can kill me: can we protect children from parents that smoke?' (1993) 13 St Louis U Public L Rev 547

Farson, R, *Birthrights*, 1974, London: Collier Macmillan

Feast, J and Howe, D, 'Adopted adults who search for background information and contact with birth relatives' (1997) 12 Adoption and Fostering 8

Federle, K, 'On the road to reconceiving rights for children: a post-feminist analysis of the capacity principle' (1993) 42 De Paul L Rev 983

Federle, KH, 'Rights flow downhill' (1994) 2 IJCR 343

Fegan, E, '"Ideology after discourse": A reconceptualisation for feminist analyses of law' (1996) 23 JLS 173

Finch, J, *Education as Social Policy*, 1984, London: Longman

Fineman, M and Mykitiuk, R (eds), *The Public Nature of Private Violence*, 1994, London: Routledge

Fineman, MA, *The Neutered Mother, the Sexual Family and Other Twentieth Century Tragedies*, 1995, New York: Routledge

Finkelhor, D and Korbin, J, 'Child abuse as an international issue' (1988) 12 Child Abuse and Neglect 3

Finley, L, 'A break in the silence: including women's issues in torts course' (1989) 1 Yale J Law and Feminism 41

Finley, L, 'Breaking women's silence in law: the dilemma of the gendered nature of legal reasoning' (1989) 64 Notre Dame L Rev 886

Fionda, J, 'R v Secretary of State for the Home Department ex p Venables and Thompson: the age of innocence? The concept of childhood in the punishment of young offenders' (1998) 10 CFLQ 77

Firestone, S, The Dialectic of Sex, 1970, New York: Bantam

Flude, M and Hammer, M (eds), The Education Reform Act 1988: Its Origins and Implications, 1990, London: Falmer

Fontana, D, Your Growing Child: From Birth to Adolescence, 1990, London: Fontana

Fortin, J, Children's Rights and the Developing Law, 1998, London: Butterworths

Foucault, M, Power/Knowledge: Selected Interviews and Other Writings, 1976, New York: Pantheon

Fowler, RB, The Dance with Community: The Contemporary Debate in American Political Thought, 1991, Kansas: Kansas UP

Frazer, E and Lacey, N, The Politics of Community: A Feminist Critique of the Liberal-Communitarian Debate, 1994, Buffalo, New York: Toronto UP

Freeman, M (ed), Divorce: Where Next?, 1996, Aldershot: Dartmouth

Freeman, M and Lewis, A, Law and Medicine, 2000, Oxford: OUP

Freeman, M, 'Children are unbeatable' (1999) 13 Children and Society 130

Freeman, M, 'Towards a critical theory of family law' (1985) 38 CLP 153

Freeman, M, Child Welfare and the Law, 1998, London: Sweet & Maxwell

Freeman, MDA, 'The sociology of childhood and children's rights' (1998) 6 IJCR 433

Freeman, MDA, The Moral Status of Children, 1997, The Hague: Kluwer

Freeman, MDA, Violence in the Home: A Socio-Legal Study, 1979, Farnborough: Saxon House

Friedmann, M, 'Feminism and modern friendship: dislocating the community' (1989) 99 Ethics 275

Frug, M, 'Rescuing impossibility doctrine: a postmodern feminist analysis of contract law' (1992) 140 Pennsylvania UL Rev 1029

Furlong, A and Cartmel, F, Young People and Social Change, 1997, Buckingham: OU Press

Furstenberg, F and Cherlin, AJ, Divided Families: What Happens to Children when Parents Part, 1991, Cambridge, Mass: Harvard UP

Gardner, JF, *Women in Roman Law and Society*, 1986, London: Croom Helm

Gatens, M, *Imaginary Bodies: Ethics, Power and Corporeality*, 1996, London: Routledge

General Council of the Bar, *Code of Conduct of the Bar of England and Wales*, 1991, London: Bar Council

Gibson, I, *The English Vice: Beating, Sex and Shame in Victorian England and After*, 1978, London: Duckworth

Giddens, A, *Modernity and Self-Identity*, 1991, Cambridge: Polity

Giddens, A, *The Third Way*, Cambridge: Polity

Giddens, A, *The Transformations of Intimacy*, 1992, Cambridge: Polity

Gilligan, C, *In a Different Voice: Psychological Theory and Women's Development*, 2nd edn, 1993, Cambridge, Mass: Harvard UP

Glaser, D and Frosh, S, *Child Sexual Abuse*, 1988, Basingstoke: Macmillan

Glazebrook, PR, 'Human beginnings' [1984] CLJ 209

Goldson, B (ed), *Youth Justice: Contemporary Policy and Practice*, 1999, Aldershot: Ashgate

Gooneskere, SK, *Children, Law and Justice*, 1998, New Delhi: Sage

Graycar, R, 'Hoovering as a hobby and other stories – gendered assessments of personal injury damages' (1997) 31 British Columbia UL Rev 17

Green, K and Lim, H, 'What is this thing about female circumcision?' (1998) 7 SLS 365

Greven, P, *Spare The Child*, 1991, New York: Alfred A Knopf

Griffin, A, *Representations of Youth: The Study of Youth and Adolescence in Britain and America*, 1993, Cambridge: Polity

Griffin, S, *Made From this Earth*, 1982, London: The Women's Press

Groner, J, *Hilary's Trial*, 1991, New York: Basic

Gross, K, 'The debtor as modern day peon: a problem of unconstitutional conditions' (1990) 88 Michigan L Rev 1506

Grosz, E, *Volatile Bodies: Toward a Corporeal Feminism*, 1994, Bloomington: Indiana UP

Gutmann, A, 'Communitarian critics of liberalism' (1985) 14 Philosophy and Public Affairs 308

Hagell, A and Newburn, T, *Persistent Young Offenders*, 1994, London: Policy Studies Institute

Haimes, E, 'Secrecy' (1988) 2 IJLPF 46

Hallett, JP, *Fathers and Daughters in Roman Society*, 1984, Princeton: Princeton UP

Harper, J, 'What does she look like? What children want to know about their birth parents' (1993) 7 Adoption and Fostering 27

Harris, A, 'Race and essentialism in feminist legal theory' (1990) 42 Stan L Rev 581

Harris, N (ed), *Children, Sex Education and the Law*, 1996, London: National Children's Bureau

Harris, N, *Law and Education: Regulation, Consumerism and the Educational System*, 1993, London: Sweet & Maxwell

Harrison, ARW, *The Law of Athens Volume I: The Family and Property*, 1968, Oxford: Clarendon

Hartley-Brewer, E, *Positive Parenting: Raising Children with Self-Esteem*, 1995, London: Cedar

Hayes, M and Williams, C, *Family Law: Principles, Policy and Practice*, 1999, London: Buterworths

Hayes, M, 'Reconciling protection for children with justice for parents' (1997) 17 LS 1

Heilbrun, C, *Hamlet's Mother and Other Women*, 1990, New York: Columbia UP

Heinze, E (ed), *Of Innocence and Autonomy, Children, Sex and Human Rights*, 2000, Aldershot: Dartmouth

Hekman, S, *Gender and Knowledge: Elements of a Post-Modern Feminism*, 1990, Cambridge: Polity

Helfer, R and Kempe, CH, *Child Abuse and Neglect*, 1976, Cambridge, Mass: Ballinger

Hendrick, H, *Children, Childhood and English Society, 1880–1990*, 1997, Cambridge: CUP

Herman, D, *The Antigay Agenda: Orthodox Vision and the Christian Right*, 1997, Chicago: Chicago UP

Herring, J, 'The Human Rights Act and the welfare principle in family law – conflicting or complementary?' (1999) 11 CFLQ 223

Hertz, JH, *The Pentateuch*, 1956, London: Soncino

Hester, M and Radford, L, *Domestic Violence and Child Contact Arrangements in England and Denmark*, 1996, Bristol: Policy

Hester, M, Kelly, L and Radford, J (eds), *Women, Violence and Male Power*, 1996, Milton Keynes: OU Press

Hester, M, Pearson, C and Radford, L, *Domestic Violence: A National Survey of Court Welfare and Voluntary Sector Mediation Practice*, 1997, Bristol: Policy

Hewitt, J, *Dilemmas of the American Self*, 1989, Philadelphia: Temple UP

Hewitt, K, 'Divorce and parental disagreement' (1996) 26 Fam Law 368

Hilton, G, '"Boys will be boys" – won't they? The attitudes of playgroup workers to gender and play experiences' (1991) 3(3) Gender and Education 311

HM Inspector of Prisons, *Women in Prison: A Thematic Review*, 1997

HMSO, *Teenage Pregnancy – Report by the Social Exclusion Unit*, 1999, London: HMSO

Hockey, J and James, A, *Growing Up and Growing Old: Ageing and Dependency in the Life Course*, 1996, London: Sage

Hodgson, D, *The Human Right to Education*, 1998, Aldershot: Ashgate

Holland, J, Ramazanoglu, C, Sharpe, S and Thomson, R, *The Male in the Head: Young People, Heterosexuality and Power*, 1998, London: Tufnell

Hollway, W and Jefferson, T, 'The risk society in an age of anxiety: situating fear of crime' (1997) 48(2) Br J Soc 255

Holt, J, *Escape from Childhood*, 1975, Harmondsworth: Penguin

Home Office, *Crime, Justice and Protecting the Public*, Cm 965, 1990, London: HMSO

Home Office, *Criminal Statistics for England and Wales*, Cm 3764, 1996, London: HMSO

Home Office, *Detention in a Young Offender Institution for 18–20 Year Olds: A Consultation Paper*, 1999, London: HMSO

Home Office, *Statistics of Offences Against Prison Discipline and Punishment in England and Wales*, Cm 3715, 1997, London: HMSO

Home Office, *Supporting Families: A Consultation Document*, 1998, London: HMSO

hooks, b, *Talking Back*, 1989, London: Sheba

Howard League, 'Prison ends for girls' (1999) 17(2) *Howard League Magazine*, p 3

Howard League, *Lost Inside: The Imprisonment of Teenage Girls*, 1997, London: Howard League for Penal Reform

Hoyles, JA, *Punishment in the Bible*, 1986, London: Epworth

Hudson, B, 'Lost inside' (1997) 30 Criminal Justice Matters 24

Hudson, J, Galaway, B, Morris, A and Maxwell, G, *Family Group Conferences: Perspectives on Policy and Practice*, 1996, Sydney: Federation

Hughes, H, 'Psychological and behavioural correlates of family violence in child witnesses and victims' (1988) 58 Am J Ortho-Psychiatry 77

Human Fertilisation and Embryology Authority, *Code of Practice*, 4th edn, July 1998, London: HFEA

Human Fertilisation and Embryology Authority, *Report of the Committee of Inquiry into Human Fertilisation and Embryology*, Cmnd 9314, 1984

Humphreys, C, 'Judicial alienation syndrome – failures to respond to post-separation violence' (1999) 29 Fam Law 313

Hunt, D, *Parents and Children in History: The Psychology of Family Life in Early Modern France*, 1970, New York: Harper

Hutchinson, A and Green, L (eds), *Law and the Community: The End of Individualism?*, 1989, Cambridge, Mass: Harvard UP

Huxtable, R, '*Re M (Medical Treatment: Consent)*: time to remove the "flax jacket"?' (2000) 12 CFLQ 83

Ingam, T, 'Contact and the obdurate parent' (1996) 26 Fam Law 615

Ingham, R, *The Development of an Integrated Model of Sexual Conduct Amongst Young People*, End of Award Report No H52427501495, 1997, London: Economic and Social Research Council

Irigaray, L, *The Sex Which Is Not One*, 1985, Ithaca: Cornell UP

Jackson, D, *Do Not Disturb: Benefits of Relaxed Parenting for You and Your Child*, 1993, London: Bloomsbury

Jackson, SE, 'Family group conferences in youth justice: the issues or implementation in England and Wales' (1998) 37(1) Howard J Crim Justice

Jaffe, P, Wolfe, D and Wilson, S, *Children of Battered Women*, 1990, Newbury Park, Cal: Sage

James, A and Prout, A (eds), *Constructing and Reconstructing mer Contemporary Issues in the Sociological Study of Childhood*, 1997, Lo

James, A, Jenks, C and Prout, A, *Theorizing Childhood*, 1998, Cambridge: Polity

James, AL and James, A, 'Pump up the volume: listening to children in separation and divorce' (1999) 6 Childhood 189

James, AL and Richards, MPM, 'Sociological perspectives, family policy, family law and children: adult thinking and sociological tinkering' (1999) 21 JSWFL 23

Jefferson, T, 'Review' (1996) 36(2) Br J Crim 323

Jenkins, H (ed), *The Children's Culture Reader*, 1998, New York: New York UP

Jenks, C, *Childhood*, 1996, London: Routledge and Kegan Paul

Johnsen, D, 'The creation of fetal rights: conflicts with women's constitutional rights to liberty, privacy, and equal protection' (1986) 95 Yale LJ 599

Johnson, A, 'Access – the basics' (1990) 20 Fam Law 483

Johnson, A, Wadsworth, J, Wellings, K and Field, J, *Sexual Attitudes and Lifestyles*, 1994, London: Blackwell Scientific

Johnson, N (ed), *Marital Violence*, 1985, London: Routledge

Jones, G and Bell, R, *Balancing Acts: Youth, Parenting and Public Policy*, Report to Joseph Rowntree Foundation, November 1999

Just, R, *Women in Athenian Law and Life*, 1989, London: Routledge

Kaganas, F and Piper, C, 'Domestic violence and divorce mediation' (1994) 16 JSWFL 265

Kaganas, F, 'Responsible or feckless fathers? *Re S (Parental Responsibility)*' (1996) 8 CFLQ 165

Karp, D, Stone, G and Yoeb, W, *Being Urban: A Sociology of City Life*, 1991, New York: Praeger

Karst, K, 'Women's constitution' (1994) Duke LJ 447

Katz, C and Monk, J (eds), *Full Circles: Geographies of Women Over the Life Course*, 1996, London: Routledge

Kaye, M, 'Domestic violence, residence and contact' (1996) 8(4) CFLQ 285

Kelly, J, 'Children's post-divorce adjustment' (1991) 21 Fam Law 52

Kennedy, I and Grubb, A, *Medical Law: Text with Materials*, 1994, London: Butterworths

King, M (ed), *Moral Agendas for Children's Welfare*, 1999, London: Routledge

King, M and Piper, C, *How the Law Thinks about Children*, 1995, Aldershot: Gower

King, M, '"Being sensible": images and practices of the new family lawyers' (1999) 19 J Social Policy 249

King, M, 'The "truth" about autopoiesis' (1993) 20 JLS 1

King, M, 'The James Bulger murder trial: moral dilemmas, and social solutions' (1995) 3 IJCR 167

King, M, *A Better World for Children*, 1997, London: Routledge

Kirkland, A *et al*, 'Comparison of attitudes of donors and recipients to occyte donation' (1992) 7 Human Reproduction 355

Kitwood, T, 'Psychotherapy, post-modernism and morality' (1990) 3 J Moral Education 3

Klock, SC, Jacob, MC and Maier, D, 'A comparison of single and married recipients of donor insemination' (1996) 11 Human Reproduction 2554

Knutsson, KE, 'Children and the future: worthy causes or worthy citizens?' (1996) 1 Development 12

Kohlberg, L, *The Philosophy of Moral Development*, 1981, San Francisco: Harper and Row

Krug, R, 'Adult male report of childhood sexual abuse by mothers: case descriptions, motivations and long-term consequences' (1989) 13 Child Abuse and Neglect 111

Kunz, J, 'The status of the Holy See in international law' (1952) 49 AJIL 308

Lacey, N, *Unspeakable Subjects*, 1998, Oxford: Hart

Lansdown, R and Walker, M, *Your Child's Development from Birth to Adolescence*, 1996, London: Frances Lincoln

Laslett, P, *The World We Have Lost*, 1971, London: Methuen

Law Commission, *Consent and Offences Against the Person*, No 134, 1994, London: HMSO

Law Commission, *Consent in the Criminal Law*, No 139, 1995, London: HMSO

Law Commission, *Facing the Future: A Discussion Paper on the Ground for Divorce*, No 170, 1988, London: HMSO

Law Commission, *Illegitimacy (Second Report)*, Cmd 157, 1986, London: HMSO

Law Commission, *Illegitimacy*, No 74, 1979, London: HMSO

Law Commission, *Review of Child Law: Guardianship and Custody*, No 172, 1988, London: HMSO

Leach, P, *Getting Positive About Discipline: A Guide for Today's Parents*, 1997, Ilford: Barnardo's

Lee, R and Morgan, D (eds), *Birthrights: Law and Ethics at the Beginnings of Life*, 1989, London: Routledge

Legrand, P, 'Comparative legal studies and commitment to theory' (1995) 58 MLR 262

Lesnik-Oberstein, K (ed), *Children in Culture, Approaches to Childhood*, 1998, London: Macmillan

Levine, D, 'To assert children's legal rights or promote children's needs: how to attain both goals' (1996) 64 Fordham L Rev 2023

Levitas, R (ed), *The Ideology of the New Right*, 1986, Bristol: Policy

Lim, H, 'Caesareans and cyborgs' (1999) 7 FLS 133

Lindon, J and Lindon, L, *Your Child from Five to Eleven*, 1993, London: Headway

Lord Chancellor's Department, *A Report to the Lord Chancellor on the Question of Parental Contact in Cases where there is Domestic Violence*, 2000, London: HMSO

Lord Chancellor's Department, *Court Procedures for the Determination of Paternity: The Law on Parental Responsibility for Unmarried Fathers – Consultation Paper*, 1998, London: HMSO

Lord Chancellor's Department, *Information Meetings and Associated Provisions within the Family Law Act 1996: Summary of Research in Progress*, 1999, London: HMSO

Lord Chancellor's Department, *Looking to the Future: Mediation and the Ground for Divorce*, Cm 2799, 1995, London: HMSO

Lord Chancellor's Department, *Principles and Practice in Guidance and Regulations*, 1990, London: HMSO

Lowe, N and Douglas, G (eds), *Families Across Frontiers*, 1996, The Hague: Martinus Nijhoff

Lowe, N and Juss, S, 'Medical treatment – pragmatism and the search for principle' (1993) 56 MLR 865

Lucier, JP, 'Unconvential rights: children and the United Nations' (1992) 5(3) Family Policy 1

Luhmann, N, 'Differentiation in society' (1977) 2(2) Canadian J Soc 29

Luhmann, N, 'Law as a social system' (1989) 83 Northwestern UL Rev 136

Luhmann, N, *Ecological Communications*, 1989, Cambridge: Polity

Lui, SC and Weaver, SM, 'Attitudes and motives of semen donors and non-donors' (1996) 11 Human Reproduction 2061

Luker, K, *Abortion and the Politics of Motherhood*, 1984, Berkeley: California UP

Lury, C, *Consumer Culture*, 1996, Cambridge: Polity

Lyon, C, 'What's happened to the child's "right" to refuse? *South Glamorgan County Council v W and B*' (1994) 6 JCL 84

Lyon, C, Surrey, E and Timms, J, *Effective Support Services for Children and Young People when Parental Relationships Break Down*, 1999, Liverpool: Calouste Gulbenkian Foundation/NYAS/Liverpool University

Mackay (Lord), 'Family law reform' (1996) 128(3) Law and Justice 10

Maclean, S and Maclean, M, 'Keeping secrets in assisted reproduction – the tension between donor anonymity and the need of the child for information' [1996] CFLQ 243

Marshall, T, *Restorative Justice: An Overview*, 1998, London: Restorative Justice Consortium

Martin, R, 'A feminist view of the reasonable man: an alternative approach to liability in negligence for personal injury' (1994) 23 Anglo-Am L Rev 334

Mason, JK, *Medico-Legal Aspects of Reproduction and Parenthood*, 1998, Aldershot: Dartmouth

Mason, M-A, *The Custody Wars*, 1999, New York: Basic

Matthews, GB, *The Philosophy of Childhood*, 1994, Cambridge, Mass: Harvard UP

Matthews, R and Young, J (eds), *Issues in Realist Criminology*, 1992, London: Sage

Mayall, B (ed), *Children's Childhoods: Observed and Experienced*, 1994, London: Falmer

McGillivray, A (ed), *Governing Childhood*, 1997, Aldershot: Dartmouth

McIntosh, CA and Finkle, JL, 'The Cairo Conference on Population and Development: a new paradigm?' (1995) 21 Population and Development Rev 233

McLean, S (ed), *Law Reform and Human Reproduction*, 1992, Aldershot: Dartmouth

Menkel-Meadow, C, 'Portia in a different voice: speculating on women's lawyering process' (1987) 1 Berkeley Women's LJ 39

Mental Health Foundation, *Too Safe For Their Own Good*, 1999, London: Mental Health Foundation

Mercer, A, 'Councils fear loss of care expertise' (1999) *Nursery World*, 26 August

Meredith, P, *Sex Education: Political Issues in Britain and Europe*, 1989, London: Routledge

Milburn-Backett, K and McKie, L (eds), *Gendered Bodies*, 2000, London: Macmillan

Miles, S and August, A, 'Courts, gender and the "right to die"' (1990) 18 Med & Health Care 85

Miller, A, *The Untouched Key: Tracing Childhood Trauma in Creativity and Destructiveness*, 1990, New York: Doubleday

Miller, J, *Never Too Young: How Young Children Can Take Responsibility and Make Decisions: A Handbook for Early Years Workers*, 1996, London: Save the Children

Millns, S and Whitty, N, *Feminist Perspectives on Public Law*, 1999, London: Cavendish Publishing

Minow, M and Lyndon Shanley, M, 'Relational rights and responsibilities: revisioning the family in liberal political theory and law' (1996) 11 Hypatia 4

Minow, M, 'Interpreting rights: an essay for Robert Cover' (1987) 96 Yale LJ 1860

Minow, M, 'Rights for the next generation: a feminist approach to children's rights' (1986) 9 Harvard Women's LJ 1

Mirrlees-Black, C, *Estimating the Extent of Domestic Violence: Findings from the 1992 BCS Research Bulletin No 37*, 1995, London: Whiting & Birch

Mitchell, J, 'Contact orders and the obstructive parent – a third way?' (1998) 28 Fam Law 678

Mnookin, R, 'Child-custody adjudication: judicial functions in the face of indeterminacy' (1975) 39 Law and Contemporary Problems 226

Monk, D, 'School exclusions and the Education Act 1997' (1997) 9(4) Education and the Law 227

Monk, D, 'Sex education and HIV/AIDS: political conflict and legal resolution' (1998) 12 Children and Society 295

Monk, D, 'Sex education and the problematisation of teenage pregnancy, a genealogy of law and governance' (1998) 7(2) SLS 241

Montgomery, J, 'Children as property?' (1988) 51 MLR 323

Moore, JG, 'Yo-yo children: victims of matrimonial violence' (1975) 54 Child Welfare 557

Morgan, D, 'The "family man": a contradiction in terms?', Fifth Jacqueline Burgoyne Memorial Lecture, February 1994, Sheffield: Sheffield Hallam University

Morris, A and O'Donnell, T (eds), *Feminist Perspectives on Employment Law*, 1999, London: Cavendish Publishing

Morris, A, 'Once upon a time in a hospital ... the cautionary tale of *St George's Healthcare NHS Trust v S, R v Collins and Others ex p S* [1998] 3 All ER 673' (1999) 7 FLS 75

Morrison, B, *As If*, 1997, London: Granta

Morrow, V, 'Conceptualising social capital in relation to the well being of children and young people: a critical review' (1999) 47(4) Sociological Rev 744

Morton, J, *A Guide to the Criminal Justice and Public Order Act 1994*, 1994, London; Butterworths

Mount, F, *The Subversive Family*, 1982, London: Jonathan Cape

Mower, AG, *The Convention on the Rights of the Child: International Law Support for Children*, 1997, Westport: Greenwood

Mulholland, M, '*Re W (A Minor)*: autonomy, consent and the anorexic teenager' (1993) 9 Professional Negligence 21

Mullender, A and Morley, M (eds), *Children Living with Domestic Violence*, 1994, London: Whiting & Birch

Muncie, J, *Youth and Crime: A Critical Introduction*, 1999, London: Sage

Murch, M, Douglas, G, Scanlan, L, Perry, A, Lisles, C, Bader, K and Borkowski, M, *Safeguarding Children's Welfare in Uncontentious Divorce: A Study of s 41 of the Matrimonial Causes Act 1973*, Research Series, No 7, 1999, London: HMSO

Murphy, T, 'Feminism on flesh' (1997) 8 Law and Critique 37

Murray, C, *Underclass: The Crisis Deepens*, 1994, London: IEA Health and Welfare Unit

Myers, E, 'Considering child labour: the changing terms, issues and actors at the international level' (1999) 6 Childhood 13

Naess, A, 'The shallow and the deep, long range ecology movement: a summary' (1973) 16 Inquiry 95

Naffine, N and Owens, R, *Sexing the Subject of Law*, 1997, London: Sweet & Maxwell

National Association for the Education of Sick Children Research Report, *Losing the Thread*, 1997, London: National Association for the Education of Sick Children

Neale, B and Smart, C, '"Good" and "bad" lawyers? Struggling in the shadow of the new law' (1997) 19 JSWFL 377

Neale, B and Smart, C, 'Agents of dependants? Struggling to listen to children in family law and family research', *Working Paper 3*, 1998, Leeds: University of Leeds Centre for Research on Family, Kinship and Childhood

Nedelsky, J, 'Reconceiving autonomy: sources, thoughts and possibilities' (1989) 7 Yale J Law and Feminism 1

Neirinck, C, 'L'accouchement sous X: le fait et le droit' (1993) 392 *La Semaine Juridique* 143

Nelson, S, *Incest: Fact and Myth*, 1987, Edinburgh: Stramullion

Newburn, T and Stanko, EA (eds), *Just Boys Doing Business? Men, Masculinities and Crime*, 1994, London: Routledge

Nnaemeka, O (ed), *The Politics of (M)othering*, 1997, London: Routledge

O'Brien, M, *The Politics of Reproduction*, 1981, Boston: Routledge and Kegan Paul

O'Donovan, K, 'A right to know one's parentage?' (1998) 2 IJLPF 27

O'Donovan, K, 'The medicalisation of infanticide' [1984] Crim LR 259

O'Donovan, K, *Family Law Matters*, 1993, London: Pluto

O'Donovan, K, *Sexual Divisions in Law*, 1985, London: Weidenfeld & Nicolson

Okin, SM, *Justice, Gender and the Family*, 1989, New York: Basic

Oldfield, A, *Citizenship and Community: Civic Republicanism and the Modern World*, 1990, London: Routledge

Olsen, F, 'Children's rights: some feminist approaches to the United Nations Convention on the Rights of the Child' (1992) 6 IJLF 192

Olsen, F, 'The family and the market: a study of ideology and legal reform' (1983) 96(7) Harv L Rev 1497

Overall, C, *Ethics and Human Reproduction: A Feminist Analysis*, 1987, Boston: Allen & Unwin

Parkinson, P and Humphreys, C, 'Children who witness domestic violence – the implications for child protection' (1998) 10 CFLQ 147

Partington, M and Jowell, J (eds), *Welfare Law and Policy*, 1979, London: Frances Pinter

Pateman, C, *The Disorder of Women*, 1989, Cambridge: Polity

Pearson, G, *Hooligan: A History of Respectable Fears*, 1983, London: Macmillan

Penn, H (ed), *Early Childhood Services: Theory, Policy and Practice*, 2000, Milton Keynes: OU Press

Pennings, G, 'The "double track" policy for donor anonymity' (1997) 12 Human Reproduction 2839

Peterson, A and Bunton, R (eds), *Foucault: Health and Medicine*, 1997, London: Routledge

Piaget, J, *The Language and Thought of the Child*, 1924, London: Routledge

Piaget, J, *The Moral Judgment of the Child*, 1932 (4th reprint 1965), London: Routledge

Piper, C, 'Divorce reform and the image of the child' (1996) 23 JLS 364

Piper, C, 'How do you define a family lawyer?' (1999) 19 LS 93

Platt, A, *The Child Savers: The Invention of Delinquency*, 1969, Chicago: Chicago UP

Plummer, K, *Telling Sexual Stories: Power, Change and Social Worlds*, 1995, London: Routledge

Pollock, F and Maitland, FW, *The History of English Law*, 1968, Cambridge: CUP

Pratt, J, *Governing the Dangerous*, 1997, Sydney: Federation

Price, F and Cook, R, 'The donor, the recipient and the child – human egg donation in UK licensed centres' [1995] CFLQ 145

Price-Cohen, C, 'The United Nations Convention on the Rights of the Child: a feminist landmark' (1997) 3 William and Mary J Women and the Law 29

Pringle, K, *Men, Masculinities and Social Welfare*, 1995, London: UCL

Pugh, G (ed), *Contemporary Issues in the Early Years*, 1996, London: National Children's Bureau

Quality and Curriculum Authority, *Early Learning Goals*, 1999, London: QCA/DfEE

Quality and Curriculum Authority, *The Review of the Desirable Learning Outcomes for Children's Learning on Entering Compulsory Education*, 1999, London: QCA

Qvortrup, J, Bardy, M, Sgritta, G and Wintersberger, H (eds), *Childhood Matters: Social Theory, Practice and Politics*, 1994, Aldershot: Averbury

Qvortrup, J, *Childhood as a Social Phenomenon: Lessons from an International Project*, 1993, Vienna: European Centre for Social Welfare, Policy and Research

Raitt, F, 'Domestic violence and divorce mediation' (1996) 18 JSWFL 11

Raitt, F, 'Informal justice and the ethics of mediating in abusive relationships' [1997] Juridical Rev 76

Rawson, B, *The Family in Ancient Rome*, 1986, London: Croom Helm

Reece, H, 'Divorcing responsibly' (2000) 8(65) FLS 1

Reece, H, 'The paramountcy principle – consensus or construct?' (1996) 49 CLP 267

Reitsma-Street, M, 'Justice for Canadian girls: a 1990s update' (1999) Canadian J Crim, July 335

Reynolds, C and Norman, R (eds), *Community in America: The Challenge of Habits of the Heart*, 1988, Berkeley, Cal: California UP

Rhode, D, 'Feminist critical theories' (1990) 42 Stan L Rev 617

Rhode, D, *Justice and Gender*, 1989, Cambridge, Mass: Harvard UP

Rich, A, *Of Woman Born: Motherhood as Experience and Institution*, 1976, New York: WW Norton

Richardson, D, 'Sexuality and citizenship' (1998) 32(1) Sociology 83

Riley, D, *The Defiant Child: A Parent's Guide to Oppositional Defiant Disorder*, 1997, Dallas, Texas: Taylor

Robinson, JN *et al*, 'Attitudes of donors and recipients to gamete donation' (1991) 6 Human Reproduction 307

Roche, J, 'Children: rights, participation and citizenship' (1999) 6 Childhood 475

Rosenbaum, A, 'Children of marital violence: a closer look at the unintended victims' (1985) 55 Am J Ortho-Psychiatry 260

Rubellin-Devichi, J, 'Droits de la mère et droits de l'enfant: reflexions sur les formes de l'abandon' (1991) Revue Trimestrielle de Droit Civil 90

Rubellin-Devichi, J, 'Le principe de l'interet de l'enfant dans la loi et la jurisprudence françaises' (1999) I *La Semaine Juridique* 3739

Rubellin-Devichi, J, *Droit de la Famille*, 1999, Paris: Dalloz

Rutherford, J (ed), *The Art of Life*, 2000, London: Lawrence & Wishart

Sandel, M, 'Morality and the liberal ideal' (1984) *New Republic*, 7 May, p 15

Sarat, A and Felstiner, WLF, *Divorce Lawyers and their Clients*, 1995, Oxford: OUP

Saunders, A, *It Hurts Me Too: Children's Experiences of Refuge Life*, 1995, Bristol: Women's Aid Federation England/Childline/National Institute for Social Work

Sawyer, C, 'Conflicting rights for children: implementing welfare, autonomy and justice within family proceedings' (1999) 21 JSWFL 99

Sawyer, C, 'One step forward, two steps back – the European Convention on the Exercise of Children's Rights' (1999) 11 CFLQ 151

Scales, A, 'The emergence of feminist jurisprudence: an essay' (1986) 95 Yale LJ 1373

Scambler, G and Scambler, A (eds), *Rethinking Prostitution: Purchasing Sex in the 1990s*, 1997, London: Routledge

Schilling, C, 'Social space, gender inequalities and educational differentiation' (1991) 12(1) Br J Sociology of Education 23

Schuler, MA (ed), *From Basic Needs to Basic Rights: Women's Claim to Human Rights*, 1995, Washington; Institute for Women, Law and Development

Scraton, P (ed), *'Childhood' in 'Crisis'?*, 1998, London: UCL

Segal, L, *Straight Sex: The Politics of Pleasure*, 1994, London: Virago

Sen, G, 'The world programme of action: a new paradigm for population' (1995) 37 Environment 10

Sevenhuijsen, S, *Citizenship and the Ethics of Care Feminist Considerations on Justice, Morality and Politics*, 1998, London: Routledge

Sex Education Forum, *Response to Social Exclusion Unit Consultation Document on Teenage Pregnancy*, 1999, London: National Children's Bureau

Seymour, J and Bagguley, R (eds), *Relating Intimacies: Power and Resistance*, 1999, London: Macmillan

Shanley, ML and Narayan, U (eds), *Reconstructing Political Theory*, 1997, Cambridge: Polity

Shaw, I and Butler, I, 'Understanding young people and prostitution: a foundation for practice?' (1998) 28 Br J Social Work 177

Sheldon, S and Thomson, M (eds), *Feminist Perspectives on Health Care Law*, 1998, London: Cavendish Publishing

Sheldon, S and Wilkinson, S, 'Female genital mutilation and cosmetic surgery: regulating non-therapeutic body modification' (1998) 12 Bioethics 263

Sherman, A, 'Five year olds' perception of why we go to school' (1997) 11(2) Children and Society 117

Silvern, L and Kaersvang, L, 'The traumatised children of violent marriages' (1989) 68 Child Welfare 421

Skeggs, B, 'Challenging masculinity and using sexuality' (1991) 12 Br J Sociology of Education 127

Skelton, C, 'Sex, male teachers and young children' (1994) 6(1) Gender and Education 87

Smart, C (ed), *Regulating Motherhood: Historical Essays on Marriage, Motherhood and Sex*, 1992, London: Routledge

Smart, C and Neale, B, 'Arguments against virtue – must contact be enforced?' (1997) 27 Fam Law 332

Smart, C and Neale, B, *Family Fragments*, 1999, Cambridge: Polity

Smart, C and Sevenhuijsen, S (eds), *Child Custody and the Politics of Gender*, 1989, London: Routledge

Smart, C, 'A history of ambivalence and conflict in the discursive construction of the "child victim" of sexual abuse' (1999) 8 SLS 392

Smart, C, 'The legal and moral ordering of child custody' (1991) 18 JLS 485

Smart, C, 'The woman of legal discourse' (1992) 1 SLS 29

Smart, C, *Feminism and the Power of Law*, 1989, London: Routledge

Smart, C, *The Ties That Bind*, 1984, London: Routledge

Smart, C, Wade, A and Neale, B, 'Objects of concern? – children and divorce' (1999) 11 CFLQ 365

Smidt, S (ed), *The Early Years: A Reader*, 1999, London: Routledge

Smith, LJF, *Domestic Violence: An Overview of the Literature*, 1989, London: HMSO

Snowden, R and Mitchell, GD, *The Artificial Family*, 1981, London: Allen & Unwin

Snowden, R and Snowden, E, *The Gift of a Child*, 1984, London: Allen & Unwin

Social Exclusion Unit, *Teenage Pregnancy*, Cm 4342, 1999, London: Cabinet Office

Spallone, P and Stenberg, DL (eds), *Made to Order*, 1987, Oxford: Pergamon

Spallone, P, *Beyond Conception: The New Politics of Reproduction*, 1989, London: Macmillan

Spock, B, *Parenting*, 1990, London: Penguin

Stainton Rogers, R and Stainton Rogers, W, *Stories of Childhood: Shifting Agendas of Childhood Concern*, 1992, New York: Harvester Wheatsheaf

Stanley, M, *Clubs for Working Girls*, 1890, London: Macmillan

Stanworth, M, *Reproductive Technologies: Gender, Motherhood and Medicine*, 1987, Cambridge: Polity

Stefan, S, 'Silencing the different voice: competence, feminist theory and law' (1993) 47 Miami UL Rev 763

Stephens, S (ed), *Children and the Politics of Culture*, 1995, Princeton: Princeton UP

Stevens, JH and Matthews, M (eds), *Mother-Child, Father-Child Relations*, 1979, Washington DC: National Association for the Education of Young Children

Stone, N, 'Out of sight but not out of mind' (1988) 18 Fam Law 216

Struering, K, 'Feminist challenges to the new familialism: lifestyle experimentation and the freedom of intimate association' (1996) 11 Hypatia 135

Sutherland, E and McCall-Smith, A (eds), *Family Rights: Family Law and Medical Advance*, 1990, Edinburgh: Edinburgh UP

Tatar, M, *The Classic Fairy Tales*, 1999, New York: Norton

Tattum, DP and Lane, DA (eds), *Bullying in Schools*, 1989, Stoke on Trent: Trentham

Taylor-Browne, J, 'A crying shame: young people involved in prostitution' (1999) 11 Focus on Police Research and Development 24

Thery, I, *Couple, Filiation et Parente Aujourd'hui*, 1998, Paris: Editions Odile Jacob

Thomson, R and Scott, S, *Learning About Sex*, 1991, London: Tufnell

Thomson, R, 'Dream on: the logic of sexual practice' (2000) 3(3) J Youth Studies 8

Thomson, R, 'Moral rhetoric and public health pragmatism: the recent politics of sex education' (1994) 48 Feminist Rev (Autumn) 40

Thomson, R, Henderson, S, Holland, J, McGrellis, S and Sharpe, S, *Youth Values: Identity, Diversity and Social Change*, End of Award Report No L129251020, 1999, London: Economic and Social Research Council, available at www.sbu.ac.uk/fhss/ssrc/youth.shtml

Thornton, R, 'Minors and medical treatment – who decides?' [1994] CLJ 34

Trinder, L, 'Competing constructions of childhood: children's rights and children's wishes in divorce' (1997) 19 JSWFL 219

Triseliotis, J, *In Search of Origins*, 1973, London: Routledge

Tronto J, *Moral Boundaries: A Political Argument for an Ethic of Care*, 1993, London: Routledge

Turkel, G, 'Michel Foucault: law, power and knowledge' (1990) 17 JLS 170

UNAIDS, *1998 World AIDS Campaign Briefing Paper*, 1998

United Nations, *Report of the Ad Hoc Committee of the Whole of the 21st Special Session of the General Assembly*, UN Doc A/S-21/5/Add.1

United Nations, *Report of the International Conference on Population and Development*, UN Doc A/CONF171/13/Rev.1

United Nations, 'Summary of the 21st Special Session of the General Assembly (ICPD +5)' (1999) 6(61) Earth Negotiations Bulletin, 5 July

United Nations Population Fund, *State of World Population*, 1997

Vagg, J and Newburn, T, *Emerging Themes in Criminology*, 1998, Loughborough: British Criminology Conferences Selected Proceedings, Vol 1

van Bueren, G (ed), *Childhood Abused*, 1998, Dartmouth: Ashgate

van Bueren, G, *The International Law on the Rights of the Child*, 1995, The Hague: Martinus Nijhoff

Vernon, J and Smith, C, *Day Nurseries at a Crossroads*, 1994, London: National Children's Bureau

Victor Hall, J, 'Domestic violence and contact' (1997) 27 Fam Law 813

Walkerdine, V, 'Beyond developmentalism' (1993) 3(4) Theory and Psychology 451

Wallace, W, 'Double standards' (1999) *Nursery World*, 15 July

Wallbank, J, 'Castigating mothers: the judicial response to "willful" women in disputes over paternal contact in English law' (1998) 20(4) JSWFL 357

Wallbank, J, 'The campaign for change of the Child Support Act 1991: reconstituting the "absent" father' (1997) 6(2) SLS 191

Wallerstein, J and Kelly, J, *Surviving the Breakup*, 1980, New York: Basic

Walsh, E, 'The Wallerstein experience' (1991) 21 Fam Law 49

Warner, M, *From the Beast to the Blonde*, 1994, New York: Farrar, Strauss & Giroux

Wattenberg, E, 'In a different light: a feminist perspective on the role of mothers in father-daughter incest' (1985) 64 Child Welfare 203

Weeks, J, *Invented Moralities: Sexual Values in an Age of Uncertainty*, 1995, Cambridge: Polity

West, R, 'Jurisprudence and gender' (1988) 55 Chicago UL Rev 1

West, R, *Caring for Justice*, 1997, New York: New York UP

Widdett, C and Thomson, M, 'Justifying treatment and other stories' (1997) 5 FLS 77

Wilkinson, S and Kitzinger, S (eds), *Heterosexuality: A Feminism and Psychology Reader*, 1993, London: Sage

Willbourne, C and Cull, L, 'The emerging problem of parental alienation' (1997) 27 Fam Law 807

Williams, F, *Social Policy: A Critical Introduction*, 1989, Cambridge: Polity

Williams, P, 'Alchemical notes: reconstructing ideals from deconstructed rights' (1987) 22 Harv Civil Rights-Civil Liberties Rev 401

Williams, P, *The Alchemy of Race and Rights*, 1991, London: Virago

Williams, P, *The Rooster's Egg*, 1995, Cambridge, Mass: Harvard UP

Willow, C and Hyde, T, 'The myth of the loving smack' (1999) 154 Childright 18

Wilson, S, 'Identity, genealogy and the social family' (1997) 11 IJLPF 270

Wishik, H, 'To question everything: the inquiries of feminist jurisprudence' (1986) 1 Berkeley Women's LJ 64

Women's Aid Federation England, 'Women's aid and contact' (1997) 27 Fam Law 649

Worrall, A, *Offending Women: Female Lawbreakers and the Criminal Justice System*, 1990, London: Routledge

Worrall, A, *Punishment in the Community: The Future of Criminal Justice*, 1997, Harlow: Longman

Wright, W, 'Exporting teen sex: UNFPA's radical agenda', 27 August 1999, available at www.cwfa.org

Wyn, J and White, R, *Rethinking Youth*, 1997, London: Sage

Young, A, *Imagining Crime*, 1996, London: Sage

Youth Forum, *Report of the Youth Forum ICPD +5*, The Hague, Netherlands, 6–7 February 1999, available at www.ngo.forum.org/files/youth/final

Youth Forum, *Sexual and Reproductive Health of Young People*, 28 January 1999

Zipes, J, *Fairy Tale as Myth, Myth as Fairy Tale*, 1994, Lexington: University of Kentucky

Zipes, J, *Happily Ever After*, 1997, New York: Routledge

INDEX